DIVINE DYNAMICS

EXPLORING ANCIENT MESOPOTAMIAN MYTHOLOGY, RIVALRIES, AND SPIRITUAL LEGACIES

VOLUME 2

M. L. Ruscsak

Divine Dynamics

Trient Press
3375 S Rainbow Blvd
#81710, SMB 13135
Las Vegas,NV 89180

Ordering Information:
Quantity sales. Special discounts are available on quantity purchases by corporations, associations, and others. For details, contact the publisher at the address above.
Orders by U.S. trade bookstores and wholesalers. Please contact Trient Press: Tel: (775) 996-3844; or visit www.trientpress.com.

Printed in the United States of America

Publisher's Cataloging-in-Publication data
Ruscsak, M.L.
A title of a book : Divine Dynamics: Exploring Ancient Mesopotamian Mythology, Rivalries, and Spiritual Legacies volume 2

ISBN
Hard Cover   979-8-88990-109-9

Paper Back   979-8-88990-110-5

Ebook   979-8-88990-111-2

Exploring Ancient Mesopotamian Mythology, Rivalries, and Spiritual Legacies
volume 2

Divine Dynamics: Exploring Ancient Mesopotamian Mythology, Rivalries, and Spiritual Legacies volume 2

Exploring Ancient Mesopotamian Mythology, Rivalries, and Spiritual Legacies
volume 2

Chapter 1: Unveiling Ancient Mesopotamia: A Journey into Myth, Spirituality, and Rivalries

Mesopotamia: The Cradle of Civilization

Mesopotamia, often referred to as the "Cradle of Civilization," was a region located in the eastern Mediterranean, between the Tigris and Euphrates rivers. This ancient land encompassed the territory of modern-day Iraq, Kuwait, parts of Syria, and Turkey. Mesopotamia holds immense significance as one of the earliest cradles of human civilization, where various cultural, scientific, and spiritual developments took place.

The fertile land between the rivers provided the necessary resources for the growth of agriculture, leading to the establishment of permanent settlements. With the advent of agriculture, communities flourished, and complex social structures emerged. Mesopotamia witnessed the birth of writing, legal codes, mathematical systems, and monumental architectural achievements, all of which laid the foundations for later civilizations.

Significance of Mesopotamian Mythology, Rivalries, and Spiritual Legacies

Mesopotamian mythology played a central role in the lives of its inhabitants, shaping their beliefs, rituals, and social structures. These ancient narratives provided explanations for the mysteries of the natural world, human existence, and the relationships between gods and mortals. Understanding Mesopotamian mythology is crucial to comprehending the worldview and cultural practices of this ancient civilization.

Rivalries among gods and goddesses were a recurring theme in Mesopotamian mythology. These divine conflicts reflected the complexities of human nature and societal dynamics, offering valuable insights into power struggles, authority, and moral choices. Exploring these rivalries allows us to delve deeper into the human condition and examine the dynamics of power and control in both ancient and contemporary societies.

The spiritual legacies of Mesopotamia continue to influence modern religious and spiritual practices. Concepts such as divination, magic, and the worship of multiple deities find resonance in various traditions, including witchcraft, divination, herbalism, shamanism, and ecospirituality. Recognizing the roots of these practices in ancient Mesopotamia enhances our understanding of the diverse spiritual landscape of the present day.

Overview of Divine Dynamics: Exploring Ancient Mesopotamian Mythology, Rivalries, and Spiritual Legacies Volume 2

"Divine Dynamics: Exploring Ancient Mesopotamian Mythology, Rivalries, and Spiritual Legacies Volume 2" is the continuation of our captivating journey into the depths of Mesopotamian culture and spirituality. Building upon the foundation established in Volume 1, this volume offers a comprehensive exploration of new themes, deities, and cultural aspects of ancient Mesopotamia.

By delving into the rich tapestry of Mesopotamian mythology, this book unveils the intricate relationships between gods and mortals, the origin stories that shaped their cosmology, and the rituals that connected them with the divine realm. It goes beyond a mere retelling of myths and instead presents an in-depth analysis of the historical, cultural, and spiritual context surrounding these narratives.

Through a multidisciplinary approach, drawing upon fields such as witchcraft, divination, herbalism, shamanism, and ecospirituality, we aim to provide a comprehensive understanding of the Mesopotamian worldview and its relevance to contemporary spiritual practices. By examining diverse examples and case studies, we encourage students to engage in critical thinking and explore the parallels and divergences between ancient Mesopotamian spirituality and modern belief systems.

Purpose and Structure of the Book

The purpose of "Divine Dynamics: Exploring Ancient Mesopotamian Mythology, Rivalries, and Spiritual Legacies Volume 2" is to serve as a comprehensive resource for students seeking to deepen their understanding of ancient Mesopotamian spirituality. It aims to bridge the gap between historical research and contemporary spiritual practices, fostering a nuanced appreciation for the roots of modern belief systems.

The book is organized into distinct chapters, each focusing on a specific aspect of Mesopotamian mythology, rivalries, or spiritual practices. By examining these topics through the lens of various fields such as witchcraft, divination, herbalism, shamanism, and ecospirituality, students gain a holistic understanding of the intricate interplay between ancient and modern belief systems.

Throughout the book, examples, problems, and exercises are integrated to facilitate active learning, critical thinking, and classroom discussions. These resources encourage students to apply their knowledge, engage with the material on a deeper level, and explore alternative perspectives.

In conclusion, the introduction sets the stage for a fascinating exploration of ancient Mesopotamian mythology, rivalries, and spiritual legacies in "Divine Dynamics: Exploring Ancient Mesopotamian Mythology, Rivalries, and Spiritual Legacies Volume 2." By understanding the historical and cultural context, students will gain a comprehensive understanding of the significance of Mesopotamia, its mythology, and its enduring influence on diverse spiritual traditions.

Understanding the Historical and Cultural Context

Mesopotamian Geography and Civilization

To fully grasp the significance of ancient Mesopotamian mythology, rivalries, and spiritual legacies, it is essential to understand the geographical and historical context in which they emerged. Mesopotamia, meaning "land between rivers," was situated in the fertile region between the Tigris and Euphrates rivers. This strategic location provided the necessary resources for agricultural development and led to the establishment of early civilizations.

The availability of water and fertile soil supported the growth of crops, enabling the emergence of settled communities. The advent of agriculture marked a pivotal shift from a nomadic lifestyle to a sedentary one, as people began to cultivate the land and establish permanent settlements. This transition laid the groundwork for the development of complex societies and the flourishing of various cultural practices.

Socio-Political Structures and Power Dynamics

Within Mesopotamian society, a hierarchical structure governed the socio-political organization. City-states, such as Uruk, Ur, and Babylon, emerged as centers of power and influence. Each city-state had its own ruler, often referred to as a king or ensi, who exercised political, military, and religious authority. These rulers claimed divine legitimacy, emphasizing their connection to the gods and their role as intermediaries between the divine and mortal realms.

The elite class, consisting of priests, scribes, and nobles, held significant power and wealth. They played crucial roles in administering religious rituals, maintaining social order, and preserving knowledge through the development of writing systems. The common people, including farmers, artisans, and laborers, formed the majority of the population, contributing to the economic prosperity and societal functioning.

Role of Religion and Mythology in Mesopotamian Society

Religion and mythology played a central role in shaping the beliefs, values, and practices of Mesopotamian society. The ancient Mesopotamians were polytheistic, worshiping a pantheon of gods and goddesses associated with various natural phenomena, celestial bodies, and aspects of human life. Each deity had specific attributes, responsibilities, and mythological narratives associated with them.

Mythology served multiple functions within the society. It provided explanations for the origins of the universe, the creation of humanity, and the natural forces at work. Myths also offered moral lessons, guiding individuals in ethical conduct and societal norms. Rituals and ceremonies were conducted to appease the gods, seek their favor, and ensure the well-being of the community.

Impact of Mesopotamian Culture on Later Civilizations

The cultural achievements of ancient Mesopotamia left an indelible impact on subsequent civilizations. Mesopotamian innovations in writing, mathematics, astronomy, and architecture influenced not only neighboring cultures but also civilizations far beyond its geographical boundaries.

The development of cuneiform writing, one of the earliest writing systems, revolutionized communication and record-keeping. This writing system spread to other regions, including ancient Egypt and Anatolia, influencing the emergence of their own writing systems. Mesopotamian mathematical concepts, such as the base-60 numeral system, laid the foundation for modern mathematics.

The architectural marvels of Mesopotamia, such as ziggurats and monumental palaces, served as models for later civilizations' construction projects. The code of Hammurabi, a famous legal code, influenced the development of subsequent legal systems, emphasizing principles of justice and accountability.

In summary, understanding the historical and cultural context is crucial for comprehending the significance of ancient Mesopotamian mythology, rivalries, and spiritual legacies. By examining the geography, socio-political structures, religious practices, and cultural impact of Mesopotamia, students can gain a holistic perspective on the enduring influence of this remarkable civilization.

Examples, problems, and exercises throughout the chapter will prompt students to critically analyze the connections between Mesopotamian culture and various fields, including witchcraft, divination, herbalism, shamanism, ecospirituality, and magic in ancient Mesopotamia.

Mythology, Rivalries, and Spiritual Beliefs

Key Themes and Symbols in Mesopotamian Mythology

Mesopotamian mythology encompasses a rich tapestry of narratives and symbols that shed light on the ancient civilization's spiritual beliefs and worldview. Understanding the key themes and symbols is essential for comprehending the intricate layers of meaning embedded in their mythological stories.

One prominent theme in Mesopotamian mythology is the struggle between order and chaos. This dichotomy is reflected in various myths, such as the Enuma Elish, which narrates the battle between the primordial forces of Tiamat, representing chaos, and Marduk, representing order and kingship. This conflict symbolizes the eternal struggle between the forces of creation and destruction, with order ultimately triumphing to establish a stable cosmos.

Another recurring motif is the concept of divine kingship. Mesopotamian rulers, as the intermediaries between the divine and mortal realms, were believed to derive their authority from the gods. Mythological stories often depict the divine selection and empowerment of a king, highlighting the close relationship between political power and religious legitimacy.

Exploration of Divine Rivalries and Power Struggles

Mesopotamian mythology is replete with stories of rivalries and power struggles among the gods and goddesses, reflecting the complex dynamics of divine relationships and their impact on human affairs. These narratives serve as allegories for the conflicts and tensions inherent in the human experience.

One notable example is the rivalry between the brothers Enki and Enlil, who embody contrasting aspects of cosmic order. Enki, associated with wisdom and creativity, represents the fertile and life-giving forces, while Enlil symbolizes the powers of authority and judgment. Their interactions shape not only the mythological narratives but also influence the fate of humanity and the natural world.

The Role of Gods and Goddesses in Mesopotamian Spiritual Life

The gods and goddesses held a central position in the spiritual life of ancient Mesopotamians, influencing every aspect of their existence. Each deity possessed unique attributes, powers, and symbolic representations, and was revered for their role in maintaining the cosmic order and guiding human affairs.

For instance, Inanna (also known as Ishtar) was the Queen of Heaven and the Goddess of Love and War. She embodied the multifaceted nature of life, ruling over love, fertility, and warfare. Inanna's worship involved rituals and offerings aimed at seeking her blessings for matters of the heart, fertility, and protection in battle.

Beliefs about Creation, Cosmology, and the Divine Order

Mesopotamian mythology offers insights into the ancient civilization's beliefs about the creation of the world, the structure of the cosmos, and the divine order governing the universe. Creation myths, such as the Enuma Elish, describe the emergence of the universe from a primordial state of chaos, portraying the gods as architects of the cosmos.

Cosmology in Mesopotamian belief centered around the notion of a tiered universe, with multiple celestial layers inhabited by gods and celestial bodies. The ziggurats, towering temple structures, were seen as gateways connecting the earthly realm to the divine realms, enabling communication and interaction between humans and gods.

In their conception of the divine order, the ancient Mesopotamians emphasized the importance of maintaining harmony and fulfilling cosmic obligations. They believed that neglecting these responsibilities could lead to divine wrath and disruption of the natural and social order.

Literature and Epic Tales

Mesopotamia, the cradle of civilization, boasts a rich literary tradition that has captivated audiences for millennia. Exploring Mesopotamian literature provides invaluable insights into the cultural, social, and spiritual dynamics of the ancient civilization. From epic tales to hymns and laments, these literary works reflect the values, beliefs, and aspirations of Mesopotamian society.

The Epic of Gilgamesh: Myth and Legend

One of the most renowned works of Mesopotamian literature is the Epic of Gilgamesh. This epic poem, written on ancient clay tablets, recounts the adventures of Gilgamesh, the legendary king of Uruk. Through Gilgamesh's encounters with gods, mortals, and mythical creatures, the epic delves into profound themes of mortality, friendship, heroism, and the quest for immortality.

Themes and Symbolism in Mesopotamian Literature

Mesopotamian literature is replete with rich themes and symbolic imagery that offer deeper layers of meaning for interpretation and analysis. The concepts of divine kingship, the struggle between order and chaos, the exploration of human nature, and the search for wisdom and immortality are recurrent motifs throughout these literary works.

For example, in the Epic of Gilgamesh, the theme of mortality and the inevitability of death resonates deeply. Gilgamesh's journey to seek immortality reflects the universal human desire for transcendence and the quest for meaning in the face of our finite existence.

Understanding the Moral and Cultural Values Embedded in Mythical Narratives

Mesopotamian literature not only entertains but also serves as a vehicle for conveying moral and cultural values. The mythical narratives embedded within these literary works provide insights into the societal norms, ethical principles, and religious beliefs of the time.

By examining the epic tales and other literary compositions, students can gain a nuanced understanding of the moral dilemmas, social hierarchies, and gender dynamics prevalent in ancient Mesopotamian society. They will be prompted to critically analyze the values embedded in these narratives and consider how they reflect or challenge contemporary perspectives.

Rituals, Offerings, and Sacrifices

Rituals, offerings, and sacrifices held great significance in the religious and spiritual landscape of ancient Mesopotamia. These practices formed a vital link between humans and the divine realm, providing a means for communication, reverence, and the establishment of cosmic order. By delving into the world of Mesopotamian rituals, we can gain a deeper understanding of the culture's belief systems and the transformative power of these sacred acts.

Importance of Rituals and Ceremonies in Mesopotamian Culture

Rituals played a central role in the daily lives of Mesopotamians, permeating various aspects of their existence. From birth to death, from agriculture to warfare, rituals were intricately woven into the fabric of Mesopotamian society. They were seen as essential for maintaining cosmic harmony, appeasing deities, and ensuring the well-being of individuals, communities, and the entire civilization.

To comprehend the significance of rituals, students must explore the multifaceted nature of Mesopotamian culture and recognize the diverse contexts in which these ceremonies were performed. By examining examples from fields such as witchcraft, divination, herbalism, shamanism, and ecospirituality, students can grasp the cross-cultural dimensions of rituals and appreciate their universality as vehicles for spiritual transformation and connection.

Significance of Offerings and Sacrifices as Acts of Worship

Central to Mesopotamian rituals were offerings and sacrifices, which embodied the act of worship and expressed devotion to the divine. These offerings ranged from food and drink to precious objects and animal sacrifices. Each offering held symbolic value, representing the gratitude, respect, and supplication of the worshipper to the gods and goddesses.

To comprehend the significance of offerings and sacrifices, students can analyze comparative examples from diverse fields such as herbalism, where the use of specific plants as offerings connects to their inherent properties and symbolism. By engaging in exercises that involve creating symbolic offerings or discussing the symbolism behind different types of sacrifices, students can deepen their understanding of the ritual practices in Mesopotamia.

Exploring the Magical and Enchanting Aspects of Mesopotamian Rituals

Mesopotamian rituals were imbued with a sense of magic and enchantment, as practitioners sought to harness supernatural forces and establish a profound connection with the divine realm. Incantations, spells, and invocations were integral components of these rituals, invoking the power of gods and goddesses and calling upon cosmic energies.

By drawing upon examples from witchcraft and shamanism, students can explore the magical aspects of Mesopotamian rituals and understand the transformative potential of ritual practice. Exercises involving the creation of personal incantations or the exploration of different ritual tools and techniques will empower students to delve into the mystical dimensions of these ancient practices.

Communication with the Divine through Ritual Practices

Mesopotamian rituals served as a means of communication with the divine, enabling individuals to seek guidance, protection, and blessings. Through the performance of rituals, worshippers established a direct connection with the gods and goddesses, fostering a reciprocal relationship based on mutual exchange.

To grasp the intricacies of communication with the divine, students can engage in exercises that involve the interpretation of ancient divination methods or the creation of personal ritual practices inspired by Mesopotamian techniques. These exercises will encourage students to reflect on the role of rituals in their own spiritual journeys and develop a deeper appreciation for the ways in which ritual practices facilitate connection and transcendence.

Life, Death, and the Afterlife
In this chapter, we will delve into the captivating realm of Mesopotamian beliefs and practices surrounding life, death, and the afterlife. By exploring the rich tapestry of their cultural and spiritual traditions, we can gain valuable insights into the profound questions that have puzzled humanity throughout the ages. Through a comprehensive examination of Mesopotamian concepts, rituals, and mythological narratives, we will unravel the mysteries of their perspectives on mortality, funerary practices, and the journey of the soul.

Beliefs and Concept of Death in Mesopotamian Society

To comprehend the Mesopotamian worldview, we must first examine their beliefs and concepts regarding death. Mesopotamians regarded death as an integral part of the natural cycle of life, viewing it not as an end but as a transition to another existence. Their understanding of death was intertwined with their cosmological and religious beliefs, emphasizing the interconnectedness between the mortal realm and the divine.

To illustrate these beliefs, let us consider the parallels with witchcraft, where the cycles of life and death are often symbolized through the phases of the moon. By engaging in exercises that explore the symbolism of these cycles and discussing the concept of death as a transformative process, students can deepen their understanding of the Mesopotamian perspective on mortality.

Funerary Practices and Rituals Surrounding Death

The rituals and practices associated with death played a vital role in Mesopotamian society. Funerary customs were meticulously observed to ensure the proper passage and well-being of the deceased in the afterlife. These rituals varied depending on social status, religious beliefs, and regional customs, reflecting the diversity and complexity of Mesopotamian culture.

To grasp the significance of funerary practices, students can engage in exercises that involve analyzing burial artifacts or discussing the symbolism behind specific rituals. By drawing upon examples from fields such as divination or herbalism, where rituals are also central, students can compare and contrast the various approaches to death-related practices across different cultures and belief systems.

Understanding the Mesopotamian Notions of the Afterlife

The concept of the afterlife held a prominent place in Mesopotamian mythology and spiritual beliefs. Mesopotamians envisioned the afterlife as a realm where the souls of the deceased continued their existence, albeit in a different form. These notions of the afterlife were intricately connected to their beliefs about the divine order and the role of deities in the cosmic realm.

To facilitate comprehension of the Mesopotamian notions of the afterlife, students can engage in exercises that involve analyzing mythological narratives, such as the story of the goddess Inanna's descent to the underworld. By examining the symbolism and messages embedded within these myths, students can reflect on the universal human quest for meaning and the concept of life beyond death.

Mythological Connections to the Journey of the Soul

Mythological narratives played a crucial role in shaping Mesopotamian views on the journey of the soul. Through epic tales and legends, Mesopotamians sought to understand the cyclical nature of life, death, and rebirth. These myths provided a framework for comprehending the complexities of the human experience and offered insights into the ultimate fate of the soul.

To illustrate the mythological connections to the journey of the soul, students can analyze comparative examples from fields such as shamanism or ecospirituality, where the quest for spiritual transformation and enlightenment is also central. By engaging in exercises that involve exploring the symbolism in mythological narratives or discussing personal interpretations, students can develop a deeper appreciation for the power of storytelling and its role in shaping cultural and spiritual beliefs.

Through the exploration of Mesopotamian beliefs and practices surrounding life, death, and the afterlife, students will be invited to reflect on their own perspectives and engage in critical thinking about the nature of existence and the human experience. By incorporating examples, problems, and exercises throughout the chapter, we aim to foster a rich and interactive learning experience that encourages students to delve into the depths of ancient wisdom and develop a nuanced understanding of these profound subjects.

Influence and Legacy

In this chapter, we will explore the enduring influence of Mesopotamian religion, mythology, and spiritual practices on later cultures. By examining the intricate web of cultural transmission and assimilation, we can unravel the threads that connect ancient Mesopotamia to modern beliefs and traditions. Through a comprehensive analysis of historical evidence and cross-cultural comparisons, we will shed light on the profound impact that Mesopotamian mythology and spirituality have had on shaping the spiritual landscape of the world.

Mesopotamian Religion and Its Impact on Later Cultures

The religious and mythological beliefs of ancient Mesopotamia left an indelible mark on the development of subsequent civilizations. From the early civilizations of the Near East to the classical cultures of Greece and Rome, traces of Mesopotamian religious concepts, deities, and rituals can be found. Understanding this influence allows us to appreciate the interconnectedness of human cultures and the enduring relevance of ancient wisdom.

To illustrate this influence, let us examine the parallels between Mesopotamian and modern witchcraft practices. By analyzing the historical and cultural contexts, students can gain insights into the shared elements, symbolism, and beliefs that bridge the gap between these seemingly disparate traditions. Engaging in exercises that involve comparing ancient Mesopotamian spells or incantations with modern magical practices can further enrich the learning experience.

Cultural Transmission and Assimilation of Mesopotamian Beliefs

Throughout history, the ideas and beliefs of ancient Mesopotamia traveled across vast distances, assimilating with the cultures they encountered along the way. Through trade routes, conquests, and cultural exchanges, Mesopotamian spiritual traditions left their imprint on diverse civilizations, including those of Egypt, Persia, and India. Understanding the mechanisms of cultural transmission and assimilation helps us trace the complex web of influences that have shaped religious and spiritual landscapes worldwide.

To illustrate cultural transmission and assimilation, let us consider the impact of Mesopotamian divination practices on ancient Egyptian culture. By examining the similarities and differences between Mesopotamian and Egyptian divinatory techniques, students can gain a deeper understanding of the interplay between cultures and the transformative power of cross-cultural exchange. Engaging in exercises that involve analyzing ancient texts or artifacts can further enhance students' critical thinking and analytical skills.

Traces of Mesopotamian Spirituality in Modern Religions and Traditions

The influence of Mesopotamian spirituality extends far beyond the ancient world. Traces of their myths, symbols, and beliefs can be found in various modern religions and spiritual traditions. By exploring these connections, we can discern the enduring resonance of Mesopotamian wisdom in contemporary spiritual practices.

To illustrate the traces of Mesopotamian spirituality in modern religions, let us examine the parallels between Mesopotamian and shamanic practices. By delving into the shared elements of spiritual journeying, healing, and connection with the spirit world, students can gain a deeper appreciation for the cross-cultural fertilization of ideas and the universal human quest for spiritual meaning. Engaging in exercises that involve comparative analysis of rituals or exploring modern interpretations of Mesopotamian myths can further enrich students' understanding of this complex interplay.

Recognizing the Enduring Influence of Mesopotamian Mythology

The enduring influence of Mesopotamian mythology can be seen in various aspects of contemporary culture, from literature and art to popular media and entertainment. Recognizing and appreciating these connections allows us to grasp the timeless power and relevance of ancient narratives in shaping human imagination.

To illustrate the enduring influence of Mesopotamian mythology, let us explore its echoes in modern fantasy literature, such as J.R.R. Tolkien's "The Lord of the Rings." By analyzing the themes, characters, and mythical motifs that resonate between these works, students can gain insights into the universal archetypes and storytelling techniques that transcend time and culture. Engaging in exercises that involve creative writing or critical analysis of contemporary adaptations of Mesopotamian myths can further enhance students' appreciation of this enduring legacy.

By delving into the influence and legacy of Mesopotamian religion and mythology, students will develop a deeper understanding of the interconnectedness of human cultures, the transformative power of cross-cultural exchange, and the timeless wisdom embedded in ancient traditions. Through examples, problems, and exercises, we encourage students to engage in critical thinking and discussion, fostering a rich and interactive learning experience that connects the ancient with the modern, the past with the present, and the individual with the collective human experience.

Modern Interpretations and Revivals

In this chapter, we will explore the modern interpretations and revivals of ancient Mesopotamian spirituality. As contemporary seekers delve into the rich tapestry of Mesopotamian mythology, rivalries, and spiritual practices, new understandings and applications emerge. By examining the ways in which ancient wisdom is being rediscovered, reinterpreted, and revived, we can appreciate the relevance and resurgence of Mesopotamian spirituality in the modern world.

Rediscovering Ancient Mesopotamian Spirituality

Rediscovering the spiritual heritage of ancient Mesopotamia involves a rigorous exploration of historical texts, archaeological discoveries, and scholarly research. By piecing together fragments of ancient wisdom, contemporary scholars and practitioners have sought to reconstruct a comprehensive understanding of Mesopotamian spirituality.

For example, let us consider the revival of ancient Mesopotamian divination practices. By studying ancient texts such as the Enuma Anu Enlil, students can gain insights into the methods and symbolism used in divination. Engaging in exercises that involve interpreting ancient omens or casting replica clay tablets can deepen students' understanding of the intricacies of divination in Mesopotamian culture.

Contemporary Approaches to Interpreting Mesopotamian Mythology and Rivalries

Contemporary scholars and practitioners approach the interpretation of Mesopotamian mythology and rivalries with a diverse array of perspectives and methodologies. By drawing from fields such as anthropology, comparative religion, and psychology, they offer fresh insights into the underlying meanings and symbolism embedded in ancient narratives.

To illustrate this, let us explore the work of a contemporary scholar who employs a psychological approach to interpret the rivalry between the gods Enki and Enlil. By analyzing the psychological archetypes and dynamics at play, students can gain a deeper understanding of the human psyche and the universal themes that transcend time and culture. Engaging in exercises that involve analyzing mythological narratives through different interpretive lenses can further enrich students' critical thinking skills.

Modern Revivals of Mesopotamian Rituals and Practices

In recent years, there has been a resurgence of interest in reviving and practicing ancient Mesopotamian rituals and magical traditions. Contemporary practitioners draw inspiration from historical sources and adapt these practices to suit modern contexts, creating vibrant and evolving spiritual communities.

For example, let us explore the modern revival of Mesopotamian purification rituals. By examining the adaptations made by contemporary practitioners, students can gain insights into the ways in which ancient rituals are reimagined and integrated into modern spiritual practices. Engaging in exercises that involve designing and performing a contemporary adaptation of a Mesopotamian purification ritual can foster students' creativity and deepen their understanding of the role of ritual in spiritual transformation.

Exploring the Relevance and Resurgence of Mesopotamian Spirituality

The resurgence of interest in Mesopotamian spirituality speaks to its enduring relevance in the modern world. From its ecological wisdom to its emphasis on the interconnectedness of all beings, Mesopotamian spirituality offers valuable insights and practices that resonate with contemporary seekers.

To illustrate the relevance of Mesopotamian spirituality, let us explore its connections with modern ecological and environmental movements. By examining the ecological principles embedded in ancient myths and rituals, students can explore the ways in which Mesopotamian spirituality offers a framework for reconnecting with the natural world and cultivating a sense of ecological responsibility. Engaging in exercises that involve designing a nature-based ritual inspired by Mesopotamian principles can deepen students' understanding of the ecological wisdom inherent in ancient spiritual traditions.

Through examples, problems, and exercises, we encourage students to critically engage with the modern interpretations and revivals of Mesopotamian spirituality. By delving into these explorations, students will gain a deeper appreciation for the resilience and adaptability of ancient wisdom in meeting the needs of contemporary seekers.

Religious Institutions and Influence

In this chapter, we will explore the religious institutions of ancient Mesopotamia and their significant influence on society. Understanding the power structures, roles of priests and priestesses, sacred spaces, and the broader social and political impact of Mesopotamian religion will provide valuable insights into the spiritual landscape of this ancient civilization.

Power Structures and Hierarchy in Mesopotamian Religious Institutions

Mesopotamian religious institutions were characterized by a hierarchical structure that reflected the societal power dynamics of the time. At the top of the hierarchy were the high priests and priestesses, who held significant influence and were seen as intermediaries between the divine and mortal realms. They wielded both spiritual and political power, often advising rulers and participating in important decision-making processes.

To grasp the intricate power structures within Mesopotamian religious institutions, let us consider an example from contemporary witchcraft traditions. In some covens, there may be a similar hierarchical structure, with a high priestess or high priest serving as the spiritual leader, guiding the coven's rituals and practices. Engaging in exercises that involve exploring the dynamics of power and authority within a coven or religious group can provide students with a practical understanding of how hierarchical structures manifest in spiritual communities.

Roles and Responsibilities of Priests and Priestesses

Priests and priestesses in Mesopotamia played crucial roles in maintaining and conducting religious rituals and ceremonies. Their responsibilities included performing sacrifices, interpreting omens, and offering prayers on behalf of the community. They were seen as mediators between the human realm and the divine, ensuring the harmony and well-being of both.

To further comprehend the roles and responsibilities of priests and priestesses, let us draw an analogy from herbalism. Just as herbalists carry the responsibility of gathering, preparing, and administering medicinal plants for the well-being of their communities, priests and priestesses in Mesopotamia took on the task of tending to the spiritual needs of their society. Engaging in exercises that involve creating an herbal remedy and discussing the parallel responsibilities of herbalists and priests/priestesses can deepen students' understanding of the role of spiritual practitioners in different cultural contexts.

Temples, Ziggurats, and Sacred Spaces as Centers of Spiritual Authority

Temples and ziggurats were significant structures in Mesopotamian society, serving as centers of spiritual authority and communal worship. These sacred spaces were believed to be the dwelling places of the gods and goddesses, and their construction and maintenance were of utmost importance.

To illustrate the significance of sacred spaces, let us consider the importance of the circle in modern witchcraft traditions. Circles are created as sacred spaces for rituals and ceremonies, representing a connection to the divine and the containment of magical energy. Engaging in exercises that involve designing and consecrating a sacred circle can help students grasp the symbolism and purpose of sacred spaces in different spiritual traditions.

Understanding the Social and Political Impact of Mesopotamian Religion

Mesopotamian religion had a profound impact on the social and political fabric of the civilization. The rituals, beliefs, and values associated with Mesopotamian spirituality influenced various aspects of daily life, including governance, law, and social norms. Religion served as a unifying force, providing a shared set of beliefs and a sense of communal identity.

To explore the social and political impact of religion, let us consider the influence of religious ethics in modern society. Just as religious principles shape societal values and inform laws and regulations, Mesopotamian religious beliefs and rituals influenced the ethical standards and governance of their time. Engaging in exercises that involve discussing the influence of religious ethics on contemporary legal systems can foster critical thinking and awareness of the interplay between spirituality and societal structures.

Through examples, problems, and exercises, we have delved into the fascinating realm of Mesopotamian religious institutions and their profound influence on the ancient civilization. By studying the power structures, roles of priests and priestesses, sacred spaces, and the social and political impact of Mesopotamian religion, we gain valuable insights into the complex dynamics of spiritual authority and its broader implications.

Conclusion

As we conclude this volume, we extend a warm invitation to you, dear reader, to continue your exploration of the rich and diverse world of Mesopotamian myth and spirituality. By immersing yourself in Volume 2 of Divine Dynamics, you will delve deeper into the realms of literature, rituals, the afterlife, and the enduring influence of Mesopotamian spirituality.

To enhance your learning experience, we encourage you to engage in exercises and thought-provoking discussions with your peers. Consider analyzing the symbolism and themes in Mesopotamian literature, reflecting on the significance of rituals and sacrifices in your own spiritual practices, or contemplating the connections between ancient mythologies and contemporary belief systems.

May your journey into the Mesopotamian world of myth ignite your curiosity, deepen your understanding, and inspire you to uncover the timeless wisdom embedded within these ancient traditions.

Safe travels, and may the spirits of old guide your path!

Chapter 2: Magic and Rituals: Spells, Incantations, and Enchantments

Magic and rituals held profound significance in the religious and cultural contexts of ancient Mesopotamia. Mesopotamian civilization, located in the fertile land between the Tigris and Euphrates rivers, gave birth to a rich tapestry of beliefs and practices that incorporated magic and rituals into their worldview. This section aims to explore the importance of magic and rituals within Mesopotamian society, shedding light on their integral role in religious ceremonies, cultural practices, and the lives of individuals.

The ancient Mesopotamians believed in a complex pantheon of gods and goddesses who governed various aspects of the natural world, human affairs, and the cosmos. Magic and rituals were considered powerful means of establishing communication and connection with the divine realm. These practices were intricately intertwined with the religious beliefs and cosmological frameworks of the Mesopotamians.

Objectives and Structure of the Chapter

Welcome to Chapter 7 of Divine Dynamics: Exploring Ancient Mesopotamian Mythology, Rivalries, and Spiritual Legacies. In this chapter, we will embark on a comprehensive exploration of the significance of magic and rituals in Mesopotamian religious and cultural contexts. By the end of this chapter, you will have gained a deep understanding of the objectives, functions, and social implications of these practices in ancient Mesopotamia.

➤ Historical and Cultural Background of Ancient Mesopotamia

We will begin our journey by delving into the historical and cultural background of ancient Mesopotamia. Understanding the unique context in which magic and rituals flourished is essential for comprehending their significance. Through a detailed examination of the religious beliefs, social structures, and cultural practices of the Mesopotamians, we will establish a solid foundation for further exploration.

➤ Objectives and Functions of Magic and Rituals

In this section, we will explore the objectives and functions of magic and rituals in Mesopotamian society. These practices were employed to address a wide range of needs, such as healing, protection, fertility, divination, and the pursuit of personal and communal goals. By examining specific examples from different fields such as witchcraft, divination, herbalism, shamanism, and ecospirituality, we will illustrate the versatility and adaptability of magic and rituals in meeting the diverse aspirations of the Mesopotamians.

➤ Role of Priests and Priestesses

Priests and priestesses played a central role in performing magical rites and rituals in Mesopotamia. In this section, we will delve into their specialized knowledge, skills, and responsibilities. By examining their crucial role as intermediaries between the human and divine realms, we will gain insight into the intricate web of communication and interaction between mortals and gods. Additionally, we will explore the social and religious significance of priests and priestesses, highlighting their integral position within Mesopotamian society.

Examples, Problems, and Exercises

To enhance your learning experience and engage in critical thinking, let's explore some examples, problems, and exercises related to the topics covered in this chapter:

Problem:
Imagine you are a priest or priestess in ancient Mesopotamia. Design a ritual that addresses a specific communal need, such as ensuring a bountiful harvest or protecting the city from harm. Outline the steps involved, the materials required, and the intended outcomes of the ritual.

Exercise:
Research the concept of sympathetic magic and its manifestations in Mesopotamian culture. Compare and contrast it with similar practices found in other ancient civilizations, such as ancient Egypt or ancient Greece. Reflect on the underlying principles and symbolism of sympathetic magic and its relevance in contemporary magical practices.

By engaging with these examples, problems, and exercises, you will deepen your understanding of the significance of magic and rituals in Mesopotamian society and cultivate critical thinking skills that will enrich your exploration of ancient spiritual practices.

Now, let us embark on this enlightening journey into the realm of Mesopotamian magic and rituals. Open your mind to the mystical world of ancient practices and the profound impact they had on the lives of the Mesopotamian people.

Preview of Key Topics and Themes

Welcome to Chapter 7 of Divine Dynamics: Exploring Ancient Mesopotamian Mythology, Rivalries, and Spiritual Legacies. In this chapter, we will delve into the fascinating world of magic and rituals in ancient Mesopotamia. By exploring key topics and themes, you will gain a profound understanding of the diverse practices and beliefs that shaped the spiritual landscape of this ancient civilization.

➢ Types of Magic and Rituals

In this section, we will explore the various types of magical practices and rituals that were prevalent in Mesopotamia. Through an examination of spellcasting, incantations, divination, exorcism, and offerings, you will gain insight into the structures, components, and intended outcomes of these rituals. By analyzing examples from fields such as witchcraft, divination, herbalism, shamanism, and ecospirituality, you will see the breadth and depth of magical practices in Mesopotamian society.

➢ Magical Objects and Tools

Magical objects and tools played a significant role in Mesopotamian rituals. In this section, we will delve into the significance of objects such as amulets, talismans, figurines, and ceremonial instruments. You will explore their functions and symbolism, understanding how these objects were believed to harness magical energies and invoke the powers of the divine. By examining the material remains and textual references, you will gain a deeper appreciation for the material culture associated with Mesopotamian magic and rituals.

➢ Mythology and Cosmology

The mythological and cosmological foundations of Mesopotamian magic and rituals are crucial to understanding their context and significance. In this section, we will explore the creation myths, the pantheon of gods and goddesses, and the cosmic order that shaped the Mesopotamian worldview. By examining the rich mythological narratives and their connections to magical practices, you will uncover the intricate relationship between the divine, the human, and the natural world.

➢ Ethical Considerations

Magic and rituals raise important ethical considerations, and Mesopotamia was no exception. In this section, we will delve into the ethical dimensions of Mesopotamian magic and rituals. You will explore questions of responsibility, intention, and consequences surrounding the use of magic. Ethical dilemmas inherent in beneficent and maleficent practices will be examined, encouraging you to engage in critical thinking and ethical reflection. By considering different perspectives and drawing from examples across various spiritual traditions, you will develop a nuanced understanding of the ethical complexities surrounding magical practices.

Examples, Problems, and Exercises

To deepen your understanding and stimulate critical thinking, let's explore some examples, problems, and exercises related to the topics covered in this chapter:

Problem:
Imagine you are a Mesopotamian priest or priestess tasked with performing a healing ritual. Design a ritual that incorporates elements of spellcasting, offerings, and incantations to address a specific ailment or disease. Justify your choices based on Mesopotamian magical beliefs and practices.

Exercise:
Reflect on the ethical considerations surrounding the use of magic in contemporary society. Compare and contrast ethical frameworks and approaches in different modern spiritual traditions, such as witchcraft, Wicca, and neo-paganism. Consider the ways in which ethical guidelines can shape and inform magical practices today.

By engaging with these examples, problems, and exercises, you will deepen your knowledge of Mesopotamian magic and rituals, develop critical thinking skills, and cultivate ethical awareness. Prepare yourself for an enchanting journey into the world of ancient Mesopotamian spirituality, where magic and rituals were deeply intertwined with the fabric of everyday life.

Understanding Mesopotamian Magic

Mesopotamia, often referred to as the "Cradle of Civilization," was a land rich in culture, religion, and ancient wisdom. Within this vast and complex civilization, the practice of magic held a prominent place, intertwining with the religious, social, and cultural fabric of the society. This section aims to provide students with a comprehensive understanding of Mesopotamian magic, unraveling its intricacies, purposes, and significance within the ancient world.

Historical and Cultural Context:

In this section, we will delve into the historical and cultural context that shaped the practices and beliefs of ancient Mesopotamia. Understanding the unique backdrop against which magic thrived is essential to grasp the intricacies of this ancient civilization.

➢ Geography and Settlements

Mesopotamia, situated between the Tigris and Euphrates rivers, boasted fertile lands that supported the growth of agriculture. This favorable geographical location allowed for the establishment of thriving settlements. City-states, such as Sumer, Babylon, and Assyria, emerged as centers of political, economic, and cultural activity. You will explore the impact of geography on the development of Mesopotamian society and its subsequent influence on magical practices.

➢ Social Structures and Institutions

Mesopotamian society was structured hierarchically, with rulers and nobles at the top, followed by priests and priestesses, scribes, merchants, farmers, and slaves. This section will delve into the social structures and institutions that played a role in shaping magical practices. You will examine the significance of the ruling elite and their connections to religious and magical endeavors. Through examples from fields such as witchcraft, divination, herbalism, and shamanism, you will gain insights into how social dynamics influenced magical beliefs and practices.

➢ Religion and Mythology

Religion played a central role in Mesopotamian society, permeating all aspects of life. The polytheistic belief system revolved around a pantheon of gods and goddesses who governed various aspects of the world. In this section, we will explore the complex mythology and the intertwined relationship between religion and magic. By analyzing myths and their connections to magical rituals, you will develop a deeper appreciation for the religious framework within which magic operated.

➢ Cultural Practices and Beliefs

The cultural practices and beliefs of Mesopotamia encompassed a wide range of aspects, including magic, rituals, divination, medicine, and astrology. This section will examine the interplay between these cultural elements and magical practices. By examining examples from diverse fields, such as witchcraft, divination, herbalism, shamanism, and ecospirituality, you will uncover the rich tapestry of beliefs and practices that shaped Mesopotamian culture.

Examples, Problems, and Exercises:

To further engage with the historical and cultural context of Mesopotamian magic, let's explore some examples, problems, and exercises:

Problem:
Imagine you are an archaeologist uncovering a Mesopotamian burial site. Design an excavation plan that incorporates the study of burial practices, grave goods, and any evidence of magical rituals. Discuss how these findings can shed light on the role of magic in the afterlife beliefs of the Mesopotamians.

Exercise:
Reflect on the influence of Mesopotamian culture on modern magical practices. Choose a contemporary magical tradition, such as Wicca or neo-paganism, and identify elements that can be traced back to Mesopotamian beliefs and practices. Discuss the significance of this cultural continuity.

By engaging with these examples, problems, and exercises, you will deepen your knowledge of the historical and cultural context surrounding Mesopotamian magic. Prepare yourself for a captivating journey into the world of ancient Mesopotamia, where magic and belief intertwined to shape a civilization that continues to inspire and intrigue us today.

Geography and Environment:

Welcome to Chapter 3 of our exploration into ancient Mesopotamia. In this chapter, we will delve into the geographical features and environmental aspects that profoundly impacted the development of this remarkable civilization. By understanding the unique relationship between the land and its inhabitants, we can gain deeper insights into the beliefs and practices that emerged in this ancient culture.

➤ The Land between the Rivers

Mesopotamia, which means "the land between the rivers" in Greek, was a remarkable region located in the eastern Mediterranean area. This section will provide you with an in-depth understanding of the geographical layout of Mesopotamia, focusing on the two mighty rivers that flowed through it: the Tigris and Euphrates. By exploring the significance of these rivers, we can unravel the profound impact they had on the lives, beliefs, and practices of the ancient Mesopotamians.

◆ The Tigris and Euphrates Rivers:

Situated between these two prominent rivers, Mesopotamia benefited from their abundant waters and fertile soil. The Tigris and Euphrates rivers were vital sources of life, providing water for drinking, irrigation, and agriculture. The Mesopotamians recognized the immense importance of these rivers, not only for sustenance but also for their symbolic significance. The rivers represented a connection between the earthly and the divine realms, embodying the cycle of life, fertility, and prosperity.These two rivers were not merely sources of sustenance for the ancient Mesopotamians, but also held immense symbolic significance in their worldview and spiritual beliefs.

✧ Abundant Waters and Vital Sources of Life:

The Tigris and Euphrates rivers were the lifelines of Mesopotamia, providing the necessary water for the survival and well-being of its inhabitants. The rivers offered a reliable source of drinking water, ensuring the hydration and nourishment of the population. Beyond quenching their thirst, the rivers played a crucial role in sustaining agriculture through irrigation. The Mesopotamians ingeniously developed an intricate system of canals and channels to divert the river waters to their fields, enabling them to cultivate crops and ensure bountiful harvests. This agricultural abundance supported the growth of cities, the flourishing of civilization, and the establishment of prosperous communities.

✧ Symbolic Significance:

The Mesopotamians, deeply attuned to the natural world, recognized the rivers' profound symbolic significance. The Tigris and Euphrates rivers represented a profound connection between the earthly and the divine realms. They were seen as channels through which the gods and goddesses communicated with humanity, bestowing blessings or delivering messages. The rhythmic flow of the rivers mirrored the cycle of life, echoing the ancient understanding of birth, growth, death, and rebirth. As such, the rivers became powerful symbols of the cyclical nature of existence and the continuous renewal of life.

✧ Embodiment of Life, Fertility, and Prosperity:

In Mesopotamian cosmology, the rivers embodied the fundamental principles of life, fertility, and prosperity. The regular flooding of the rivers brought fertile sediment, enriching the soil and creating a thriving agricultural landscape. This abundant fertility was linked to the gods and goddesses associated with the rivers, such as Enki and Enlil, who were revered as divine patrons of agriculture and fertility. The Mesopotamians celebrated the rivers' life-giving properties through rituals, offerings, and prayers, seeking their blessings for successful harvests, healthy livestock, and overall prosperity.

◆ Essential Resources:

The presence of the Tigris and Euphrates rivers endowed Mesopotamia with a rich array of natural resources. As you delve deeper into this topic, you will discover how the rivers supported agricultural productivity by depositing nutrient-rich silt during their annual flooding. This fertile soil allowed the Mesopotamians to cultivate crops such as barley, wheat, and dates. Additionally, the rivers facilitated transportation and trade, contributing to economic growth and the development of advanced civilizations.

The presence of the Tigris and Euphrates rivers bestowed upon Mesopotamia a treasure trove of natural resources, fostering the flourishing of this ancient land. As we delve into this topic, we will explore how the rivers played a vital role in supporting agricultural productivity, enhancing economic growth, and contributing to the development of advanced civilizations.

✧ Agricultural Productivity:

The annual flooding of the Tigris and Euphrates rivers brought immense benefits to the Mesopotamian farmers. As the rivers overflowed their banks, they deposited nutrient-rich silt across the floodplains, enriching the soil with vital minerals and organic matter. This fertile soil provided the ideal conditions for agricultural cultivation. Mesopotamian farmers skillfully harnessed the rivers' waters through a sophisticated irrigation system, channeling the water to their fields and ensuring the continuous nourishment of their crops. The cultivation of staple crops such as barley, wheat, and dates thrived in this fertile landscape, allowing for abundant harvests and sustained food production.

✧   Transportation and Trade:

The Tigris and Euphrates rivers served as natural highways, facilitating transportation and trade throughout the region. The Mesopotamians, recognizing the advantages of this waterborne mode of transport, utilized boats and rafts to navigate the rivers' currents. This efficient means of transportation enabled the movement of goods, resources, and people across vast distances. The rivers connected various cities and settlements, fostering trade networks and economic exchange. Mesopotamian merchants transported goods such as textiles, pottery, metals, and agricultural produce, facilitating commerce and contributing to the growth of thriving urban centers.

✧   Economic Growth and Civilizational Development:

The abundant natural resources provided by the Tigris and Euphrates rivers fueled the economic growth and development of advanced civilizations in Mesopotamia. The fertile agricultural lands supported a surplus of food production, allowing for population growth and the emergence of specialized occupations beyond agriculture. The surplus food and the availability of diverse resources facilitated the development of complex societies, the establishment of cities, and the formation of intricate social and economic structures. The rivers acted as arteries of economic prosperity, attracting traders, artisans, and professionals, who contributed to the advancement of Mesopotamian civilization.

Examples:

Advanced Irrigation Techniques: Mesopotamian farmers developed innovative irrigation techniques to harness the waters of the rivers for agricultural purposes. Canals, dikes, and reservoirs were constructed to effectively distribute water to the fields and manage irrigation cycles, ensuring optimal growth conditions for crops.

Trade Routes: The Tigris and Euphrates rivers formed crucial trade routes that connected Mesopotamia with neighboring regions. For instance, the rivers provided access to the Persian Gulf, facilitating maritime trade with civilizations such as the Indus Valley civilization and the Gulf states.

Economic Specialization: The surplus agricultural production made it possible for individuals to engage in specialized occupations beyond farming. Craftsmen, merchants, scribes, and religious functionaries emerged, contributing to the diversification of the economy and the growth of urban centers.

By understanding the significance of the Tigris and Euphrates rivers in supporting agricultural productivity, facilitating transportation and trade, and fostering economic growth, we gain valuable insights into the foundations of Mesopotamian civilization. The rivers served as lifelines for the development of prosperous societies, laying the groundwork for cultural achievements and advancements that would shape the course of human history.

◆ Influence on Settlement Patterns:

The influence of the Tigris and Euphrates rivers on settlement patterns in Mesopotamia cannot be overstated. In this section, we will explore how the availability of water resources, along with the natural barriers provided by the rivers, shaped the establishment of cities and urban centers, contributing to the development of sophisticated societies in this ancient land. Through examples from fields such as divination, herbalism, and shamanism, we will gain a deeper understanding of how the rivers influenced settlement patterns and provided a sense of security to the inhabitants.

✦ Availability of Water Resources:

The Tigris and Euphrates rivers served as the lifeblood of the Mesopotamian civilization, providing a steady supply of water for various purposes. The availability of water resources, including drinking water and water for irrigation, was a determining factor in the choice of settlement locations. The rivers ensured the sustenance of agricultural practices, allowing communities to cultivate crops and thrive in fertile lands adjacent to the riverbanks. Settlements that were situated near the rivers could harness the water for their daily needs, agricultural activities, and the development of advanced irrigation systems. This proximity to abundant water resources fostered the growth and prosperity of these settlements, eventually leading to the formation of urban centers.

✦ Natural Barriers and Protection:

Beyond their role as a water source, the Tigris and Euphrates rivers acted as natural barriers, offering a degree of protection to the settlements along their banks. The rivers, with their powerful currents and unpredictable flooding patterns, created physical barriers that impeded the advancement of potential invaders. This natural defense mechanism provided a sense of security to the inhabitants, allowing them to focus on the development of their communities without constant fear of external threats. The rivers also served as a means of transportation, facilitating communication and trade between settlements while acting as a natural buffer against hostile forces.

Examples:

City of Babylon: The ancient city of Babylon, located on the banks of the Euphrates River, exemplifies the influence of the rivers on settlement patterns. The presence of the river allowed for the construction of impressive water management systems, such as canals and reservoirs, ensuring a reliable water supply for the city's inhabitants. The strategic positioning of Babylon on the riverbanks provided both access to water resources and a natural defense against potential invaders.

Ur: The city of Ur, situated near the mouth of the Euphrates River, owed its prominence to the river's influence. The river facilitated maritime trade, connecting Ur to various trading partners across the region. The water resources of the Euphrates River supported the agricultural activities of Ur, ensuring a stable food supply for the city's inhabitants and contributing to its growth and prosperity.

Security and Protection: Mesopotamian myths and rituals often featured the rivers as symbols of protection and guardianship. For example, in the epic of Gilgamesh, the hero encounters water-related challenges and confronts fearsome creatures in his quest for immortality. These narratives illustrate the Mesopotamians' perception of the rivers as both life-sustaining forces and protective entities guarding against external dangers.

By recognizing the influence of the Tigris and Euphrates rivers on settlement patterns and the sense of security they provided, we gain valuable insights into the interconnected relationship between humans and their environment. The rivers not only shaped the physical landscapes but also influenced the cultural and spiritual beliefs of the Mesopotamian people. They fostered the growth of urban centers, facilitated trade and communication, and played a significant role in the formation of advanced societies.

◆ Impact on Daily Life and Spiritual Beliefs:

By examining examples from fields such as divination, herbalism, and shamanism, we can gain valuable insights into how the Tigris and Euphrates rivers influenced the daily lives and spiritual beliefs of the Mesopotamians. For instance, divination practices often involved the observation of natural phenomena, including the flow of rivers, to gain insights into future events or divine intentions. Herbalism, too, relied on the fertile soil near the rivers to cultivate medicinal plants and herbs. Shamanic rituals, on the other hand, drew upon the rivers' symbolism of life and renewal in their ceremonies.

Examples:

Divination: Mesopotamian diviners would closely observe the flow and behavior of the Tigris and Euphrates rivers, interpreting the patterns and movements as omens and messages from the gods. For example, a sudden change in the river's course might be seen as a sign of impending disaster or upheaval.

Herbalism: The fertile soil near the rivers provided ideal conditions for growing medicinal plants. Ancient Mesopotamian herbalists would gather herbs like licorice root, chamomile, and cumin, utilizing their healing properties in various remedies and potions.

Shamanism: During shamanic rituals, the rivers served as sacred spaces where the shaman would connect with the spiritual realm. By immersing themselves in the flowing waters, shamans believed they could cleanse their souls, receive divine guidance, and access hidden knowledge.

By exploring the significance of the Tigris and Euphrates rivers in the context of divination, herbalism, and shamanism, you will develop a comprehensive understanding of how these waterways shaped the daily lives and spiritual beliefs of the ancient Mesopotamians. Prepare yourself for a captivating journey into a world where rivers were more than just bodies of water—they were lifelines connecting humanity with the divine forces that governed their existence.

➢ Fertile Soil and Agricultural Productivity

One of the most remarkable aspects of Mesopotamia's geography was its fertile soil, nourished by the annual flooding of the rivers. This section will delve into the significance of fertile soil in supporting agricultural productivity. You will learn about the development of irrigation systems, such as canals and dikes, which allowed for efficient water management and crop cultivation. By examining examples from fields like herbalism and ecospirituality, you will discover the interconnectedness between the land, agriculture, and spiritual practices.

Within the remarkable geography of Mesopotamia, the presence of fertile soil stands as a testament to the region's agricultural productivity. In this section, we will explore the significance of this fertile soil and its direct impact on the cultivation of crops, as well as the development of sophisticated irrigation systems.

Through examples from fields such as herbalism and ecospirituality, we will deepen our understanding of the profound connection between the land, agricultural practices, and spiritual beliefs.

✧ Fertile Soil and Agricultural Abundance:

Mesopotamia's fertile soil owes its richness to the annual flooding of the Tigris and Euphrates rivers. These floods, while initially disruptive, brought forth a gift—the deposition of nutrient-rich silt across the river valleys. The sediments carried by the rivers replenished the soil, making it exceptionally fertile for agricultural cultivation. This fertile soil supported the growth of a diverse range of crops, including barley, wheat, dates, vegetables, and fruits. The abundance of agricultural resources not only sustained the local population but also facilitated trade and economic development, contributing to the overall prosperity of the region.

✧ Development of Irrigation Systems:

To harness the benefits of the rivers' flooding and ensure consistent water supply for crops, the Mesopotamians developed elaborate irrigation systems. Canals, dikes, and reservoirs were constructed to redirect and control the flow of water, allowing for efficient distribution across farmland. These irrigation systems required advanced engineering techniques and collective efforts, demonstrating the ingenuity and collaborative spirit of the Mesopotamian civilization. By effectively managing water resources, the Mesopotamians maximized agricultural productivity and mitigated the risks of drought or irregular flooding.

Examples:

Herbalism: The cultivation and use of medicinal plants in Mesopotamia were deeply intertwined with the region's agricultural practices. Herbalists recognized the importance of fertile soil in growing plants with potent healing properties. For example, the Sumerians utilized various herbs and plants in their medicinal practices, such as licorice, thyme, and aloe vera. They believed that the vitality of these healing herbs was directly linked to the fertile soil in which they were cultivated, emphasizing the connection between the land, agricultural abundance, and the healing arts.

Ecospirituality: The agricultural fertility of Mesopotamia held profound spiritual significance for its inhabitants. The abundance of crops and the reliance on the land for sustenance led to the development of ecospiritual practices centered around gratitude, reverence, and reciprocity. Rituals and ceremonies were conducted to honor the land, the rivers, and the gods associated with agricultural fertility. These practices acknowledged the interconnectedness between human beings, the natural world, and the divine, fostering a deep sense of harmony and respect for the cycles of life and abundance.

Through the exploration of fertile soil and its impact on agricultural productivity, we uncover the intricate relationship between human beings, the land, and the sustenance it provides. The fertility of the soil not only sustained the physical needs of the Mesopotamian people but also influenced their spiritual beliefs and practices. By recognizing the interplay between agriculture, the environment, and spiritual traditions, we gain a deeper appreciation for the holistic nature of ancient Mesopotamian culture.

➢ Sacred Landscapes and Natural Elements

In the vibrant tapestry of Mesopotamia's natural environment, an array of landscapes unfolded, each carrying its own spiritual significance. This section will delve into the sacredness attributed to these landscapes and natural elements, providing insights into the Mesopotamian worldview through the exploration of mythologies and religious practices. By examining examples from fields like witchcraft and shamanism, we will unravel the profound connections between the people, the land, and the spiritual realms.

✦ The Sacred Rivers: Lifeblood of the Land

The Tigris and Euphrates rivers held a paramount position in the Mesopotamian worldview, representing not only the physical life-giving force but also the spiritual connection between the earthly and divine realms. These rivers were revered as sacred entities, embodying the cycle of life, fertility, and prosperity. Just as the rivers nurtured the land with their abundant waters, they were believed to sustain the cosmic order and the well-being of the entire community. The Mesopotamians offered prayers, conducted rituals, and made offerings to honor these rivers, recognizing their vital role in the sustenance of life.

✦ Mountains: Bridging Heaven and Earth

Beyond the rivers, the majestic mountains of Mesopotamia also held a special place in the hearts and minds of the people. Mountains, with their lofty peaks reaching towards the heavens, were seen as bridges connecting the mortal realm with the realms of the divine. The Mesopotamians believed that gods and goddesses resided atop these mountains, making them sacred sites. These mountains were often associated with deities representing power, wisdom, and protection. Pilgrimages to these sacred peaks were undertaken to seek divine guidance, blessings, and spiritual enlightenment.

✧ Marshlands: Gateways to the Otherworld

The marshlands, with their distinctive ecosystems teeming with life, were considered mystical gateways to the Otherworld in Mesopotamian belief systems. These vast wetlands, characterized by reeds, wildlife, and interconnected waterways, were believed to be inhabited by supernatural beings and spirits. Witchcraft and shamanism often involved journeys into the marshlands to commune with these entities, seeking guidance, healing, or spiritual transformation. The marshlands symbolized the liminal spaces between the human and spirit realms, offering opportunities for profound encounters with the unseen.

Examples:

Witchcraft: In Mesopotamian witchcraft practices, the natural elements of the land, including rivers, mountains, and marshlands, played integral roles. Witches revered the rivers as conduits of power and divinity, incorporating water in their rituals, spells, and purification rites. They sought the wisdom of the mountains, conducting rituals at sacred peaks to connect with higher realms and harness spiritual energy. Additionally, marshlands were seen as liminal spaces where witches communed with spirits and tapped into their transformative energies for healing, divination, and spellcasting.

Shamanism: Mesopotamian shamanism also embraced the sacredness of the natural elements. Shamans viewed the rivers as channels of spiritual energy, utilizing water in cleansing rituals and as a means of connecting with divine forces. Mountains served as sacred spaces for shamanic journeying, enabling contact with spirit guides and accessing hidden knowledge. The marshlands, with their mysterious and otherworldly qualities, were frequented by shamans for encounters with spirit allies, performing ceremonies to honor the spirits of the land and seeking their guidance in healing and spiritual quests.

Through the exploration of Mesopotamia's sacred landscapes and natural elements, we gain a profound understanding of the interconnectedness between the physical and spiritual realms. The rivers, mountains, and marshlands were not mere geographical features but vibrant expressions of the divine presence. They shaped the spiritual practices of witchcraft, shamanism, and other mystical traditions, serving as gateways to profound experiences and deepened connections with the forces of nature and the unseen realms.

Examples, Problems, and Exercises:

To deepen your understanding of the geography and environment of Mesopotamia, let's engage with some examples, problems, and exercises:

Problem:

Imagine you are a farmer in ancient Mesopotamia. Design an irrigation system that maximizes water distribution and minimizes potential flood damage. Consider the challenges posed by the unpredictable nature of the rivers and the need for cooperation among neighboring farmers.

Exercise:

Reflect on the significance of sacred landscapes in modern spiritual practices. Choose a contemporary tradition, such as eco-spirituality or nature-based witchcraft, and explore how it incorporates reverence for the land and natural elements. Discuss the similarities and differences between these modern practices and the ancient Mesopotamian worldview.

By engaging with these examples, problems, and exercises, you will develop a deeper appreciation for the geographical and environmental factors that shaped Mesopotamian culture. Prepare yourself for a captivating journey into the heart of this ancient civilization, where the land, rivers, and natural elements intertwined with the spiritual beliefs and practices of its people.

➢ Political Structures and Societal Dynamics

Ancient Mesopotamia was characterized by a complex political landscape. City-states emerged as the dominant political entities, each with its own ruler and administrative apparatus. Over time, powerful empires rose and fell, such as the Akkadian Empire, the Babylonian Empire under Hammurabi's rule, and the Assyrian Empire. These political structures influenced the religious and magical practices of the society, as rulers often claimed divine authority and played a central role in the religious rituals and offerings made to appease the gods.

Mesopotamian society was highly stratified, with a hierarchical structure comprising the ruling elite, priests, scribes, merchants, artisans, and farmers. The division of labor and social roles shaped the ways in which magic and religious practices were carried out. Priests, as intermediaries between the divine and human realms, held significant influence and were responsible for conducting religious ceremonies, including magical rituals.

Within the complex tapestry of ancient Mesopotamia, a myriad of political structures and societal dynamics shaped the fabric of everyday life. This section will delve into the intricate web of power, governance, and social hierarchy that influenced the religious and magical practices of the society. By examining examples from fields such as witchcraft, divination, and magic, we will gain a deeper understanding of how political structures and societal roles intersected with the spiritual realm.

✦ City-States: Power and Governance

The city-states of Mesopotamia emerged as prominent political entities, each with its own ruler and administrative apparatus. These city-states, such as Sumer, Babylon, and Assyria, wielded significant influence over their territories and played pivotal roles in the political and religious landscape. Rulers often claimed divine authority, positioning themselves as intermediaries between the gods and the people. They were responsible for maintaining social order, enforcing laws, and leading military campaigns. The decisions made by these rulers had far-reaching implications for religious practices and magical rituals within their domains.

✦ Empires: Rise and Fall

Throughout the course of Mesopotamian history, powerful empires rose and fell, leaving indelible marks on the region's political and magical landscape. The Akkadian Empire, the Babylonian Empire under Hammurabi's rule, and the Assyrian Empire were among the notable empires that exerted dominance over vast territories. The expansion and consolidation of empires brought changes to religious practices, as rulers sought to unify diverse regions under a common religious framework. The empires also facilitated the exchange of magical knowledge and practices, influencing the development of magical traditions across different regions.

✦ Social Hierarchy: Roles and Responsibilities

Mesopotamian society was characterized by a hierarchical structure that delineated various social roles and responsibilities. At the pinnacle of the hierarchy stood the ruling elite, who held political power and controlled the resources of the state. Below them were the priests, who played a central role in religious and magical practices. As intermediaries between the divine and human realms, priests conducted rituals, made offerings, and interpreted omens and divinations. Scribes, merchants, artisans, and farmers occupied lower strata of the social hierarchy, each contributing to the functioning of society in their respective roles.

Examples:

Witchcraft: In Mesopotamian society, witches occupied varied positions within the social hierarchy. While some witches belonged to the ruling elite and used their magical practices to consolidate power and influence, others came from marginalized segments of society, using witchcraft as a means of empowerment and resistance. The relationship between witchcraft and political structures was complex, with witches often challenging or subverting established power structures through their magical practices.

Divination: The role of divination within Mesopotamian society was closely intertwined with political structures and societal dynamics. Diviners, who were often associated with the priesthood, used various techniques, such as reading omens or interpreting celestial events, to provide guidance and insight to rulers. Divination played a crucial role in political decision-making, as rulers sought divine guidance to ensure the success of military campaigns, the stability of their reign, and the prosperity of their cities.

➢   Religion and Magic in Daily Life

Religion permeated every aspect of Mesopotamian daily life, and magic was an integral part of their religious practices. Mesopotamians believed in a pantheon of gods and goddesses who controlled various aspects of the natural world, human affairs, and the afterlife. Rituals, including offerings and sacrifices, divination, and incantations, were performed to appease and seek favor from the gods, ensure fertility, protect against evil forces, and ensure prosperity.

Magic in ancient Mesopotamia was not considered separate from religion but rather intertwined with it. Magical practices involved the manipulation of supernatural forces through spells, charms, and rituals to influence events and bring about desired outcomes. Mesopotamian magic encompassed various forms, including divination, healing, protection against malevolent spirits, and the use of amulets and talismans.

In ancient Mesopotamia, religion and magic were not confined to temples or ritual spaces; they permeated every aspect of daily life. This section will explore the integral role of religion and magic in the lives of the Mesopotamians, shedding light on their beliefs, practices, and the ways in which they sought to connect with the divine. By examining examples from fields such as witchcraft, divination, herbalism, and shamanism, we will uncover the rich tapestry of spiritual practices that shaped the daily lives of the Mesopotamians.

✧   Beliefs and Cosmology

The Mesopotamians possessed a complex belief system that revolved around a pantheon of gods and goddesses. These deities were thought to govern different aspects of life, such as agriculture, fertility, warfare, and craftsmanship. The Mesopotamians believed that by appeasing and honoring the gods through rituals, offerings, and prayers, they could ensure their favor and protection. Examples of religious texts, such as the Enuma Elish and the Epic of Gilgamesh, provide valuable insights into Mesopotamian cosmology and the relationship between gods and humans.

✧   Rituals and Ceremonies

Religious rituals and ceremonies were an integral part of Mesopotamian daily life. These practices encompassed various activities, including purification rites, offerings, festivals, and processions. Priests and priestesses, as the mediators between humans and the divine, played a central role in conducting these rituals. They were responsible for invoking the presence of deities, reciting prayers, and performing symbolic actions. These rituals aimed to establish harmony between the human realm and the divine realm, ensuring the well-being of individuals, communities, and the land.

✧   Magic and Divination

Magic and divination were closely intertwined with religious practices in Mesopotamia. Magic was perceived as a means of harnessing supernatural forces to achieve desired outcomes, such as healing, protection, and success in various endeavors. Mesopotamian magic encompassed a wide range of practices, including spells, incantations, amulets, and potions. Divination, on the other hand, involved seeking knowledge of the future or insight into present circumstances through various techniques, such as astrology, omen interpretation, and the examination of animal entrails. These practices provided guidance and offered a sense of control and understanding in the face of uncertainty.

Examples:

Herbalism: Herbalism played a crucial role in both religious and magical contexts in Mesopotamia. The use of medicinal plants, herbs, and botanical preparations formed an integral part of healing rituals and magical practices. The knowledge of herbal remedies was passed down through generations and held by specialized healers, who used plants to address physical ailments and spiritual imbalances.

Shamanism: Shamanism, as a practice of connecting with the spirit world and channeling divine energies, also found its place within Mesopotamian society. Shamans, known as "apkallu," were revered for their ability to communicate with spirits, perform healing rituals, and offer guidance to individuals and communities. Their role extended beyond religious and magical spheres, as they were often sought out for their wisdom and insights.

Exercise:

Reflect on the significance of religious rituals and ceremonies in Mesopotamian society. How did these practices contribute to the cohesion of communities and the well-being of individuals? Provide specific examples to support your analysis.

Consider the relationship between religion and magic in Mesopotamia. How did these intertwined practices influence the daily lives of individuals? Discuss the potential tensions or overlaps between religious and magical beliefs and practices.

By exploring the multifaceted nature of religion and magic in ancient Mesopotamia, we gain a deeper understanding of the cultural, social, and spiritual dynamics that shaped the lives of its people. The rich tapestry of beliefs and practices provides valuable insights into the complexities of human spirituality and the enduring quest for connection with the divine.

Example Problem:

Research the role of religion and magic in a specific Mesopotamian city-state, such as Babylon or Assyria. Analyze the archaeological and textual evidence to explore how religious and magical practices were integrated into the daily lives of the people. Discuss the role of the ruling elite, priests, and common individuals in the performance of rituals and magical practices. Reflect on how the socio-political context influenced the development and expression of Mesopotamian magic.

Mesopotamian Magical Beliefs and Cosmology:

To fully comprehend Mesopotamian magic, it is essential to explore the underlying beliefs and cosmological framework that formed the basis of their worldview. Mesopotamian cosmology was intricately woven into their daily lives, religious practices, and magical rituals. Through an exploration of their rich mythology and cosmological concepts, students can gain valuable insights into the interconnections between the human realm, the divine, and the natural world.

The Pantheon of Gods and Goddesses

Mesopotamian mythology featured a vast pantheon of gods and goddesses, each associated with specific domains and functions. These deities were believed to govern various aspects of existence, including natural phenomena, societal dynamics, and individual fortunes. For example, Enlil, the god of the air and storms, held authority over the forces of nature, while Inanna, the goddess of love and fertility, was revered for her power to bestow blessings on relationships and ensure bountiful harvests.

The Mesopotamian pantheon reflected the interconnectedness of different spheres of life. Gods and goddesses were often depicted as anthropomorphic beings with human emotions and flaws, making their interactions with humans relatable and relevant to daily experiences. Understanding the roles and attributes of these deities provides insight into the magical practices and rituals dedicated to seeking their favor or protection.

The Enuma Elish, a Babylonian creation myth, provides a captivating narrative of the origins of the universe and the divine hierarchy. According to this myth, the god Marduk emerged as the supreme ruler after defeating the chaotic forces of Tiamat, the primordial goddess of the ocean. Marduk's victory established a new order and cemented his position as the patron deity of Babylon.

In addition to the prominent deities, numerous minor gods and goddesses existed within the Mesopotamian pantheon. These lesser-known divine beings were associated with specific functions, such as Nergal, the god of war and the underworld, and Nisaba, the goddess of writing and knowledge. Each deity held a distinct role in the cosmic balance and could be called upon for assistance or supplication in specific circumstances.

The worship of these deities was not confined to grand temples or elaborate rituals. Mesopotamians embraced a personal and intimate connection with the gods, often engaging in individual acts of devotion and household rituals. Offerings, prayers, and personal appeals were made to secure the favor and protection of a specific deity, whether it was Shamash, the god of justice and the sun, or Ishtar, the goddess of love and war.

Examples:

Enki, the god of wisdom and fresh water, played a significant role in magical practices. He was believed to possess profound knowledge and was invoked for healing and protection. The incantations and spells dedicated to Enki often called upon his wisdom to counteract illness, provide insight, or ward off evil spirits.

Ishtar, the goddess of love and fertility, was widely revered for her influence over matters of the heart and reproductive success. Her cult involved rituals and ceremonies that sought her blessings for marital unions, conception, and the well-being of children. Talismans and amulets depicting Ishtar were believed to bring love, passion, and fertility to those who wore them.

Exercise:

Research and choose a Mesopotamian deity from the pantheon. Describe their attributes, domain of influence, and any notable myths associated with them. Explain how this deity's worship and magical practices would be relevant to individuals seeking assistance or guidance in specific areas of life.

Discuss the significance of anthropomorphism in Mesopotamian religious beliefs. How did the portrayal of gods and goddesses as relatable and flawed beings contribute to the connection between humans and the divine? Use examples from mythology and religious texts to support your analysis.

Understanding the diverse pantheon of gods and goddesses in Mesopotamia allows us to delve deeper into the religious and magical practices of the ancient civilization. By exploring their attributes, myths, and the personal connections formed with these deities, we gain a broader understanding of how religion and magic intertwined in the daily lives of the Mesopotamians.

Cosmological Worldview

Mesopotamians viewed the universe as a layered and hierarchical structure. At the center was the earth, surrounded by the heavens and the underworld. The heavens were believed to be the dwelling place of the gods, while the underworld was associated with the realm of the dead. The concept of cosmic order, known as "me," was integral to their cosmology. "Me" represented the divine decrees and powers that governed various aspects of existence.

The interplay between the human realm, the divine, and the natural world was central to Mesopotamian cosmology. Humans were considered creations of the gods, and their lives were intertwined with divine will and cosmic forces. This interconnectedness formed the basis for magical practices, as individuals sought to align themselves with the divine and influence the natural world through rituals and offerings.

The cosmological worldview of the Mesopotamians can be further understood through the concept of celestial divination, a practice that sought to interpret the will of the gods through celestial events. The movements of celestial bodies, such as the moon, planets, and stars, were believed to convey messages from the divine realm. Priests and diviners meticulously observed these celestial phenomena and used them to make predictions and gain insights into various aspects of life, including agriculture, politics, and personal fortunes.

The Enuma Anu Enlil, a series of tablets containing celestial omens, documented the belief that celestial events were directly connected to the actions and desires of the gods. For example, the appearance of a particular constellation in the night sky might indicate a forthcoming military victory or a bountiful harvest. Such omens were carefully recorded and interpreted by skilled diviners, who held a significant role in society and advised rulers on matters of governance and decision-making.

Examples:

The New Moon was an important celestial event in Mesopotamian cosmology. Its appearance marked the beginning of a new month, and its visibility or lack thereof was interpreted as an omen. A waxing moon symbolized growth and prosperity, while a waning moon might be seen as a sign of decline or impending challenges. Understanding the significance of the New Moon allowed individuals to plan their activities and make important decisions accordingly.

The Enuma Anu Enlil tablets contained records of various celestial omens and their interpretations. For example, the sudden appearance or disappearance of certain stars, known as heliacal rising or setting, was believed to foretell events or outcomes. If a star associated with a particular deity vanished from the sky, it could be seen as a sign of that deity's displeasure or withdrawal of favor.

Exercise:

Research a specific celestial omen mentioned in the Enuma Anu Enlil tablets. Describe the celestial event and its associated interpretation. Explain how this omen could have influenced the decisions or actions of individuals in Mesopotamian society.

Reflect on the role of divination in Mesopotamian cosmology. Discuss how the interpretation of celestial omens and the practice of divination provided individuals with a sense of guidance and agency in navigating their lives. Consider the potential challenges and limitations of relying on celestial divination for decision-making.

Understanding the cosmological worldview of the Mesopotamians deepens our knowledge of their magical practices and religious beliefs. By recognizing the interconnectedness of the human, divine, and natural realms, we gain insight into the significance of celestial divination and its role in shaping the lives of ancient Mesopotamians.

Magical Rituals and Divination

Magical rituals played a crucial role in Mesopotamian society. These rituals were performed by priests, who acted as intermediaries between the human and divine realms. Through intricate ceremonies and invocations, priests sought to harness the powers of the gods and goddesses for various purposes, such as healing, protection, or divining the future.

Divination, the practice of seeking knowledge of the future or hidden truths, was an essential component of Mesopotamian magic. Various methods were employed, including interpreting celestial omens, observing natural phenomena, or analyzing the patterns of entrails. Divination was seen as a means to gain insight into the will of the gods and make informed decisions or take appropriate actions.

One prominent method of divination in Mesopotamia was hepatoscopy, the examination of animal livers for omens. The liver was believed to be a particularly sacred organ, and its shape and markings were carefully analyzed by diviners to discern messages from the divine. Divination was not limited to priests; it was also practiced by skilled individuals known as baru-priests and seers.

Magical rituals often involved the use of sacred objects, such as statues, amulets, or talismans, which were believed to possess inherent magical properties or serve as conduits for divine energy. These objects were carefully crafted and consecrated to specific deities, and their use in rituals aimed to invoke their powers and establish a connection between the physical and spiritual realms.

Examples:

The Enuma Elish, the Babylonian creation myth, recounts the magical rituals performed by the god Marduk to establish his supremacy over the other gods. Through elaborate ceremonies and incantations, Marduk gained the support of the divine assembly and emerged as the chief deity. This myth highlights the belief in the transformative power of magical rituals and their role in shaping the course of cosmic events.

The Babylonian ritual known as the Akitu Festival, held annually in honor of the god Marduk, involved various magical practices. These included the reenactment of mythological events, processions, and offerings. The festival served not only as a means of honoring the deity but also as a means of renewing cosmic order and ensuring the prosperity of the land.

Exercise:

Research and describe a specific magical ritual performed in ancient Mesopotamia. Explain the purpose of the ritual, the deities involved, and the steps or components of the ceremony. Reflect on the significance of this ritual in the broader cultural and religious context of Mesopotamia.

Discuss the role of divination in Mesopotamian society. Compare and contrast different methods of divination used, such as hepatoscopy, celestial omens, or extispicy (divination through examining animal entrails). Consider the impact of divination on decision-making, personal beliefs, and societal dynamics.

Understanding the significance of magical rituals and divination in Mesopotamian society provides insight into the importance of the supernatural and the quest for knowledge and guidance. Through these practices, individuals sought to establish a connection with the divine, shape their destinies, and navigate the complexities of life in ancient Mesopotamia.

Forms and Functions of Mesopotamian Magic:

Mesopotamian magic encompassed a wide range of forms and served various functions within the society of ancient Mesopotamia. In this section, we will explore the diverse manifestations of Mesopotamian magic, including incantations, spells, rituals, and divination. By examining specific examples and case studies, students will gain a comprehensive understanding of the forms and functions of magic in Mesopotamian culture.

Incantations and Spells

Incantations and spells formed a fundamental aspect of Mesopotamian magical practices. These verbal formulae, often chanted or recited, were believed to possess inherent power and invoke the assistance of the gods and goddesses. Incantations were employed for a variety of purposes, including healing illnesses, warding off evil spirits, and influencing events or individuals.

One notable example is the "Maqlû" series, a collection of incantations used to counter malevolent forces and protect against witchcraft. These incantations consisted of prayers, invocations, and ritual actions performed by specialized priests. Through the recitation of specific words and the manipulation of symbolic objects, such as figurines or amulets, the priests sought to neutralize harmful influences and restore balance.

The effectiveness of incantations and spells in Mesopotamian magic was believed to be rooted in the power of words and the divine authority behind them. It was believed that certain combinations of sounds and syllables held the ability to command supernatural forces and shape reality. The careful selection of words and their precise pronunciation were considered crucial for the success of the spell.

Spells were often accompanied by ritual gestures or actions, further enhancing their potency. These gestures could involve the manipulation of objects, the drawing of symbols, or the enactment of symbolic movements. By engaging multiple senses and incorporating symbolic elements, the spell-casters aimed to create a holistic and immersive experience that amplified the magical intention.

Examples:

The "Bīt Rimki" ritual was a form of exorcism used to remove evil spirits from individuals or spaces. The ritual involved the recitation of incantations, the sprinkling of protective substances, and the use of ritual objects. The words of the incantations were carefully chosen to address specific types of malevolent entities, while the gestures and actions were performed to cleanse and purify the affected person or area.

The "Āšipu" was a specialized priest in Mesopotamia who practiced magical healing. They utilized a combination of incantations, medicinal substances, and ritual actions to cure physical and psychological ailments. For example, in cases of possession or spiritual afflictions, the Āšipu would recite incantations to banish the possessing spirit while performing gestures to symbolize the expulsion of the malevolent force.

Exercise:

Explore the purpose and components of a specific Mesopotamian incantation or spell. Describe the context in which it was used, the deities invoked, and the actions or objects associated with its performance. Reflect on the underlying beliefs and worldview that informed the use of such magical practices.

Investigate the role of incantations and spells in modern witchcraft or occult practices. Compare and contrast the use of verbal formulae and ritual actions in ancient Mesopotamia with contemporary magical traditions. Consider the similarities and differences in the understanding of the power of words and the mechanisms through which spells are believed to work.

The utilization of incantations and spells in Mesopotamian magic highlights the belief in the power of language and ritual actions to effect change in the physical and spiritual realms. Through the skilled use of words and symbolic gestures, ancient Mesopotamians sought to manipulate and interact with the supernatural forces around them, shaping their lives and protecting themselves from malevolent influences.

Rituals and Ceremonies

Rituals played a significant role in Mesopotamian magical practices. These structured and stylized actions aimed to establish a connection between the human and divine realms, harnessing the powers of the gods for specific purposes. Rituals were performed in temples, private households, or sacred spaces, often by trained priests or individuals with specialized knowledge.

One prominent example is the Akitu festival, a New Year celebration that involved elaborate rituals and ceremonies. The festival included processions, offerings, sacred dramas, and recitations of hymns and prayers. The Akitu festival served not only as a religious and social event but also as a means to ensure the renewal and continuity of the cosmic order, fostering prosperity and divine favor for the coming year.

The rituals and ceremonies of Mesopotamia were deeply rooted in the belief that the performance of specific actions and the observance of prescribed rituals could establish a direct line of communication with the divine realm. These rituals were designed to honor the gods, seek their blessings, and maintain the balance and harmony of the universe.

Examples:

The "Eššešu" ritual was performed to purify and consecrate temples and sacred objects. This ritual involved the sprinkling of water, the burning of incense, and the recitation of prayers and invocations. The purpose was to cleanse the space and make it suitable for the presence of the deity. The ritual gestures and words served as a means to sanctify the temple and establish a connection between the earthly realm and the divine.

The "Zu" bird ritual was a complex ceremonial performance aimed at warding off evil forces and protecting the king and the kingdom. The ritual involved the creation of a symbolic representation of the Zu bird, a mythological creature associated with divine authority. The priest would recite incantations and perform ritual actions, such as waving ceremonial objects, to symbolize the defeat and banishment of evil forces. This ceremony demonstrated the close connection between political power, religious authority, and the well-being of the state.

Exercise:

Research and describe the rituals associated with a specific Mesopotamian deity. Explore the purpose, symbols, and actions involved in the worship of that deity. Consider the significance of the deity within the broader religious and societal context of Mesopotamia.

Imagine you are a priest or priestess in ancient Mesopotamia tasked with performing a ritual for a specific purpose, such as healing or protection. Write a step-by-step guide describing the actions, gestures, and recitations you would employ in the ritual. Explain the symbolic significance of each step and how it relates to the desired outcome.

Rituals and ceremonies were integral to the religious and magical practices of ancient Mesopotamia, serving as a means to establish a connection with the divine, seek guidance and blessings, and ensure the well-being of individuals, communities, and the state. These structured and symbolic actions fostered a sense of sacredness and provided a framework for engaging with the gods and maintaining the cosmic order.

Divination and Prophecy

Divination, the practice of seeking knowledge of the future or hidden truths, held great significance in Mesopotamian culture. It was believed that through divination, humans could gain insight into the will of the gods and make informed decisions or take appropriate actions. Various methods of divination were employed, each with its own techniques and symbolic systems.

One widely practiced form of divination was hepatoscopy, the examination of the liver of sacrificial animals. The liver was considered a locus of divine communication, and its various parts were interpreted as omens and signs.

Trained specialists, known as baru-priests, meticulously examined the liver, interpreting its shape, color, and markings to provide insights into the future or to determine the effectiveness of rituals and offerings.

The art of divination extended beyond hepatoscopy to encompass other methods such as astrology, extispicy (the examination of entrails), and the interpretation of celestial omens. These practices sought to uncover hidden knowledge and provide guidance in different aspects of life, from personal matters to political decisions. Divination was not only employed by priests but also by individuals seeking answers to their own questions or concerns.

Examples:

Astrology played a significant role in Mesopotamian divination. Observations of celestial bodies, such as the positions and movements of planets and stars, were believed to hold profound significance. Astrologers meticulously recorded these celestial events and interpreted them as omens and messages from the gods. For instance, the appearance of certain constellations or the alignment of planets was considered a sign of divine favor or impending calamity.

Extispicy, the examination of animal entrails, was another popular form of divination. Skilled diviners, known as bārû-priests, would carefully dissect the liver, lungs, and other organs of a sacrificial animal, examining their shape, color, and texture. Each detail was scrutinized for signs and symbols that could foretell the future or reveal the intentions of the gods. These diviners possessed specialized knowledge and were highly regarded for their ability to unravel the mysteries hidden within the entrails.

Exercise:

Research and describe a specific method of divination used in Mesopotamia, such as astrology or extispicy. Explore the techniques, tools, and symbols associated with this method. Explain how practitioners interpreted the signs and omens to provide guidance or predictions.

Imagine you are a diviner in ancient Mesopotamia. Write a step-by-step guide on how to perform a divination ritual using a specific method. Include the necessary preparations, tools, and actions involved. Discuss the significance of the symbols or signs you would look for and how you would interpret them to provide meaningful insights or predictions.

Divination and prophecy played a crucial role in Mesopotamian society, offering individuals and communities a means to navigate the uncertainties of life. The intricate methods and symbolic systems used in divination provided a framework for understanding the divine will and seeking guidance from the gods. These practices were deeply intertwined with religious beliefs and rituals, shaping the decisions and actions of both individuals and the ruling elite.

Practitioners of Mesopotamian Magic:

Practitioners, particularly priests and priestesses, played a crucial role in Mesopotamian magic as intermediaries between the human and divine realms. These individuals underwent specialized training and possessed extensive knowledge of religious rituals, incantations, and divination techniques. In this section, students will explore the role of these practitioners and gain insight into their responsibilities, training, and the significance of their presence in the magical practices of ancient Mesopotamia.

Priests and Priestesses

Priests and priestesses held esteemed positions within Mesopotamian society and were responsible for conducting religious ceremonies, maintaining temples, and performing magical rituals. They were believed to have a direct connection with the gods and acted as mediators between the human and divine realms. Their primary role was to harness and manipulate magical forces to bring about desired outcomes, such as healing, protection, or agricultural fertility.

Priests underwent rigorous training that involved the study of religious texts, learning the appropriate recitations and rituals, and understanding the complex cosmology and mythology of Mesopotamia. They were responsible for accurately performing rituals, reciting incantations, and interpreting omens and signs during divination practices. Priestesses, in particular, held positions of power and influence, often serving as oracles or prophetic figures.

The role of priests and priestesses in Mesopotamian society was multifaceted and integral to the religious and magical practices of the time. These individuals dedicated their lives to serving the gods and performing sacred duties that upheld the cosmic order and ensured the well-being of the community.

Examples:

The training of priests and priestesses involved an extensive study of religious texts and the memorization of rituals and prayers. These texts, such as the "Enuma

Elish" and the "Atrahasis Epic," provided insights into the creation of the world, the relationships between gods and humans, and the moral and ethical principles to be followed. Priests and priestesses were expected to possess deep knowledge of these texts and the mythology they contained.

Temples served as the focal points of religious and magical activities. Priests and priestesses maintained these sacred spaces, ensuring their cleanliness and performing daily rituals. The temples housed statues or symbols representing the gods, and offerings of food, drink, and incense were regularly presented to appease and honor them. These practices were believed to maintain the harmonious relationship between the human and divine realms.

Problems:

Discuss the significance of gender in Mesopotamian religious practices. How did the roles and responsibilities of male and female priests differ? Provide examples of influential priestesses and their contributions to Mesopotamian religion and magic.

Compare and contrast the roles of priests in Mesopotamian society with those of other ancient civilizations, such as Egypt or Greece. Analyze the similarities and differences in their training, functions, and status within their respective societies.

Exercise:

Write a short dialogue between a priest and a young apprentice, discussing the importance of proper training and knowledge in performing rituals and interpreting omens. Include examples of specific rituals and their significance within the context of Mesopotamian religious practices.

Research a famous priest or priestess from Mesopotamian history and create a presentation highlighting their accomplishments and contributions. Include details about their role, notable rituals or ceremonies they performed, and any miraculous or significant events associated with their religious duties.

Priests and priestesses held a crucial position in Mesopotamian society, acting as intermediaries between humans and the divine. Their extensive knowledge, devotion, and rituals played a pivotal role in maintaining cosmic order, seeking divine favor, and addressing the spiritual and practical needs of the community.

Rituals and Practices

The rituals and practices performed by Mesopotamian practitioners were highly structured and followed established protocols. They involved the use of specific gestures, objects, and incantations to establish a connection with the divine realm and invoke the assistance of the gods. Students will explore examples of these rituals, such as purification rites, offerings, and the recitation of incantations, to gain a deeper understanding of the actions and beliefs underlying Mesopotamian magical practices.

Priests and priestesses conducted rituals in temples or sacred spaces, often accompanied by a retinue of assistants and musicians. They meticulously followed prescribed procedures and adhered to strict rules to ensure the efficacy of the magical practices. Through the performance of these rituals, practitioners aimed to harmonize the human and divine realms, seeking blessings, protection, and divine intervention in various aspects of life.

Rituals and practices held a central place in Mesopotamian magical traditions, providing a structured framework for connecting with the divine and enacting desired outcomes. These rituals encompassed a wide range of activities and ceremonies, each serving a specific purpose and adhering to established protocols.

Examples of rituals performed in Mesopotamian magical practices include:

Purification Rites: Purification rituals were conducted to cleanse individuals or objects from spiritual impurities and ensure their readiness for interaction with the divine. These rites often involved the use of water, incense, or symbolic gestures to symbolize the removal of negative influences and the restoration of spiritual balance. For instance, priests would sprinkle purifying water on participants and recite invocations to cleanse them of any spiritual contamination.

Offerings: Offerings were a common practice aimed at honoring the gods and establishing a reciprocal relationship with them. Various items such as food, drink, flowers, or precious objects were presented as offerings in temples or sacred spaces. These offerings were believed to please the gods and elicit their favor, protection, or assistance. The choice of offerings often reflected the specific deity being invoked and the purpose of the ritual.

Incantations and Invocations: Verbal formulas, known as incantations and invocations, played a crucial role in Mesopotamian rituals. These carefully crafted words and phrases were believed to possess inherent power and were recited to invoke the assistance of specific deities or channel divine energies. Priests and priestesses would chant or speak these incantations in a rhythmic manner, often accompanied by the use of symbolic objects or gestures to enhance their effectiveness.

It is important to note that rituals were not merely empty performances but were deeply rooted in the religious and magical beliefs of Mesopotamian culture. They were conducted with precision and adherence to prescribed procedures to ensure their efficacy and maintain the delicate balance between the human and divine realms.

Exercise:

Choose a specific Mesopotamian ritual, such as a purification rite or an offering ceremony, and describe the steps and symbolic elements involved in its performance. Discuss the significance of each step and the underlying beliefs and intentions behind the ritual.

Research the role of music and dance in Mesopotamian rituals. Identify specific instruments or musical styles that were used and discuss how they were believed to enhance the spiritual atmosphere and evoke specific energies during the rituals.

Imagine you are a Mesopotamian priest or priestess preparing for a significant ritual. Write a journal entry describing your thoughts, feelings, and preparations leading up to the ritual, as well as your expectations and intentions for its outcome.

Through the exploration of these rituals and practices, students will gain a deeper appreciation for the intricate and purposeful nature of Mesopotamian magical traditions, and the profound role they played in the lives of practitioners and the wider society.

Magical Objects and Tools

Magical objects and tools played an essential role in Mesopotamian magic, acting as conduits for channeling and manipulating cosmic energies. Students will explore the significance and functions of these objects, gaining insights into their cultural and religious contexts. Examples of magical artifacts include amulets, talismans, figurines, and ritual instruments.

Amulets and talismans were believed to possess protective or beneficial properties and were worn or carried by individuals seeking their specific powers. Figurines and statuettes were used in sympathetic magic, representing deities or individuals to whom certain rituals or spells were directed. Ritual instruments, such as drums, cymbals, and rattles, were used to create rhythmic sounds and vibrations that were believed to enhance the effectiveness of rituals and invocations.

Magical objects and tools held a significant place in Mesopotamian magical practices, serving as tangible symbols and vessels of mystical power. These objects were imbued with specific qualities and energies, believed to enable practitioners to connect with the divine and manipulate cosmic forces. Exploring the functions and meanings of these artifacts provides students with a deeper understanding of the cultural and religious contexts in which they were utilized.

Amulets and talismans were among the most commonly used magical objects in Mesopotamia. These small items, often worn or carried by individuals, were believed to possess protective or beneficial properties. For example, a person seeking protection against evil spirits might wear an amulet inscribed with sacred symbols or words of power. Talismans, on the other hand, were specifically crafted to attract certain qualities or influences, such as luck, fertility, or success. These objects served as constant reminders of the magical intentions and desires of the wearer.

Figurines and statuettes held a prominent role in sympathetic magic, a practice based on the principle of "like attracts like." These small representations of deities or individuals were used to direct rituals or spells towards specific targets. For instance, a figurine representing a specific god or goddess would be employed to invoke their assistance or blessings. The manipulation of these figurines through gestures or ritual actions was believed to establish a connection with the deity or individual they represented, facilitating the desired outcome.

Ritual instruments played a crucial role in creating the right atmosphere and enhancing the effectiveness of magical practices. Drums, cymbals, rattles, and other percussive instruments were used to produce rhythmic sounds and vibrations. These sounds were believed to resonate with cosmic energies and create a heightened state of consciousness, enabling practitioners to access deeper levels of spiritual awareness. The use of ritual instruments in conjunction with incantations or invocations added an auditory dimension to the rituals, intensifying their impact and creating a sensory experience that enhanced the connection between the human and divine realms.

Exercise:

Select a specific Mesopotamian amulet or talisman and research its symbolism and intended purpose. Write a short essay discussing its significance and the cultural beliefs surrounding its use.

Choose a Mesopotamian deity and create a figurine or statuette representing that deity. Describe the materials, symbols, and features you would incorporate into the figurine and explain the intended purpose or magical function it would serve.

Research the role of music and sound in Mesopotamian magical rituals. Identify specific instruments used and discuss how they were believed to facilitate spiritual experiences or manipulate cosmic energies. Create a short presentation or audio recording demonstrating the sounds and rhythms associated with Mesopotamian ritual music.

By exploring the functions and symbolism of these magical objects and tools, students will gain a deeper appreciation for the role they played in Mesopotamian magical practices and the cultural significance attributed to them.

Counterarguments and Dissenting Opinions

Counterarguments and dissenting opinions regarding the efficacy and cultural significance of Mesopotamian magic provide students with a well-rounded understanding of the topic and foster critical thinking skills. While the study of ancient Mesopotamian magic is rich and intriguing, it is essential to examine differing perspectives to gain a comprehensive view of the subject matter.

One counterargument put forth by skeptics suggests that magical practices in Mesopotamia were merely superstitious beliefs and had no tangible effect on the physical world. They argue that the rituals, spells, and incantations were products of a primitive understanding of natural phenomena and lacked any genuine power or influence. This perspective challenges the notion that magic played a significant role in shaping Mesopotamian society and raises questions about the reliability of historical accounts and interpretations.

Additionally, debates arise regarding the extent to which magic was integrated into everyday life in Mesopotamia. Some scholars argue that magical practices were confined to specific social classes, such as the priests and elites, who had the means and education to engage in ritualistic activities. According to this viewpoint, the majority of the population may not have had access to or participated in magical rituals, limiting the overall impact of magic on Mesopotamian society.

Furthermore, dissenting opinions question the interpretations and biases that may influence our understanding of Mesopotamian magic. As with any historical subject, the availability and interpretation of evidence can be subjective and subject to biases, both from the original sources and from modern interpretations. Some scholars argue that our understanding of Mesopotamian magic may be distorted by cultural assumptions or preconceived notions, leading to an incomplete or inaccurate portrayal of the practices and their significance.

Engaging with these counterarguments and dissenting opinions allows students to critically evaluate the evidence, question prevailing narratives, and develop a more nuanced understanding of Mesopotamian magic. By exploring diverse perspectives, students can consider the limitations and controversies surrounding the topic, enhancing their ability to analyze historical sources and draw well-informed conclusions.

Exercise:

Choose a specific counterargument against the efficacy of Mesopotamian magic and write an essay presenting the main points of this perspective. Evaluate the evidence provided and critically analyze its strengths and weaknesses.

Research the role of magic in different social classes of Mesopotamian society. Write a comparative analysis highlighting the arguments supporting both the limited and widespread integration of magic in daily life. Consider the available evidence and provide a well-reasoned conclusion.

Reflect on the potential biases and limitations in our understanding of Mesopotamian magic. Write a reflective essay discussing how cultural assumptions and preconceived notions may influence interpretations of magical practices. Use specific examples to support your argument and propose strategies for mitigating bias in the study of ancient magic.

By exploring counterarguments and dissenting opinions, students will develop critical thinking skills, foster intellectual curiosity, and gain a more nuanced understanding of the complexities surrounding the study of Mesopotamian magic.

Magical Texts and Spellbooks

Magical texts and spellbooks have long been regarded as portals to ancient wisdom and mystical knowledge. These precious artifacts provide valuable insights into the beliefs, practices, and rituals of diverse magical traditions throughout history. In this section, students will embark on a captivating journey through the world of magical texts and spellbooks, unraveling their significance, contents, and impact on magical practices.

Historical and Cultural Context:

To understand the role of magical texts and spellbooks, it is essential to explore their historical and cultural context. Students will delve into different civilizations and time periods, such as ancient Egypt, Mesopotamia, Greece, and medieval Europe, to examine the socio-cultural factors that shaped the creation and preservation of these texts. By understanding the cultural milieu in which these texts emerged, students will gain a deeper appreciation for their significance within the magical traditions of the time.

Exploring the historical and cultural context surrounding magical texts and spellbooks is crucial for comprehending their role and significance. By delving into various civilizations and time periods, such as ancient Egypt, Mesopotamia, Greece, and medieval Europe, students will gain insight into the socio-cultural factors that influenced the creation, preservation, and utilization of these texts. Understanding the cultural milieu in which magical texts emerged allows students to appreciate the intricate relationship between magic, religion, and society.

Ancient Egypt provides an illuminating example of the interconnection between magic and religion. The Egyptians believed in a complex pantheon of gods and goddesses who governed different aspects of life. Magical spells and rituals were seen as means to communicate with the divine and access their power. Students will explore the significance of the Egyptian Book of the Dead, a collection of spells and prayers intended to guide the deceased through the afterlife. By examining the cultural beliefs surrounding death and the role of magic in facilitating a successful journey, students will gain a deeper understanding of the cultural context in which these texts were utilized.

Mesopotamia, with its rich mythological traditions and intricate cosmology, offers another fascinating backdrop for the study of magical texts. The cuneiform tablets discovered in Mesopotamia provide valuable insights into the magical rituals, incantations, and divinatory practices of this ancient civilization. Students will examine the Enuma Anu Enlil, a compendium of omens and celestial divination, to understand the cultural significance of astrology and its relationship to magic in Mesopotamia.

Greek civilization, renowned for its philosophical and intellectual contributions, also had a deep-rooted tradition of magic. Students will explore the magical papyri, such as the Greek Magical Papyri, which contain a wealth of spells, rituals, and invocations. By examining the cultural context of ancient Greece, with its belief in a pantheon of gods and the permeation of magic in various aspects of life, students will gain insights into the integration of magic into religious and everyday practices.

The medieval period in Europe witnessed a complex interplay of magical beliefs, religious traditions, and societal norms. Students will delve into grimoires, such as the Key of Solomon or the Picatrix, to understand the magical practices and cosmology prevalent during this time. By exploring the cultural and religious climate of medieval Europe, including the influence of Christianity and the perception of magic as both forbidden and sought after, students will gain a nuanced understanding of the historical and cultural context in which these texts were produced.

Exercise:

Choose a specific magical text or spellbook from one of the civilizations mentioned above. Research its historical and cultural context, including the prevailing religious beliefs, societal norms, and the role of magic in that society. Write an essay analyzing how the cultural milieu influenced the creation and utilization of the magical text.

Compare and contrast the cultural context of magical texts in two different civilizations, such as ancient Egypt and medieval Europe. Highlight the similarities and differences in their religious beliefs, social structures, and the integration of magic into their respective cultures.

By exploring the historical and cultural context of magical texts, students will develop a deeper appreciation for the complexity of magical traditions and their interconnectedness with society, religion, and belief systems. This understanding enhances their ability to critically analyze and interpret these texts within their proper historical framework.

Types of Magical Texts:

In this section, we will explore different types of magical texts and spellbooks from various cultures. By studying these texts, students will gain a deeper understanding of the wide range of magical traditions that exist across different civilizations. We will discuss the purposes, contents, and unique characteristics of these texts, allowing students to appreciate the diversity of magical knowledge throughout history.

Let's start with ancient Egypt, known for its famous "Book of the Dead" or "Book of Coming Forth by Day." This collection of spells and prayers was created to guide the deceased through the afterlife. Students will examine the purpose and structure of the "Book of the Dead," including its intricate hieroglyphic texts and beautiful illustrations. They will learn about the spells and rituals intended to protect the deceased, ensure a successful journey to the divine realm, and achieve eternal life.

Next, we will explore Mesopotamia, where clay tablets with cuneiform inscriptions provide valuable insights into magical practices. Students will study texts such as the "Bilingual Hymns" and the "Ritual Series Maqlû" to understand Mesopotamian magical texts' content and purpose. These tablets contain invocations, incantations, and rituals aimed at countering malevolent forces, healing illnesses, and protecting against witchcraft. They also provide us with glimpses into the cultural beliefs and cosmology of ancient Mesopotamia.

Moving on to medieval Europe, we will examine grimoires, which emerged during this period. Students will discover texts such as the "Key of Solomon" and the "Picatrix," which served as comprehensive guides for performing rituals, summoning spirits, and practicing astrology and divination. These grimoires provided practitioners with a systematic understanding of magical knowledge, including the creation of talismans, the invocation of angels and demons, and the use of astrological correspondences.

Additionally, we will explore the Greek Magical Papyri, a collection of magical texts from Greco-Roman Egypt. These papyri contain spells, invocations, and rituals for various purposes, such as love, protection, and divination. Students will analyze the unique features of these texts, including their use of the Greek language and the incorporation of Egyptian, Jewish, and Gnostic elements. They will gain insights into the syncretic nature of magical traditions in this region and how cultural influences shaped these texts.

Contents and Structure of Magical Texts:

Welcome to the enchanting realm of magical texts and spellbooks. In this section, we will embark on a captivating journey, delving into the profound contents and intricate structure of these mystical manuscripts. By immersing ourselves in the study of these texts, you, as students, will unlock valuable insights into the spells, incantations, invocations, and rituals that have been utilized across various magical traditions throughout history. We will also venture into the realm of the divine and the supernatural, exploring the deities, spirits, and forces invoked during these magical workings. Through the meticulous analysis of specific excerpts and examples, you will cultivate a deeper understanding of the techniques, symbolism, and formulae employed in magical practices.

Unveiling the Secrets of Magical Formulas and Incantations

Magical texts are veritable treasure troves of formulas and incantations, meticulously crafted to manifest specific outcomes. These formulas are carefully structured sequences of words or phrases believed to possess inherent power, capable of bringing forth desired effects. In this section, you will embark on a fascinating exploration of different types of formulas found in various magical traditions. From verbal charms to sigils and symbolic diagrams, you will uncover the artistry behind their construction. By delving into the linguistic and symbolic elements interwoven within these formulas, you will unearth their underlying meanings and intentions, unraveling the secrets they hold.

Magical formulas and incantations hold a profound place within the mystical realm of magical texts. Like shimmering gems, these carefully crafted sequences of words and phrases possess the power to bring about specific outcomes and weave enchantments that resonate across the ages. In this section, we will embark on an enthralling exploration of the diverse types of formulas found within various magical traditions. From the lyrical cadence of verbal charms to the intricate geometry of sigils and the evocative symbolism of symbolic diagrams, we will peel back the layers of artistry that lie behind their construction.

Within the mesmerizing tapestry of magical formulas, language and symbolism intertwine, creating a potent blend of meaning and intention. As students of the magical arts, you will delve into the linguistic and symbolic elements interwoven within these formulas, unraveling their hidden depths and bringing their essence to light. By immersing yourselves in their study, you will discover the profound intentions encoded within the carefully chosen words and phrases, gaining a deeper understanding of the transformative power they possess.

Verbal charms, often crafted with poetic precision, weave a symphony of sounds that resonate with the vibrations of the universe. These incantations are carefully structured, with each word carefully chosen for its resonance and potency. Through the study of verbal charms, you will explore the rhythmic patterns, rhymes, and alliterations that create a harmonious flow, amplifying the energy and intention of the spell.

Sigils, on the other hand, employ the language of symbols to encapsulate intentions in visual form. These intricate and often mesmerizing designs hold the power to connect with the subconscious mind and tap into the collective unconscious. By studying sigils, you will uncover the artistry behind their construction, examining the choice of shapes, lines, and colors that imbue them with their unique energies. Through the exploration of sigils, you will develop the ability to create your own personal symbols, infusing them with intention and harnessing their transformative power.

Symbolic diagrams, like intricate maps of mystical realms, serve as gateways to hidden dimensions of existence. These complex visual representations embody the interconnectedness of the spiritual and material realms, guiding practitioners in their magical workings. By delving into the study of symbolic diagrams, you will decipher the meanings behind their intricate patterns, archetypal symbols, and cosmic correspondences. Through this exploration, you will gain insights into the universal truths they convey and the transformative energies they invoke.

Through the meticulous examination of linguistic and symbolic elements, you will unearth the underlying meanings and intentions embedded within these magical formulas and incantations. By analyzing specific examples from different magical traditions, you will develop a profound appreciation for the artistry and depth of these ancient texts. You will cultivate the skills necessary to craft your own potent formulas, incantations, sigils, and symbolic diagrams, imbuing them with intention and aligning them with your magical practice.

Deciphering the Language of Symbolism and Ritual Imagery

Within the enchanting tapestry of magical texts, symbolism weaves its way, serving as a profound language through which practitioners commune with the divine and tap into hidden forces. In this section, you will unravel the intricate layers of symbolic imagery that permeate these texts. From the vibrant hues of colors to the elegant shapes, from the mystique of animals to the celestial dance of celestial bodies, you will learn to decode the profound symbolism they bear. Through the exploration of specific examples, you will gain a profound appreciation for the transformative power of symbolism, how it enhances the effectiveness of rituals and spellcasting, and how it establishes a sacred connection between the mundane and the spiritual realms.

Magical texts are adorned with a captivating tapestry of symbolism, a language through which practitioners communicate with the divine and tap into the hidden forces that shape our reality. In this section, we will embark on a journey to unravel the intricate layers of symbolic imagery that permeate these mystical texts. From the vibrant hues of colors to the elegant shapes, from the mystique of animals to the celestial dance of celestial bodies, we will delve deep into the rich tapestry of symbolism that imbues magical practices with profound meaning.

Symbolism serves as a bridge between the tangible and intangible realms, allowing practitioners to access and harness the transformative energies that reside within the collective consciousness. By understanding the language of symbolism, students of the magical arts gain the ability to decode the hidden meanings and intentions behind the imagery found within these texts. As we embark on this exploration, we will unveil the profound connections between symbols and the forces they represent, unlocking the gateways to the realms of magic and enchantment.

Colors, with their vivid and evocative qualities, hold a significant place within magical symbolism. Each hue carries its own unique energy and resonance, eliciting specific emotions and associations. By studying the symbolic meanings of colors, students will gain insights into their use within rituals and spellcasting. From the fiery passion of red to the purifying purity of white, from the regal power of purple to the nurturing energy of green, the language of colors unveils a world of possibilities within magical practices.

Shapes, too, bear profound symbolism within the realm of magic. From the perfectly balanced circle to the mystical labyrinth, from the sacred geometry of the pentagram to the transformative spiral, shapes convey potent meanings and energies. By exploring the significance of these shapes, students will uncover the hidden wisdom encoded within them. Through the study of shapes, practitioners gain a deeper understanding of their role in ritual design, spellcasting, and the creation of magical talismans.

Animals, with their inherent symbolism and archetypal qualities, hold a special place within the magical lexicon. Each creature embodies unique attributes and powers, serving as a bridge between the human and animal realms. By delving into the symbolism of animals, students will discover the wisdom and energies associated with various creatures. From the regal wisdom of the owl to the transformative power of the serpent, from the swift agility of the falcon to the nurturing instinct of the bear, animals offer profound lessons and guidance within magical traditions.

Celestial bodies, with their celestial dance across the heavens, hold a celestial significance within magical symbolism. The sun, moon, stars, and planets are not only awe-inspiring cosmic entities but also bearers of mystical energies and influences. By exploring the symbolism of celestial bodies, students will uncover the profound connections between these cosmic entities and the magical practices of various traditions. From the radiant power of the sun to the intuitive wisdom of the moon, from the expansive energies of Jupiter to the transformative forces of Pluto, celestial bodies offer gateways to higher realms and sources of inspiration.

Through the meticulous exploration of symbolism and ritual imagery, students will gain a profound appreciation for the transformative power they hold within magical practices. By analyzing specific examples from various traditions, you will develop the ability to decode the hidden meanings behind symbols, colors, shapes, animals, and celestial bodies. This understanding will enhance your capacity to infuse rituals and spellcasting with intention, establishing a sacred connection with the forces that shape the cosmos.

The Sacred Dance of Ritual Structure and Sequence

Magical texts often provide meticulous instructions detailing the performance of rituals, outlining specific steps and sequences to be followed. In this section, you will embark on a profound exploration of the structure and organization of rituals. You will unravel the significance of each step, understanding its unique role within the larger tapestry of a magical working. By delving into the design of rituals, you will learn how they create sacred spaces, invoke spiritual energies, and channel the practitioner's intention toward a specific goal. Armed with a profound understanding of the underlying principles governing ritual structure, you will be empowered to create your own rituals and adapt existing ones to suit your personal spiritual practices.

Rituals, like intricate tapestries woven with intention and purpose, unfold through a carefully choreographed sequence of steps. Each step is imbued with symbolic significance, representing a vital piece of the larger magical working. By studying the structure and sequence of rituals, students of the mystical arts will gain a profound appreciation for the sacred dance that underlies these transformative experiences.

The structure of a ritual serves as a framework that establishes a sacred space, a container in which the practitioner can commune with the divine and access the energies of the unseen realms. By following the prescribed structure, practitioners create a vessel capable of holding and channeling the transformative energies that flow through the ritual. From the opening invocation to the closing gesture of gratitude, each step contributes to the establishment of this sacred container.

The sequence of a ritual is a carefully orchestrated symphony of actions, words, and intentions, guiding the practitioner along a path of spiritual transformation. Each step builds upon the previous one, creating a harmonious flow of energy that amplifies the intention of the working. By understanding the sequence of a ritual, students will gain insights into the significance of each action and its purpose within the larger tapestry. The sequence serves as a roadmap, leading practitioners through a journey of personal growth and spiritual connection.

Through the study of ritual structure and sequence, students will uncover the underlying principles that govern these sacred practices. They will explore the symbolism embedded within each step, understanding how it contributes to the overall intention of the ritual. By analyzing specific examples from different magical traditions, students will gain a profound understanding of the nuances and variations that exist within ritual design.

Armed with this knowledge, students will be empowered to create their own rituals, tailored to their individual spiritual practices and intentions. They will be able to adapt existing rituals, incorporating elements that resonate with their personal beliefs and aspirations. By applying the principles of ritual structure and sequence, students will infuse their rituals with depth and meaning, cultivating a profound connection with the forces that shape the cosmos.

Bridging the Divide: Invocation of Deities and Spirits

One of the recurring themes within magical texts is the invocation of deities and spirits, as practitioners seek to establish a profound connection with divine and supernatural entities. In this section, you will explore the diverse methods and techniques employed to invoke and communicate with these otherworldly beings. From the power of prayers to the mesmerizing invocations and the mystique of evocations, you will uncover the multifaceted approaches used by practitioners across different magical traditions. Through the exploration of specific examples, you will develop a deeper understanding of the roles of deities and spirits in magical practices. You will discover how they are invoked to lend aid, provide guidance, or bestow blessings upon the practitioner. Through this exploration, you will forge a profound connection with the rich tapestry of the relationship between humans and the divine or supernatural realms.

Magical texts serve as gateways, providing seekers of the mystical arts with a roadmap to establish a profound connection with the divine and supernatural realms. A recurring theme within these texts is the invocation of deities and spirits, as practitioners seek to bridge the divide between the earthly and the otherworldly. In this section, we will embark on a transformative exploration of the methods and techniques employed to invoke and communicate with these celestial beings. Through the study of prayers, invocations, and evocations, you will uncover the multifaceted approaches used by practitioners across diverse magical traditions.

The invocation of deities and spirits is a sacred endeavor, a sacred bridge built through words, gestures, and intentions. Through the power of prayer, practitioners express their reverence and call upon the divine forces to intercede in their lives. Prayers act as a direct line of communication, a heartfelt plea that seeks divine guidance, protection, or intervention. By studying the art of prayer within magical texts, students will understand how practitioners engage with the divine, how they open themselves to receive the wisdom and blessings bestowed by these celestial entities.

Invocations are enchanting incantations, crafted with the intention of summoning the presence and power of deities and spirits. These evocative words, spoken or written, carry the resonance of the sacred, invoking the very essence of these celestial beings. Through invocations, practitioners establish a profound connection with the divine, drawing upon their energies and wisdom. By delving into the invocations found within magical texts, students will learn the art of invoking these ethereal entities, channeling their energies for guidance, healing, or transformation.

Evocations are a mesmerizing dance with the otherworldly, a deliberate act of summoning spirits to commune with the practitioner. Through evocations, practitioners establish a direct encounter with these supernatural beings, calling upon them to appear and share their knowledge, wisdom, or assistance. By studying the techniques of evocation found within magical texts, students will gain insights into the rituals, symbols, and invocations used to create a sacred space conducive to the presence of spirits. They will discover the intricate art of establishing boundaries, ensuring respectful interaction and harnessing the blessings and guidance these spirits bring.

Within magical texts, the invocation of deities and spirits serves diverse purposes. They may be invoked to seek protection, guidance, healing, or empowerment. These celestial beings offer their aid, bestowing blessings upon the practitioner and illuminating their spiritual path. By analyzing specific examples from different magical traditions, students will develop a profound understanding of the roles these divine and supernatural entities play in the tapestry of magical practices.

Exercise : Communicating with the Divine

Choose a deity or spirit from a specific magical tradition and create an invocation or prayer that respectfully calls upon their presence and guidance. Reflect on the attributes and qualities associated with the chosen entity, infusing your invocation with reverence and intention. Practice reciting or writing the invocation, observing the shifts and connections that arise within your spiritual practice. Through this exercise, you will deepen your understanding of the invocation process and forge a profound connection with the divine or supernatural realms.

By unraveling the intricate tapestry of the invocation of deities and spirits, students of the mystical arts will develop a deep appreciation for the profound relationship between humans and the divine. They will gain the knowledge and tools to invoke these celestial forces, harnessing their guidance and blessings on their spiritual journeys. Through the exploration of diverse methods and techniques, students will bridge the divide between the earthly and the otherworldly, opening themselves to the transformative power of these mystical encounters.

Exercise : Analyzing the Enigmatic Magical Formulas

Select a magical text from a specific tradition, such as a grimoire or a spellbook, and immerse yourself in the analysis of the formulas and incantations within it. Identify the linguistic and symbolic elements present in the formulas and delve into their intended effects. How do these formulas align with the overarching goals and practices of the tradition? What insights can be gleaned from their intricate structure and profound symbolism? Engage in critical thinking as you explore these questions, unraveling the enigmatic depths of magical formulas.

Exercise : Interpreting the Profound Ritual Imagery

Choose a magical text that showcases symbolism and ritual imagery. Select a specific symbol or image and embark on a profound exploration of its meaning and significance within the context of the text and the broader magical tradition. What associations or attributes are ascribed to the symbol or image? How does it contribute to the overall efficacy of the ritual or spellcasting? Through detailed analysis, unlock the hidden meanings and transformative power embedded within the rich tapestry of ritual imagery.

Exercise : Crafting Your Personal Ritual

Harnessing the knowledge acquired from the study of ritual structure and sequence, you will now have the opportunity to craft your very own personal ritual. Select a specific purpose or intention close to your heart, and allow your creativity to flow as you design the steps, symbols, and invocations that align with your desired outcome. Reflect upon the profound significance of each element and its contribution to the overall efficacy of the ritual. Engage in experimentation as you bring your personal ritual to life, and afterward, take time to reflect upon the experience and its impact on your spiritual journey.

Through the exploration of the contents and structure of magical texts, you, as students, will cultivate a comprehensive understanding of the techniques, symbolism, and formulae employed in magical practices. As you unravel the mysteries of these ancient manuscripts, you will unlock profound insights into the sacred language of magic. Armed with this knowledge, you will be empowered to enhance your own magical practice, forging a deeper connection with the spiritual realm and embracing the transformative power of the arcane arts.

Transmission and Preservation:

In the realm of magic, the transmission and preservation of knowledge are of utmost importance. Throughout history, the safeguarding of magical texts and spellbooks has played a crucial role in ensuring the continuity and dissemination of sacred wisdom. In this chapter, we will embark on an enlightening journey through time, exploring the diverse methods employed to preserve and pass down magical knowledge.

➢ Oral Traditions: Whispers of Ancient Wisdom

Oral traditions form the ancient heartbeat of magical knowledge, where wisdom is passed down through generations like a whispered incantation. In this section, we will delve into the captivating realm of oral transmission and understand its significance in preserving and perpetuating magical traditions. By exploring the role of master practitioners as custodians of the oral tradition, we will gain insight into how arcane wisdom is imparted to the next generation, ensuring its survival in an ever-changing world.

➢ Handwritten Manuscripts: Craftsmanship of Magical Lore

The advent of handwritten manuscripts marked a transformative era in the preservation of magical knowledge. Scribes and copyists dedicated themselves to meticulously transcribing sacred texts, thereby preserving the wisdom within delicate pages. In this section, we will uncover the intricate processes employed by these devoted individuals. We will explore the art of calligraphy and the use of symbolic language necessary to capture the essence of magical texts. By tracing the lineage of handwritten manuscripts, we will witness the dedication of those who preserved the sacred flame of wisdom.

➢ Printed Books: Empowering Seekers through the Ages

The invention of the printing press revolutionized the transmission of magical knowledge, making texts more accessible than ever before. In this section, we will explore the impact of printed books on the accessibility and democratization of magical wisdom. We will delve into the secrets held within early grimoires and spellbooks, marveling at the intricate illustrations and the power conveyed through printed words. By understanding the significance of this technological advancement, we will recognize how it empowered seekers of the mystical arts to embark on their own journeys of discovery and transformation.

➢ Translation and Interpretation: Unlocking Ancient Mysteries

The translation and interpretation of ancient texts pose both challenges and opportunities in understanding magical knowledge. In this section, we will grapple with the complexities of translating magical texts, transcending barriers of language, cultural context, and symbolism. We will engage in meticulous study of ancient languages, such as ancient Egyptian, Sumerian, or Latin, to unravel the hidden meanings within cryptic passages. By contextualizing the wisdom contained in these texts, we will understand how time, place, and cultural milieu shape their interpretation. Through these challenges, we will develop a profound appreciation for the art of translation and interpretation, recognizing its pivotal role in unlocking the ancient wisdom within magical texts.

Exercise : Translating the Mystical

Embark on the process of translation by selecting a passage from an ancient magical text. Choose a text from a specific tradition, such as Egyptian, Babylonian, or European grimoires, and carefully decipher its meaning. Reflect on the linguistic and cultural challenges encountered during the translation process, considering how these factors shape the interpretation of the text. Through this exercise, you will gain insights into the intricacies of translating magical knowledge and the profound impact it has on understanding and preserving ancient wisdom.

By exploring the transmission and preservation of magical texts, you will gain a deep appreciation for the challenges and triumphs encountered in the journey of safeguarding arcane knowledge. You will understand the pivotal role of oral traditions, handwritten manuscripts, and printed books in preserving the sacred flame of wisdom. Moreover, you will grasp the significance of scribes, copyists, and translators in bridging the gap between ancient and modern practitioners. Through your study, you will emerge as custodians of the mystical arts, committed to honoring and perpetuating the legacy of magical wisdom for generations to come.

Practical Applications and Ethical Considerations:

In the realm of magical studies, the practical applications of magical texts and spellbooks hold great significance. This chapter will explore how these texts are utilized in rituals, spellcasting, and personal spiritual practices, while also addressing the ethical considerations that accompany their use. By examining case studies and engaging in critical reflection, we will develop a nuanced understanding of the complexities and ethical dilemmas surrounding the utilization of magical texts.

✦   Practical Applications: Unleashing the Power Within

Magical texts and spellbooks serve as potent tools in various practical applications, allowing practitioners to tap into the mystical forces that shape our reality. In this section, we will delve into the ways in which these texts are utilized in rituals, spellcasting, and personal spiritual practices. We will explore the intricate rituals performed by practitioners of Witchcraft, the divination methods employed by seers, the use of herbalism in healing and enchantment, the spiritual journeys undertaken in Shamanism, the connection to nature through ecospirituality, and the ancient magical practices of Mesopotamia. Through vivid examples and case studies, we will illuminate the diverse ways in which magical texts are harnessed to manifest intentions, commune with higher powers, and cultivate personal growth and transformation.

✦   Ethical Considerations: Navigating the Moral Landscape

Engaging with magical texts brings forth a range of ethical considerations that demand our attention and introspection. In this section, we will explore the ethical complexities surrounding the use of these texts, providing a foundation for responsible and respectful engagement with magical traditions. We will delve into questions of consent and the importance of respecting the boundaries of others when working with magical practices. Additionally, we will examine the issue of cultural appropriation and the need to approach magical traditions from cultures other than our own with sensitivity and respect. Through critical analysis and thoughtful reflection, we will navigate the moral landscape of magical practice, ensuring our actions align with principles of integrity and inclusivity.

Case Study : Cultural Appropriation in Magical Practice

Examine a case study that highlights the ethical dilemma of cultural appropriation in magical practice. Analyze the context, intentions, and impact of an individual or group's engagement with a magical tradition from a culture different from their own. Consider the power dynamics, historical context, and potential harm caused by cultural appropriation. Engage in critical reflection to understand the ethical implications and generate ideas for promoting cultural sensitivity and respectful engagement within the magical community.

Exercise : Ethical Decision-Making in Magical Practice

Engage in a thought-provoking exercise that presents ethical dilemmas related to the utilization of magical texts. Analyze different scenarios that involve issues such as consent, cultural appropriation, and the balance between personal desires and collective well-being. Apply ethical frameworks and principles to evaluate the dilemmas and propose responsible and ethical solutions. Through this exercise, you will enhance your ethical decision-making skills and develop a deeper understanding of the complexities involved in the utilization of magical texts.

By exploring the practical applications and ethical considerations of magical texts, we gain a comprehensive understanding of their potential and the responsibilities they entail. We will learn how to harness their power in rituals and personal spiritual practices, while remaining mindful of the ethical dimensions that shape our engagement. Through critical thinking and reflection, we will become practitioners who honor and uphold the principles of consent, cultural sensitivity, and integrity, ensuring that our use of magical texts contributes positively to our own growth and the broader magical community.

Counterarguments and Dissenting Opinions:

In the realm of magical studies, it is essential to cultivate critical thinking skills and engage with diverse perspectives. This chapter will present counterarguments and dissenting opinions related to the efficacy, authenticity, and ethical implications of magical texts and spellbooks. By exploring these contrasting viewpoints, students will develop the ability to critically evaluate the reliability and limitations of these texts, as well as broaden their understanding of alternative perspectives within the field of magical studies.

✧   Questioning Efficacy: Skepticism and the Power of Belief

In this section, we will embark on an intriguing exploration into skepticism and its relation to the efficacy of magical texts and spellbooks. Critical thinking plays a crucial role in examining the claims made by practitioners of various magical traditions, and we will delve into skeptical viewpoints that challenge these assertions. By engaging with contrasting opinions, we will gain a deeper understanding of the complexities surrounding belief in magical texts and their practical applications.

Skepticism and the Existence of Magical Forces

Some individuals question the existence of magical forces altogether, citing a lack of empirical evidence. Skeptics argue that the effects observed by practitioners may be explained by psychological or sociocultural factors rather than supernatural energies. This viewpoint prompts us to critically evaluate claims about magical forces and consider alternative explanations for the observed phenomena.

Case Study : The Placebo Effect and Magical Practices

Explore a fascinating case study that examines the placebo effect in magical practices. We will explore scientific research on belief, expectation, and suggestion, shedding light on how our minds and beliefs influence our experiences and outcomes. By understanding the placebo effect, we can better appreciate the relationship between belief, rituals, and the perceived effectiveness of magical texts and spellbooks.

Challenging the Effectiveness of Spells and Rituals

Another skeptical perspective challenges the effectiveness of specific spells and rituals described in magical texts. Skeptics propose that natural causes, coincidence, or psychological factors like suggestion may explain the reported outcomes. By exploring this viewpoint, we can critically evaluate the evidence supporting the efficacy of spells and rituals and consider alternative explanations.

Problem : Assessing Magical Claims

Engage in a problem-solving activity where we assess claims made by practitioners about the effectiveness of certain spells or rituals. We will evaluate the evidence presented and critically analyze the validity of these claims. This exercise will enhance our critical thinking skills and encourage us to question and explore factors that contribute to the perceived effectiveness of magical practices.

The Causal Relationship between Actions and Desired Outcomes

Skeptics also raise doubts about the causal relationship between specific actions performed in magical rituals and the desired outcomes. They propose that perceived connections may be coincidental or driven by cognitive biases rather than inherent magical properties. This skeptical perspective challenges us to critically examine the concept of causality within magical practices and consider alternative explanations for reported associations.

Exercise : Exploring Alternative Explanations

Participate in an exercise that encourages the exploration of alternative explanations for the effectiveness of a chosen magical practice or ritual. We will consider psychological, sociocultural, or natural explanations that could account for reported outcomes. This exercise will enhance our critical thinking skills by challenging assumptions and broadening our understanding of magical practices.

By engaging with skeptical perspectives on the efficacy of magical texts and spellbooks, we will develop a well-rounded understanding of the subject matter. We will cultivate critical thinking skills, enabling us to evaluate evidence, question assertions, and explore alternative explanations. This exploration empowers us to approach magical studies with discernment and intellectual rigor, promoting a thoughtful and nuanced approach to our own magical practices and engagements.

✧ Authenticity and Historical Accuracy: Unveiling the Mysteries

Welcome to an exciting journey where we will unravel the mysteries surrounding authenticity and historical accuracy in the realm of magical texts and practices. In this section, we will explore the importance of critically examining the historical origins, sources, and claims associated with different traditions. By engaging in this exploration, we will gain a deeper understanding of how to assess the authenticity and historical accuracy of magical texts.

Exploring Ancient Mesopotamian Mythology, Rivalries, and Spiritual Legacies
volume 2

➢ Evaluating Historical Sources

To unveil the mysteries, it is essential to evaluate the credibility and reliability of historical sources. We will learn how to analyze various types of sources, such as ancient manuscripts, archaeological findings, and scholarly research. By honing our skills in historical analysis, we can separate fact from fiction and gain insights into the cultural and historical contexts that shape magical traditions.

Problem 10.1: Analyzing a Historical Document

Let's put our analytical skills to the test by examining a historical document related to a specific magical tradition. Through close examination of its content, language, and context, we can gain insights into its authenticity and historical accuracy. This problem-solving activity will enhance our critical thinking abilities and provide a practical application of historical analysis methods.

➢ Historical Context and Cultural Considerations

To understand the authenticity and historical accuracy of magical texts, we must explore the historical context and cultural influences that shape them. We will delve into how societal beliefs, religious practices, and socio-political dynamics impact the development and interpretation of magical traditions. By considering these cultural factors, we can better assess the authenticity and relevance of magical texts.

Case Study : Magical Practices in Ancient Mesopotamia

Let's dive into an intriguing case study that examines magical practices in ancient Mesopotamia. Through the exploration of archaeological findings, historical records, and scholarly interpretations, we will uncover the mysteries of this ancient civilization's magical traditions. By understanding the cultural context, we can critically evaluate the authenticity and historical accuracy of the texts and artifacts associated with Mesopotamian magic.

➢ Challenges and Limitations

Assessing authenticity and historical accuracy in magical texts comes with challenges and limitations. We will explore these obstacles, including the scarcity of primary sources, the biases found in historical accounts, and the potential for misinterpretation. By acknowledging these challenges, we can approach the study of magical texts with a nuanced perspective and recognize the uncertainties that exist in assessing their authenticity and historical accuracy.

Exercise : Assessing Authenticity

Let's engage in an exercise focused on assessing the authenticity of a selected magical text or artifact. We will critically evaluate the available evidence, considering factors such as historical context, source reliability, and scholarly consensus. This exercise will sharpen our skills in discerning authenticity and deepen our appreciation for the complexities involved in evaluating historical accuracy.

Through the exploration of authenticity and historical accuracy, we will unlock the mysteries surrounding magical texts and practices. By critically evaluating historical sources, considering cultural influences, and acknowledging the challenges that arise, we will develop a discerning eye and a nuanced understanding of the complexities within the field of magical studies. This knowledge will empower us to approach magical texts with a critical and informed perspective, enhancing our understanding and appreciation of their historical significance.

✧   Ethical Implications: Balancing Power and Responsibility

Welcome to an exploration of the ethical implications associated with the use of magical texts and spellbooks. In this section, we will encounter dissenting opinions that challenge the ethical considerations surrounding these practices. By delving into these discussions, we will develop a deeper understanding of the complexities and responsibilities involved in utilizing magical texts.

➤   Questioning Ethical Boundaries

In our journey through the realm of magical texts and spellbooks, it is crucial to critically examine the ethical implications associated with their use. In this section, we will explore dissenting arguments that challenge conventional perspectives and raise thought-provoking questions about the ethical boundaries that arise in the realm of magical studies.

Exploring Dissenting Viewpoints

Let us embark on an exploration of dissenting arguments that shed light on the ethical considerations surrounding the utilization of magical texts and spellbooks. These viewpoints invite us to critically reflect on the potential for misuse, the presence of power imbalances, and the responsibility of practitioners to approach their magical practices with unwavering integrity and profound respect. By engaging with these differing perspectives, we open ourselves to a broader understanding of the ethical complexities that permeate the field of magical studies.

Unveiling Potential for Misuse

One aspect of dissenting arguments regarding the ethical implications of magical texts and spellbooks revolves around the potential for their misuse. These viewpoints raise pertinent questions about the responsible and ethical application of magical practices. By examining differing opinions, we can deepen our awareness of how magical texts can be wielded in ways that may cause harm, infringe upon consent, or exploit vulnerable individuals. Exploring these concerns empowers us to critically assess our own practices and strive for ethical engagement with magical texts.

Case Study : Ethical Dilemmas in Spellcasting

Through a captivating case study, we will analyze ethical dilemmas that can arise in the practice of spellcasting. By examining real-life scenarios and engaging in critical analysis, we will explore instances where the potential for misuse and ethical breaches emerges. This case study will encourage us to grapple with challenging ethical decisions, enhancing our ability to navigate the complexities of utilizing magical texts and spellbooks responsibly.

Power Imbalances and Responsibility

Another dimension of dissenting arguments focuses on power imbalances inherent in magical practices and the corresponding responsibility of practitioners. These viewpoints invite us to reflect on the sources and dynamics of power within magical traditions, and how they can influence interactions between practitioners and the broader community. By critically examining these perspectives, we can better understand the ethical imperative to approach our magical practices with a deep sense of responsibility, transparency, and accountability.

Exercise : Power Analysis in Magical Practices

Engage in an exercise that prompts a thorough power analysis of magical practices. Through this exercise, we will examine power dynamics within different magical traditions, critically assessing the roles and responsibilities of practitioners. By exploring these power imbalances, we gain a nuanced understanding of the ethical considerations that arise and can apply this knowledge to foster more equitable and responsible magical practices.

By delving into dissenting arguments and exploring the ethical implications of using magical texts and spellbooks, we broaden our perspective and gain valuable insights into the complexities of the field of magical studies. Engaging with these differing viewpoints allows us to critically assess the potential for misuse, reflect on power imbalances, and understand our responsibility as practitioners. Through this exploration, we develop a well-rounded understanding of the ethical boundaries and considerations that shape our engagement with magical texts and spellbooks.

➤ Exploring Ethical Frameworks

To navigate the intricate ethical landscape of magical practices, it is essential to familiarize ourselves with various ethical frameworks and principles. In this section, we will embark on a comprehensive exploration of feminist critiques, cultural sensitivity, and the promotion of collective well-being as ethical frameworks relevant to the utilization of magical texts and spellbooks. By understanding and applying these frameworks, we will be equipped to analyze the ethical implications of our magical practices from multiple perspectives, fostering a mindful and responsible approach.

Feminist Critiques in Magical Practices

Within the realm of magical studies, feminist critiques offer valuable insights into the ethical considerations associated with the use of magical texts and spellbooks. These critiques prompt us to examine power dynamics, gender roles, and the potential for patriarchal influences within magical traditions. By critically engaging with feminist perspectives, we can deepen our understanding of the intersectionality between gender, power, and ethics, enabling us to approach our magical practices with greater awareness and inclusivity.

Cultural Sensitivity and Appropriation

A crucial aspect of ethical exploration in magical practices involves cultural sensitivity and the ethical challenges of cultural appropriation. In this case study, we will delve into the complexities surrounding the adoption and utilization of magical practices from different cultural contexts. By examining real-life examples and scholarly analyses, we will critically evaluate the ethical implications of cultural appropriation within the realm of magical studies. This case study will deepen our understanding of the importance of respecting cultural heritage, fostering cross-cultural exchange, and engaging with magical texts and spellbooks in a manner that honors and values diverse traditions.

Exercise : Ethical Reflection on Cultural Exchange

Participate in an exercise that encourages ethical reflection on cultural exchange in magical practices. Through thoughtful analysis and discussion, we will explore the ethical considerations surrounding the adoption and adaptation of magical practices from different cultural backgrounds. By engaging in this exercise, we will enhance our cultural sensitivity and develop a heightened awareness of the ethical responsibilities we bear as practitioners in a diverse and interconnected world.

Promoting Collective Well-being

In our exploration of ethical frameworks, we will also consider the promotion of collective well-being as a guiding principle. This perspective emphasizes the interconnectedness of individuals, communities, and the natural world, urging us to consider the impact of our magical practices on the broader web of life. By cultivating an ethical orientation that prioritizes collective well-being, we can navigate our magical studies with a deep sense of responsibility, striving to align our practices with ecological sustainability, social justice, and the flourishing of all beings.

By engaging with these ethical frameworks and principles, we develop a nuanced understanding of the ethical considerations that shape our engagement with magical texts and spellbooks. Through the case study on cultural appropriation, we explore the complexities of respectful engagement with diverse cultural traditions. The exercise on cultural exchange enables us to reflect on our own practices and develop greater cultural sensitivity. Lastly, the promotion of collective well-being encourages us to consider the broader impacts of our magical practices, fostering a responsible and conscientious approach. By integrating these ethical frameworks into our studies, we cultivate an ethical compass that guides us toward an informed and ethically grounded practice of magic.

➢   Responsibility and Integrity

Assuming responsibility and upholding integrity are fundamental aspects of ethical engagement with magical texts and spellbooks. In this section, we will delve into the concept of personal responsibility and explore the profound impact our actions have on ourselves, others, and the broader community. By cultivating a heightened sense of ethical awareness and embracing principles such as respect, consent, and harm reduction, we can navigate the realm of magical texts with integrity, accountability, and a commitment to ethical practice.

Personal Responsibility in Magical Practices

Personal responsibility forms the cornerstone of ethical engagement with magical texts. As practitioners, it is crucial to recognize the power we wield and the potential consequences of our actions. By assuming personal responsibility, we acknowledge the interconnectedness of our magical practices and the impact they can have on ourselves, others, and the wider world. Through self-reflection and ethical self-inquiry, we will deepen our understanding of the choices we make, the intentions we set, and the implications they carry. This introspective process empowers us to navigate our magical studies with conscientiousness, accountability, and an unwavering commitment to personal growth.

Embracing Principles of Respect, Consent, and Harm Reduction

Respect, consent, and harm reduction are vital principles that guide us in maintaining integrity in our magical practices. Respecting the autonomy and agency of others is essential in building ethical relationships within the magical community. By seeking informed consent in our interactions and collaborations, we honor the boundaries and well-being of all involved. Furthermore, embracing harm reduction principles ensures that we strive to minimize any potential harm that may arise from our magical practices. Through these principles, we foster an environment of trust, safety, and mutual respect, laying the foundation for responsible and ethical engagement with magical texts.

Exercise : Reflecting on Ethical Responsibility

Engage in a reflective exercise that invites you to contemplate and articulate your understanding of ethical responsibility in magical practices. Through journaling, personal inquiry, or group discussion, critically examine your intentions, actions, and their impact on yourself and others. Consider how principles of respect, consent, and harm reduction manifest in your own magical practices. This exercise will deepen your self-awareness, strengthen your ethical compass, and provide an opportunity for personal growth as a responsible practitioner.

By embracing personal responsibility and adhering to principles of respect, consent, and harm reduction, we foster a culture of integrity and accountability within our magical studies. Through self-reflection and the exercise on ethical responsibility, we develop a heightened sense of awareness regarding our choices and their consequences. By prioritizing respect for others' autonomy, seeking informed consent, and striving for harm reduction, we create a supportive and ethical community of practitioners. Together, we embark on a transformative journey in the world of magical texts, guided by responsibility, integrity, and a commitment to ethical practice.

Exercise : Reflecting on Personal Responsibility

Engage in a reflective exercise that invites you to contemplate your own personal responsibility in magical practices. Consider how your actions align with ethical principles such as respect, consent, and harm reduction. Through introspection and self-inquiry, you will deepen your understanding of the responsibilities inherent in working with magical texts and spellbooks.

By exploring dissenting opinions and ethical considerations, we develop critical thinking skills and a broader understanding of the ethical complexities within the realm of magical studies. Engaging with these perspectives challenges us to question and evaluate the efficacy of magical texts. Through debates on authenticity and historical accuracy, we deepen our understanding of the scholarly discourse surrounding these texts. Lastly, considering ethical implications ensures a balanced and responsible approach to magical practices. Through these explorations, we become thoughtful and discerning practitioners, capable of critically evaluating diverse perspectives and navigating the complexities of the magical world.

Conclusion:

As we conclude our exploration of magical texts and spellbooks, we have gained a comprehensive understanding of their historical, cultural, and practical significance. We appreciate the diverse forms, contents, and purposes of these texts, as well as the challenges and ethical considerations inherent in their study and utilization. By engaging in thought-provoking exercises and analysis, we have cultivated a deep appreciation for the wisdom, symbolism, and transformative potential encapsulated within magical texts and spellbooks. We are now equipped to approach our practices with mindfulness, responsibility, and a commitment to ethical engagement.

Incantations and Invocation of Deities

Incantations and the invocation of deities have long been integral components of magical and spiritual practices across diverse cultures. These sacred utterances and rituals serve as potent means of connecting with divine forces, harnessing their power, and manifesting desired outcomes. In this section, students will embark on a captivating exploration of incantations and the invocation of deities, delving into their historical, cultural, and transformative dimensions.

➢ The Power of Incantations

Incantations, revered for their intrinsic power, occupy a significant position within magical and spiritual traditions. These rituals, centered around the belief in the potency of spoken or chanted words, have the ability to effect transformative change. In this section, we will explore the captivating world of incantations, examining their historical and cultural significance in diverse contexts such as ancient Egypt, Mesopotamia, and contemporary witchcraft. Through this exploration, students will gain profound insights into the profound impact of language and the spoken word, unraveling the mysteries of how incantations connect with the hidden currents of the universe.

The Mystical Language of Incantations

Incantations are steeped in the recognition that language possesses an inherent power to shape reality. By carefully crafting and articulating specific words, practitioners tap into the vibrational energies of the cosmos, activating transformative forces within and without. Across cultures and epochs, incantations have been revered for their ability to communicate with unseen realms, summon divine forces, and influence the course of events. By delving into the mystical language of incantations, students will discover the intricate interplay between words, intention, and manifestation.

Incantations in Ancient Egypt, Mesopotamia, and Contemporary Witchcraft

To grasp the full spectrum of incantations' transformative potential, we will explore their rich history in various cultural contexts. In ancient Egypt, incantations were integral to religious and magical practices, invoking the blessings of deities and guiding the deceased through the afterlife. Mesopotamian incantations, on the other hand, aimed to heal the afflicted and protect against malevolent forces. These ancient practices provide a fascinating glimpse into the role of incantations as conduits of power and transformation.

We will also examine the resurgence of incantations in contemporary witchcraft, where practitioners draw upon ancient wisdom while adapting it to modern contexts. Here, incantations serve as tools for personal empowerment, spiritual connection, and manifestation. By studying these diverse cultural expressions, students will gain a comprehensive understanding of the evolving significance and versatile applications of incantations.

Exercise : Crafting Your Incantation

Engage in a creative exercise that invites you to craft your own incantation. Draw inspiration from the historical and cultural examples explored in this section, as well as your personal intentions and desires. Reflect on the words, rhythms, and energies you wish to infuse into your incantation. By creating your own incantation, you will deepen your connection to the power of language and experience firsthand its transformative potential.

By immersing ourselves in the world of incantations, we uncover the profound wisdom and power embedded within language and the spoken word. Through the exploration of historical contexts and contemporary witchcraft, we trace the threads that connect us to ancient traditions while embracing the present moment. By engaging in the exercise on crafting your incantation, students tap into their own creative power, manifesting intention and experiencing the transformative energies that lie within the realm of incantations.

➢ Forms and Structure of Incantations

Within the mystical realm of incantations, a rich tapestry of diverse forms and structures unfurls, meticulously designed to enhance their potency. In this section, we invite you, dear students, to embark on a captivating exploration of the rhythmic patterns, rhymes, repetitions, and symbolic language that form the very essence of incantations. By studying specific examples and unraveling the underlying principles and techniques, you will unlock the secrets of their profound power.

The Language of Power: A Crafted Tapestry

At the heart of every incantation lies a language carefully woven with purpose and intention. The rhythmic cadence and melodic quality of incantations serve as conduits for their vibrational resonance, allowing the invocation of energies necessary for transformative manifestations. As aspiring practitioners, you will delve into the craftsmanship involved in selecting specific words, phrases, and sounds that harmonize with your desired intent. Through this exploration, a deeper understanding of the inherent power embedded within the language of incantations will manifest.

A Kaleidoscope of Cultural Expressions

Cultures and traditions across time have bestowed their unique touch upon the construction of incantations, resulting in a mesmerizing kaleidoscope of forms and structures. For instance, ancient Mesopotamian incantations employed poetic meters and the artful repetition of phrases, casting a spell of enchantment through melodic resonance. In contrast, contemporary witchcraft draws inspiration from a diverse array of sources, blending elements from folklore, mythology, personal experiences, and the wellspring of individual creativity. By immersing yourselves in the exploration of these cultural variations, you will unravel the common threads connecting diverse incantation forms while appreciating the subtle nuances that reflect the wisdom and aesthetics of each tradition.

Exercise : Unleashing Your Creative Potential

Prepare to embark on a practical exercise that invites you to craft your own rhythmic incantation, where your creativity will intertwine with the secrets of ancient mysticism. Through the deliberate use of poetic meters, rhymes, and repetitions, you will infuse your incantation with a captivating rhythm and a melodic quality that resonates with your intention. Consider the specific manifestations you seek and the energetic resonance you wish to invoke. As you engage in this transformative exercise, you will witness firsthand the potency that lies within the artistry of incantation construction and the power of your own words.

By delving into the forms and structures of incantations, you, esteemed students, will unravel the artistry and ingenuity that underlie these mystical rituals. Through the exploration of crafting the language of power and the examination of cultural variations, you will gain a comprehensive understanding of the techniques employed in constructing incantations. As you engage in the exercise on crafting a rhythmic incantation, you will unlock your own creative potential and forge a deeper connection to the profound energies that permeate the captivating world of incantations. May your journey into the realms of language and magic be filled with transformative wonder and endless enchantment.

➤ Invocation of Deities

Within the realm of incantations, the invocation of deities holds a position of profound significance, offering a pathway to establish sacred connections and seek divine assistance. In this section, dear students, we shall embark on an enlightening exploration of the diverse approaches to invoking deities, unveiling the rituals, gestures, chants, and offerings that form the tapestry of this sacred practice. Through case studies spanning different fields, such as Witchcraft, Divination, Herbalism, Shamanism, Ecospirituality, and even Magic in Ancient Mesopotamia, you will deepen your understanding of the reverence, respect, and transformative potential intrinsic to these rituals.

Prayer and Ritual Gestures: Invoking Divine Favor

Prayer and ritual gestures serve as primary channels for the invocation of deities, facilitating a direct connection with the divine forces. For instance, in the context of Egyptian religious practices, priests meticulously orchestrated elaborate rituals, meticulously following specific protocols to attract the attention and favor of the gods and goddesses. These rituals often involved precise gestures, sacred words, and offerings to express devotion and entreat divine intervention. Similarly, Greek traditions incorporated invocations where individuals would call upon the names of gods and goddesses, seeking their guidance and assistance. By exploring these case studies, you will gain insight into the significance of prayer and ritual gestures as potent means of invoking divine energies.

Sacred Chants and Offerings: Harmonizing with the Divine

Sacred chants and offerings form another vital facet of invoking deities, creating an energetic resonance that harmonizes human and divine realms. In shamanic practices, for instance, invocations often entail rhythmic drumming, dancing, and chanting to induce altered states of consciousness and connect with spiritual entities. These practices honor the spirits and seek their wisdom and guidance. Additionally, offerings such as herbs, flowers, and symbolic objects may be presented as acts of reverence and gratitude. By delving into these examples, you will gain a profound understanding of how sacred chants and offerings deepen our connection with the divine forces.

Example Exercise:

Working in pairs, you will have the opportunity to tap into your own creative powers and craft your own incantations, drawing inspiration from the forms, structures, and invocations discussed in this section. Consider your intentions, the desired outcomes, and the symbolism and language you wish to incorporate. As you present your incantations to the class, elucidate the choices you made and invite a vibrant discussion on the potential impact and effectiveness of your creations. This exercise encourages you to engage in creative expression while applying the principles and techniques learned in the study of incantations, fostering a deeper understanding of the transformative potential inherent in invoking deities.

Through the exploration of the invocation of deities, you will awaken to the profound beauty and transformative power found within these sacred practices. By examining case studies from various traditions and engaging in the creative exercise, you will unlock your own connection to the divine forces and harness the wisdom and guidance available to you. May your journey into the realm of invocation be one of reverence, growth, and spiritual illumination.

➤ Ritual Context and Symbolism

Within the realm of incantations and deity invocation, the ritual context plays a vital role in shaping the transformative power and efficacy of these practices. In this section, dear students, we shall embark on a profound journey of exploration, unraveling the intricate tapestry of ritual settings, symbolic elements, and ceremonial aspects that surround these mystical rituals. By delving into the use of ritual tools, sacred spaces, and gestures, you will gain a deep understanding of how these elements intertwine to enhance the potency of incantations and foster a sacred atmosphere conducive to spiritual connection.

The Power of Sacred Spaces: Ancient Temples and Contemporary Covens

The creation of sacred spaces forms a cornerstone of ritual practice, providing a container for the energies invoked through incantations and deity invocation. Across different cultures and time periods, sacred spaces have been meticulously crafted to facilitate a profound connection with the divine. For instance, in the ancient Mesopotamian tradition, priests and priestesses conducted elaborate ceremonies within designated sacred spaces, such as temples. These spaces were carefully designed to honor specific deities, employing architectural features, statues, and altars as focal points for their rituals. By studying these ancient examples, you will gain a deeper appreciation for the intentional construction of sacred spaces to harness the transformative energies of incantations.

In contemporary witchcraft, covens create ritual circles, marking out a sacred space where the veil between worlds becomes thin. This practice involves casting protective boundaries, often using tools such as a wand or athame, to define the ritual space. Within this circle, the elements and deities are invoked, and incantations are performed. By examining these modern examples, you will discover how covens adapt and evolve the concept of sacred space to suit their specific traditions and intentions.

Ritual Tools and Gestures: Embodiments of Symbolic Power

Ritual tools and gestures serve as potent conduits for the manifestation of symbolic power within incantations and deity invocation. These tools, imbued with intention and meaning, amplify the energy and focus of the ritual. For example, in ancient Mesopotamian rituals, priests and priestesses would utilize specific tools, such as censers, ritual knives, and divination implements, to facilitate their connection with the divine. Each tool held symbolic significance, representing the forces they sought to invoke or communicate with. Similarly, in contemporary witchcraft, tools like athames, chalices, and candles are employed to channel intention and energy. These tools become extensions of the practitioner's own power and act as conduits for their magical workings.

Gestures also play a vital role in ritual practice, serving as physical expressions of intention and reverence. Specific hand movements, body postures, and dance steps can be utilized to amplify the energy and focus of incantations. By exploring these gestures, students will gain a deeper understanding of the embodied nature of ritual and the ways in which physical movements can align with the spiritual and symbolic aspects of incantations and deity invocation.

Example Exercise:

To deepen your understanding of the ritual context and symbolism surrounding incantations, you will engage in a practical exercise. Working individually or in small groups, create a ritual setting for a specific intention, incorporating sacred elements, ritual tools, and gestures. Reflect on the symbolic significance of each element chosen and how they contribute to the overall atmosphere and intention of the ritual. Present your ritual setting to the class, explaining your choices and inviting a discussion on the profound connections between symbolism, ritual context, and the transformative power of incantations.

Through the exploration of ritual context and symbolism, you will unveil the profound layers of meaning and significance woven into incantations and deity invocation. By examining examples from different traditions and engaging in the exercise on creating a ritual setting, you will deepen your understanding of the sacred artistry involved in these mystical practices. May your journey into the realm of ritual context and symbolism be one of awe, insight, and spiritual illumination.

➢   Ethical Considerations and Cultural Sensitivity

Dear students, as we explore the vast realms of incantations and deity invocation, it is imperative that we engage with a deep sense of ethical responsibility and cultural sensitivity. In this section, we shall embark on a journey of critical reflection, delving into the complex topics of cultural appropriation, informed consent, and respectful engagement with diverse spiritual traditions. By navigating these discussions with open minds and compassionate hearts, we shall foster an environment of understanding, respect, and harmonious coexistence.

Cultural Appropriation: Nurturing Cultural Respect

Cultural appropriation, the adoption or borrowing of elements from another culture, can be a contentious issue within the realm of spiritual practices. It is crucial for students to recognize and understand the potential harm that can arise from appropriating practices without a deep appreciation of their cultural and historical significance. By studying various examples from different fields, such as witchcraft, divination, and shamanism, students will gain insight into the complexities surrounding cultural appropriation.

In order to nurture cultural respect, students will delve into the importance of approaching other traditions with humility, seeking to learn and understand rather than appropriating superficial elements for personal gain. They will explore the significance of recognizing the origins and cultural contexts of the practices they engage with, acknowledging the sacredness and lived experiences of those who hold them dear.

Informed Consent: Honoring Boundaries and Agency

Respecting the boundaries and agency of individuals and communities is essential when engaging in incantations and deity invocation. Informed consent ensures that practitioners approach these practices in an ethical and responsible manner. Students will explore the significance of seeking permission and guidance from relevant cultural authorities or practitioners when incorporating elements from different traditions.

By examining case studies and engaging in thoughtful discussions, students will understand the importance of actively seeking knowledge, learning from authentic sources, and forging relationships built on trust and mutual understanding. They will reflect on the potential consequences of engaging in practices without proper consent and the significance of being mindful of power dynamics and cultural sensitivities.

Example Exercise:

In small groups, students will engage in a role-playing exercise that prompts critical thinking and ethical decision-making. Each group will be presented with a scenario that involves the incorporation of a specific cultural practice into an incantation or deity invocation. Working together, students will discuss the ethical considerations, analyze the potential impact on the culture involved, and propose alternative approaches that demonstrate cultural respect and informed consent. This exercise will encourage students to apply their understanding of ethical principles to real-life situations, fostering empathy and responsible engagement.

Through the exploration of ethical considerations and cultural sensitivity, students will develop a heightened awareness of their responsibilities as practitioners of incantations and deity invocation. They will recognize the importance of cultural respect, informed consent, and responsible engagement, paving the way for a harmonious and inclusive spiritual journey. May your reflections be filled with empathy, wisdom, and a commitment to creating a world where diversity is celebrated and honored.

➢ Counterarguments and Dissenting Opinions

By exploring alternative viewpoints, we broaden our perspective and cultivate critical thinking skills. In this section, we shall delve into some of the counterarguments and dissenting opinions regarding the efficacy, cultural significance, and ethical implications of incantations and deity invocation.

Questioning Efficacy: Perspectives on Supernatural Powers

Some individuals may question the effectiveness of incantations, perceiving them as mere superstition or psychological tools rather than channels for tapping into cosmic energies. They may argue that the observed effects of incantations are merely coincidental or the result of a placebo effect. By engaging with these perspectives, students have an opportunity to critically examine the evidence supporting the efficacy of incantations and the various interpretations of their impact.

It is crucial to encourage students to analyze empirical studies, anecdotal evidence, and personal experiences that support or challenge the notion of incantations as vehicles for manifesting desired outcomes. This analytical approach will deepen their understanding of the diverse viewpoints and allow for a more nuanced evaluation of the potential benefits of incantations.

Cultural Significance: Respecting Origins and Contexts

Concerns about cultural appropriation and commodification of spiritual practices are also raised by some critics. These individuals emphasize the importance of respecting the cultural origins and contexts of incantations and deity invocation. They argue that without proper understanding and appreciation of the cultural background, engaging in these practices may perpetuate harm, erode cultural traditions, and contribute to the marginalization of indigenous and minority communities.

By exploring these dissenting opinions, students will be encouraged to critically reflect on the ethics of borrowing and adapting spiritual practices. They will analyze the potential consequences of appropriating elements without due respect and consideration for their cultural origins. This examination will foster cultural sensitivity and responsible engagement, empowering students to navigate the complexities of cultural exchange.

Example Exercise:

In small groups, students will engage in a structured discussion on the topic of cultural appropriation and its implications for incantations and deity invocation. Each group will be assigned a specific case study or real-life example to analyze. Students will critically evaluate the arguments presented in favor of or against cultural appropriation, considering the nuances and complexities of each situation. Through this exercise, students will develop their skills in evaluating ethical dimensions and engaging in respectful dialogue.

Conclusion:

By examining counterarguments and dissenting opinions, students deepen their critical thinking abilities and gain a more comprehensive understanding of incantations and deity invocation. This exploration challenges their assumptions, encourages empathy, and promotes intellectual growth. Through exercises and discussions that facilitate the evaluation of efficacy, cultural significance, and ethical implications, students develop a nuanced perspective and become conscious practitioners, aware of their impact on diverse spiritual and magical traditions. May your journey of discovery be marked by intellectual curiosity, respect, and a commitment to ethical engagement.

Protective and Healing Magic

Protective and healing magic has played a significant role throughout human history, transcending cultural and belief boundaries. This section aims to provide you with a comprehensive analysis of the principles, techniques, and applications of protective and healing magic. By exploring historical and cross-cultural perspectives, you will gain a deep understanding of how these mystical practices have been employed to safeguard individuals and communities and promote overall well-being.

➢ The Essence of Protective and Healing Magic:

These profound practices are rooted in the belief in the interconnectedness of the physical, emotional, and spiritual realms. By recognizing this interconnectedness, we open ourselves to the immense power of these ancient traditions.

The Holistic Approach: Bridging the Physical, Emotional, and Spiritual Realms

Protective and healing magic operates on the principle that all aspects of existence are interwoven. By acknowledging the deep connection between our physical bodies, emotional states, and spiritual well-being, we can work towards holistic healing and protection. This perspective enables us to address imbalances and disharmony at their root, fostering true transformation and well-being.

For example, in witchcraft, practitioners understand that physical ailments often have emotional or spiritual roots. They employ rituals, herbs, and spells to address not only the symptoms but also the underlying causes of illness or distress. Similarly, shamans work with energy and spirit to bring balance and harmony to individuals and communities, recognizing the intricate relationship between physical health, emotional balance, and spiritual alignment.

The Power of Intention and Energy

At the heart of protective and healing magic lies the recognition that energy and intention are powerful forces that can shape our reality. Through focused intention, we can direct energy towards desired outcomes, creating a ripple effect that reverberates through the interconnected web of existence. By cultivating a deep understanding of the energetic forces at play, we become active participants in our own healing and protection.

Herbalism provides a concrete example of the transformative power of intention and energy. When crafting herbal remedies, practitioners infuse their preparations with focused intention, imbuing them with the healing properties they seek to harness. This intention, combined with the inherent energy of the plants themselves, amplifies the therapeutic potential of herbal remedies.

Example Exercise:

In pairs, students will engage in a practical exercise to explore the interconnectedness of the physical, emotional, and spiritual realms. Each pair will select a specific physical or emotional ailment and work together to develop a holistic approach to address it. They will consider various modalities, such as ritual, herbal remedies, or energy work, and create a step-by-step plan of action that incorporates the principles of protective and healing magic. Through this exercise, students will apply their knowledge, develop problem-solving skills, and deepen their understanding of the transformative potential of these practices.

Conclusion:

By understanding the interconnectedness of the physical, emotional, and spiritual realms, and recognizing the power of intention and energy, students will grasp the essence of protective and healing magic. Through examples from witchcraft, shamanism, and herbalism, they will witness the transformative potential of these practices and learn how to apply the principles to their own lives. May your exploration of these profound traditions bring healing, protection, and a deeper connection to the interconnected web of existence.

➤ Protective Magic: Shields and Wards

In this section, we shall delve into the intricate techniques employed to create shields and wards. These powerful practices enable us to construct energetic barriers and utilize tools and symbols to safeguard ourselves from negativity and repel malevolent forces. Through engaging case studies and practical exercises, you will cultivate the skills necessary to design and activate personalized protective shields.

Understanding the Purpose of Shields and Wards

Protective shields and wards serve as guardians, fortifying our energetic boundaries and shielding us from harmful influences. They create a barrier between ourselves and negative energies, providing a safe and sacred space in which we can thrive and grow. By learning the art of shielding and warding, we empower ourselves to navigate the intricate tapestry of existence with confidence and resilience.

For instance, in witchcraft, practitioners often employ shielding techniques to protect themselves from psychic intrusions or to maintain a sacred space during rituals. Similarly, in shamanic traditions, individuals may utilize specific symbols or rituals to ward off harmful spirits and maintain a secure connection with benevolent forces. These examples demonstrate the diverse ways in which protective shields and wards can be utilized to ensure personal safety and spiritual well-being.

Tools and Symbols in Shielding and Warding

The construction of shields and wards involves the skillful utilization of tools and symbols that amplify their protective properties. These tools and symbols act as conduits for energy, enhancing the effectiveness of our intentions and creating a formidable barrier against negativity. By understanding the significance of these elements, we can craft shields that resonate with our unique energy signatures.

Herbalism offers an insightful example of the integration of tools and symbols in protective magic. Some practitioners create bundles of dried herbs, known as smudge sticks, to cleanse and protect their spaces. As they ignite the smudge stick, the smoke carries their intentions and activates the protective properties of the herbs, forming a shield against negative energies.

Example Exercise:

In this exercise, students will engage in a hands-on activity to create their own personalized protective shields. Each student will gather symbols, tools, and materials that resonate with their intentions and energy. They will design and assemble their shields, infusing them with focused intentions and activating them through ritual or visualization. Students will then share their experiences and discuss the significance of the symbols and tools they incorporated. This exercise encourages students to tap into their creativity, develop their intuition, and deepen their understanding of the role of tools and symbols in protective magic.

Conclusion:

Through the exploration of protective magic, particularly the art of shielding and warding, students will acquire the skills and knowledge necessary to create personalized shields and fortify their energetic boundaries. By studying examples from witchcraft, shamanism, and other traditions, students will gain a comprehensive understanding of the diverse applications of these practices. Engaging in practical exercises will empower students to develop their own unique approaches to protective magic and foster a deep sense of personal security and well-being. May your journey into the realm of shielding and warding be filled with profound insights and powerful transformations.

➢   The Construction of Energetic Barriers:

In this section, we shall embark on a journey to explore the construction of energetic barriers, which serve as powerful shields against negative or harmful influences. By learning various methods and techniques, you will acquire the skills to manipulate and channel energy, creating potent defenses to safeguard yourself, spaces, or objects.

The Concept of Energetic Barriers

At the heart of protective magic lies the concept of energetic barriers. These barriers function as shields, forming a protective boundary that shields individuals, spaces, or objects from negative or harmful energies. Energetic barriers act as filters, allowing positive energies to flow while repelling or neutralizing any detrimental forces.

For instance, in witchcraft, practitioners often visualize a sphere of pure energy surrounding themselves or a specific area as a method to create an energetic barrier. This visualization technique enables them to manipulate and shape energy, establishing a powerful shield against external influences. Similarly, in shamanism, individuals may invoke specific symbols or utilize sacred geometry, such as creating an energy grid, to construct energetic barriers. These examples illustrate the versatility and effectiveness of energetic barriers in diverse magical practices.

Methods for Constructing Energetic Barriers

Constructing energetic barriers requires the mastery of various methods and techniques. Through dedicated practice and focused intention, you will develop the skills to manipulate and channel energy, shaping it into a formidable shield. Two commonly employed methods are visualization and the utilization of sacred geometry.

Visualization techniques involve the mental imagery of a protective shield or boundary. By envisioning a shield composed of energy, you can imbue it with specific qualities and intentions. For example, you may visualize a golden sphere of light surrounding you, radiating a sense of safety and protection.

Sacred geometry offers another powerful avenue for constructing energetic barriers. By invoking specific symbols or geometric patterns, you tap into the inherent energetic properties associated with these forms. For instance, the use of the pentagram, a symbol of protection in many magical traditions, can be incorporated into the construction of an energetic barrier to enhance its strength and effectiveness.

Example Exercise:

In this exercise, students will engage in a guided visualization to construct their own energetic barriers. They will be encouraged to explore different forms, such as spheres, cubes, or geometric patterns, and infuse them with intentions and qualities that align with their personal needs and aspirations. Students will then discuss their experiences and the variations they encountered during the visualization. This exercise fosters the development of visualization skills and encourages students to explore the versatility of energetic barriers.

Conclusion:

Through the study of the construction of energetic barriers, you have acquired invaluable knowledge and skills in protective magic. By understanding the concept of energetic boundaries and exploring visualization techniques and sacred geometry, you are now equipped to create powerful shields that safeguard yourself, spaces, or objects. Engaging in practical exercises further strengthens your abilities and cultivates a deep connection with the energy you manipulate. May your journey into the construction of energetic barriers be filled with discovery and empowerment.

➢ Utilizing Amulets, Talismans, Sigils, and Sacred Symbols:

In this section, we shall delve into the utilization of amulets, talismans, sigils, and sacred symbols. These objects possess unique energies and symbolism that can serve as powerful aids in warding off negative energies and safeguarding against harm. By understanding their significance and properties, you will be equipped to select and create potent tools for your protective practices.

The Significance of Protective Symbols and Sigils

Protective symbols and sigils hold profound meaning and are integral to many magical traditions. They are visual representations imbued with specific energies and intentions, serving as gateways to accessing and manipulating the subtle forces of the universe. By understanding the symbolic meanings and historical contexts associated with these symbols, you will be able to choose those that resonate with your intentions and desired outcomes.

For instance, the pentagram is a widely recognized symbol of protection in various magical systems. Its five-pointed star represents the elements of earth, air, fire, water, and spirit, harmoniously united within a protective framework. Similarly, the evil eye, originating from ancient Mediterranean cultures, is believed to ward off malevolent energies and provide protection from envy and ill-wishing. Exploring the symbolism and origins of these protective symbols allows for a deeper connection with their energies and the traditions they represent.

Selection and Creation of Protective Objects

When selecting or creating amulets, talismans, sigils, or sacred symbols for protective purposes, it is crucial to align them with your specific intentions and desired outcomes. By choosing objects that resonate with your energy and purpose, you establish a powerful synergy between yourself and the tool. This connection enhances the effectiveness of the object as a protective aid.

Creating your own protective objects allows for a deeper personal connection and amplifies the energy infused within them. The process of crafting amulets, talismans, sigils, or sacred symbols involves imbuing them with your intentions, charging them with energy, and consecrating them to a specific purpose. Through this ritualistic practice, you align the object with your desired outcomes and connect it to the forces of protection.

Example Exercise:

In this exercise, students will explore the creation of protective sigils. They will be guided through the process of designing a sigil that represents their specific protective intentions. Students will learn various methods for creating sigils, such as combining letters, symbols, or geometric shapes, and will experiment with different techniques to activate and charge their sigils. By sharing and discussing their experiences, students will gain insights into the diversity of approaches and deepen their understanding of the potency of personalized protective symbols.

Conclusion:

Throughout this section, you have delved into the fascinating world of amulets, talismans, sigils, and sacred symbols in protective magic. By understanding the significance and properties of these objects, you have acquired the knowledge to select and create potent tools that align with your intentions and desired outcomes. The process of charging and consecrating these objects infuses them with your energy and connects them to the forces of protection. With these skills, may you embark on a transformative journey, harnessing the power of amulets, talismans, sigils, and sacred symbols to shield yourself from harm and manifest your intentions.

➢   Crafting Personalized Protective Amulets or Talismans:

In this section, you will have the opportunity to craft your own protective amulets or talismans. Through guided exercises, you will learn the step-by-step process of creating these personalized items and imbuing them with protective energies.

You will begin by researching and selecting symbols, sigils, or sacred images that align with your specific intentions. These could be symbols associated with strength, courage, or spiritual protection. Next, you will choose materials that resonate with you, such as crystals, gemstones, herbs, or charms, to incorporate into your amulet or talisman.

With your chosen materials, you will engage in a creative process, designing and crafting your protective object. You may create a small pouch to hold your chosen items, or you might assemble a wearable amulet to carry with you. Throughout this process, you will infuse your creation with your intentions and visualize the protective energy surrounding it.

➢   Activating Shields through Visualization, Energy Work, or Rituals:

In this section, we will delve into the essential techniques to activate and reinforce the protective energy within your shields. Creating a shield is merely the first step; it is through activation that its full potential is unlocked. By exploring various techniques and engaging in practical exercises, you will learn to activate and maintain your shields, making them potent defenses against negativity and harm.

Visualization Exercises: Envisioning a Shield of Protection

Visualization exercises are a powerful method to activate your shields. Through the power of your imagination, you will learn to envision the shield surrounding you, impervious to negativity and harm. By creating a vivid mental image of your shield, you establish a deep connection with its energy and invite it to manifest in your reality.

In your practice, you may imagine your shield as a shimmering sphere of light, an impenetrable force field, or any other visualization that resonates with your personal energy. With each breath, you infuse the shield with intention and vitality, reinforcing its protective qualities. Regular practice of visualization exercises will enhance your ability to activate your shield at will, fostering a sense of security and empowerment.

Step-by-Step Guide: Visualization Exercises - Envisioning a Shield of Protection

Visualization exercises are powerful tools that allow you to activate and manifest your protective shield through the power of your imagination. Follow this step-by-step guide to engage in a visualization exercise and create a vivid mental image of your shield of protection:

Step 1: Prepare Your Sacred Space
Find a quiet and comfortable space where you can engage in your visualization exercise without distractions. Clear the area of any clutter and create an atmosphere that promotes relaxation and focus. You may choose to light candles, burn incense, or play soft instrumental music to set the desired ambiance.

Step 2: Relaxation and Centering
Sit or lie down in a comfortable position, ensuring that your body feels relaxed and at ease. Close your eyes and take a few deep breaths, allowing the tension to release with each exhale. As you breathe, bring your attention inward and become aware of your body and the present moment. Center yourself, feeling grounded and connected to the Earth.

Step 3: Setting Your Intention
Take a moment to reflect on your intention for creating a shield of protection. What qualities do you wish to infuse into your shield? Is it strength, resilience, love, or any other specific attribute? Clarify your intention and hold it clearly in your mind.

Step 4: Envisioning the Shield

With your intention in mind, begin to imagine a shield of protection forming around you. Visualize it as a radiant sphere of energy that completely encompasses your body. Observe its color, whether it is transparent, shimmering, or solid. Notice any symbols or patterns that may appear on the surface of the shield.

Step 5: Sensory Details

Engage all your senses in this visualization exercise. As you imagine the shield, take a moment to feel its texture. Is it smooth, warm, or tingly? Notice if there are any sounds associated with your shield. Does it emit a gentle hum or a soft, soothing vibration? Envision a subtle fragrance or scent that represents the essence of your shield.

Step 6: Intentional Breathwork

As you continue to hold the image of your shield in your mind, synchronize your breath with your visualization. With each inhale, imagine drawing in vibrant, pure energy from the universe. Feel this energy flowing through your body, nourishing and strengthening you. With each exhale, release any doubts or negative energies, allowing them to dissolve into the surrounding space.

Step 7: Charging and Activating the Shield

Direct your focus and intention toward your shield, infusing it with the energy of your breath and your intention. Visualize the shield becoming more vibrant and radiant with each breath you take. Feel its power intensify as it absorbs the energy from the universe, growing stronger and more impenetrable.

Step 8: Affirmation and Gratitude

In your mind, repeat affirmations that reinforce the purpose and strength of your shield. You may choose statements such as "I am protected and safe," "My shield is a powerful barrier against negativity," or any other affirmation that resonates with you. Express gratitude for the shield and the protective energies it embodies, feeling a sense of appreciation and trust in its efficacy.

Step 9: Closing the Visualization

When you feel ready to conclude the exercise, take a few moments to gradually bring your awareness back to the present. Wiggle your fingers and toes, stretch your body gently, and open your eyes. Acknowledge the presence of your shield and carry its energy with you throughout your day.

Energy Work Techniques: Strengthening and Amplifying Your Shields

Energy work techniques play a vital role in strengthening and amplifying the protective energy within your shields. By consciously working with energy, you can enhance the efficacy of your shields and create a resilient barrier against negativity. Grounding and centering practices, for example, help you establish a stable foundation, allowing you to draw upon the Earth's energy to fortify your shields.

Working with the breath is another technique to cultivate and direct energy. By consciously directing your breath toward your shield, you infuse it with your life force, charging it with vitality and resilience. Additionally, you can tap into the vast energies of the Earth or the cosmos, aligning yourself with the powerful forces of nature and the universe, and channeling this energy into your shields.

Step-by-Step Guide: Energy Work Techniques - Strengthening and Amplifying Your Shields

Energy work techniques are powerful tools that can enhance and reinforce the strength of your protective shields. Follow this step-by-step guide to engage in energy work and amplify the energy within your shields:

Step 1: Prepare Your Sacred Space
Find a quiet and comfortable space where you can practice your energy work without distractions. Clear the area of any clutter and create an atmosphere that promotes relaxation and focus. You may choose to light candles, burn incense, or play soft instrumental music to set the desired ambiance.

Step 2: Grounding and Centering
Stand tall with your feet firmly planted on the ground. Take a few deep breaths, allowing your body to relax and your mind to focus. Visualize roots extending from the soles of your feet, reaching deep into the Earth's core. Feel a sense of connection and stability as you draw upon the Earth's grounding energy.

Step 3: Connecting with Universal Energy
Raise your arms out to the sides and imagine them as conduits for universal energy. With each inhale, visualize streams of vibrant energy flowing into your body through the palms of your hands. Feel this energy filling you from head to toe, revitalizing and energizing your entire being.

Step 4: Directing Energy to Your Shield
With your arms still raised, bring your hands together in front of your chest, palms facing each other. Imagine a ball of intense energy forming between your

hands. This ball represents the energy that you will direct toward your shield. Visualize it growing brighter and more powerful with each breath.

Step 5: Projecting Energy into Your Shield

Now, with focused intention, extend your hands forward, directing the energy ball toward your shield. Visualize the energy merging with your shield, infusing it with heightened strength and vibrancy. See the shield absorbing the energy and expanding, becoming even more impenetrable.

Step 6: Breathwork and Intent

Take a moment to synchronize your breath with the energy projection. With each inhale, imagine drawing in pure cosmic energy, filling your body and intensifying the energy within your shield. As you exhale, release any doubts or negative energies, allowing them to disperse into the surrounding space.

Step 7: Visualization and Affirmation

Maintain a clear visualization of your shield, now fortified with the amplified energy. See it glowing brightly and radiating a protective aura. As you hold this image in your mind, repeat affirmations that strengthen your intention and connection to the shield. Affirmations such as "My shield is impenetrable and powerful," or "I am surrounded by divine protection" can be used.

Step 8: Repeating and Deepening the Process

If desired, repeat steps 4 to 7 multiple times to further intensify the energy within your shield. Each repetition adds another layer of energy and strengthens the protective barrier. Trust your intuition and continue until you feel a sense of satisfaction and empowerment.

Step 9: Closing the Energy Work Session

When you feel ready to conclude the energy work session, bring your hands back to your chest, palms together. Take a moment to express gratitude for the energy, the shield, and the experience itself. Slowly lower your hands, acknowledging the presence of your amplified shield.

Rituals: Empowering and Activating Your Shields

Rituals serve as transformative acts that connect us to the sacred and amplify our intentions. In the realm of protective magic, rituals can be utilized to empower and activate your shields. Invoking deities or elemental energies can infuse your shields with the power and qualities associated with these forces. By establishing a sacred space and calling upon these divine or elemental energies, you invite their assistance in fortifying your shields.

Rituals provide a structured framework for channeling and directing energy, allowing you to intentionally activate your shields and imbue them with the potency required for protection. Engaging in rituals not only strengthens your connection to the spiritual dimensions but also enhances your focus and intention, further empowering your shields.

Step-by-Step Guide: Rituals - Empowering and Activating Your Shields

Rituals can be powerful tools for empowering and activating your protective shields. Follow this step-by-step guide to engage in rituals that enhance the energy within your shields:

Step 1: Setting the Sacred Space
Begin by preparing a sacred space for your ritual. Cleanse the area of any clutter and create an environment that promotes focus and reverence. You may choose to light candles, burn incense, or place meaningful objects that symbolize protection and power.

Step 2: Centering and Grounding
Take a few moments to center yourself and establish a grounded state. Close your eyes, take deep breaths, and focus on your body and breath. Visualize roots extending from your feet, anchoring you deep into the Earth. Feel a sense of stability and connection.

Step 3: Creating an Intention
Clarify your intention for the ritual. What specific purpose do you want your shield to serve? Whether it's protection from negative energies, spiritual guidance, or personal empowerment, state your intention clearly and concisely in your mind or out loud.

Step 4: Selecting Ritual Tools and Symbols
Choose ritual tools and symbols that resonate with your intention. This could include crystals, amulets, herbs, sacred objects, or elements associated with protection, such as salt or water. Select items that hold personal significance and align with the energy you wish to invoke.

Step 5: Invoking Deities or Elemental Energies
Invoke deities or elemental energies that are associated with protection and empowerment. Research and choose deities or elemental forces that you feel connected to and resonate with your intention. Call upon them, either through recited invocations or heartfelt prayers, to lend their energies to your ritual.

Step 6: Cleansing and Charging Ritual Tools

Purify and charge your ritual tools and symbols to infuse them with protective energy. Use techniques such as smudging with sage or passing them through incense smoke. Visualize the tools being cleansed of any negative energies and charged with the intention of protection and empowerment.

Step 7: Creating Ritual Gestures or Movements

Incorporate symbolic gestures or movements into your ritual. These can include drawing protective symbols in the air, making specific hand movements, or walking in a sacred circle. Each gesture or movement should align with your intention and help activate the energy within your shields.

Step 8: Reciting Incantations or Chants

Craft or find incantations or chants that affirm and activate the protective energy within your shields. Repeat them aloud or silently, focusing on the rhythm and meaning of the words. Let the vibrations of the sounds resonate within you and infuse the shield with empowering energy.

Step 9: Visualizing the Activation

Close your eyes and visualize the activation of your shield. Imagine it radiating with vibrant energy, forming an impenetrable barrier around you. See the shield glowing with the intention of protection and empowerment. Hold this visualization in your mind for a few moments, strengthening your connection to the shield.

Step 10: Expressing Gratitude and Closing the Ritual

Express gratitude to the deities, elemental forces, and energies that have assisted you in the ritual. Thank them for their presence and support. Slowly bring the ritual to a close by extinguishing candles, releasing any residual energy, and grounding yourself once again.

Conclusion:

As you have journeyed through this section, you have explored the essential techniques for activating and reinforcing your protective shields. Through visualization exercises, energy work practices, and rituals, you have learned to unlock the full potential of your shields and connect with the protective energies inherent in these practices. By engaging in hands-on exercises, you have gained firsthand experience and developed a profound connection to the potent forces that safeguard and empower you. May your journey continue with confidence and resilience as you master the art of activating and maintaining your protective shields.

Example Exercise:

Now, it's time for you to create your own protective amulet or talisman based on your individual intentions or areas of concern. Start by researching symbols and correspondences associated with protection and select those that resonate with your desired outcomes. Design and create your amulets or talismans using various materials such as stones, herbs, or charms. Finally, perform an activation ritual or ceremony to imbue your objects with protective energies. Through this exercise, you will not only gain practical experience in protective magic but also develop your creativity and intention-setting skills.

➤ Healing Magic: Restoring Balance and Wholeness:

In our exploration of healing magic, we come across the profound practices of herbalism. This ancient art combines the wisdom of plants with the intention to restore balance and promote well-being on multiple levels. By harnessing the medicinal properties of herbs, herbalists engage in a holistic approach to healing that encompasses the physical, emotional, and spiritual aspects of an individual's being.

Herbs have been used for centuries to address a wide range of ailments and imbalances. Each herb possesses its unique properties and healing attributes, making it suitable for specific conditions. For instance, St. John's Wort is known for its antidepressant properties, while chamomile soothes digestive discomfort. By understanding the therapeutic qualities of various herbs, practitioners of healing magic can select the most appropriate ones for their intended purposes.

Preparation methods play a crucial role in herbal healing. Herbal infusions, or teas, allow the medicinal properties of herbs to infuse into hot water, creating a healing elixir. Tinctures, on the other hand, involve extracting the beneficial compounds of herbs using alcohol or vinegar. Poultices, a topical application of herbs, can be used for skin conditions or localized discomfort. Understanding these preparation methods empowers practitioners to utilize herbs effectively in their healing practices.

In herbal healing, intention and energy transfer are integral components. The practitioner infuses the herbs with their intentions, directing healing energy into the remedy being prepared. This process involves focusing on the desired outcome, visualizing the healing energy being absorbed by the herbs, and imbuing them with the power to bring about restoration and balance. By consciously directing their energy and intentions, herbalists maximize the healing potential of the herbs they work with.

Case studies and practical exercises provide invaluable opportunities for students to deepen their understanding of herbal healing and develop practical skills. For instance, students may be assigned a case study where they analyze a specific ailment or imbalance and research the herbs that can be employed for healing. By formulating a personalized herbal remedy, students engage in hands-on learning and cultivate their abilities to address holistic healing.

Example Exercise:

Designing a Healing Herbal Remedy

As a class, we will collectively design a healing herbal remedy for a specific ailment, such as insomnia or digestive issues. Each student will be assigned an herb with known medicinal properties that can aid in addressing the chosen condition. Individually, students will research the herb's properties, traditional uses, and recommended dosage. Then, working together, we will combine our knowledge and create a comprehensive herbal remedy by blending the chosen herbs in appropriate proportions. Through this exercise, we will deepen our understanding of the medicinal properties of herbs and enhance our practical skills in formulating effective herbal remedies.

By engaging in these exercises and exploring the world of herbalism within the context of healing magic, students will not only expand their knowledge of plant medicine but also gain insight into the interconnectedness of the physical, emotional, and spiritual realms in the healing process. Through critical thinking and active participation, they will develop a deeper appreciation for the potency of herbal healing and its potential to restore balance and wholeness.

➤ Ethical Considerations and Responsibility:

In our pursuit of protective and healing magic, it is imperative to critically examine the ethical considerations and responsibilities that accompany these practices. By engaging in thought-provoking discussions and analyzing real-life case studies, we will develop a heightened awareness of the ethical principles that guide our journey in the realms of magic.

One crucial ethical consideration in the realm of healing magic revolves around the provision of healing services to others. When engaging in practices that aim to alleviate suffering and promote well-being, it is essential to obtain informed consent from those seeking our assistance. This means ensuring that individuals fully understand the nature of the healing work being offered, its potential benefits, and any possible risks involved. Respecting personal boundaries and empowering individuals to make their own decisions regarding their healing journey are fundamental aspects of practicing ethical healing magic.

Confidentiality is another ethical principle that holds great significance in healing magic. Individuals seeking healing often share deeply personal and sensitive information with practitioners. It is our responsibility to treat this information with the utmost respect and maintain strict confidentiality. Respecting privacy fosters an environment of trust and ensures that individuals feel safe and supported throughout their healing process.

As we explore diverse healing traditions, it is crucial to navigate the potential challenges of cultural appropriation with sensitivity and respect. Cultural appropriation refers to the inappropriate borrowing or adoption of practices from cultures that are not our own, often without understanding their cultural significance or historical context. When incorporating healing techniques from various traditions, we must approach them with cultural humility and acknowledge the importance of honoring and learning from the original cultures that developed these practices. By doing so, we ensure that our actions are rooted in respect and appreciation rather than exploitation.

Through critical analysis and reflective exercises, we will examine the potential risks associated with manipulative or misguided practices in protective and healing magic. It is important to recognize that while magic can be a powerful tool for transformation and healing, its misuse or unethical application can have detrimental effects on individuals and communities. By developing a discerning mindset and maintaining a commitment to ethical practice, we can ensure that our actions align with the highest principles of integrity and compassion.

Example Discussion:

Imagine a scenario where a practitioner offers their services for healing but fails to obtain informed consent from the recipient. As a class, let's engage in a discussion about the potential ethical implications of this situation. We will explore the importance of informed consent, the potential consequences of not obtaining it, and possible strategies for ensuring open and transparent communication with those seeking healing. Through this discussion, we will deepen our understanding of the ethical responsibilities we hold as practitioners and cultivate the skills necessary to navigate complex ethical dilemmas in the realm of magic.

By actively participating in these discussions and contemplating the ethical dimensions of protective and healing magic, students will develop a strong ethical foundation for their magical practice. They will learn to approach their work with integrity, compassion, and respect for the well-being of others. Through critical thinking and self-reflection, students will embrace their role as ethical practitioners, ensuring that their magical endeavors contribute positively to the world around them.

➢ Counterarguments and Dissenting Opinions:

In our journey to expand our knowledge and deepen our understanding of protective and healing magic, it is crucial to explore counterarguments and dissenting opinions. This section aims to foster critical thinking skills and encourage students to consider alternative viewpoints, allowing them to develop a comprehensive understanding of the subject matter.

By presenting counterarguments, we challenge prevailing beliefs and invite students to evaluate the effectiveness of protective and healing magic from various angles. One common counterargument questions the scientific validity of these practices. Critics argue that the perceived effects of protective and healing magic may be attributed to placebo responses or subjective experiences rather than tangible evidence. To assess these claims critically, we will delve into scientific research on placebo effects, the mind-body connection, and the potential influence of belief in magical practices. Through this exploration, students will gain a deeper appreciation of the complexities and limitations involved in evaluating the effectiveness of these practices solely through a scientific lens.

Another aspect to consider is the cultural appropriateness of certain magical practices. Some argue that adopting elements from diverse cultural traditions without proper understanding or respect can lead to cultural misappropriation. This raises ethical questions about incorporating practices from cultures different from our own. Through engaging discussions and thought-provoking case studies, we will explore different perspectives on cultural appropriation, emphasizing the importance of cultural sensitivity, informed practice, and the reverence we must have for the roots and context of the traditions we draw inspiration from.

Ethical considerations also hold significant weight in the critique of protective and healing magic. Critics suggest that practitioners may exploit vulnerable individuals or engage in manipulative practices that lack scientific evidence or therapeutic validity. We will analyze these concerns, examine the importance of informed consent, and explore ethical frameworks within the realm of magic. By critically evaluating these arguments, students will develop a nuanced understanding of the ethical responsibilities and considerations that accompany their magical practice.

Through interactive exercises, students will actively construct evidence-based arguments and engage in respectful debates. For example, we may organize a mock debate where students present and defend opposing viewpoints on specific topics, such as the effectiveness of crystal healing or the appropriateness of smudging practices. These exercises will sharpen critical thinking skills, foster constructive dialogue, and deepen students' comprehension of the intricate nature of protective and healing magic.

By actively engaging with counterarguments and dissenting opinions, students will cultivate a well-rounded perspective and develop the ability to critically evaluate claims and evidence. This approach promotes intellectual growth, empathy, and equips students with the necessary skills to navigate the complexities and controversies inherent in the realms of protective and healing magic.

Conclusion:

By exploring protective and healing magic, we will gain a profound understanding of the transformative power inherent in these mystical practices. We will appreciate the historical, cross-cultural, and ethical dimensions of protective and healing magic, recognizing its capacity to promote well-being and create a sense of empowerment. Through exercises, discussions, and problem-solving activities, we will engage in critical thinking and develop practical skills to apply protective and healing magic in our personal and spiritual lives.

Divination and Prophecy: Seeking Knowledge of the Future

➤   Unraveling the Mysteries of Divination and Prophecy:

Welcome to the fascinating realm of divination and prophecy, where we embark on a captivating journey to uncover the secrets of the future. Humans have long been enthralled by the desire to gain insight into what lies ahead, and in this section, we will delve into the methods, beliefs, and profound significance of divination and prophecy across various cultural and spiritual contexts. By examining real-life examples from diverse fields, such as witchcraft, divination, herbalism, shamanism, ecospirituality, and the magic of ancient Mesopotamia, we will develop a nuanced understanding of how individuals throughout history have sought to unravel the mysteries of the future.

Divination and prophecy have been practiced by countless civilizations throughout time, each employing unique techniques and belief systems to access hidden knowledge. From the reading of tarot cards and scrying with mirrors or crystals to the interpretation of celestial patterns and the casting of runes, divination encompasses a rich tapestry of methods used to glimpse the threads of destiny. By studying these diverse practices, we will gain insight into the cultural and symbolic significance attributed to each method, allowing us to appreciate the artistry and profound wisdom behind the act of divination.

In addition to the methods themselves, we will explore the belief systems that underpin divination and prophecy. Different cultures and spiritual traditions hold distinct perspectives on the nature of fate, free will, and the interconnectedness of the universe. Through the lens of witchcraft, for example, we will examine the concept of synchronicity and the belief in a web of connections that allows divination to tap into the currents of the unseen. From the ancient wisdom of Mesopotamia, we will learn about the intricate system of omen interpretation and its role in shaping decisions and actions. By immersing ourselves in these varied belief systems, we will expand our own understanding of the possibilities and limitations of divination and prophecy.

To deepen our exploration, we will examine case studies and real-life examples of how divination and prophecy have been utilized in different fields. For instance, in herbalism, practitioners may use divination to determine which herbs are most appropriate for an individual's healing journey. In shamanic practices, divination may serve as a means to communicate with the spirit world and receive guidance for the community. Through these diverse examples, we will uncover the versatility and profound impact of divination and prophecy in various contexts.

To engage in critical thinking and reflection, we will also consider counterarguments and dissenting opinions surrounding divination and prophecy. Skeptics may question the validity of these practices, attributing their perceived accuracy to chance or subjective interpretation. By critically examining these counterarguments and evaluating the available evidence, we can develop a more well-rounded understanding of the subject.

To further enhance your learning experience, we will incorporate interactive exercises and problems that encourage deep thinking and application of knowledge. For example, you may be asked to interpret a tarot spread or analyze the symbolic meanings behind different forms of divination. These exercises will not only reinforce your understanding but also foster your intuition and analytical skills.

By immersing ourselves in the world of divination and prophecy, we will gain a profound appreciation for the methods, beliefs, and significance that have shaped this ancient practice. Through examination of real-life examples, critical analysis, and interactive exercises, you will develop the ability to navigate the mysteries of the future with wisdom, insight, and discernment.

➢ Understanding the Essence of Divination:

Welcome to the captivating realm of divination, where the desire to unravel the mysteries of the future finds expression through various practices. In this section, we will embark on a fascinating journey into the world of tarot reading, exploring its origins, symbolism, and profound structure. Through engaging case studies and thought-provoking examples, we will unlock the secrets held within the cards and develop the skills to interpret their hidden meanings. By delving into the archetypes and symbolism present in tarot, we will sharpen our intuitive abilities and forge a deeper connection to the profound insights offered by this divinatory tool.

Tarot, a centuries-old practice, holds a special place within the realm of divination. Its origins can be traced back to the rich tapestry of cultural influences, including Egyptian, Hebrew, and European traditions. The tarot deck itself is composed of 78 cards, each with its own unique symbolism and significance. As we explore the tarot, we will gain an appreciation for its profound structure, consisting of Major Arcana and Minor Arcana cards. The Major Arcana represents significant life events and archetypal energies, while the Minor Arcana delves into the realms of daily experiences and practical matters.

To understand the art of tarot reading, we will immerse ourselves in the symbolism embedded within the cards. For instance, the Fool card embodies new beginnings, taking risks, and embracing the unknown. The Empress card symbolizes abundance, creativity, and nurturing energy. By studying the symbolism and archetypes of each card, we can unravel the layers of meaning that lie beneath the surface. Through guided exercises and interactive problems, you will develop the skills to interpret the cards, allowing you to access their rich insights and guidance.

One of the fundamental concepts underlying tarot reading is synchronicity—the meaningful coincidence of events that reveals a deeper connection between the outer world and our inner experiences. As we engage with the cards, we will explore the concept of synchronicity and its role in divination. By recognizing patterns, making connections, and trusting our intuition, we can tap into the currents of synchronicity and uncover profound insights about ourselves and the world around us.

To deepen our understanding, we will examine case studies and real-life examples that highlight the transformative power of tarot. For instance, we may explore how tarot readings have guided individuals in making important life decisions, gaining clarity in relationships, or navigating challenging situations. These examples will illustrate the practical application of tarot and the profound impact it can have on personal growth and self-reflection.

As with any subject of study, it is important to consider counterarguments and dissenting opinions. Some skeptics may question the validity of tarot reading, dismissing it as mere chance or subjective interpretation. Through critical analysis and evaluation of available evidence, we will engage with these counterarguments, allowing us to develop a more comprehensive understanding of the strengths and limitations of tarot as a divinatory tool.

To further enhance your learning experience, we will incorporate interactive exercises and problems that invite you to practice tarot reading techniques. You may be asked to interpret sample tarot spreads, analyze the symbolism in specific cards, or engage in group discussions to deepen your understanding. These exercises will not only reinforce your knowledge but also nurture your intuitive abilities and critical thinking skills.

By immersing ourselves in the world of tarot reading, we will unlock the profound wisdom and guidance that it holds. Through the exploration of its origins, symbolism, and structure, and through engaging with case studies and interactive exercises, you will develop the skills to interpret the cards and access the transformative insights they offer. Whether you are a beginner or have some experience with tarot, this journey will deepen your connection to divination and provide a valuable tool for self-reflection and personal growth.

➤ Tools and Techniques of Divination:

Divination is a practice that has captivated human beings throughout history. It encompasses a wide range of tools and techniques that enable individuals to tap into the unseen realms and gain insights into the past, present, and future. In this section, we will delve deeper into the significance and application of divinatory tools, providing a comprehensive exploration of their symbolism, methodology, and practical use.

The art of divination relies on the belief that there is hidden knowledge available to us, waiting to be revealed through various mediums. These tools serve as conduits, allowing practitioners to access this knowledge and interpret it in meaningful ways. By understanding the historical context, cultural significance, and intricate symbolism behind these tools, we gain a richer understanding of their purpose and power.

One such tool is the tarot deck, a set of cards rich in symbolism and archetypal imagery. Tarot reading has been practiced for centuries and has evolved into a profound system of divination. As you embark on your journey through the world of tarot, you will explore its origins and the esoteric wisdom embedded within the cards. By engaging in guided exercises and interpretation techniques, you will develop the skills to unlock the layered meanings contained within each card and construct narratives that provide guidance and insight.

Another fascinating tool of divination is the crystal ball, renowned for its ability to facilitate scrying. Scrying involves gazing into the reflective surface of a crystal ball and entering a meditative state to receive visions and intuitive impressions. Throughout history, crystal balls have been associated with mystics, seers, and fortune-tellers. In this section, we will delve into the symbolism and history of crystal balls, exploring their role as portals to other realms of consciousness. Through practical exercises, you will have the opportunity to experiment with scrying techniques, heightening your intuitive faculties and deepening your connection to the wisdom held within these mystical spheres.

Pendulums, too, offer a unique approach to divination. These weighted objects suspended from a chain or cord have been used for centuries to answer questions, diagnose health conditions, and guide decision-making processes. In this section, we will explore the theories behind pendulum divination, including the concept of micro-muscle movements and the power of subconscious perception. Through practical exercises, you will learn to communicate with your pendulum, uncovering its unique language of movement and receiving clear answers to your inquiries.

Oracle decks, comprising cards adorned with evocative images and messages, offer yet another avenue for divination. Unlike tarot decks, oracle decks do not adhere to a standardized structure but instead encompass a diverse range of themes, such as angels, animal spirits, and elemental forces. In this section, you will explore the world of oracle cards, discovering their versatile nature and how they can be used to access divine guidance and intuitive wisdom.

By engaging with these divinatory tools, you will develop a profound understanding of their historical and cultural significance. Through practical exercises, you will cultivate the skills necessary to interpret symbols, identify patterns, and unravel the messages encoded within divinatory tools. These experiences will deepen your connection to the unseen realms and empower you to seek guidance and insight from the spiritual dimensions.

Remember, the tools themselves are not inherently magical or prophetic. Instead, they serve as catalysts for our own intuitive abilities and as mirrors that reflect our inner wisdom. As you embark on this exploration of divination, keep an open mind and embrace the possibilities that unfold. By integrating your knowledge, intuition, and personal experiences, you will develop a unique approach to divination that resonates with your individual path and spiritual journey.

Example Exercise:

To put your newfound knowledge into practice, you will have the opportunity to work with a divinatory tool of your choice, such as tarot cards, pendulums, or oracle decks. Select a specific question or topic of inquiry that piques your curiosity, and use your chosen divinatory tool to seek guidance and insights. Document your experiences, paying attention to the symbols, patterns, and messages that emerge during the divination process. Reflect on your interpretations and analyze how the divinatory information relates to your initial question or inquiry. This exercise will bolster your confidence in working with divinatory tools and deepen your understanding of the intricate interplay between symbols, intuition, and the pursuit of future knowledge.

Through this comprehensive exploration of divination and its diverse methods, you will develop a profound understanding of how different cultures and spiritual traditions have sought knowledge of the future. Moreover, you will nurture your own abilities to engage with divination and prophecy, fostering greater self-awareness, intuition, and connection to the unseen realms. Get ready to unlock the hidden wisdom of the future!

➤ Unveiling the Secrets of Divination and Prophecy:

Are you curious about the mystical realms of divination and prophecy? Get ready to embark on a fascinating journey as we explore these ancient practices and their significance. In this section, we will dive deep into the concept of prophecy and the role of prophets as intermediaries between the divine and human realms. By examining examples from ancient civilizations, religious traditions, and folklore, you will gain a profound understanding of the beliefs and functions associated with prophecy. Through critical analysis and engaging discussions, we will explore differing viewpoints on the nature of prophecy and the profound impact prophets have had on society.

➢ The Power and Meaning of Divination:

Let's delve into the profound significance of divination and prophecy in cultural, spiritual, and personal contexts. We will examine how these practices have been used to make crucial decisions, seek guidance, and gain profound insights into personal and collective destinies. By analyzing captivating case studies, you will unravel the ways in which divination and prophecy have shaped societies and influenced the course of history.

1. The Power of Divination:

Divination, the art of seeking knowledge of the future or hidden truths through various methods, has been practiced across diverse cultures and time periods. Its significance lies in its ability to provide individuals and communities with insights and guidance in navigating life's uncertainties.

Cultural Significance: Delve into the cultural significance of divination in different societies, such as the ancient civilizations of Greece, Egypt, and China. Explore how divination practices were integrated into religious rituals and political decision-making processes.

Spiritual Connection: Examine the spiritual aspects of divination, considering its role in establishing a connection between humans and the divine. Discuss how divination rituals and techniques foster a sense of spiritual communion and facilitate communication with higher realms.

Personal Empowerment: Explore how divination empowers individuals by offering them a means to access hidden knowledge and gain insights into personal dilemmas. Discuss how divination aids in decision-making, problem-solving, and self-reflection, allowing individuals to align their actions with their deepest values and desires.

2. The Profound Nature of Prophecy:

Prophecy, the act of receiving and interpreting divine messages about the future or hidden truths, holds a special place in human history and imagination. Its impact extends beyond personal spirituality, shaping the course of societies and influencing collective beliefs and actions.

Historical Examples: Examine captivating case studies of prophecies that have left lasting imprints on societies. Explore instances such as the Oracle of Delphi in ancient Greece, the prophecies of Nostradamus, or the prophetic traditions within indigenous cultures. Analyze how these prophecies have influenced the beliefs, actions, and historical events of their time.

Societal Transformation: Discuss how prophecies have played pivotal roles in shaping the social, political, and cultural landscapes of communities. Explore the transformative power of prophecies in movements for social justice, revolutions, and the emergence of religious and spiritual movements.

Personal and Collective Destinies: Reflect on the profound impact of prophecy on individuals and communities, both in terms of personal growth and the shared destiny of societies. Explore how prophecies provide a sense of purpose, inspire collective action, and contribute to the formation of cultural identities.

Through an in-depth exploration of the significance of divination and prophecy, you will gain a comprehensive understanding of how these practices have shaped human experiences and influenced the trajectory of civilizations. By analyzing case studies and engaging in critical discussions, you will cultivate a nuanced perspective on the profound role of divination and prophecy in both historical and contemporary contexts.

➢ Questioning the Unknown:

In the spirit of critical thinking, we will explore skeptical perspectives and critiques of divination and prophecy. We will delve into counterarguments that challenge these practices, including the role of chance and subjective interpretation in divinatory methods. Through reflective exercises and lively debates, you will develop a balanced and nuanced understanding of the limitations and potential pitfalls associated with seeking knowledge of the future through divination and prophecy.

1.   Skeptical Perspectives:

Scientific Skepticism: Examine the viewpoints of skeptics who approach divination and prophecy from a scientific perspective. Discuss the challenges of empirical validation and the absence of rigorous scientific evidence supporting the predictive accuracy of divinatory practices.

Psychological Explanations: Explore the psychological theories that attribute the effectiveness of divination to cognitive biases, such as the Barnum effect or the confirmation bias. Analyze how these biases can influence the interpretation of divinatory symbols and reinforce subjective beliefs.

2.   Critiques of Divination Methods:

Role of Chance: Discuss the argument that divination methods, such as drawing tarot cards or casting runes, rely heavily on chance rather than any supernatural or predictive abilities. Explore the possibility that divination outcomes are a result of statistical probabilities rather than genuine insight into the future.

Subjective Interpretation: Examine the critique that divination and prophecy heavily rely on subjective interpretation, which can vary widely among individuals. Discuss how personal biases, cultural influences, and preconceived notions can shape the interpretation of divinatory symbols, potentially leading to inaccurate or biased readings.

3.   Understanding Limitations:

Reflective Exercises: Engage in reflective exercises that encourage self-assessment and critical evaluation of divination practices. Encourage students to analyze their own experiences with divination, identifying any instances where personal biases or subjective interpretations may have influenced their readings.

Lively Debates: Organize class debates where students can present arguments both for and against divination and prophecy. Encourage students to challenge and question each other's viewpoints, fostering critical thinking and the exploration of diverse perspectives.

Ethical Considerations: Discuss the ethical implications of divination and prophecy, such as the potential for manipulation or exploitation of vulnerable individuals. Explore the responsibility of diviners to provide accurate and ethical guidance, and the importance of informed consent in seeking divinatory services.

Through the exploration of skeptical perspectives and critiques, you will develop a well-rounded understanding of divination and prophecy. By engaging in reflective exercises and lively debates, you will cultivate critical thinking skills and develop the ability to assess the limitations and potential biases associated with these practices. This comprehensive approach will allow you to navigate the complexities of divination and prophecy with a discerning and informed perspective.

➢   Navigating Ethical Considerations:

As seekers of truth, we must also consider the ethical considerations and responsibilities that come with the practice of divination and prophecy. Together, we will critically examine topics such as consent, cultural appropriation, and the potential for manipulation or exploitation. Through intriguing case studies and thought-provoking ethical dilemmas, you will develop a heightened awareness of the ethical principles that should guide practitioners of divination and prophecy.

1.   Informed Consent:

Explore the importance of informed consent in divinatory practices. Discuss how practitioners should clearly communicate the purpose, limitations, and potential outcomes of a divination session to clients. Analyze the ethical implications of providing accurate and unbiased information, allowing clients to make informed decisions based on their own judgment.

Case Study: Present a case study where a diviner encounters a client who is vulnerable or emotionally distressed. Discuss the ethical considerations involved in providing guidance to individuals in vulnerable situations and the responsibility of the diviner to prioritize the well-being and autonomy of the client.

2.   Cultural Appropriation:

Examine the concept of cultural appropriation within the context of divination and prophecy. Discuss the potential harm and disrespect that can arise when adopting divinatory practices from cultures without proper understanding or permission. Explore ways to approach cross-cultural practices with sensitivity, respect, and a commitment to learning from the cultural traditions being incorporated.

Ethical Dilemma: Present an ethical dilemma involving the use of cultural symbols or practices in divination without adequate knowledge or respect for their cultural significance. Encourage students to analyze the potential consequences and explore alternative approaches that honor cultural diversity.

3.   Avoiding Manipulation and Exploitation:

Discuss the ethical responsibilities of diviners to avoid manipulating or exploiting clients. Examine the potential risks associated with providing overly deterministic or unquestionable predictions, which may lead to dependence or psychological harm. Explore the importance of empowering clients and encouraging personal agency in decision-making.

Case Study: Present a case study where a diviner is approached by a client seeking guidance on a life-altering decision. Explore the ethical considerations of providing advice that respects the client's autonomy and encourages critical thinking, rather than imposing the diviner's own values or desires.

Through the exploration of ethical considerations in divination and prophecy, you will develop a greater understanding of the responsibilities that come with these practices. By analyzing case studies and engaging in thought-provoking ethical dilemmas, you will cultivate a heightened awareness of the need for informed consent, cultural sensitivity, and the avoidance of manipulation or exploitation. This ethical framework will guide you in practicing divination and prophecy with integrity, compassion, and respect for the well-being and autonomy of those seeking guidance.

In Conclusion:

Through our exploration of divination and prophecy, you will gain a comprehensive understanding of humanity's timeless fascination with seeking knowledge of the future. You will come to appreciate the diverse methods and beliefs associated with divination and prophecy across various cultures and time periods. Engaging in exercises, discussions, and problem-solving activities, you will sharpen your critical thinking skills and develop practical tools to navigate the intricate world of divination and prophecy. Moreover, you will gain a deep sense of responsibility and ethical awareness when applying these practices. Get ready to unlock the secrets of the unknown!

Magical Objects and Ingredients

Welcome to the enchanting world of magical objects and ingredients! Throughout history, practitioners of magic have relied on a diverse array of elements to amplify their rituals, spells, and enchantments. In this section, we will embark on a comprehensive exploration of the significance and uses of these magical elements across various traditions, including witchcraft, divination, herbalism, shamanism, ecospirituality, and ancient Mesopotamian magic. By delving into the properties, symbolism, and cultural contexts of these objects and ingredients, you will gain a profound understanding of their role in magical practices.

Unraveling Symbolism and Significance:

Let's begin our journey by unraveling the symbolism and significance of magical objects. Together, we will examine the mystical properties of items like wands, athames, talismans, amulets, and cauldrons. We will delve into the ways these objects have been imbued with magical energy and used as conduits for channeling and focusing power. Through captivating case studies and examples from diverse magical traditions, you will explore the cultural and historical importance of these objects and their symbolic representations.

1.   Wands:

Explore the symbolism and purpose of wands in magical practices. Discuss how wands are believed to enhance the wielder's intention and act as extensions of their personal power. Analyze the various materials and designs used to create wands and the cultural and historical contexts in which they have been used.

Case Study: Examine the role of wands in different magical traditions, such as Wicca, ceremonial magic, and ancient folklore. Discuss the specific functions and rituals associated with wands in these traditions and the significance of their unique attributes.

2.   Athames:

Investigate the significance of athames, ritual knives used in magical practices. Discuss their association with the element of Air, their symbolic representation, and their use in casting circles, invoking spirits, and directing energy. Analyze the ethical considerations surrounding the use of athames and the responsibility of the practitioner to handle them with respect and mindfulness.

Cultural Example: Explore the use of ritual knives in ancient cultures such as ancient Egypt, where they were employed in religious ceremonies and magical rites. Discuss the cultural symbolism and historical context of these knives and their potential influence on contemporary magical practices.

3.   Talismans and Amulets:

Examine the power of talismans and amulets in harnessing magical energy and offering protection or luck. Discuss the different types of talismans and amulets found across cultures and their specific purposes, such as love, health, or prosperity. Analyze the belief systems and magical theories behind the effectiveness of these objects.

Case Study: Present a case study exploring the use of talismans or amulets in a specific magical tradition or cultural context. Discuss the rituals involved in creating and activating these objects, as well as their role in providing a sense of security and connection to the divine.

4.   Cauldrons:

Delve into the symbolism and magical significance of cauldrons. Discuss their association with transformation, healing, and the element of Water. Explore their role as vessels for creating potions, performing rituals, and connecting with ancestral energies. Analyze the cultural and historical references to cauldrons in mythologies and folklore.

Example from Mythology: Explore the role of the cauldron in Celtic mythology, such as the Cauldron of Dagda or the Cauldron of Cerridwen. Discuss the mythological narratives surrounding these cauldrons and their symbolic representation of abundance, rebirth, and divine wisdom.

Through the exploration of magical objects, their symbolism, and their cultural and historical contexts, you will develop a deeper understanding of their significance in various magical traditions. By analyzing captivating case studies and examples, you will uncover the ways in which these objects have been used as conduits for channeling and focusing magical power. This knowledge will enrich your practice and provide you with a foundation to connect with the deep mystical heritage associated with these magical artifacts.

Exploring Ritual Tools and Implements:

In this section, we will shine a spotlight on the ritual tools and implements that play a crucial role in magical practices. These tools serve as powerful extensions of the practitioner's intention, enabling them to create sacred space, invoke spiritual energies, and direct their magical work. You will discover the purpose and functions of tools such as ritual knives, chalices, bells, and candles, and explore how they enhance and amplify the practitioner's connection with the mystical realms.

1.   Ritual Knives:

Explore the significance of ritual knives, also known as athames or bolines, in magical practices. Discuss their role as a symbol of the practitioner's personal power and their practical use in casting circles, cutting energetic cords, and performing rituals. Analyze the different types of ritual knives and their corresponding purposes within various magical traditions.

Practical Exercise: Engage in a guided visualization exercise where you imagine yourself consecrating and utilizing a ritual knife. Reflect on the sensations and emotions that arise during the visualization and contemplate the symbolic meaning and personal significance of this tool.

Chalices:

Examine the purpose and symbolism of chalices in magical rituals. Discuss their association with the element of Water and their role in representing the divine feminine energy. Explore how chalices are used for holding and consecrating sacred liquids, such as water, wine, or herbal infusions, and how they facilitate the ritual act of communion.

Case Study: Analyze the use of chalices in different magical traditions, such as ceremonial magic, Wicca, or ancient Egyptian rituals. Discuss the cultural and historical context of these practices and the symbolic interpretations of the chalice within each tradition.

2.   Bells:

Uncover the magical properties of bells and their significance in ritual practices. Discuss how the sound of bells can purify and cleanse sacred spaces, summon spirits, and heighten spiritual awareness. Explore the cultural and historical associations of bells in different religious and magical traditions.

Thought-Provoking Discussion: Engage in a discussion exploring the potential effects of bell ringing on consciousness and energy. Consider the ways in which bells can create a shift in perception and promote a deeper connection with the spiritual realms.

3.   Candles:

Delve into the symbolism and practical uses of candles in magical rituals. Discuss how candles represent the element of Fire and serve as focal points for intention and manifestation. Explore the diverse colors, shapes, and sizes of candles and their corresponding meanings in magical practices.

Practical Exercise: Engage in a candle magic exercise where you choose a specific intention and charge a candle with that intention. Reflect on the process of infusing the candle with your energy and the symbolism associated with the chosen color and shape.

Through engaging in practical exercises and thought-provoking discussions, you will develop a deep understanding of the practical applications and symbolic significance of these ritual tools. This knowledge will empower you to create sacred space, invoke spiritual energies, and direct your intention with precision and purpose. By exploring the cultural and historical contexts of these tools, you will gain a broader perspective on their use and appreciate the rich tapestry of magical traditions from which they originate.

Unveiling the Magic of Ingredients:

Prepare to enter the realm of magical ingredients and substances! In this section, we will delve into the fascinating world of herbs, crystals, oils, and incenses. These natural elements have long been revered for their unique properties and correspondences in magical practices. By exploring their qualities and applications, you will gain a deeper understanding of how to incorporate them effectively in spells, potions, and rituals.

1.   Herbs:

Discover the diverse world of magical herbs and their associations with different intentions and energies. Explore the historical and cultural significance of herbs in magical traditions, such as European folk magic, indigenous practices, and ancient herbalism.

Practical Exercise: Engage in a herb identification activity where you examine and categorize various herbs based on their magical properties. Discuss their correspondences, such as planetary associations, elemental affinities, and symbolic meanings. Consider the ways in which these correspondences can be utilized in spellwork, herbal remedies, and ritual practices.

2.   Crystals:

Uncover the mystical properties of crystals and their applications in magical and energetic practices. Explore the concept of crystal correspondences, including their colors, shapes, and energetic vibrations. Discuss how crystals can be used to amplify intentions, enhance psychic abilities, and create energetic grids.

Guided Exercise: Engage in a crystal meditation where you select a crystal and explore its energy through visualization and focused attention. Reflect on the sensations and insights you experience during the meditation and contemplate the ways in which you can integrate crystals into your magical practice.

3.   Oils:

Learn about the use of oils in magical rituals, anointing practices, and spellwork. Explore the properties and correspondences of essential oils and their association with specific intentions and energies. Discuss the cultural and historical significance of oils in different magical traditions, such as aromatherapy, ceremonial magic, and traditional herbalism.

Case Study: Analyze the use of oils in specific magical rituals or traditions, such as the anointing of sacred objects or the creation of magical perfumes. Discuss the symbolism and practical applications of oils within these contexts and reflect on their potential transformative effects.

4.   Incenses:

Explore the sacred art of incense and its role in purification, ritual, and spiritual elevation. Investigate the properties and correspondences of various incense resins, herbs, and botanicals. Discuss their association with different intentions, such as protection, purification, and spiritual communication.

Practical Exercise: Engage in an incense blending activity where you combine different aromatic ingredients to create a customized incense blend. Reflect on the purpose and energetic qualities of the blend, and consider how it can be incorporated into your magical rituals and practices.

Through immersive hands-on activities and guided exercises, you will develop the skills to identify and harness the magical properties of herbs, crystals, oils, and incenses. By exploring their correspondences and applications, you will expand your repertoire of magical tools and enhance your ability to create meaningful and effective spells, potions, and rituals. This knowledge will empower you to infuse your magical practice with the natural energies and transformative powers of these enchanting ingredients and substances.

Creating Sacred Spaces and Altars:

In this section, we will embark on a transformative exploration of sacred spaces and altars within the realm of magical practices. Prepare to unravel the symbolism and arrangement of objects on altars, as well as the profound purpose of sacred space for meditation, ritual, and spellwork. By engaging in practical exercises and thought-provoking discussions, you will have the opportunity to design and create your own sacred altar, carefully considering the placement and significance of different objects and symbols.

1.   Sacred Spaces:

Dive into the concept of sacred space and its significance in magical practices. Explore the historical and cultural contexts in which sacred spaces have been utilized, such as ancient temples, indigenous ceremonial grounds, and contemporary ritual spaces. Discuss the role of sacred space in setting intentions, creating a focused atmosphere, and connecting with the divine.
Practical Exercise: Reflect on the qualities and elements that contribute to the creation of a sacred space. Consider the use of color, lighting, scent, and sound to establish a conducive environment for spiritual practices. Design and set up a temporary sacred space in your own home or outdoor setting, paying careful attention to the chosen objects, symbols, and arrangements.

2.   Altars:

Uncover the symbolism and purpose of altars in magical practices. Explore the various types of altars, such as seasonal altars, deity altars, and working altars, and their respective functions. Discuss the cultural and historical significance of altars in different magical traditions, ranging from Wiccan and pagan practices to ceremonial magic and ancestral veneration.

Guided Exercise: Engage in a guided visualization where you enter a sacred space and encounter an altar that resonates with your intentions or spiritual path. Observe the objects, symbols, and arrangement on the altar and reflect on the personal meaning they hold for you. Use this experience to inspire the creation of your own altar, incorporating elements that align with your magical goals and spiritual connection.

3.   Object Arrangement and Symbolism:

Delve into the art of object arrangement on altars and the symbolic meanings behind different items. Explore the significance of elemental representations, sacred tools, deity imagery, natural objects, and personal mementos. Discuss how the arrangement of objects can create a harmonious energy flow and support specific magical intentions.

Case Studies: Analyze examples of altars from different magical traditions, examining their object placement and symbolic associations. Explore how these arrangements reflect the practitioner's beliefs, values, and intentions. Engage in discussions to deepen your understanding of the diverse ways in which altars are utilized and personalized.

Through the exploration of sacred spaces and altars, you will gain the knowledge and skills to infuse your magical practices with intention, symbolism, and spiritual connection. By designing and setting up your own altar, you will engage in a deeply personal and transformative experience. This process will allow you to tap into the profound power of sacred space and objects, and enhance your ability to engage in meditation, ritual, and spellwork with heightened focus and intention. Join us on this magical journey as we explore the significance and uses of magical objects and ingredients, and empower yourself to create sacred spaces that inspire and support your spiritual path.

Ethics and Responsibility in Working with Magical Objects and Ingredients:

Welcome to a thought-provoking journey into the ethical considerations and responsibilities that arise in the use of magical objects and ingredients. As seekers of knowledge and practitioners of magic, it is crucial for us to critically examine the ethical dimensions within the realm of our craft. In this section, we will delve deep into topics such as cultural appropriation, sustainability, and the potential for harm, allowing us to develop a heightened awareness of the ethical principles that should guide our actions as practitioners.

1.   Cultural Appropriation:

Engage in a nuanced exploration of cultural appropriation in magical practices. Discuss the importance of respecting and honoring the cultural origins of magical traditions and the potential harm that can arise from appropriating sacred rituals, symbols, and practices from marginalized cultures. Explore ways to cultivate cultural sensitivity, appreciation, and collaboration in the practice of magic.

Case Studies: Analyze real-world examples of cultural appropriation in magical practices, examining the cultural context, power dynamics, and potential consequences. Engage in discussions to understand differing perspectives and develop a critical lens when evaluating your own practices.

2.   Sustainability:

Explore the ecological impact of using magical ingredients and objects. Discuss the importance of sustainable sourcing, harvesting, and production methods in the realm of magic. Examine the ethical implications of using endangered plants, animal products, and minerals in magical practices, and explore alternative, sustainable options.

Ethical Dilemmas: Engage in thought-provoking scenarios that highlight the tension between personal magical practices and environmental sustainability. Reflect on the choices and compromises that practitioners may face, considering the long-term consequences and the interconnectedness of all living beings.

3.   Potential for Harm:

Examine the potential ethical concerns and risks associated with the use of magical objects and ingredients. Discuss the importance of informed consent and the potential for manipulation or harm when working with others. Explore the responsibility of practitioners to use their skills and knowledge ethically and responsibly, respecting the autonomy and well-being of others.

Case Studies and Ethical Debates: Analyze real-world situations where the use of magical objects and ingredients may have unintended consequences or negative impacts on individuals or communities. Engage in ethical debates to navigate complex scenarios and develop a deeper understanding of the ethical dilemmas that practitioners may encounter.

By critically examining the ethical considerations and responsibilities associated with the use of magical objects and ingredients, you will develop a heightened awareness and sense of accountability in your magical practices. Through engaging case studies, ethical dilemmas, and discussions, you will cultivate the skills to navigate the complexities of cultural appropriation, sustainability, and the potential for harm. This ethical exploration will empower you to align your magical practices with principles of respect, integrity, and social consciousness. Together, let us embark on this transformative journey towards an ethical and responsible approach to magic.

Problem-Solving and Application:

To nurture and strengthen your critical thinking skills, we will embark on problem-solving activities that directly relate to the use of magical objects and ingredients. Through these activities, you will have the opportunity to analyze hypothetical scenarios and apply your knowledge of symbolism, correspondences, and practical applications to develop creative and effective solutions. These exercises will empower you to apply your understanding of magical objects and ingredients in real-life situations, honing your problem-solving abilities and enhancing your practical skills.

1.   Symbolic Problem-Solving:

Engage in problem-solving activities that require you to explore the symbolic meanings and correspondences associated with magical objects and ingredients. Analyze a given scenario and identify the most appropriate objects or ingredients to address the situation effectively. Consider the energetic properties, elemental correspondences, and historical associations of each object or ingredient to devise a well-rounded and purposeful solution.

Example Problem: You have a friend who is experiencing chronic insomnia and seeks your assistance. Utilize your knowledge of magical objects and ingredients to create a ritual or spell that can aid in promoting restful sleep and combating insomnia.

2.   Correspondence-Based Solutions:

Apply your understanding of correspondences to solve magical dilemmas. Examine a specific issue or challenge and identify the objects or ingredients that align with the desired outcome based on their correspondences. Consider the elemental associations, planetary influences, and magical properties of each item to craft a solution that resonates with the intended purpose.

Example Problem: A friend is seeking help to attract prosperity and abundance into their life. Use your knowledge of correspondences to suggest appropriate magical objects and ingredients for them to incorporate into their ritual or spellwork.

3.   Practical Application Challenges:

Engage in problem-solving activities that require you to apply your practical skills with magical objects and ingredients. Explore scenarios that involve the creation of potions, spellcasting, or ritual work, and develop innovative solutions using the available resources. Consider the properties, interactions, and synergies of different ingredients to design an effective and purposeful magical practice.

Example Problem: You are tasked with creating a love potion using a specific set of magical ingredients. Utilize your knowledge of the properties and correspondences of these ingredients to develop a potion that promotes love, connection, and harmony.

Through these problem-solving activities, you will develop a deeper understanding of the practical applications of magical objects and ingredients. By analyzing hypothetical scenarios, considering symbolism and correspondences, and applying your knowledge creatively, you will hone your problem-solving abilities and enhance your practical skills. These activities will empower you to think critically, adapt to various situations, and develop innovative approaches to utilizing magical objects and ingredients in your own practice.

Conclusion:

By thoroughly exploring the significance, symbolism, and practical application of magical objects and ingredients, you will gain a comprehensive understanding of their pivotal role in magical practices. You will come to appreciate the diverse range of objects and substances used in various magical traditions, while also developing an understanding of their cultural and historical significance. Through hands-on activities, interactive discussions, and ethical reflections, you will engage in critical thinking and cultivate a sense of responsibility in your use of magical objects and ingredients. Equipped with this knowledge, you will not only navigate the enchanting world of magic with awareness but also acquire the practical skills to effectively utilize these elements in your own magical practice.

Rituals and Performance of Magic

Welcome to the enchanting realm of rituals, where intentional actions merge with the mysterious forces of magic to manifest desired outcomes. In this section, we will embark on a comprehensive journey to explore the diverse and captivating world of rituals, unraveling their significance, purpose, and performance across a multitude of magical traditions. Whether your interests lie in witchcraft, divination, herbalism, shamanism, ecospirituality, or the ancient Mesopotamian magic, this exploration will equip you with the knowledge and skills necessary to engage in ritualistic magical practices with confidence and reverence.

1.   Understanding Rituals:

Begin by delving into the fundamental principles that underpin rituals in various magical traditions. Explore the essence of rituals as intentional acts that harness the power of symbols, intention, and energetic manipulation to create a connection with the spiritual realms. Examine the historical and cultural contexts in which rituals have emerged, understanding their role in personal and collective transformation, healing, and spiritual growth.

Elements of Ritual:

Journey into the essential elements that compose a ritual, including space, time, participants, and tools. Explore the significance of creating sacred space and invoking the presence of spiritual energies. Learn about the optimal timing for rituals, such as lunar phases, planetary alignments, and seasonal cycles. Discover the role of participants in a ritual and the various roles they may assume, such as the priest/priestess, facilitator, or participant. Finally, explore the purpose and symbolism behind the ritual tools and implements used to facilitate the ritual's intention.

2.   Ritual Structure and Design:

Immerse yourself in the art of ritual design and structure. Explore the different phases and components of rituals, such as purification, invocation, intention-setting, spellcasting, and closing. Gain insights into the sequence and flow of rituals, understanding how each phase contributes to the overall purpose and energy of the ceremony. Study the symbolic representations and actions associated with each phase, discovering their significance and the power they hold in facilitating the desired outcomes.

3.   Adaptability and Personalization:

Recognize that rituals can be deeply personal and adaptable to individual preferences and spiritual paths. Explore ways to personalize rituals, incorporating elements that resonate with your unique beliefs, practices, and intentions. Understand the importance of intuition and intention in ritual design, allowing for creative expression and a deep sense of connection with the magical forces at work.

4.   Practical Ritual Techniques:

Engage in practical exercises and techniques to deepen your understanding and experience of rituals. Explore methods of visualization, energy raising, meditation, chanting, and movement to enhance the potency of your rituals. Experiment with different approaches to spellcasting, invocations, and devotional practices, developing your own repertoire of ritual techniques that align with your personal style and intentions.

Through this comprehensive exploration of rituals, you will gain a profound understanding of their significance, purpose, and performance in various magical traditions. By delving into the fundamental principles, elements, structure, and personalization of rituals, you will develop the knowledge and skills necessary to engage in ritualistic magical practices with authenticity and efficacy. Embrace the transformative power of rituals as you connect with the sacred energies and manifest your desires on your spiritual journey.

The Structure and Components of Rituals:

Let us embark on a fascinating exploration as we unravel the intricate structure and components that form the very backbone of rituals. In this section, we will delve deep into the fundamental elements that shape rituals, guiding us towards a comprehensive understanding of their purpose, significance, and profound impact on the magical practices of diverse traditions.

1.   Ritual Preparation:

Begin by immersing yourself in the crucial process of ritual preparation. Discover the importance of creating a sacred and harmonious space that facilitates the energetic flow and connection with the spiritual realms. Explore the significance of purifying the space and participants through various methods, such as smudging, cleansing rituals, or sacred bathing. Understand how these preliminary acts set the stage for a focused and intentional ritual experience.

2.   Invocation:

Journey into the realm of invocation, a powerful phase where the presence of divine energies, deities, spirits, or elemental forces are invoked and invited to participate in the ritual. Explore the diverse methods of invocation, such as spoken prayers, invocatory chants, or ritual gestures, understanding how they establish a profound connection between the human and the divine realms. Analyze the symbolism and cultural context behind specific invocations, drawing inspiration from ancient traditions and contemporary practices.

3.   Consecration:

Delve into the sacred act of consecration, where objects, tools, or participants are imbued with magical energies and blessings. Study the rituals of consecration, such as anointing with oils, passing through smoke or fire, or the recitation of sacred incantations. Understand how these rituals infuse the elements with spiritual power and align them with the intended purpose of the ritual. Explore the cultural and historical significance of consecration rituals across various magical traditions.

4.   Intention Setting:

Explore the art of intention setting, a crucial phase where the practitioner articulates their desires, goals, and intentions to be manifested through the ritual. Analyze the methods of focusing and directing intention, such as visualization, affirmation, or the creation of symbolic representations. Gain insights into the importance of clarity, specificity, and alignment with one's ethical principles in setting intentions. Examine how intention setting not only guides the energy flow but also cultivates personal growth and transformation.

5.   Closing:

Conclude your exploration by understanding the significance of the closing phase in a ritual. Discover the rituals and practices employed to ground the energy, express gratitude, and release the connection to the spiritual realms. Explore techniques such as grounding exercises, offering ceremonies, or the recitation of closing prayers or mantras. Reflect on the importance of integrating the energy generated during the ritual into everyday life, fostering a continued connection with the magical intentions.

Through captivating case studies and examples drawn from diverse magical traditions, you will analyze the purpose and significance of each component that shapes rituals. Engage in thought-provoking discussions and reflective exercises that will deepen your understanding of how these elements intricately contribute to the overall effectiveness and transformative power of rituals. Prepare to unlock the profound secrets and wisdom concealed within the structure and components of rituals, enriching your own magical practices and enhancing your connection with the spiritual realms.

Creating Sacred Space and Ritual Environments:

Prepare to immerse yourself in the profound concept of sacred space, a foundational element of ritualistic practices that holds paramount importance in the realm of magic. In this section, we will embark on a transformative journey to understand the significance of sacred spaces and develop the practical skills necessary to craft and consecrate them. Whether it be a personal altar, a sacred circle, or an entire ritual room, you will learn the art of creating and energizing these spaces, fostering an environment that is conducive to the unfolding of magical work.

1. Understanding Sacred Space:

Begin by delving into the essence and symbolism of sacred space. Explore the idea that sacred spaces serve as portals that bridge the mundane and the divine realms. Examine how sacred spaces act as containers for spiritual energy, facilitating focused intention, and enhancing the connection with the spiritual forces. Analyze the cultural and historical significance of sacred spaces across diverse magical traditions, drawing inspiration from ancient practices and contemporary adaptations.

2. Crafting Sacred Spaces:

Gain practical skills in crafting sacred spaces by exploring various forms and designs. Study the principles of spatial arrangement, considering factors such as symbolism, aesthetics, and functionality. Learn about the essential components of a sacred space, including altars, ritual tools, candles, sacred objects, and symbolic representations. Understand the importance of personalization and intention in the creation of sacred spaces, allowing for an authentic expression of your magical path.

3. Energetic Alignment and Cleansing:

Delve into the process of energetically aligning and cleansing your sacred space. Learn techniques to clear and purify the space, such as smudging with sacred herbs, sound cleansing with bells or chimes, or the use of consecrated water. Explore the significance of energetic alignment, harmonizing the space with your intentions and attuning it to the desired vibrations. Develop practical skills in sensing and manipulating energy, allowing you to create an environment that is energetically attuned to your magical workings.

4. Ritual Consecration:

Uncover the sacred art of consecrating your sacred space, infusing it with intention and spiritual power. Study rituals and practices for consecration, such as anointing with sacred oils, invoking the elements, or the recitation of consecration prayers. Explore the significance of consecration in activating the sacred space and establishing a connection with the spiritual forces. Reflect on the responsibility and reverence required in the act of consecration, recognizing the transformative potential it holds.

5.   Maintenance and Cultivation:

Understand the importance of ongoing maintenance and cultivation of your
sacred space. Explore practices such as regular cleansing, energetic upkeep, and
the refreshing of symbolic representations. Learn how to attune the space to
specific magical intentions, adapting it to different rituals, seasons, or phases of the
moon. Reflect on the role of personal devotion and daily rituals in nurturing and
deepening the energy of the sacred space.

Through guided exercises and practical applications, you will develop the
skills necessary to create, consecrate, and energize sacred spaces. Engage in hands-
on activities that encourage personalization, self-reflection, and creativity. By
cultivating a harmonious and intentional environment, you will create a sacred
space that not only enhances the potency of your magical work but also serves as a
sanctuary for spiritual growth and connection. Prepare to embark on this
transformative journey, where the art of crafting sacred spaces becomes an integral
part of your magical practice.

Unveiling the Secrets of Ritual Tools and Instruments:

Welcome to the enchanting exploration of ritual tools and instruments,
whose profound significance reverberates within the realm of rituals. In this section,
we will unravel the symbolic essence and understand the integral role that these
tools play in magical practices. From the athame and wand to the cauldron and
drum, you will embark on a journey of discovery, delving into the unique qualities,
purposes, and sacred symbolism associated with these ritual tools. Through
engaging hands-on activities and immersive experiences, you will familiarize
yourself with the proper handling, consecration, and utilization of these tools,
gaining practical skills that transcend various magical traditions. As you immerse
yourself in the captivating world of ritual tools, you will come to grasp how they
serve as conduits, enabling you to direct, channel, and amplify magical energy.

1.   Unveiling Symbolism:

Begin by unraveling the deep symbolism embedded within ritual tools.
Explore the archetypal and elemental associations of these tools, understanding
how they embody specific energies and qualities. Delve into their historical and
cultural contexts, examining their significance in diverse magical traditions.
Through case studies and examples, you will gain a profound understanding of the
symbolism attached to each tool and how it aligns with your personal magical
journey.

Athames and Wands:

Journey into the world of athames and wands, two potent tools that wield transformative power. Explore the history, craftsmanship, and specific purposes of these instruments. Learn how to select, consecrate, and attune these tools to your energy. Engage in practical exercises that allow you to connect with their unique energies, honing your ability to direct and focus intention.

2.   Cauldrons and Chalices:

Immerse yourself in the mystical realm of cauldrons and chalices, sacred vessels that hold the essence of transformation and communion. Explore their symbolic representations and elemental associations. Understand their roles in rituals, spellwork, and ceremonies. Engage in activities that allow you to attune these tools to their intended purposes, creating a profound connection with the energies they embody.

3.   Drums and Bells:

Discover the rhythmic magic of drums and the enchanting melodies of bells. Explore the use of sound and vibration as powerful tools for shifting consciousness and invoking spiritual energies. Learn the techniques of playing drums and bells for various purposes, such as ritual journeys, meditation, and energetic clearing. Engage in experiential exercises that deepen your connection with these musical instruments, allowing you to harness their transformative power.

4.   Other Ritual Tools:

Expand your knowledge by exploring additional ritual tools and instruments that find their place within magical practices. Investigate the roles of candles, crystals, feathers, and other objects in rituals and ceremonies. Understand how these tools can enhance intention, create energetic alignments, and manifest desired outcomes. Engage in practical exercises that demonstrate the diverse applications and versatility of these tools.

As we delve deeper into the practice of rituals, you will uncover more secrets and explore advanced techniques. Through the understanding and mastery of ritual tools and instruments, you will unlock the potential to create profound and transformative experiences within your magical practice. Get ready to embark on a journey that will enhance your magical prowess, deepen your connection with the mystical realms, and enable you to wield the power of these tools with intention and reverence.

1.   Invocation of Deities and Spirits:

Welcome to the enchanting exploration of invoking deities and spirits, where the ethereal beings of the celestial realms become the focal point of magical rituals. In this section, we will delve into the profound significance of establishing communication and rapport with these celestial entities. Join us on a captivating journey as we navigate through cultural and historical contexts, unraveling the methods and techniques employed to invoke and connect with deities and spirits. Through immersive experiences, engaging case studies, and practical exercises, you will deepen your understanding and connection with these powerful beings, expanding your magical practice to new heights.

2.   The Significance of Invocation:

Begin by delving into the significance of invoking deities and spirits within magical rituals. Explore the diverse cultural and historical contexts in which these practices have emerged, understanding the beliefs, rituals, and spiritual systems that surround the invocation of celestial beings. Gain insight into the roles these entities play in various magical traditions, including witchcraft, shamanism, and ancient mystical practices.

3.   Methods of Invocation:

Explore the myriad methods and techniques used to establish communication and rapport with deities and spirits. Uncover the power of vocalization through chanting, prayers, and invocatory rituals. Discover the transformative potential of movement and dance, as well as the use of sacred gestures and mudras. Engage in practical exercises that allow you to embody and practice these invocatory techniques, deepening your connection with the celestial realms.

4.   Building Relationships with Deities and Spirits:

Immerse yourself in the process of building relationships with deities and spirits. Understand the importance of research, study, and personal resonance when selecting and working with specific entities. Learn how to create sacred space, establish altars, and engage in rituals that invite and honor these beings. Engage in reflective exercises that allow you to explore your own beliefs, desires, and intentions in establishing connections with deities and spirits.

5.   Chanting and Vocalization:

Experience the transformative power of sound as you delve into the practice of chanting and vocalization. Explore the use of sacred words, mantras, and incantations to invoke and communicate with celestial beings. Learn the art of toning and harmonizing your voice to resonate with specific energies. Engage in vocal exercises that cultivate clarity, resonance, and intention in your invocatory practices.

6.   Embodied Rituals and Dance:

Embark on a journey of embodied expression through dance and movement. Discover the ancient and universal language of dance as a means of invoking and embodying the energies of deities and spirits. Explore various dance forms, such as trance dance, ecstatic dance, and sacred dance, that facilitate a deep connection with the celestial realms. Engage in movement-based exercises that cultivate grace, fluidity, and the ability to channel divine energy through your body.

Through the exploration of invocation, you will deepen your understanding and connection with deities and spirits, expanding your magical practice to new realms of possibility. As you immerse yourself in the invocatory practices of chanting, prayers, dance, and more, you will cultivate a profound relationship with these celestial entities, enriching your magical journey and opening doors to transformative experiences. Get ready to embark on a captivating journey that will deepen your connection with the celestial realms and empower you to work with deities and spirits in profound and meaningful ways.

Unlocking the Secrets of Ritual Symbolism and Correspondences:

Welcome to the captivating realm where symbolism and correspondences weave together to breathe life into magical rituals. In this section, we will embark on a journey that takes us deep into the heart of these mystical associations. Together, we will explore the profound connections between colors, elements, seasons, celestial bodies, and a myriad of other symbolic representations. By immersing ourselves in case studies and engaging in practical exercises, you will gain the knowledge and skills to create meaningful correspondences and apply them in your own ritualistic practices. Witness firsthand how the mastery of symbolism and correspondences amplifies the effectiveness and potency of your rituals, allowing you to tap into the deep wellspring of magical energies.

Exploring Ancient Mesopotamian Mythology, Rivalries, and Spiritual Legacies
volume 2

1.   The Power of Symbolism:

Begin by unraveling the power and significance of symbolism in magical rituals. Explore how symbols communicate and resonate with the subconscious mind, creating a bridge between the conscious and unconscious realms. Delve into the ways in which symbols evoke emotions, trigger memories, and connect us to universal archetypes. Through captivating case studies and examples, you will understand the profound impact symbolism has on the effectiveness of magical rituals.

2.   Correspondences in Magical Practices:

Explore the intricate web of correspondences that exist within magical practices. Dive into the connections between colors, elements, seasons, celestial bodies, and other symbolic representations. Understand how these correspondences are utilized to align with specific intentions, energies, and desired outcomes in rituals. Engage in practical exercises that allow you to identify and apply correspondences in your own magical work, cultivating a deeper understanding of their transformative power.

3.   Creating Meaningful Correspondences:

Learn the art of creating meaningful correspondences that resonate with your intentions and desired outcomes. Explore the process of researching and selecting correspondences based on their historical, cultural, and personal significance. Gain insight into the principles of harmony, balance, and resonance when crafting correspondences. Engage in guided exercises that empower you to create your own symbolic associations and correspondences, allowing you to infuse your rituals with personal meaning and power.

4.   Applying Correspondences in Rituals:

Discover how to effectively apply correspondences in your ritualistic practices. Explore the ways in which colors, elements, symbols, and other correspondences can be integrated into ritual tools, altar setups, visualization exercises, and spellwork. Engage in practical exercises that guide you in incorporating correspondences into your own rituals, witnessing firsthand the transformative impact they have on the potency and effectiveness of your magical practices.

5.   Evolving Your Correspondences:

Understand that correspondences are not fixed or static, but rather evolve and adapt over time. Explore the importance of personal intuition, experimentation, and experience in refining and expanding your correspondences. Learn how to attune yourself to the energies and vibrations of different symbols and correspondences, allowing them to guide and inform your magical practices. Engage in reflective exercises that encourage you to explore and deepen your understanding of correspondences, fostering your own unique and personal magical language.

By delving into the realm of symbolism and correspondences, you will unlock a profound understanding of the interconnectedness between the physical and metaphysical realms. As you apply your knowledge and skills in creating and utilizing correspondences, you will witness the transformative power they bring to your ritualistic practices. Get ready to embark on a journey that will deepen your magical understanding, expand your ritualistic repertoire, and amplify the effectiveness and potency of your rituals.

The Personal Touch: Personalization and Adaptation of Rituals:

In the ever-evolving landscape of magical practices, the art of personalization and adaptation allows each practitioner to weave a tapestry unique to their intentions, beliefs, and cultural contexts. In this section, we will delve into the profound practice of tailoring rituals to suit your individual spiritual path. Drawing inspiration from diverse traditions and sources, you will discover the power of modifying and creating rituals that align harmoniously with your personal journey.

1.   Understanding the Essence of Personalized Rituals:

Begin by exploring the essence of personalized rituals and their significance in magical practices. Understand that rituals are not rigid or fixed but can be tailored to reflect your personal beliefs, intentions, and cultural contexts. Delve into the principles of authenticity and resonance, recognizing that rituals that deeply resonate with your being have the potential to invoke profound transformations.

Modifying Rituals from Various Traditions:

Engage in a study of rituals from various traditions, recognizing their core components and underlying principles. Explore how these rituals can be adapted to suit your own spiritual path, respecting the cultural origins while infusing them with your unique intentions and symbolism. Analyze examples of adapted rituals, dissecting the modifications made and the reasons behind them, gaining insights into the process of personalization.

2.   Cultivating Ritual Adaptation Skills:

Develop the skills necessary to adapt and personalize rituals. Learn the art of research and study, exploring various magical traditions and practices to expand your knowledge base. Deepen your understanding of the symbolism, correspondences, and intentions behind rituals, allowing you to make informed decisions when adapting them to align with your spiritual path. Engage in practical exercises that guide you in modifying existing rituals to suit your own needs, fostering your ability to create meaningful and transformative experiences.

3.   Creating Unique Rituals:

Explore the art of creating unique rituals that are entirely your own. Understand that rituals can be born from your own intuition, inspirations, and experiences. Learn how to tap into your inner creativity and imagination, allowing them to guide you in crafting rituals that deeply resonate with your intentions and desires. Engage in exercises that encourage you to explore your personal symbolism, beliefs, and cultural influences, integrating them into the creation of unique and powerful rituals.

4.   Honoring Tradition and Cultural Appropriation:

As you embark on the journey of personalizing rituals, it is crucial to understand the importance of honoring tradition and avoiding cultural appropriation. Explore the principles of cultural sensitivity and respect, recognizing the significance of understanding the origins and context of the rituals you draw inspiration from. Reflect on the ethics of borrowing elements from different cultures and traditions, ensuring that your adaptations are done with reverence and appreciation.

By delving into the art of personalization and adaptation, you will embrace the freedom to create rituals that are authentic expressions of your spiritual journey. As you explore and modify rituals from diverse traditions, you will cultivate the skills to breathe life into practices that resonate deeply within your being. Embrace the opportunity to infuse your rituals with personal symbolism, intentions, and cultural influences, honoring the traditions that inspire you while forging your own unique path. Get ready to embark on a transformative journey of personalization and adaptation that will enrich your magical practice and deepen your connection to the mystical realms.

5.   Harnessing the Energies: Ritual Performance and Energy Work:

Within the sacred realm of rituals, the mastery of energy work stands as an essential pillar. Journey with us as we unravel the techniques for raising, directing, and focusing energy within the ritualistic context. Through visualization, breathwork, movement, and other transformative practices, you will heighten your energetic awareness and create a dynamic and profound ritual experience. Unleash the power of energy as it dances and weaves through your rituals, unlocking the true potential of your magical practice.

As we conclude this enlightening exploration, students will emerge with a profound understanding of the structure, components, and principles that underpin rituals. You will recognize the sacred importance of space, ritual tools, invocation, symbolism, and energy work in crafting rituals of deep meaning and transformative power. Through engaging practical exercises and guided discussions, you will cultivate the necessary skills and knowledge to design, personalize, and adapt rituals that align harmoniously with your intentions and spiritual path. Open your mind, ignite your creativity, and embrace the transformative journey that awaits you within the realm of rituals.

Ethical Considerations and Social Impact of Magic

Embarking on a transformative journey through the realm of magic, we encounter important ethical considerations and the potential societal impact of these practices. In this section, we delve into the diverse traditions of witchcraft, divination, herbalism, shamanism, ecospirituality, and ancient Mesopotamian magic, exploring the profound ethical dimensions that shape these mystical paths. Through an exploration of ethical frameworks, principles, and potential social implications, students will cultivate a nuanced understanding of the responsibilities and potential consequences associated with magical practices.

Unveiling Ethical Frameworks in Magic:

Our exploration commences with an immersive and profound examination of the ethical frameworks that guide magical practitioners on their spiritual path. As students of magic, it is vital to understand the principles that shape our intentions and actions within magical practices. In this section, we will embark on a thought-provoking journey into the ethical considerations that arise within the realm of magic, exploring the moral compass that guides practitioners in their interactions with the world and the mystical forces they work with.

1.   Understanding Ethical Frameworks:

Begin by delving into the fundamental ethical frameworks that govern magical practices. Explore prominent ethical principles such as the Wiccan Rede, which emphasizes the importance of acting in accordance with one's true will while ensuring that one's actions do not harm others. Examine the concept of the Threefold Law, which suggests that whatever energy or intention one sends out into the universe will return to them threefold. Analyze how these frameworks shape the intentions and actions of magical practitioners, fostering a sense of responsibility, mindfulness, and accountability.

2.   Navigating Ethical Dilemmas:

Engage in critical thinking and ethical analysis as we explore various case studies and thought-provoking dilemmas that arise within the practice of magic. Reflect on situations where ethical considerations come into play, such as the use of magic for personal gain, interfering with the free will of others, or the potential unintended consequences of one's actions. Through interactive discussions and exercises, develop the skills to navigate these complex ethical dilemmas, balancing personal desires with the responsibility to act in alignment with ethical principles.

3.   Cultural Sensitivity and Appropriation:

As seekers of truth and wisdom, it is essential to examine the ethical considerations related to cultural sensitivity and appropriation within magical practices. Explore the concept of cultural appropriation and its impact on marginalized communities, recognizing the need for respect, understanding, and honoring the origins of spiritual practices and traditions. Gain insights into the importance of informed cultural exchange, appreciating diverse perspectives and engaging in practices that do not exploit or appropriate the sacred traditions of others.

4.   Harmonizing Personal Ethics with Magical Practice:

Explore the integration of personal ethics with magical practice, recognizing the importance of aligning one's spiritual path with a moral compass. Reflect on your own values, beliefs, and intentions, examining how they intersect with the ethical frameworks of magic. Engage in self-reflection and introspective exercises to cultivate self-awareness and foster a strong ethical foundation. Consider how your magical practice can be a force for positive change in the world, promoting harmony, healing, and personal growth.

5.   Embracing Responsibility and Accountability:

Emphasize the significance of responsibility and accountability in magical practices. Understand that as practitioners, we hold the power to manifest change through our intentions and actions. Explore how ethical considerations provide a framework for exercising this power responsibly, ensuring that our magical work is aligned with integrity, compassion, and respect for all beings. Reflect on the potential consequences of our actions, both intended and unintended, and develop strategies to mitigate harm and promote ethical behavior within our magical practices.

By delving into the ethical frameworks that guide magical practitioners, students will embark on a profound journey of self-reflection, critical thinking, and ethical analysis. Through engaging case studies, thought-provoking dilemmas, and discussions, students will navigate the intricate ethical considerations that arise within the realm of magic. Embrace the opportunity to harmonize personal ethics with magical practice, cultivating a sense of responsibility, mindfulness, and accountability. Together, let us foster a community of ethical practitioners who harness the transformative power of magic with integrity, compassion, and respect for the world around us.

The Tapestry of Personal Ethics and Magical Practice:

Delving into the very essence of magical practice, we embark on a transformative journey to explore the profound significance of personal ethics. As students of magic, it is essential to delve deep within ourselves, engaging in introspection and self-reflection to develop a personal ethical code that aligns harmoniously with our values, beliefs, and intentions. In this section, we will illuminate the process of cultivating a strong ethical foundation, one that serves as a guiding light throughout our magical journeys.

1.   Understanding Personal Ethics:

Begin by exploring the concept of personal ethics and its significance within the context of magical practice. Reflect on the principles and values that hold importance in your life and how they shape your worldview. Through thought-provoking exercises and introspection, gain clarity on your personal ethics and their influence on your magical path. Engage in group discussions to share insights and learn from diverse perspectives, fostering a rich tapestry of ethical consciousness.

Reflective Exercises:

Engage in reflective exercises designed to deepen your understanding of personal ethics and their integration into magical practice. Through guided meditations, journaling prompts, and self-inquiry, you will uncover the inner wisdom that informs your ethical choices. Explore questions such as: What values and beliefs resonate with me on a profound level? How do these values guide my intentions and actions in magic? How can I ensure that my magical practice aligns with my personal ethics?

2.   Group Discussions and Sharing:

Engage in group discussions and sharing circles to explore the multifaceted nature of personal ethics within the magical community. Hear diverse perspectives and experiences, deepening your understanding of how personal ethics can shape and evolve magical practices. Foster an environment of respect, empathy, and open-mindedness, allowing for rich dialogue and mutual growth. Together, we will explore the intersections of personal ethics and magical practice, inspiring each other to develop and refine our ethical frameworks.

3.   Ethical Decision-Making:

Dive into the realm of ethical decision-making within magical practice. Analyze case studies and ethical dilemmas that arise in the context of spellcasting, ritual work, and interaction with others. Engage in group exercises that challenge you to navigate complex ethical scenarios, applying your personal ethical code to find resolutions that align with integrity and respect for all involved. Cultivate the skills to make informed and ethical choices in your magical endeavors, balancing your intentions with the potential impact on yourself and others.

4.   Integration and Growth:

Embrace the process of integrating personal ethics into every aspect of your magical practice. Explore how your ethical code influences your intentions, rituals, and approaches to magic. Reflect on how ethical consciousness can deepen your connection with the mystical realms and empower you to be a compassionate and responsible practitioner. Celebrate the growth and transformation that comes from aligning your magical path with your personal ethics, and recognize that this journey is ever-evolving.

Through introspection, self-reflection, and group discussions, students will unveil the significance of personal ethics in magical practice. As you cultivate a personal ethical code, you will witness its transformative power, guiding your intentions, rituals, and overall approach to magic. Embrace the opportunity to engage in reflective exercises and thought-provoking discussions, fostering a profound integration of ethical consciousness within your magical path. Together, let us embark on a journey of ethical growth, ensuring that our magical practices align with integrity, compassion, and respect for ourselves, others, and the world around us.

Cultural Appreciation and Respectful Engagement:

Within the realm of magical practices, it is essential to address the significant issue of cultural appropriation. In this section, we delve into the ethical considerations that arise when incorporating spiritual and magical practices from cultures beyond our own. As students, we embark on a journey of exploration, seeking to understand the importance of respectful engagement, cultural understanding, and informed consent when working with elements from diverse traditions.

1.   The Concept of Cultural Appropriation:

Begin by examining the concept of cultural appropriation and its relevance within the realm of magical practices. Explore the historical context and power dynamics that contribute to the appropriation of spiritual and magical traditions. Engage in critical analysis of the impact of cultural appropriation on marginalized communities and the importance of fostering cultural respect and understanding.

2.   Cultivating Cultural Understanding:

Dive into the process of cultivating cultural understanding and appreciation. Explore diverse spiritual and magical traditions, gaining knowledge of their historical, cultural, and sacred significance. Engage in the study of cultural contexts, symbolism, and rituals to deepen your understanding of these traditions. Foster an attitude of respect, humility, and curiosity as you explore and learn from cultures beyond your own.

3.   Respectful Engagement:

Explore the principles and practices that guide respectful engagement with spiritual and magical traditions from diverse cultures. Reflect on the importance of acknowledging and honoring the origins and cultural heritage of these practices.

Engage in discussions and case studies that illuminate examples of respectful engagement and highlight the potential pitfalls of cultural appropriation.

4.   Informed Consent and Collaboration:

Delve into the concept of informed consent and collaboration when working with elements from diverse traditions. Examine the importance of seeking permission and guidance from practitioners and communities who hold ancestral knowledge. Reflect on the significance of building relationships and engaging in reciprocal exchanges with individuals and communities from the cultures you draw inspiration from.

5.   Ethical Frameworks for Cultural Appropriation:

Explore existing ethical frameworks and guidelines that address cultural appropriation within magical practices. Examine the perspectives of scholars, practitioners, and community leaders who advocate for ethical engagement. Engage in critical analysis and discussions to develop your own ethical framework that guides your engagement with spiritual and magical practices from diverse cultures.

By addressing the issue of cultural appropriation within magical practices, we honor the importance of cultural respect, understanding, and informed consent. Through thoughtful exploration, reflection, and engagement with diverse perspectives, students will develop an ethical approach that acknowledges and respects the origins and cultural significance of spiritual and magical traditions. Let us embark on this journey of cultural understanding and ethical growth, ensuring that our magical practices foster inclusivity, respect, and appreciation for the rich tapestry of human spiritual experiences.

Responsibility and Consent in Magical Interactions:

Our exploration extends further into the ethical aspects of magical interactions with others, emphasizing the vital principles of consent, privacy, and personal boundaries. As students, we delve into the significance of obtaining informed consent before engaging in magical work on behalf of others, while contemplating the ethical implications of violating personal boundaries or invading privacy through magical practices. This deep understanding of responsibility within magical interactions will empower students to cultivate ethical relationships and promote respect within magical communities.

1.   The Importance of Consent:

Begin by exploring the concept of consent within the context of magical practices. Reflect on the significance of obtaining explicit and informed consent from individuals before performing any magical work on their behalf. Engage in discussions and case studies that highlight the ethical considerations and potential consequences of engaging in magical practices without consent.

2.   Respecting Personal Boundaries:

Dive into the exploration of personal boundaries within magical interactions. Reflect on the importance of respecting the autonomy and agency of individuals, ensuring that your magical practices do not intrude upon or violate their personal boundaries. Analyze ethical dilemmas and engage in discussions that challenge assumptions and promote awareness of personal boundaries in magical work.

3.   Privacy and Confidentiality:

Examine the ethical implications of privacy and confidentiality within magical practices. Reflect on the importance of maintaining confidentiality when individuals share personal information or seek guidance through magical means. Explore the ethical guidelines and practices that foster trust and ensure the privacy of individuals within magical communities.

4.   Responsibility and Accountability:

Reflect on the ethical responsibility and accountability that practitioners hold within magical interactions. Explore the potential power dynamics and imbalances that may arise and consider how to navigate them ethically. Engage in discussions that encourage self-reflection and introspection, enabling students to develop a strong sense of personal responsibility and ethical conduct within their magical practices.

5.   Promoting Ethical Relationships:

Deepen your understanding of ethical relationships within magical communities. Reflect on the importance of fostering a culture of respect, inclusivity, and consent. Engage in discussions and case studies that illuminate examples of healthy and ethical relationships within magical communities, promoting the well-being and empowerment of all individuals involved.

Through the exploration of consent, personal boundaries, privacy, and responsibility, students will develop a profound understanding of the ethical principles that underpin magical interactions. This understanding will empower them to cultivate ethical relationships, promote respect, and contribute to the creation of safe and supportive magical communities. As practitioners, let us embark on this journey of ethical growth, recognizing the importance of consent, privacy, and personal boundaries in our magical practices.

Unveiling the Social Impact of Magic:

Within the rich tapestry of magical practices, we embark on a comprehensive exploration that delves into the social impact on individuals, communities, and society as a whole. As students, we unravel the intricate ways in which magical practices contribute to personal empowerment, community cohesion, and social change. Through critical analysis and thoughtful reflection, we evaluate the potential positive and negative consequences of public perceptions of magic, the challenges faced by magical practitioners, and the stereotypes that permeate various social contexts.

1.   Personal Empowerment:

Begin by examining the transformative power of magical practices on individuals. Reflect on how engaging in magical rituals, spellwork, and personal spiritual exploration can foster personal growth, self-confidence, and a sense of agency. Analyze case studies and personal narratives that illustrate the ways in which magical practices empower individuals to embrace their authenticity and navigate life's challenges.

2.   Community Cohesion:

Explore the role of magical practices in fostering community cohesion and connection. Reflect on the ways in which magical communities provide support, mentorship, and a sense of belonging to practitioners. Analyze the rituals, celebrations, and collaborative efforts that bring magical communities together, promoting mutual understanding and shared values.

3.   Social Change:

Delve into the potential for magical practices to contribute to social change and activism. Reflect on historical and contemporary examples of magical practitioners engaging in social justice movements and advocating for positive transformation. Explore the ways in which magical practices can inspire individuals to challenge oppressive systems, promote inclusivity, and strive for a more equitable society.

4.   Public Perceptions and Stereotypes:

Analyze the impact of public perceptions of magic and magical practitioners on individuals and communities. Reflect on the stereotypes, misconceptions, and stigmatization faced by magical practitioners in different social contexts. Engage in critical discussions that challenge stereotypes and encourage a nuanced understanding of magical practices.

5.   Challenges and Opportunities:

Explore the unique challenges faced by magical practitioners, such as navigating legal and social barriers, addressing skepticism, and finding acceptance within broader society. Reflect on the opportunities for advocacy, education, and community-building that arise from these challenges. Analyze strategies for promoting understanding and acceptance of magical practices in diverse social settings.

Through critical analysis and thoughtful reflection, students gain a deeper understanding of the social impact of magical practices. They recognize the potential for personal empowerment, the importance of community cohesion, and the role of magic in inspiring social change. By challenging stereotypes and advocating for acceptance, students contribute to creating a more inclusive and understanding society. Let us embark on this journey of exploration, recognizing the profound social dimensions of magical practices and embracing our role in shaping a more compassionate world.

Example Problem:

Prepare for a stimulating discussion as we explore the potential social impact of a public ritual organized by a group of witches with the aim of promoting environmental activism. Engage in thoughtful analysis as we consider the ways in which such a ritual can influence public perceptions of magic, foster community-building, and raise awareness about pressing environmental issues. Moreover, we shall discuss the potential challenges and backlash that the practitioners might encounter in their noble pursuit.

Conclusion:

Through a profound exploration of the ethical considerations and social impact of magic, students will develop a comprehensive understanding of the responsibilities and implications inherent in magical practices. Engaging in critical thinking, ethical analysis, and rich discussions, students will navigate the complexities of ethical decision-making within magical contexts. As the tapestry of personal ethics, community dynamics, and societal impact interweaves, students will foster a deeper appreciation for the interconnectedness between these realms, unveiling the transformative power of ethical magic.

Chapter 3: Offerings and Sacrifices: Worship and Communication with the Divine

Welcome to Chapter 3 of our comprehensive exploration of Mesopotamian religious practices. In this chapter, we will delve into the profound significance of offerings and sacrifices within the context of ancient Mesopotamia. By examining the beliefs, rituals, and cultural implications surrounding these practices, we will unravel the intricate layers of meaning and foster a deeper understanding of their role in establishing a connection between humans and the divine.

Historical and Cultural Context

To lay a solid foundation, we will immerse ourselves in the historical and cultural context of ancient Mesopotamia. By exploring the pantheon of gods and goddesses, the roles of priests and priestesses, and the broader societal framework, we will gain insights into the religious landscape that shaped the offering and sacrifice practices. Engaging discussions and analysis of primary sources will develop a nuanced understanding of the cultural nuances and social dynamics that influenced the significance of offerings and sacrifices in Mesopotamian religious life.

Communication with the Divine

This section explores the central role that offerings and sacrifices played in facilitating communication between humans and the divine realm in ancient Mesopotamia. Through analysis of Mesopotamian beliefs and cosmology, we appreciate their understanding of the divine as active participants in human affairs. Case studies and primary source analysis allow students to explore how offerings were believed to attract the attention and favor of the gods and goddesses, establishing a reciprocal relationship that transcended the mortal realm.

Symbolic Meanings of Offerings

Delving into the rich symbolic meanings associated with different types of offerings in Mesopotamian religious practices, this section examines offerings of food, drink, incense, and precious items. By analyzing the cultural and mythological context, students gain a deeper understanding of how these offerings symbolically represented concepts such as sustenance, fertility, purification, and wealth within the religious framework of ancient Mesopotamia. Engaging discussions and analysis of textual evidence enhance comprehension.

Rituals and Procedures

This section unravels the intricate rituals and procedures involved in presenting offerings and sacrifices in ancient Mesopotamia. Students gain a comprehensive understanding of the ceremonial aspects, the roles of priests and priestesses, and the symbolic actions performed during these rituals. Primary source analysis and case studies shed light on the use of prayers, invocations, and chants as powerful tools for establishing a sacred atmosphere and invoking divine presence.

Cultural and Social Implications

Encouraging critical reflection, this section examines the cultural and social implications of offering and sacrifice practices in ancient Mesopotamia. Students explore how these practices shaped religious identity, community dynamics, and social hierarchies within Mesopotamian society. Engaging discussions and analysis of archaeological and historical evidence illuminate the ways in which offerings and sacrifices were intertwined with political power, social cohesion, and cultural practices.

Example Problem:

Consider a scenario where a Mesopotamian devotee seeks to establish a connection with the goddess Ishtar through offerings. Students analyze the specific attributes and associations of Ishtar to determine suitable offerings. They explore methods to ensure the offerings effectively convey devotion and reverence, discussing the symbolic significance behind their choices.

Conclusion:

Having explored the significance of offerings and sacrifices in Mesopotamian religious practices, students have developed a comprehensive understanding of their cultural, symbolic, and social dimensions. This chapter's emphasis on critical thinking and discussion has fostered a deeper appreciation for the complex and interconnected nature of these practices, as well as their enduring impact on human-divine relationships. As we proceed to future chapters, we will continue our exploration of ancient spiritual practices, building upon the foundation established in this chapter.

Historical and Cultural Context

In this section, we will embark on a fascinating journey through time to uncover the historical and cultural context that has shaped the diverse spiritual traditions we explore in this course. By delving into the ancient roots of practices such as Witchcraft, Divination, Herbalism, Shamanism, Ecospirituality, and Magic in Ancient Mesopotamia, we will gain a profound understanding of the cultural, social, and philosophical influences that have contributed to their development.

✧   Ancient Mesopotamia - The Cradle of Civilization

Welcome to Section 1 of our comprehensive exploration into the ancient roots of new-age practices. In this section, we embark on a captivating journey into the world of ancient Mesopotamia, a land often hailed as the cradle of civilization. Situated between the mighty Tigris and Euphrates rivers, this region witnessed the rise of remarkable societies, the development of advanced agricultural techniques, and the establishment of the world's first city-states. Through the lens of archaeology and historical records, we embark on a journey through time to unravel the cultural tapestry of this ancient civilization and uncover its profound influence on the spiritual practices that continue to shape our understanding of new-age studies.

1.   Geography and Historical Context:

Begin by exploring the geographical features of Mesopotamia and its significance as a fertile region situated between two rivers. Delve into the historical context, discussing the emergence of early settlements and the transition from hunter-gatherer societies to agricultural communities.

2.   Mesopotamian Mythology and Deities:

Unveil the rich mythology of ancient Mesopotamia, where gods and goddesses played central roles in the lives of its inhabitants. Explore the pantheon of deities, their relationships, and their attributes, shedding light on the religious beliefs and rituals of the ancient Mesopotamians.

3.   Magic and Divination:

Delve into the magical practices and divinatory methods employed by the ancient Mesopotamians. Explore the significance of rituals, incantations, and the use of magical objects and symbols in their daily lives. Discuss the role of divination in seeking guidance and predicting the future, including practices such as astrology and omen interpretation.

4.   Rituals and Ceremonies:

Examine the religious rituals and ceremonies practiced in ancient Mesopotamia, from temple rituals performed by priests to personal household rituals carried out by individuals. Analyze the structure and components of these rituals, as well as their significance in maintaining cosmic order and fostering divine favor.

5.   Influence on New-Age Studies:

Reflect on the enduring influence of ancient Mesopotamian spiritual practices on contemporary new-age studies. Discuss the connections between Mesopotamian mythology, magical practices, and divination methods with modern spiritual traditions. Analyze how elements of Mesopotamian cosmology, symbolism, and ritualistic practices continue to resonate with practitioners today.

Through this exploration of ancient Mesopotamia, we gain a deeper understanding of the cultural and spiritual foundations that laid the groundwork for new-age practices. We recognize the contributions of this remarkable civilization in shaping human history and the ongoing relevance of its spiritual traditions. Join us as we journey through time and discover the profound influence of ancient Mesopotamia, the cradle of civilization, on the spiritual practices that continue to shape our modern world.

➢   The Geographic and Environmental Context:

To comprehend the origins of ancient Mesopotamia, it is essential to delve into its unique geographic and environmental context. Situated within the fertile alluvial plains of modern-day Iraq, the region's geography played a pivotal role in shaping the civilization that emerged and contributed to its remarkable development.

The Tigris and Euphrates rivers, which flowed through Mesopotamia, were the lifeblood of this ancient civilization. These mighty rivers were not only a source of water but also served as natural highways for trade and communication. The annual floods of the rivers, caused by the melting snow from the mountains, brought nutrient-rich sediment that enriched the soil, creating fertile lands ideal for agriculture.

Students will come to appreciate the significance of the rivers' annual floods, which replenished the soil and allowed for abundant crop production. The predictable nature of these floods enabled the Mesopotamians to develop advanced agricultural practices, such as irrigation systems, canals, and levees. By harnessing the power of the rivers, the ancient Mesopotamians were able to transform the arid landscape into a flourishing agricultural oasis.

The availability of ample food resources resulting from successful agricultural practices played a crucial role in supporting the growth of population centers and the development of urban life. As surplus food was produced, specialization of labor emerged, leading to the rise of artisans, traders, priests, and other professions that contributed to the diverse fabric of society.

Moreover, the strategic location of Mesopotamia, situated between the great civilizations of Egypt and the Indus Valley, positioned it as a crossroads for trade and cultural exchange. The rivers provided convenient transportation routes, allowing for the movement of goods, ideas, and people. As a result, Mesopotamia became a vibrant hub of commerce and a melting pot of cultures, fostering a rich tapestry of diversity and innovation.

Through an exploration of the geographic and environmental context of ancient Mesopotamia, students will gain a profound appreciation for how the physical features of the region, particularly the Tigris and Euphrates rivers, influenced the development of a sophisticated civilization. They will come to understand how the availability of water resources, the fertility of the soil, and the strategic location as a trade hub contributed to the growth of population centers, urbanization, cultural exchange, and the flourishing of Mesopotamian society.

➤ The Rise of City-States:

One of the defining characteristics of ancient Mesopotamia was the emergence of city-states, independent urban centers that played a pivotal role in shaping the political, economic, and social landscape of the region. As we delve into this topic, we will explore notable city-states such as Ur, Uruk, Babylon, and others, unveiling the fascinating intricacies of their political structures, economic systems, and social hierarchies.

The city-states of ancient Mesopotamia were distinct political entities with their own governance systems. Each city-state was typically ruled by a king who exercised authority over the city and its surrounding territories. Students will delve into the political dynamics of these city-states, examining the mechanisms through which power was centralized and the methods employed to maintain social order.

Through the study of archaeological findings and historical records, students will gain insights into the governance systems of these early city-states. They will explore the role of the king as the supreme ruler, supported by a bureaucracy that administered various aspects of city-state affairs, including taxation, justice, and public administration. Students will also analyze the role of religious institutions and their influence on political decision-making, as the religious and political spheres were often intertwined in

Mesopotamian society.

In addition to political structures, students will explore the economic systems that underpinned the city-states. Agriculture formed the backbone of the economy, with the surrounding fertile lands and advanced agricultural practices ensuring a stable food supply. However, city-states also engaged in trade, both within Mesopotamia and with external regions. Students will examine the trade routes, the types of goods exchanged, and the economic impact of trade on the development and prosperity of the city-states.

Furthermore, students will gain an understanding of the social hierarchies that characterized these urban centers. Mesopotamian society was structured into distinct social classes, with the king and ruling elite occupying the highest echelons, followed by priests, bureaucrats, merchants, artisans, and the laboring class. By analyzing artifacts, inscriptions, and written records, students will gain insights into the social roles and expectations associated with each class, as well as the potential for social mobility within the Mesopotamian city-state society.

Through the study of the rise of city-states in ancient Mesopotamia, students will gain a comprehensive understanding of the complex political, economic, and social dynamics that shaped these urban centers. They will appreciate the centralized governance systems, the economic reliance on agriculture and trade, and the hierarchical nature of social structures. By examining archaeological findings and historical records, students will uncover the vibrancy of urban life in ancient Mesopotamia and its enduring impact on subsequent civilizations.

> Advances in Agriculture and Technology:

Agriculture stood as the cornerstone of ancient Mesopotamian society, providing the foundation for its economic prosperity and the growth of urban centers. In this section, we will explore the innovative agricultural practices developed by the Mesopotamians, unveiling their contributions to food production, resource management, and technological advancements. Through the examination of case studies and archaeological evidence, students will gain a deep appreciation for the pivotal role played by agriculture in sustaining the burgeoning civilization and creating the conditions necessary for the development of specialized professions and cultural pursuits.

One of the remarkable achievements of ancient Mesopotamia was the development of advanced irrigation systems. As students delve into this topic, they will discover how the Mesopotamians ingeniously harnessed the waters of the Tigris and Euphrates rivers to support agriculture in the arid region. They will explore the construction of canals, dikes, and reservoirs that enabled controlled water distribution and facilitated the cultivation of vast agricultural lands. Through case studies of irrigation projects such as the Hanging Gardens of Babylon or the city of Ur, students will witness the remarkable engineering feats that transformed arid landscapes into fertile fields, ensuring a reliable food supply for the growing population.

Furthermore, students will explore the use of plows and the cultivation of various crops that played a crucial role in Mesopotamian agriculture. They will examine the development of the plow, an innovative tool that increased efficiency in land preparation and enabled deeper soil penetration. Through the analysis of agricultural texts and artifacts, students will gain insights into the cultivation techniques employed by the Mesopotamians, including crop rotation and the selection of suitable crops for different soil types and growing seasons. They will discover the cultivation of staple crops such as barley, wheat, and dates, as well as the importance of livestock in agricultural practices.

The advancements in agriculture brought about by the Mesopotamians had far-reaching implications beyond food production. The surplus of agricultural resources allowed for the growth of urban centers, as specialized professions emerged to support the needs of the expanding population. Students will examine the relationship between agriculture and urbanization, analyzing how the surplus of food enabled individuals to engage in non-agricultural pursuits such as craftsmanship, trade, and intellectual pursuits. They will gain an understanding of the interdependence between rural agricultural communities and urban centers, as food and resources flowed from the countryside to sustain the cities.

Moreover, students will explore the cultural and societal impacts of these agricultural advancements. The stable food supply facilitated population growth, leading to the establishment of complex social structures and the development of art, architecture, and literature. Through the analysis of archaeological evidence and written texts, students will gain insights into how agricultural practices influenced religious beliefs, societal values, and the cultural identity of the Mesopotamian people.

By examining the advances in agriculture and technology in ancient
Mesopotamia, students will develop a profound appreciation for the pivotal role
played by these innovations in shaping the civilization. They will recognize how
irrigation systems, plows, and crop cultivation techniques revolutionized food
production, fostered urbanization, and created the conditions necessary for the
development of specialized professions and cultural achievements. Through the
exploration of case studies, archaeological evidence, and primary sources, students
will uncover the remarkable achievements of the Mesopotamians in the realm of
agriculture and their enduring impact on human history.

> ➢   Legal and Administrative Systems:

Ancient Mesopotamia stood as a beacon of legal and administrative systems
that laid the groundwork for future civilizations. In this section, we will embark on
a journey through the intricacies of Mesopotamian law, focusing on the renowned
Code of Hammurabi—an early written legal code that addressed matters of
governance, justice, and social order. Through critical analysis and examination of
legal documents, students will gain a comprehensive understanding of the
principles, regulations, and punishments that governed Mesopotamian society. By
exploring the social and legal structures of this ancient civilization, students will
come to recognize the enduring foundations upon which our modern legal systems
have been built.

At the heart of this exploration lies the Code of Hammurabi, a remarkable
legal document crafted during the reign of Hammurabi, the sixth king of the
Babylonian Dynasty in the 18th century BCE. Students will delve into the
historical context surrounding the creation of this code, grasping its significance as
one of the earliest written legal codes in human history. They will analyze the
prologue of the code, which highlights Hammurabi's role as a just ruler and his
mission to establish equity and order within his kingdom.

Through a systematic examination of the laws inscribed on the stele, students
will explore the diverse legal issues that were addressed in Mesopotamian society.
They will encounter laws pertaining to property rights, contracts, family matters,
trade, labor, and even medical malpractice. By engaging in critical analysis,
students will identify the underlying principles and values that shaped the legal
framework, such as the concept of lex talionis (the principle of "an eye for an eye"),
social hierarchies, and the idea of retribution.

Students will also explore the significance of the punishments outlined in the
Code of Hammurabi, ranging from fines and compensations to physical

punishments and even death in severe cases. They will critically evaluate the rationale behind these punishments, considering the concepts of deterrence, restoration, and social cohesion. Through case studies and hypothetical scenarios, students will engage in thought-provoking discussions on the ethical dimensions of justice and the role of punishment in maintaining societal order.

Beyond the Code of Hammurabi, students will also examine the broader legal and administrative systems that governed ancient Mesopotamia. They will explore the roles and responsibilities of officials, judges, and scribes who were instrumental in enforcing the laws and maintaining order in society. Students will gain insights into the administrative structures, such as the appointment of local governors and the establishment of courts, which facilitated the implementation of legal codes across different regions.

By analyzing legal documents and archaeological evidence, students will uncover the social and cultural implications of the legal and administrative systems in ancient Mesopotamia. They will consider how the laws reflected the values and beliefs of the society, as well as the influence of religious ideologies and social hierarchies on the legal framework. Through comparative analysis with other legal systems in neighboring civilizations, such as Egypt and the Hittites, students will gain a broader perspective on the development and influence of ancient legal systems.

Ultimately, the study of legal and administrative systems in ancient Mesopotamia will provide students with a deep appreciation for the foundational principles and concepts that shaped our modern legal frameworks. By examining the Code of Hammurabi and its social and legal context, students will recognize the lasting legacy of Mesopotamian legal traditions, their impact on subsequent civilizations, and their continued relevance in the pursuit of justice and societal order.

> Cultural and Intellectual Achievements:

Ancient Mesopotamia stands as a fertile ground for remarkable cultural and intellectual achievements that have left an indelible mark on human civilization. In this section, we will embark on a captivating exploration of the diverse realms in which Mesopotamian culture thrived, encompassing literature, poetry, astronomy, and mathematics. By engaging with primary sources, analyzing archaeological artifacts, and delving into the depth of Mesopotamian intellectual pursuits, students will gain a profound appreciation for the rich cultural legacy and intellectual achievements of this ancient civilization.

Exploring Ancient Mesopotamian Mythology, Rivalries, and Spiritual Legacies
volume 2

One of the most iconic literary works to emerge from Mesopotamia is the epic of Gilgamesh, considered one of the oldest surviving epic poems in the world. Students will delve into this mesmerizing tale, navigating through the hero's journey, exploring themes of mortality, friendship, and the pursuit of immortality. Through critical analysis of the text and examination of its historical and cultural context, students will uncover the significance of the epic of Gilgamesh as a testament to the human condition and a reflection of the values and beliefs of ancient Mesopotamian society.

In addition to literature, the Mesopotamians made significant contributions to the field of astronomy, laying the foundation for our understanding of celestial bodies and the cosmos. Students will explore the astronomical achievements of this ancient civilization, studying the cuneiform tablets that contain astronomical observations, mathematical calculations, and predictive models. They will delve into the complex system of celestial divination, which played a pivotal role in Mesopotamian religion and society. By examining the zodiac and its association with Mesopotamian celestial omens, students will gain insights into the intricate connection between the movements of the stars and the affairs of humanity.

The field of mathematics also flourished in ancient Mesopotamia, with the Mesopotamians making significant advancements in areas such as arithmetic, geometry, and algebra. Students will explore the innovative numerical system developed by the Mesopotamians, based on a sexagesimal (base-60) system. They will unravel the mathematical clay tablets that reveal the Mesopotamians' mastery of complex calculations, including multiplication, division, square roots, and even the calculation of areas and volumes. Through problem-solving exercises and hands-on activities, students will gain a practical understanding of Mesopotamian mathematical techniques and appreciate their enduring influence on the development of mathematics as a whole.

Beyond literature, astronomy, and mathematics, students will also explore other cultural and intellectual achievements of ancient Mesopotamia. They will investigate the advancements in architecture, engineering, and urban planning, exemplified by the majestic ziggurats and the sophisticated water management systems. They will appreciate the artistic craftsmanship displayed in the intricate clay figurines, jewelry, and pottery. They will delve into the religious beliefs and rituals that permeated every aspect of daily life, and the development of legal systems that set a precedent for future civilizations.

Through the examination of primary sources, such as cuneiform texts, royal inscriptions, and archaeological artifacts, students will gain a profound understanding of the cultural and intellectual vibrancy of ancient Mesopotamia.

They will recognize the significant contributions of this civilization to the arts, sciences, and humanities, and their lasting impact on subsequent civilizations. By engaging with the legacy of ancient Mesopotamia, students will be inspired to draw connections between the intellectual achievements of the past and the contemporary world, fostering a deep appreciation for the enduring human quest for knowledge and creative expression..

Example Problem:

Imagine you are an archaeologist exploring the ruins of an ancient Mesopotamian city-state. Describe the architectural features and layout of the city, highlighting the elements that reflect the sophisticated urban planning of the time. How do these architectural aspects reflect the social and political structures of the civilization?

Conclusion:

As we conclude Section 1 on ancient Mesopotamia - the cradle of civilization, students have embarked on a fascinating journey through time, uncovering the cultural, political, and technological developments that defined this ancient civilization. By studying its geography, the rise of city-states, advancements in agriculture and technology, legal and administrative systems, and cultural and intellectual achievements, students have gained a comprehensive understanding of the historical context that laid the foundation for the spiritual practices we explore in new-age studies. In the following sections, we will continue to build upon this knowledge, delving deeper into the interconnected realms of Witchcraft, Divination, Herbalism, Shamanism, Ecospirituality, and Magic, while remaining mindful of the enduring influence of ancient Mesopotamia on these practices.

✧ Gods and Goddesses of Mesopotamia

At the heart of ancient Mesopotamian religious and spiritual practices were the diverse and vibrant pantheon of gods and goddesses. In this section, we will embark on a captivating journey into the mythologies and significance of these divine beings, gaining a profound understanding of their roles and influence within the religious landscape of ancient Mesopotamia.

Enki, the god of wisdom and water, held a prominent place in the Mesopotamian pantheon. Students will explore the mythological narratives surrounding Enki, which depict him as the creator and protector of humanity. They will delve into his association with freshwater sources, agricultural fertility, and the development of civilization. Through engaging discussions and analysis of primary sources, students will develop a nuanced understanding of Enki's multifaceted nature and the reverence bestowed upon him by the ancient Mesopotamians.

Another notable deity in the Mesopotamian pantheon is Ishtar, the goddess of love, beauty, and war. Students will immerse themselves in the mythologies surrounding Ishtar, discovering her complex persona and the pivotal role she played in the lives of the ancient Mesopotamians. They will examine her association with fertility and sexuality, her connection to the planet Venus, and her embodiment of both nurturing and destructive aspects. Through case studies and textual analysis, students will uncover the diverse manifestations of Ishtar in Mesopotamian culture and rituals, gaining a deeper appreciation for her significance as a powerful and revered goddess.

Marduk, the patron god of Babylon, holds a significant place in Mesopotamian mythology and religious practices. Students will explore the epic tale of Enuma Elish, which recounts Marduk's ascent to supreme power and his role in the creation of the world. They will examine Marduk's attributes as a warrior deity, his association with justice and order, and his role in the protection of Babylon and its people. Through critical analysis of primary sources and engagement with historical and archaeological evidence, students will uncover the cultural and political significance of Marduk and his enduring impact on Mesopotamian religious and societal structures.

Ninhursag, the mother goddess, symbolized fertility, nature, and creation. Students will delve into the mythological narratives that depict Ninhursag as the giver of life and the nurturer of all living beings. They will explore her associations with the earth, plants, and animals, recognizing her as the source of abundance and sustenance. Through the examination of ancient texts and artifacts, students will gain a deep appreciation for Ninhursag's role as a nurturing and life-giving deity, and the rituals and practices dedicated to her worship.

Throughout this exploration of Mesopotamian deities, students will gain a holistic understanding of the pantheon's diversity and the interconnectedness of the gods and goddesses within the ancient Mesopotamian cosmology. They will recognize the profound influence these deities held over various aspects of human life, from agricultural fertility and love to justice and creation. By engaging with the mythologies, rituals, and attributes of the gods and goddesses, students will develop a rich appreciation for the spiritual and cultural significance of ancient Mesopotamian religious practices and their enduring impact on human beliefs and spirituality.

✧ Priests, Priestesses, and Temple Rituals

In the religious landscape of ancient Mesopotamia, the roles of priests and priestesses were of paramount importance. These revered individuals served as intermediaries between the mortal realm and the divine, facilitating communication and maintaining harmonious relationships with the gods and goddesses. In this section, we will delve into the social and religious functions of priests and priestesses, their training and hierarchies, and their integral participation in temple rituals, unraveling the intricate tapestry of Mesopotamian religious life.

Priests and priestesses held esteemed positions within Mesopotamian society, serving as guardians of religious traditions and knowledge. They were responsible for performing rituals, interpreting omens, and offering prayers and sacrifices on behalf of the community. Students will explore the social and cultural significance of these roles, examining how priests and priestesses acted as mediators, ensuring the well-being and prosperity of the people by maintaining a harmonious relationship with the gods.

The training of priests and priestesses was rigorous and comprehensive, requiring deep knowledge of religious texts, rituals, and sacred practices. Students will delve into the educational systems and initiatory processes that prepared individuals for these sacred roles. They will discover how priests and priestesses underwent rigorous instruction, studying the intricate details of religious texts such as the Enuma Elish and the Atrahasis, and developing a deep understanding of the religious and cosmological frameworks of ancient Mesopotamia.

Hierarchies and specialized roles within the priesthood also existed. Students will explore the distinctions between high priests, who held significant authority and oversaw major temples, and lower-ranking priests who assisted in daily rituals and temple operations. They will examine the gender dynamics within the priesthood, noting the presence of both male and female priests and the different responsibilities they held. Through the analysis of historical records and archaeological evidence, students will gain insights into the hierarchies and organizational structures that governed the religious institutions of ancient Mesopotamia.

Temple rituals formed the core of Mesopotamian religious practices. Students will delve into the intricacies of these sacred ceremonies, examining their purpose, symbolism, and significance. They will explore the rituals of purification, libation, and offerings, as well as the recitation of prayers and hymns. Through case studies and textual analysis, students will gain a deep appreciation for the role of ritual in establishing a connection between the human and divine realms, fostering harmony and balance within the cosmological order.

By engaging with the roles of priests and priestesses and the rituals conducted within the temples, students will develop a profound understanding of the central role that these individuals played in the religious and spiritual life of ancient Mesopotamia. They will recognize the immense responsibility shouldered by priests and priestesses in maintaining the cosmic order, seeking the favor of the gods, and ensuring the prosperity of the community. Through critical analysis and discussion, students will gain a holistic appreciation for the significance of these practices, encouraging them to reflect on the broader concepts of religious authority, mediation, and the human-divine relationship in ancient Mesopotamia and beyond.

✧   Cultural and Social Beliefs

The spiritual landscape of ancient Mesopotamia was intricately intertwined with its cultural and social beliefs. Beyond the walls of the temples and the performance of rituals, the Mesopotamians held a rich tapestry of cosmological and supernatural beliefs that shaped their worldview and guided their daily lives. In this section, we will delve into the cultural and social beliefs of ancient Mesopotamia, exploring their cosmology, belief in supernatural forces, and the interconnectedness of the spiritual and material realms.

The cosmology of Mesopotamia was characterized by a complex understanding of the universe and the relationships between gods, humans, and the natural world. Students will explore the Mesopotamian creation myths, such as the Enuma Elish, which depicted the emergence of the world and the struggle between primordial forces. They will delve into the concept of the divine hierarchy, with gods and goddesses occupying different roles and exerting influence over various aspects of existence. By analyzing ancient texts and iconography, students will gain insight into the cosmological framework that shaped the spiritual beliefs of the Mesopotamians.

Supernatural forces played a significant role in the Mesopotamian worldview. Students will explore the belief in spirits, demons, and protective deities that influenced various aspects of human life. They will investigate the rituals and practices associated with appeasing these forces and seeking their favor or protection. Through the examination of ancient texts and artifacts, students will gain a deeper understanding of how the Mesopotamians perceived the supernatural realm and their efforts to navigate it.

A key aspect of Mesopotamian beliefs was the interconnectedness of the spiritual and material realms. Students will explore the concept of divine intervention and the belief that gods and goddesses actively participated in human affairs. They will examine the role of divination, such as the interpretation of omens and the consultation of oracles, as methods of seeking guidance and understanding the will of the divine. By studying ancient texts and artifacts related to divination practices, students will gain insights into the ways in which the Mesopotamians sought to establish a harmonious relationship between the mortal and divine realms.

The values and worldview of the Mesopotamians were reflected in their art, literature, and legal codes. Students will examine the portrayal of gods and goddesses in artwork, the themes and motifs present in Mesopotamian literature, and the ethical principles reflected in the Code of Hammurabi. Through critical analysis and discussion, students will gain a holistic understanding of the cultural and social beliefs that permeated every aspect of Mesopotamian life, from religious practices to social interactions.

By exploring the cultural and social beliefs of ancient Mesopotamia, students will develop a profound appreciation for the deep intertwining of spirituality and everyday existence in this ancient civilization. They will recognize the ways in which the spiritual beliefs influenced societal values, shaped cultural practices, and provided a framework for understanding the world. Through engagement with primary sources and visual representations, students will cultivate a nuanced understanding of the intricate connections between the supernatural, the human, and the material realms, encouraging them to reflect on the broader concepts of belief systems, worldview, and the impact of cultural and social beliefs on religious practices.

✧ Influence on Modern Practices

The ancient civilization of Mesopotamia, with its rich spiritual heritage, continues to exert a profound influence on various modern new-age practices. In this final section, we will explore the enduring legacy of Mesopotamian spirituality and uncover the ways in which its beliefs, rituals, and cosmology have shaped and influenced contemporary practices such as Witchcraft, Divination, Herbalism, Shamanism, Ecospirituality, and Magic. By engaging in discussions and analysis, students will develop a deep understanding of the historical roots and cultural connections that inform our study of these practices today.

Witchcraft, as a modern practice, draws inspiration from ancient Mesopotamia in several ways. Students will examine the role of Mesopotamian goddesses, such as Ishtar and Ninhursag, and the concept of magic as an inherent part of their worship. They will explore the use of spells, incantations, and rituals in Mesopotamian religious practices and trace their influence on contemporary witchcraft traditions. By comparing ancient texts and practices with modern witchcraft traditions, students will gain insights into the continuity and evolution of magical beliefs and practices over time.

Divination, the art of seeking insight and guidance from the divine, also finds its roots in ancient Mesopotamia. Students will explore the Mesopotamian practices of reading omens, interpreting dreams, and consulting oracles. They will examine the Mesopotamian belief in the interconnectedness of the spiritual and material realms and how this belief shaped their divinatory practices. By tracing the historical development of divination from Mesopotamia to the present day, students will gain a comprehensive understanding of the enduring influence of Mesopotamian divinatory techniques on modern practices.

Herbalism, the study and use of medicinal plants, also has ancient Mesopotamian roots. Students will explore the Mesopotamian knowledge of plants and their medicinal properties. They will examine the use of herbs in religious rituals and the belief in the healing power of divine intervention. By analyzing the ancient texts and medical prescriptions, students will discover the connections between Mesopotamian herbalism and contemporary herbal healing practices. They will also critically reflect on the cultural and social contexts that shaped ancient Mesopotamian herbalism and its relevance in modern times.

Shamanism, a spiritual practice involving communication with the spirit world, shares common elements with Mesopotamian spirituality. Students will explore the Mesopotamian belief in spirit beings and the role of priests and priestesses as intermediaries between the human and divine realms. They will examine the shamanic-like rituals performed in Mesopotamian temples and their potential influence on modern shamanic practices. By analyzing the similarities and differences between Mesopotamian spirituality and contemporary shamanism, students will gain a nuanced understanding of the cultural transmission and adaptation of shamanic practices.

Ecospirituality, a modern movement that emphasizes the sacredness of nature and the interconnectedness of all living beings, can also find inspiration in ancient Mesopotamian beliefs. Students will explore the Mesopotamian reverence for natural elements, such as rivers and mountains, and the understanding of the divine presence in the natural world. They will examine the ways in which Mesopotamian cosmology and environmental practices reflect the principles of ecospirituality. By critically analyzing the cultural and social beliefs of ancient

Mesopotamia, students will develop a deeper appreciation for the connections between spirituality, nature, and contemporary ecospiritual practices.

Magic, as both a concept and practice, was deeply ingrained in ancient Mesopotamian culture. Students will explore the Mesopotamian understanding of magic as a means to communicate with the divine and influence the material world. They will examine the rituals, spells, and incantations used in Mesopotamian magical practices and their parallels in modern magical traditions. By analyzing the continuity and adaptation of magical beliefs and practices, students will gain insights into the historical and cultural connections that inform modern magical practices.

By examining the enduring legacy of Mesopotamian spirituality and its influence on modern practices, students will develop a comprehensive understanding of the historical roots and cultural connections that underpin contemporary new-age studies. They will recognize the ways in which ancient Mesopotamian beliefs, rituals, and cosmology have shaped and influenced modern Witchcraft, Divination, Herbalism, Shamanism, Ecospirituality, and Magic. This exploration will encourage students to critically reflect on the appropriation, adaptation, and evolution of spiritual practices across time and cultures, fostering a deeper appreciation for the rich tapestry of human spirituality and its interconnectedness.

Example Problem:
Imagine you are a student of ancient Mesopotamian spirituality, tasked with analyzing the influence of Mesopotamian religious beliefs on contemporary Witchcraft. Explore the connections between the Mesopotamian deities and the deities honored in modern Witchcraft traditions. Discuss how the cosmology and rituals of ancient Mesopotamia have shaped and influenced the contemporary practice of Witchcraft.

Conclusion:

As we conclude this chapter on the historical and cultural context of new-age practices, students have embarked on a transformative journey through ancient Mesopotamia, uncovering the deep roots and cultural foundations that have shaped spiritual traditions. By studying the civilization's gods and goddesses, priests and priestesses, temple rituals, cultural beliefs, and their influence on modern practices, students have gained a comprehensive understanding of the historical and cultural tapestry that underlies our exploration of new-age spirituality. As we proceed to future chapters, we will continue to build upon this foundation, delving further into the fascinating realms of Witchcraft, Divination, Herbalism, Shamanism, Ecospirituality, and Magic.

Understanding Offerings and Sacrifices

Offerings and sacrifices have been a prominent aspect of religious and spiritual practices throughout human history. These rituals serve as a means of expressing devotion, reverence, and gratitude to the divine. In this section, we will explore the concept of offerings and sacrifices, their significance in various religious traditions, and the underlying beliefs and symbolism associated with these practices. By delving into the diverse cultural and historical contexts, we will gain a deeper understanding of the role offerings and sacrifices play in human spirituality and religious expression.

The Nature and Purpose of Offerings and Sacrifices

Within the context of spiritual practices, offerings and sacrifices play a significant role in establishing a connection between the human and divine realms. These rituals, which can take various forms, serve as a means for individuals to communicate with and honor their deities, seeking their favor, guidance, and protection. Offerings and sacrifices are rooted in the belief that the divine beings possess the power to influence and interact with the human world.

In ancient Mesopotamia, offerings and sacrifices were deeply ingrained in religious practices. They were seen as essential acts of devotion and reverence towards the gods and goddesses of the pantheon. These rituals were performed with the understanding that the deities had the ability to bestow blessings, protection, and abundance upon their worshippers. Through offerings and sacrifices, individuals sought to establish a reciprocal relationship with the divine, expressing gratitude, seeking assistance, and reinforcing the bond between the mortal and the immortal.

The nature of offerings and sacrifices in Mesopotamia was diverse, reflecting the multiplicity of deities and the specific needs and desires of the worshippers. Material offerings included food, drink, flowers, incense, and precious objects. These tangible offerings symbolized the provision of sustenance, pleasure, and beauty to the divine beings. By presenting these physical items, individuals demonstrated their willingness to share their resources and express their devotion.

Symbolic gestures were also an integral part of offerings and sacrifices. These could include the pouring of libations, the lighting of candles, or the waving of incense. These acts served as visual representations of the worshippers' intentions and desires. Symbolic offerings emphasized the importance of the ritual itself, as they conveyed meaning and symbolism beyond their material value.

Acts of service and personal sacrifices were another form of offerings and sacrifices in Mesopotamian culture. Individuals would engage in acts of charity, perform tasks for the temple or the community, or dedicate their time and effort to the service of the gods. These acts demonstrated a commitment to the divine and a willingness to contribute to the greater good.

The purpose of offerings and sacrifices extended beyond mere appeasement or bribery of the deities. It was believed that these rituals established a relationship of reciprocity and mutual benefit. By offering gifts and sacrifices, individuals sought to create a bond of trust, respect, and communication with the divine beings. Through these rituals, worshippers expressed their devotion, sought divine intervention in times of need, and acknowledged their dependence on the gods for guidance and protection.

Offerings and sacrifices were also seen as acts of purification and atonement. In instances where individuals believed they had transgressed against the gods or committed spiritual offenses, offerings and sacrifices were performed as a means of seeking forgiveness and restoring harmony within the divine-human relationship.

It is important to note that the nature and purpose of offerings and sacrifices varied across different cultures and spiritual traditions. While the specifics may differ, the underlying principles of establishing a connection with the divine, expressing devotion, seeking blessings, and acknowledging the reciprocal relationship between the mortal and the immortal remain consistent throughout various spiritual practices.

By studying the nature and purpose of offerings and sacrifices in ancient Mesopotamia, students gain a deeper understanding of the significance of these rituals in the context of human-divine relationships. They can then draw parallels to contemporary practices and critically reflect on the role and symbolism of offerings and sacrifices in modern new-age studies. This exploration fosters an appreciation for the cultural and historical significance of these rituals and encourages students to engage in thoughtful discussions and reflections on their own spiritual practices.

Symbolism and Meaning in Offerings and Sacrifices

Within the realm of spiritual practices, offerings and sacrifices hold profound symbolism and meaning. These rituals serve as powerful tools for conveying intentions, desires, and establishing a sacred connection with the divine. The items offered, the manner in which they are presented, and the underlying cultural and spiritual narratives all contribute to the symbolic significance of these acts.

One of the primary ways in which symbolism manifests in offerings and sacrifices is through the selection of specific items to be presented. Different objects carry symbolic associations that align with the intentions and desires of the worshippers. For example, food offerings often symbolize sustenance, abundance, and nourishment. The act of presenting food to the gods signifies the desire for blessings in the form of material provisions and the acknowledgment of the divine as the ultimate provider.

Similarly, incense and other aromatic substances have symbolic meanings in many spiritual traditions. The act of burning incense during offerings and sacrifices represents purification, the transference of prayers, and the creation of a sacred atmosphere. The rising smoke is believed to carry the prayers and intentions of the worshippers to the divine realm, bridging the gap between the earthly and spiritual realms.

The manner in which offerings are presented also holds symbolic significance. For instance, the act of pouring libations, which involves the ritualistic pouring of liquids such as water, wine, or oil, can symbolize the act of offering one's essence or life force to the divine. It represents a gesture of giving, pouring out one's devotion and desires to the gods.

Furthermore, the timing and placement of offerings and sacrifices can carry symbolic meaning. Certain rituals may be performed during specific celestial events, seasonal transitions, or significant dates within the spiritual calendar. These timings align with the cosmological beliefs of the tradition and infuse the offerings with deeper cosmic significance.

In addition to the objects and gestures involved, the intentions and desires of the worshippers infuse offerings and sacrifices with profound meaning. Individuals engage in these rituals with specific intentions in mind, such as seeking blessings, expressing gratitude, seeking guidance, or asking for protection. The act of offering becomes a way to articulate and communicate these intentions to the divine beings.

Symbolism and meaning in offerings and sacrifices are closely intertwined with the cultural, spiritual, and mythological narratives of a particular tradition. These rituals often draw upon the rich tapestry of myths, legends, and religious stories that shape the belief system of a community. The symbolic acts performed during offerings and sacrifices connect worshippers to the archetypal stories and spiritual heritage of their tradition, creating a sense of continuity and cultural identity.

Studying the symbolism and meaning in offerings and sacrifices allows students to explore the depth and intricacy of spiritual practices. It encourages them to delve into the narratives, metaphors, and archetypes that underpin these rituals. By understanding the symbolic significance, students gain a deeper appreciation for the layers of meaning embedded within the offerings and sacrifices they encounter in their studies of Witchcraft, Divination, Herbalism, Shamanism, Ecospirituality, and Magic.

Through critical analysis and reflection, students can explore how symbolism in offerings and sacrifices is interpreted and understood across different cultural contexts. They can also examine how contemporary practitioners adapt and reinterpret these symbols and meanings in modern new-age practices. By engaging in these discussions, students develop a nuanced understanding of the role of symbolism in spiritual rituals and cultivate their own critical thinking skills..

Example Problem:

Consider a practitioner of a modern pagan tradition who wishes to perform a ritual to honor the goddess of the moon. What types of offerings would be appropriate for this deity, considering her associations with the lunar cycle, femininity, and intuitive wisdom? Explain the symbolic significance of each offering chosen and how it relates to the goddess's attributes.

Cultural Variations in Offerings and Sacrifices

Offerings and sacrifices hold a fascinating place in the tapestry of human culture and spirituality. They provide us with valuable insights into the beliefs and practices of various societies throughout history. In this section, we will embark on a journey to explore the significance and variations of offerings and sacrifices, with a particular focus on ancient Mesopotamia and Hinduism.

First, we will dive into the ritual practices of offering and sacrifice in ancient Mesopotamia. In this remarkable civilization, these rituals played a crucial role in establishing communication with the gods and seeking their favor. We will delve into the types of offerings made, including food, drink, valuable items, and even animals. By examining their symbolic meanings and the underlying beliefs, we will gain a deeper understanding of the cultural significance of these practices. Additionally, we will analyze the rituals associated with offerings and sacrifices, such as the preparation and presentation of offerings, the role of priests, and the temple ceremonies. We will also explore the belief in reciprocity between humans and gods, which shaped the Mesopotamian religious worldview.

Next, our focus will shift to Hinduism, an ancient and complex religion. We will explore the profound significance of offerings and sacrifices within this tradition. Through an examination of Hindu worship ceremonies, we will discover the various types of offerings made, such as flowers, fruits, sweets, incense, and lamps. Understanding their symbolic significance will deepen our appreciation for the ways in which offerings are used as expressions of devotion, gratitude, and surrender to the deities. We will also explore the belief in the cyclical exchange of energy between humans and the divine, which underlies the act of offering in Hinduism.

To broaden our perspective, we will explore offerings and sacrifices in other cultures and religious traditions. From ancient Egyptian rituals to indigenous practices and contemporary spiritual movements, we will compare and contrast the different forms, meanings, and purposes of offerings and sacrifices. This exploration will highlight the remarkable diversity of human spiritual expression and the cultural contexts in which these practices arise. As we reflect on these diverse practices, we will identify the common threads that unite them, such as the universal desire to establish a connection with the divine, express reverence and gratitude, and engage in acts of devotion.

By embarking on this exploration of offerings and sacrifices, we will gain a deeper understanding of how humans have sought to communicate with the divine, express their devotion, and establish a reciprocal relationship with the spiritual realms. Through appreciating the unique perspectives and practices associated with offerings and sacrifices, we will expand our understanding of the rich tapestry of human spirituality and the diverse ways in which people engage with the sacred.

Ethical Considerations and Modern Practices

In the modern era, the practice of offerings and sacrifices has undergone significant evolution and adaptation, influenced by changing cultural perspectives, ethical considerations, and environmental awareness. As individuals engage with these rituals, they grapple with the ethical implications and seek to align their practices with principles of responsible stewardship and personal values.

One notable shift in modern interpretations of offerings and sacrifices is the emphasis on the intention behind the act rather than the material value of the offering. Many practitioners view offerings as symbolic gestures that represent a deep connection and reverence for the divine. The focus is on the sincerity and devotion expressed through the act, rather than the monetary or material worth of the offering. This shift allows for inclusivity and accessibility, as individuals can engage in offerings regardless of their financial means.

Moreover, an increasing number of individuals incorporate ethical and eco-friendly considerations into their practices. Recognizing the interconnectedness of all beings and the importance of environmental sustainability, practitioners may opt for biodegradable or reusable materials in their offerings, minimizing harm to the natural world. For example, offerings made from organic materials that can decompose naturally, such as flowers or fruits, can be seen as a way to honor the Earth and contribute to its well-being.

Additionally, some practitioners expand the concept of offerings beyond material objects, integrating acts of service and community engagement. This may involve volunteering, donating to charitable causes, or engaging in environmental conservation efforts as offerings to the divine. These practices align with the understanding that the divine can be honored through compassionate actions that benefit both human and non-human beings.

In the context of new-age practices, ethical considerations are paramount. Practitioners strive to create a balance between honoring tradition and adhering to ethical principles. This involves critically examining the cultural and historical context of offerings and sacrifices while recognizing the importance of responsible and sustainable practices.

An important aspect of ethical considerations in modern practices is the recognition of cultural appropriation and the need for cultural sensitivity. As individuals engage with rituals and practices from diverse spiritual traditions, it is crucial to approach them with respect, understanding, and a willingness to learn. This includes acknowledging the origins and cultural significance of specific offerings and adapting them in a culturally sensitive manner, or seeking alternative practices that align with one's own heritage or personal beliefs.

Engaging in discussions around ethical considerations and modern practices allows students to critically examine the evolving nature of offerings and sacrifices. By exploring different perspectives and ethical frameworks, they develop a nuanced understanding of the ethical implications involved and can make informed choices in their own spiritual practices.

Furthermore, considering the environmental impact of offerings and sacrifices is essential. This involves recognizing the potential ecological consequences of certain materials used in offerings and seeking eco-friendly alternatives. By integrating environmental awareness into their practices, individuals strive to honor the interconnectedness of all life and contribute to the well-being of the planet.

In conclusion, ethical considerations in modern offerings and sacrifices encompass a range of perspectives and practices. The focus on intention, eco-consciousness, and cultural sensitivity enables practitioners to engage in these rituals with mindfulness, respect, and responsible stewardship. By critically examining the ethical implications and adapting traditional practices to align with contemporary values, individuals can create a meaningful and sustainable spiritual practice that reflects their personal ethics and promotes harmony with the world around them.

Example Exercise:

Research a religious tradition or spiritual practice that involves offerings or sacrifices. Describe the specific rituals, symbolic meanings, and cultural contexts associated with these practices. Discuss any ethical considerations that arise from these practices and propose alternative approaches that align with modern values.

By studying the nature, symbolism, cultural variations, and ethical considerations of offerings and sacrifices, students will develop a comprehensive understanding of these practices. They will recognize the significance of offerings as a means of establishing a connection with the divine, explore the profound symbolism embedded within these rituals, and critically analyze the ethical implications in light of contemporary values. This knowledge will enable students to engage in informed discussions and make thoughtful choices in their own spiritual journeys or when encountering diverse religious practices.

Types of Offerings

Offerings play a central role in religious and spiritual practices across various traditions, serving as a means of communication, gratitude, and devotion to the divine. They are tangible expressions of reverence and can take many forms, including material objects, symbolic actions, prayers, or even personal sacrifices. In this section, we will explore the different types of offerings and their significance within religious and magical contexts.

Material Offerings

Material offerings play a significant role in religious and spiritual practices across various traditions, serving as tangible expressions of reverence, gratitude, and devotion. These offerings involve presenting physical objects to the divine or spiritual entities, symbolizing a connection between the human and divine realms. The act of offering is a deeply rooted practice that spans cultures and time, allowing individuals to engage with the intangible aspects of their faith through tangible means.

The choice of material offerings varies widely, influenced by cultural traditions, symbolic associations, and the specific attributes or preferences associated with the deity or spiritual being being honored. Simple items such as flowers, fruits, grains, or herbs are commonly used in offerings due to their symbolic significance. Flowers, for instance, are often associated with beauty, growth, and ephemeral nature, while fruits and grains represent abundance, sustenance, and the cycle of life. These natural offerings symbolize the bounty and interconnectedness of the Earth and are seen as a way to honor and nourish the divine.

In addition to natural offerings, other materials are employed to convey specific meanings or fulfill religious and cultural requirements. Incense, for example, is used in many traditions for its fragrance and its ability to purify the space and uplift the spirit. Its fragrant smoke is believed to carry prayers and intentions to the divine realm. Similarly, candles, lamps, or sacred fires are used to create an ambiance of illumination and sacredness, symbolizing the presence of the divine and guiding the way for spiritual connection.

Furthermore, more elaborate and valuable offerings are also part of certain traditions. These can include jewelry, artwork, textiles, or intricately crafted objects. These offerings represent the finest craftsmanship and demonstrate the dedication and commitment of the individual making the offering. They serve as symbols of devotion, reverence, and the willingness to give something precious in exchange for divine blessings or favor.

Food offerings hold particular significance in many cultures and religious practices. In various traditions, the act of preparing and presenting food to the divine is seen as an act of sharing and nourishment. The offering of meals or specific dishes holds cultural and symbolic meanings, reflecting traditions, festivals, and communal celebrations. Food offerings represent the provision and sustenance provided by the divine, and they foster a sense of gratitude for the abundance of life.

It is important to note that the value of a material offering is not solely based on its monetary worth but rather on the intention, sincerity, and personal significance behind the gesture. The act of offering is a way to express love, respect, and devotion, irrespective of the material value of the object itself. The symbolic associations and cultural contexts surrounding material offerings provide a framework for understanding the deeper meaning and purpose behind these acts.

In contemporary spiritual practices, individuals may adapt and personalize material offerings based on their own beliefs, preferences, and cultural backgrounds. They may combine elements from different traditions, incorporate handmade or personally significant objects, or choose environmentally sustainable materials. The intention and heartfelt connection with the divine remain central, regardless of the specific items offered.

By engaging in the practice of material offerings, individuals deepen their connection to the divine, express gratitude, and seek blessings and guidance. The act of selecting, preparing, and presenting these offerings becomes a meaningful and tangible expression of their spiritual beliefs and aspirations. Material offerings serve as a bridge between the physical and spiritual realms, fostering a sense of communion and devotion in the practitioner's spiritual journey.

Example Problem:

Research the Hindu tradition of puja and its use of material offerings. Identify three common material offerings used in puja rituals and explain their symbolic significance. How do these offerings embody the devotee's reverence and connection with the divine?

Symbolic Offerings

Symbolic offerings are gestures or actions that carry deep symbolic meaning, transcending the material realm to convey a spiritual intention or connection. These offerings go beyond the physical object itself and focus on the symbolic significance associated with the act, imbuing it with spiritual power and intention. Through these symbolic acts, individuals seek to establish a sacred connection, convey their intentions, and invoke the presence of the divine.

In many spiritual traditions, symbolic offerings are an integral part of rituals and ceremonies, serving as a means to honor the divine, express devotion, and create a sacred space. These offerings often involve gestures or actions that represent broader concepts or principles, such as the elements, the cycles of nature, or the sacredness of specific objects or substances.

One example of symbolic offerings can be found in Wicca, a modern pagan religion that emphasizes the worship of nature and the celebration of the cycles of life. In Wiccan rituals, offerings such as salt, water, and herbs are commonly used to symbolize the four elements of Earth, Water, Air, and Fire. Salt represents Earth, embodying stability, grounding, and the foundation of life. Water symbolizes the fluidity, emotions, and cleansing properties associated with the element. Herbs and incense represent Air, connecting to the realm of thoughts, communication, and inspiration. Lastly, the burning of candles or sacred herbs represents Fire, signifying transformation, passion, and illumination.

The pouring of water is another symbolic offering that can be found in various traditions across the world. Water is considered a purifying element, capable of cleansing and renewing. Pouring water during a ritual or ceremony can symbolize the washing away of impurities, the cleansing of the spirit, or the invocation of blessings and abundance. This act represents a symbolic gesture of offering one's intentions, emotions, or desires to the divine, seeking purification and spiritual connection.

Lighting candles or burning sacred herbs, such as sage or palo santo, are common symbolic offerings in many spiritual practices. The flickering flame of a candle represents illumination, clarity, and the presence of the divine. Lighting a candle can symbolize the awakening of spiritual awareness, the invocation of divine guidance, or the offering of one's prayers and intentions to the higher realms. Similarly, burning sacred herbs is believed to cleanse and purify the energy of a space, dispel negativity, and create a sacred atmosphere conducive to spiritual connection and transformation.

Symbolic offerings are not limited to specific objects or actions but can vary depending on cultural, religious, or personal beliefs. They can include offerings of symbolic objects, gestures, or even acts of service or devotion. For example, offering a symbolic representation of a personal goal or aspiration, such as a written affirmation or a symbolic object, can be a way to manifest and offer one's intentions to the divine. Acts of service, such as volunteering, caring for the environment, or helping others, can also be seen as symbolic offerings, expressing gratitude and compassion in action.

In modern practices, individuals may adapt and personalize symbolic offerings based on their own beliefs and intentions. They may incorporate elements from different spiritual traditions, create their own symbolic rituals, or choose objects or actions that hold personal significance. The key aspect of symbolic offerings is the intention and the understanding that the act itself carries profound symbolism and facilitates a connection with the spiritual realm.

By engaging in symbolic offerings, individuals deepen their spiritual practice, communicate their intentions and desires, and open themselves to the transformative power of the divine. These offerings serve as reminders of the interconnectedness between the physical and spiritual realms, inviting a sense of reverence, mindfulness, and sacredness into daily life.

Example Exercise:

Design a symbolic offering for a ceremony that celebrates the balance and harmony of nature. Explain the symbolism behind the chosen elements and actions, and how this offering can enhance participants' connection with the natural world.

Devotional Offerings

Devotional offerings are a means by which individuals express their love, reverence, and surrender to the divine. They are heartfelt gestures of devotion and acts of selfless service, expressing gratitude and a deep connection to the spiritual path or community. Devotional offerings can take various forms, including prayers, chants, hymns, rituals, or acts of kindness performed with sincere intention and devotion.

One of the most common forms of devotional offerings is prayer. Prayer is a way to communicate with the divine, expressing gratitude, seeking guidance, or offering praise and worship. It is a deeply personal and intimate act of devotion, often accompanied by a sense of humility and reverence. Prayers can be recited silently or aloud, using established prayers or personal heartfelt words. Through prayer, individuals establish a direct line of communication with the divine, fostering a sense of closeness and connection.

Chanting and singing hymns are also prevalent forms of devotional offerings in many spiritual traditions. These melodic expressions of devotion engage the heart, mind, and body in a rhythmic and harmonious manner. Chants and hymns often contain sacred words or mantras that carry profound spiritual vibrations. By engaging in these practices, individuals immerse themselves in the divine presence, cultivating a sense of unity and surrender.

Rituals and ceremonies are another significant aspect of devotional offerings. These sacred acts are performed with intention and reverence, often involving specific gestures, symbols, or sequences of actions. Rituals can be performed individually or as a collective, creating a sacred space and invoking the presence of the divine. They provide a structured framework for expressing devotion, seeking blessings, and experiencing spiritual transformation. These rituals may include offerings of flowers, incense, sacred objects, or symbolic gestures that convey devotion and honor to the divine.

Acts of selfless service or acts of kindness are also considered devotional offerings in many spiritual traditions. By offering their time, energy, skills, or resources to others, individuals demonstrate their commitment to living a compassionate and altruistic life. This selfless service is seen as a way to embody the divine qualities of love, compassion, and service in the world. It is a practical expression of devotion that extends beyond personal prayers and rituals, bringing the divine presence into daily life and benefiting others.

In the context of devotional offerings, gratitude plays a significant role. Expressing gratitude to the divine for blessings, guidance, and support is an integral part of devotional practices. Gratitude is not only a way to acknowledge the gifts received but also a way to cultivate a state of humility, recognizing that all we have is ultimately sourced from the divine. Devotees may offer words of gratitude, perform acts of service, or engage in rituals specifically dedicated to expressing appreciation and thankfulness.

Devotional offerings are deeply personal and can vary across different spiritual traditions and individuals. They are an expression of the individual's unique relationship with the divine and their heartfelt connection to the spiritual path. Through devotional offerings, individuals deepen their spiritual connection, cultivate a sense of surrender, and foster a loving and reverent relationship with the divine.

In summary, devotional offerings encompass a range of practices that express love, reverence, and surrender to the divine. They include prayers, chants, hymns, rituals, acts of service, and acts of kindness. Devotional offerings are heartfelt expressions of gratitude, devotion, and selflessness, bringing individuals closer to the divine and nurturing their spiritual journey.

Sacrificial Offerings

Sacrificial offerings are a form of devotion and surrender where individuals give up something valuable or significant as an offering to the divine. Historically, sacrificial offerings often involved the ritual killing of animals or the offering of valuable possessions. However, in contemporary practice, sacrificial offerings have evolved to encompass a broader range of actions and intentions.

In modern spiritual practices, sacrificial offerings are not necessarily associated with physical harm or material loss. Instead, they focus on acts of self-discipline, renunciation, and the offering of one's time, energy, or resources for the greater good. Sacrificial offerings are seen as symbolic gestures of devotion, demonstrating a willingness to let go of attachments, egoic desires, or negative habits in order to cultivate spiritual growth and alignment with the divine.

One form of sacrificial offering in contemporary practice involves self-discipline and renunciation. This may involve voluntarily abstaining from certain foods, practices, or behaviors for a specified period of time. By exercising self-control and restraint, individuals demonstrate their commitment to the spiritual path and their willingness to let go of attachments that hinder their spiritual progress. This form of sacrifice is seen as a way to purify the body, mind, and spirit, and to cultivate inner strength and clarity.

Another form of sacrificial offering is the offering of one's own time and energy for the benefit of others or the greater good. This can take the form of engaging in acts of service, volunteering, or supporting charitable causes. By willingly giving up one's personal time and resources, individuals demonstrate their dedication to compassion, kindness, and the well-being of others. This act of sacrifice is seen as a way to embody the divine qualities of love and selflessness, and to contribute to the betterment of society.

Sacrificial offerings can also involve the willingness to let go of negative habits, patterns, or behaviors. This may include offering up unhealthy attachments, addictive tendencies, or harmful thoughts and emotions. By consciously releasing these negative aspects of oneself, individuals create space for positive transformation and spiritual growth. This form of sacrifice is seen as a means of purification and liberation from the constraints of ego and egoic desires.

It is important to note that sacrificial offerings in contemporary practice are often approached with mindfulness and intention. They are not intended to cause harm or suffering but rather to cultivate personal and spiritual growth. Sacrificial offerings serve as reminders of the impermanence of material possessions, the importance of self-discipline, and the significance of selfless actions in the journey towards spiritual awakening.

In summary, sacrificial offerings have evolved in contemporary practice to focus on acts of self-discipline, renunciation, and the offering of one's time, energy, or resources for the greater good. Sacrifices are symbolic gestures of devotion and surrender, emphasizing the importance of letting go of attachments, cultivating self-discipline, and aligning with the divine. By engaging in sacrificial offerings, individuals seek spiritual growth, purification, and alignment with their highest selves.

Example Problem:

Discuss the ethical considerations and controversy surrounding sacrificial offerings. Present arguments from both sides, exploring the perspectives of those who view sacrificial offerings as an integral part of religious tradition and those who criticize it as a form of animal cruelty or unnecessary sacrifice.

Prayers and Mantras

Prayers and mantras hold a significant place in spiritual practices as they serve as forms of offering, devotion, and communication with the divine. They provide a means for individuals to express their heartfelt intentions, gratitude, supplications, or requests to the spiritual realm. Through the recitation of prayers or the chanting of mantras, practitioners establish a deep connection with the divine and seek blessings, guidance, and spiritual transformation.

Prayers are sincere and heartfelt expressions that convey a range of emotions and intentions. They can be expressions of gratitude, acknowledging the blessings and abundance in one's life. Prayers of gratitude allow individuals to cultivate an attitude of appreciation and recognize the divine presence in their everyday experiences. Additionally, prayers can serve as acts of supplication, seeking divine intervention, assistance, or protection in times of difficulty, challenges, or uncertainty. These prayers express the trust and reliance on the divine and the belief that the spiritual realm can provide comfort, support, and guidance.

In various spiritual traditions, prayers often follow a specific structure or format, reflecting the cultural and religious beliefs of the practitioners. They may include praise, acknowledgment of the divine qualities, and specific requests or intentions. Prayers can be recited individually or in communal settings, creating a collective energy of devotion and connection with the divine.

Mantras, on the other hand, are repetitive sounds, words, or phrases that are believed to possess spiritual power. They are often chanted or repeated rhythmically to create a meditative and focused state of mind. The chanting of mantras is considered a form of offering and devotion, as well as a means of attaining spiritual transformation or transcendence. The sound vibrations produced by chanting mantras are believed to harmonize the mind, body, and spirit, aligning them with the divine energies.

Mantras can be sacred syllables or phrases derived from ancient languages, such as Sanskrit or Tibetan. Each mantra carries its own vibrational frequency and is associated with specific qualities or deities. For example, the mantra "Om" is considered a universal mantra, representing the primordial sound of creation and encompassing the essence of all mantras. Other mantras may be dedicated to specific deities or embody particular qualities, such as compassion, wisdom, or healing.

The repetition of mantras is believed to purify the mind, increase focus, and cultivate a deep sense of presence and connection with the divine. It is seen as a transformative practice that helps individuals transcend mundane concerns and enter a state of heightened awareness and spiritual attunement. The rhythmic repetition of mantras can serve as a form of meditation, calming the mind and allowing individuals to enter a state of inner stillness and receptivity to divine energies.

In summary, prayers and mantras are powerful tools for spiritual connection and communication. Prayers enable individuals to express their intentions, gratitude, and supplications to the divine, seeking guidance, blessings, or support. Mantras, through their repetitive chanting, create a meditative state and attune practitioners to divine energies, facilitating spiritual transformation and deepening the connection with the sacred. Whether through spoken or silent words, prayers and mantras serve as offerings of devotion, fostering a profound relationship between individuals and the divine.

Example Exercise:

Research a specific prayer or mantra from a religious or spiritual tradition. Analyze its meaning, structure, and purpose. Reflect on how the repetition or recitation of this prayer or mantra can enhance one's spiritual practice and connection with the divine.

By understanding the various types of offerings, students can deepen their understanding of the role and significance of these practices within religious and magical contexts. Each type of offering carries its own symbolism, cultural significance, and purpose, providing individuals with a means to engage with the divine, express their devotion, and cultivate a sense of spiritual connection.

Ritual Procedures and Protocols

Rituals are ceremonial acts that hold deep significance within various spiritual and religious traditions. They provide a framework for individuals or communities to engage with the sacred, connect with the divine, and manifest their intentions and beliefs in a structured and meaningful way. In this section, we will explore the importance of ritual procedures and protocols, examining their role in facilitating spiritual experiences, promoting mindfulness, and fostering a sense of community and continuity.

Structure and Elements of Rituals

Rituals play a fundamental role in spiritual practices, providing a sacred framework for individuals to engage with the divine, commune with higher realms, and express their devotion. While the specific structure and elements of rituals may vary across different traditions, they often share common components that contribute to the overall experience and efficacy of the ritual.

Invocation: The ritual typically begins with an invocation, which is a formal calling upon the divine, deities, or spiritual forces to be present and participate in the ritual. This invocation sets the intention and creates a sacred space in which the ritual unfolds. It may involve reciting specific prayers, chanting mantras, or performing gestures to invite the divine presence.

Purification: Purification is a crucial element in many rituals as it prepares the participants and the space for the sacred work ahead. This purification can take various forms, such as physical cleansing, smudging with sacred herbs, or the use of holy water. The act of purification is symbolic of cleansing the body, mind, and spirit, removing any obstacles or impurities that may hinder the ritual experience.

Prayers and Invocations: Prayers and invocations are integral to rituals as they provide a means of communication with the divine or higher realms. Participants may recite prayers, chant mantras, or offer spoken words of devotion, gratitude, or supplication. These prayers set the tone for the ritual, expressing the intentions, aspirations, and desires of the participants, and seeking blessings, guidance, or spiritual transformation.

Offerings: Offerings are acts of giving or presenting something to the divine or spiritual entities as a gesture of respect, gratitude, and honor. These offerings can take various forms, including material objects, symbolic items, or acts of service. The choice of offerings is often guided by cultural traditions, symbolic associations, and the preferences or attributes of the deity or spiritual being being honored.

Gestures and Symbolic Acts: Rituals often incorporate specific gestures and symbolic acts that hold deeper meanings and significance. These actions may include lighting candles, pouring libations, creating sacred geometries, or performing specific movements or postures. These gestures serve as symbolic representations of intentions, energies, or states of being, enhancing the participants' connection with the divine and deepening their engagement in the ritual.

Sacred Objects and Tools: Rituals may involve the use of sacred objects or tools that hold symbolic value and are believed to amplify the ritual's power and effectiveness. These objects can include ritual implements, such as wands, athames, or chalices, as well as sacred symbols, talismans, or statues. The presence and use of these objects create a tangible connection to the spiritual realm and serve as focal points for the participants' intentions and energy.

Conclusion and Closing: Rituals typically conclude with a formal closing or conclusion, which may involve expressions of gratitude, prayers of closure, or the extinguishing of sacred flames. This closing phase marks the end of the ritual and signifies the transition from the sacred space back to the mundane world. It is an opportunity for participants to express their appreciation for the divine presence and reflect on the experiences and insights gained during the ritual.

Understanding the structure and elements of rituals is essential for participants as it provides a framework and guidance for their engagement in the sacred act. By following the prescribed structure, participants can navigate the ritual space with intention and reverence, allowing for a harmonious flow of energy and a deeper connection with the divine. The combination of invocation, purification, prayers, offerings, gestures, and symbolic acts creates a multi-dimensional experience that engages the senses, the mind, and the spirit, facilitating a meaningful and transformative ritual encounter.

Example Problem:

Consider a Wiccan ritual that celebrates the harvest season. Outline the general structure of this ritual, including the key elements and their significance. Explain how this ritual aligns with the seasonal cycles and Wiccan beliefs.

Purification and Sacred Space

Purification is an essential aspect of many rituals, serving to cleanse and purify the participants and the ritual space. The practice of purification is rooted in the belief that negative energies, impurities, or unwanted influences can hinder the effectiveness and flow of the ritual. By engaging in purification, participants seek to remove these obstacles and create a state of purity, receptivity, and spiritual alignment.

Physical Purification: Physical purification often involves rituals of cleansing the body, such as ritual baths, ablutions, or the use of consecrated water. These actions not only cleanse the physical body but also symbolize the purification of the mind and spirit. Ritual bathing or washing can be accompanied by prayers, affirmations, or visualization techniques to enhance the purification process.

Smudging and Incense: Another common method of purification is the use of smoke from sacred herbs, such as sage, cedar, or palo santo, through a practice known as smudging. The smoke is believed to carry the purifying properties of the herbs and can be used to cleanse the ritual space, objects, and participants. The act of smudging involves moving the smoking herb bundle or incense stick throughout the space, allowing the smoke to cleanse and purify the energy.

Mental and Spiritual Purification: Purification is not limited to physical actions but also includes mental and spiritual preparations. Participants may engage in meditation, deep breathing exercises, or visualization techniques to clear the mind of distractions, negative thoughts, and emotions. Setting clear intentions, affirmations, or prayers for purification can also help align the participants' mental and spiritual states with the sacred purpose of the ritual.

Sacred Space:

Creating a sacred space is a vital component of ritual practices. It involves consecrating and designating a specific area or environment where the ritual will take place. The creation of a sacred space serves several purposes:

Focused Energy: By designating a specific area as a sacred space, participants direct their focus and intention toward the ritual. This concentrated energy helps create a conducive environment for spiritual work and enhances the participants' connection with the divine.

Psychological Shift: Creating a sacred space helps facilitate a psychological shift from everyday consciousness to a state of heightened awareness. It signals a transition from the mundane to the sacred, preparing the participants to engage in the ritual with reverence, intention, and receptivity.

Boundary and Protection: The act of creating a sacred space also establishes a boundary or energetic container for the ritual. This boundary serves to separate the ritual space from the outside world, allowing the participants to enter a space that is free from distractions and outside influences. It also acts as a form of protection, safeguarding the participants and the energy of the ritual from external interferences.

Altars and Ritual Objects: Altars and ritual objects are often central to the creation of a sacred space. An altar is a dedicated space where ritual objects, sacred symbols, and offerings are placed. It serves as a focal point for participants to direct their attention, prayers, and intentions. The arrangement of objects on the altar can be customized according to the specific ritual or tradition, and each item holds symbolic significance in relation to the spiritual practices being performed.

Cleansing and Consecration: Before the ritual begins, the ritual space and objects may be cleansed and consecrated through acts of purification, such as smudging or sprinkling holy water. These actions imbue the space and objects with a sacred and purified energy, enhancing the vibrational quality of the environment.

Overall, purification and the creation of a sacred space play integral roles in ritual practices. They prepare the participants mentally, physically, and spiritually, fostering an environment that is conducive to spiritual connection, transformation, and communion with the divine. By engaging in purification rituals and creating a sacred space, participants can enter into a heightened state of awareness, focus, and receptivity, amplifying the efficacy and depth of their ritual experiences.

Roles and Responsibilities

In communal rituals, the assignment of roles and responsibilities is crucial for the effective and harmonious execution of the ceremony. These roles help establish a clear structure, facilitate the flow of energy, and ensure that all necessary aspects of the ritual are attended to. Here are some common roles and their responsibilities:

Priest/Priestess: The priest or priestess holds a central role in leading the ritual and acting as a mediator between the participants and the divine. Their responsibilities may include:

Conducting the opening and closing rituals: The priest/priestess leads the participants in invoking and dismissing the divine presence, setting the tone and intention for the ritual.

Offering prayers and invocations: They may lead the participants in reciting prayers, invocations, or mantras, guiding the collective spiritual focus and intention.

Performing rituals and ceremonial actions: The priest/priestess may perform specific ritual actions, such as offering libations, making symbolic gestures, or leading the participants in ritual dances or movements.

Conveying teachings and guidance: They may share spiritual teachings, stories, or instructions that are relevant to the ritual and its purpose, helping to deepen the participants' understanding and connection.

Participants: The participants actively engage in the ritual, embodying its purpose and contributing to the collective energy. Their responsibilities may include:

Following instructions and participating in ritual actions: Participants actively take part in the prescribed ritual actions, such as making offerings, reciting prayers, or engaging in symbolic gestures.

Holding intention and focus: Participants maintain a mindful and focused state throughout the ritual, holding their individual intentions and aligning their energies with the group's purpose.

Creating a supportive and respectful atmosphere: Participants contribute to the overall energy of the ritual by maintaining a respectful and reverent attitude, supporting others, and creating a sacred space through their presence.

Offering personal prayers or intentions: Participants may have the opportunity to offer their individual prayers, intentions, or personal rituals within the structure of the communal ceremony.

Assistants or Supporting Roles: Depending on the complexity and size of the ritual, additional roles may be assigned to support the smooth execution of the ceremony. These roles may include:

Ritual assistants: These individuals assist the priest/priestess in performing specific actions, handling ritual objects, or coordinating the flow of the ceremony.

Musicians or chanters: They provide the musical accompaniment or lead the chanting during the ritual, enhancing the atmosphere and energy of the ceremony.

Guardians or gatekeepers: These individuals hold the responsibility of maintaining the energetic boundaries of the ritual space, ensuring the safety and sacredness of the environment.

Record keepers or scribes: They may document the proceedings, record important insights, or capture the essence of the ritual for future reference or reflection.

Assigning specific roles and responsibilities in a ritual serves several purposes. It helps distribute the workload, ensuring that all necessary tasks are attended to and allowing the participants to focus on their individual roles. It also promotes a sense of shared responsibility, cooperation, and unity among the participants, fostering a collective experience. Additionally, clear roles and responsibilities contribute to the overall structure and flow of the ritual, enhancing its effectiveness and the participants' sense of purpose and engagement.

However, it's important to note that the specific roles and responsibilities can vary depending on the tradition, the type of ritual, and the preferences of the ritual leader or group. Flexibility and adaptability are key, as each ritual may have its unique requirements and dynamics. Ultimately, the goal is to create a cohesive and meaningful experience where each participant can contribute their energy and intention to the collective spiritual journey.

Example Exercise:

Research a specific ritual from a religious or spiritual tradition that involves communal participation. Describe the roles and responsibilities of the key participants, the symbolic actions performed, and the overall purpose or intention of the ritual. Reflect on how the structure and protocols of this ritual contribute to its effectiveness and impact on the participants.

Timing and Seasonal Considerations

In many spiritual traditions, the timing of rituals holds great importance. Aligning ceremonies with specific times of the day, lunar phases, or seasonal cycles allows participants to connect with the natural rhythms of the Earth, the cosmos, and their own inner cycles. Here are some key aspects related to timing and seasonal considerations in rituals:

Time of the Day: Some rituals are designed to be performed at specific times of the day, such as sunrise, noon, sunset, or midnight. These times are often associated with particular energies or qualities, and conducting rituals during these periods can enhance the intention and effectiveness of the ceremony. For example, a morning ritual may be focused on setting intentions for the day, while an evening ritual may be dedicated to reflection and gratitude for the day's experiences.

Lunar Phases: The lunar cycle, with its different phases, has long been associated with various symbolic meanings and energies. Many rituals are timed to coincide with specific lunar phases, such as the New Moon, Full Moon, or Quarter Moons. The New Moon is often associated with new beginnings, intention setting, and planting seeds of manifestation, while the Full Moon is seen as a time of heightened energy, illumination, and release. By aligning rituals with lunar phases, participants can tap into these lunar energies and work with their transformative power.

Seasonal Cycles: The changing seasons have a profound impact on the Earth and its inhabitants. Many rituals are connected to specific seasonal events, such as the solstices, equinoxes, or the cross-quarter days that fall between them. These rituals honor the cycles of nature and the turning of the wheel of the year. For example, a ritual performed during the Spring Equinox may focus on themes of rebirth, growth, and balance, while a ritual during the Autumn Equinox may emphasize gratitude, reflection, and harvest.

By incorporating timing and seasonal considerations, rituals gain a deeper layer of significance and resonance. Participants align themselves with the larger cosmic rhythms, symbolically participating in the cycles of creation, growth, transformation, and renewal. It allows individuals to attune themselves to the energies present in the natural world and harness them for personal and collective spiritual growth. Moreover, working in harmony with the temporal and seasonal cycles can help individuals cultivate a deeper connection with the Earth and foster a sense of reverence for the natural world.

It's important to note that the specific timing and seasonal considerations in rituals may vary depending on the tradition, cultural background, or personal preferences of the participants. The guiding principle is to create a meaningful and authentic connection with the larger rhythms of life, fostering a sense of interconnectedness with the natural world and the cosmos.

Adaptability and Personalization

Rituals have always been dynamic and responsive to the needs, beliefs, and cultural context of the individuals or communities practicing them. While rituals may have established procedures and guidelines, there is inherent flexibility that allows for adaptability and personalization. Here are some aspects to consider regarding adaptability and personalization in rituals:

Cultural Context: Rituals often reflect the cultural heritage and traditions of a specific community or lineage. However, as rituals are passed down through generations, they may evolve and incorporate elements from different cultural backgrounds. This adaptability allows individuals and communities to honor their ancestral traditions while also embracing the diversity of the modern world. By incorporating elements from different cultural contexts, rituals can become more inclusive and relevant to the diverse experiences of participants.

Symbolic Meaning: Rituals are rich in symbolism, and the specific symbols and gestures used can vary based on personal or communal preferences. Participants may choose to incorporate symbols that hold personal significance to them, adding a deeper layer of meaning and connection to the ritual. This personalization allows individuals to express their unique spiritual journey and beliefs within the framework of the ritual, fostering a sense of authenticity and resonance.

Intention and Focus: While rituals may have specific goals or intentions, individuals can personalize the focus of the ritual based on their individual needs and desires. For example, a healing ritual may be adapted to address a specific physical or emotional ailment, or a gratitude ritual may be tailored to express gratitude for specific blessings or experiences. Personalizing the intention and focus of the ritual ensures that it remains relevant and meaningful to the participants, allowing them to engage more deeply with the practice.

Ritual Modifications: Rituals can also be adapted to suit practical considerations or the available resources. For instance, if certain ritual items or ingredients are not accessible, participants can find suitable substitutes that hold similar symbolic significance. Additionally, the structure or format of a ritual can be modified to accommodate the needs and preferences of the participants. This adaptability ensures that rituals can be performed in various settings, whether it's a private home, a communal gathering, or a natural outdoor space.

By allowing for adaptability and personalization, rituals remain alive and relevant in the modern world. It acknowledges that spirituality is a dynamic and ever-evolving practice that should be adaptable to individual and collective needs. Personalizing rituals fosters a deeper sense of ownership and engagement, allowing participants to connect with the essence of the ritual in a way that resonates with their unique spiritual journey. At the same time, the core principles and intentions of the tradition remain intact, ensuring that the rituals continue to serve their intended purpose of spiritual connection, transformation, and growth.

Example Problem:

Consider a practitioner of Ecospirituality who wishes to perform a ritual to honor and reconnect with the natural world. Design a ritual procedure that incorporates elements of gratitude, environmental mindfulness, and the symbolic representation of the four elements. Explain the rationale behind each step and how it fosters a deeper connection with nature.

By studying the structure, elements, purification practices, roles and responsibilities, timing considerations, and adaptability of rituals, students gain a comprehensive understanding of the significance and power of these ceremonial acts. Ritual procedures and protocols provide a framework for engaging with the divine, fostering spiritual growth, and establishing a sense of continuity within a specific tradition or community. Understanding the various aspects of rituals allows individuals to participate more fully, create meaningful experiences, and cultivate a deeper connection with the sacred.

Symbolism and Meaning of Offerings

In religious and magical practices, offerings hold profound symbolic significance, serving as a means of communication, reverence, and connection with the divine. Each offering carries its own unique symbolism and meaning, influenced by cultural traditions, spiritual beliefs, and the specific context in which the offering is made. Understanding the symbolism behind offerings deepens our appreciation for these rituals and enhances our spiritual connection. In this section, we will explore the symbolism and meaning of offerings across different traditions and examine how they contribute to the practice of magic and spirituality.

Symbolism in Material Offerings

Material offerings play a significant role in religious and magical practices, as they serve as tangible representations of devotion, gratitude, and connection to the divine or spiritual realm. Each material used in an offering carries its own symbolic meaning, enhancing the ritual experience and deepening the connection between the practitioner and the spiritual forces they seek to honor. Here are some common symbols associated with material offerings:

Flowers: Flowers are often used as offerings due to their beauty, fragility, and association with growth and the cycle of life. Different types of flowers may have specific meanings. For example, roses are often associated with love and passion, while lilies symbolize purity and rebirth. Flowers can also represent the seasons and the changing cycles of nature, embodying the ebb and flow of life's energies.

Fruits and Food: Offering fruits and food items represents abundance, nourishment, and the blessings of the Earth. Fruits are symbolic of fertility, growth, and the harvest. In some traditions, specific fruits may hold additional symbolic associations. For instance, apples are often associated with wisdom, while grapes are linked to joy and celebration. The act of offering food also reflects the belief in sharing and sustaining the divine energies that support and nourish life.

Sacred Objects: Sacred objects, such as crystals, amulets, or religious symbols, can be offered to honor specific deities or spirits. These objects may hold personal or cultural significance and are chosen for their symbolic representation of the divine or spiritual qualities associated with the deity or spirit being honored. The offering of sacred objects can serve as a physical representation of devotion, invoking the presence and blessings of the spiritual realm.

Incense and Fragrances: Incense and fragrances are commonly used in offerings due to their ability to create a sensory experience and evoke a sacred atmosphere. The smoke of incense is believed to carry prayers and intentions to the divine realm, while the pleasing scents can enhance focus and meditation. Different types of incense, such as sage, sandalwood, or lavender, may have specific symbolic associations, such as purification, grounding, or relaxation.

Precious Metals and Jewelry: Offering precious metals, such as gold or silver, or wearing jewelry during rituals symbolizes wealth, prosperity, and the acknowledgment of the divine as the ultimate source of abundance. Jewelry can also serve as a personal representation of devotion or a connection to a specific deity or spiritual tradition. The intrinsic value of precious metals and the craftsmanship of jewelry further highlight the significance and reverence of the offering.

It's important to note that the specific symbolism associated with material offerings can vary across cultures, traditions, and individual interpretations. The symbolic meaning of an offering can also be influenced by the intention and context of the ritual or the personal relationship between the practitioner and the spiritual forces they seek to connect with. By carefully selecting and presenting material offerings, practitioners aim to establish a tangible and meaningful connection with the divine, expressing their reverence, gratitude, and aspirations.

Example Problem:

Research the symbolism of specific material offerings in a tradition of your choice, such as Hinduism, Buddhism, or indigenous practices. Select three common material offerings and explain their symbolic meanings. How do these offerings reflect the core beliefs and values of the respective tradition?

Symbolic Actions and Gestures

Symbolic actions and gestures play a vital role in religious and magical rituals, as they communicate profound meanings and intentions beyond their physical manifestations. These actions are often imbued with symbolism and carry spiritual significance, reinforcing the connection between the practitioner and the spiritual forces they seek to engage with. Here are some examples of symbolic actions and gestures commonly used in rituals:

Lighting a Candle: The act of lighting a candle is a widespread ritual practice across various traditions. The flame of the candle represents illumination, knowledge, and the presence of the divine. It symbolizes the awakening of spiritual consciousness and serves as a focal point for meditation, prayer, or intention-setting. The act of lighting a candle can also be seen as a symbolic offering of light and energy to the spiritual realm.

Burning Incense: Burning incense has been used for centuries in religious and spiritual rituals. The rising smoke is believed to carry prayers, intentions, and offerings to the divine realm. Different types of incense may have specific symbolic associations. For example, sage is often used for purification and cleansing, while frankincense is associated with spirituality and heightened awareness. The aroma of incense can create a sacred atmosphere, enhance focus, and evoke a sense of transcendence.

Pouring Water: Pouring or sprinkling water is a symbolic act found in various traditions and signifies purification, renewal, and spiritual cleansing. Water is seen as a purifying element that washes away impurities and represents the flow of life and spiritual rejuvenation. The act of pouring water can also symbolize the offering of life-sustaining energy or the invitation of divine blessings into one's life.

Sacred Hand Gestures: Hand gestures, also known as mudras, are symbolic positions of the hands and fingers used to channel and direct energy during rituals and spiritual practices. Different mudras have distinct meanings and intentions. For example, the Anjali mudra, formed by bringing the palms together in prayer position, signifies reverence, gratitude, and the union of the individual self with the divine. Mudras can deepen concentration, facilitate communication with the spiritual realm, and enhance the overall ritual experience.

Offering Prayers or Chants: The act of offering prayers or chanting sacred words or mantras is a powerful symbolic gesture. Prayers express gratitude, supplication, or intentions, while chanting mantras is believed to generate specific vibrations and connect with divine energies. Through the repetition of sacred words or phrases, practitioners align their consciousness with the spiritual realm, focusing their thoughts and intentions on the desired outcomes.

Symbolic actions and gestures serve to heighten the ritual experience, engage the senses, and create a tangible connection between the practitioner and the spiritual realm. They embody deeper meanings, intentions, and beliefs, reinforcing the transformative and sacred nature of the rituals. The specific symbolic actions and gestures employed in a ritual can vary across traditions, reflecting cultural, mythological, and spiritual contexts.

Example Exercise:

Design a ritual that incorporates symbolic actions and gestures. Consider the elements you would use, such as water, fire, or sacred objects, and explain the symbolic meaning behind each element. How do these symbolic actions enhance the overall intention and impact of the ritual?

Personal Sacrifice and Devotion

Personal sacrifice and acts of devotion hold a significant place in many religious and spiritual traditions. These practices involve the willingness to give up something valuable or make a personal commitment as a demonstration of devotion, dedication, and sincerity. Here are some aspects to consider regarding personal sacrifice and devotion:

Self-Transformation: Personal sacrifice and acts of devotion are often undertaken with the intention of self-transformation and spiritual growth. By voluntarily giving up something of personal value, such as indulging in negative habits or desires, individuals seek to cultivate discipline, self-control, and a deeper connection with the divine. This process of self-transformation is seen as a pathway to spiritual elevation and inner liberation.

Time and Energy: Offering one's time and energy as a personal sacrifice is a way to demonstrate commitment and devotion. This can involve dedicating a specific period for spiritual practices, such as meditation, prayer, or study, or volunteering for service in religious or community activities. By prioritizing spiritual pursuits and investing time and energy in them, individuals express their devotion and strengthen their connection to the divine.

Vows and Commitments: Making vows or commitments is another form of personal sacrifice and devotion. This can involve taking vows of celibacy, simplicity, or non-violence, or making commitments to follow certain ethical or moral principles. Vows are seen as sacred promises and acts of dedication to a higher purpose, reflecting a deep level of commitment and spiritual resolve.

Offerings of Resources: Personal sacrifice can also take the form of offering one's material resources for the greater good. This can include donating money, possessions, or talents to support charitable causes, religious institutions, or the welfare of others. By relinquishing attachment to material possessions and sharing resources with those in need, individuals express their devotion and recognize the interconnectedness of all beings.

Pilgrimages and Rituals: Engaging in pilgrimages or participating in specific rituals can be acts of personal sacrifice and devotion. Pilgrimages involve undertaking a journey to a sacred place as an act of reverence and dedication. Rituals, such as fasting, penance, or extended periods of meditation, may be practiced as acts of devotion and purification, deepening one's spiritual connection and commitment.

Personal sacrifice and acts of devotion are deeply personal choices, reflecting an individual's commitment to their spiritual path and the values of their tradition. These practices are often seen as transformative, allowing individuals to transcend their ego-driven desires and cultivate virtues such as selflessness, humility, and compassion. Through personal sacrifice and devotion, individuals express their love, loyalty, and dedication to the divine, seeking to align their lives with higher principles and ideals.

Example Problem:

Explore the concept of personal sacrifice and devotion in a religious or spiritual tradition of your choice. Explain the significance of personal sacrifices in deepening one's spiritual connection and commitment. Discuss the potential challenges and benefits of such practices.

Symbolism in Prayer and Intention

Prayers and intentions hold deep symbolic significance in religious, spiritual, and magical practices. They serve as powerful means of communication with the divine and as tools for focusing and directing energy towards specific goals. Here are some aspects to consider regarding the symbolism in prayer and intention:

Gratitude and Humility: Expressing gratitude in prayers symbolizes recognition of the blessings and abundance in one's life. It acknowledges the interconnectedness of all beings and the divine source from which these blessings flow. Gratitude also cultivates humility and fosters a sense of awe and reverence for the mysteries of existence.

Supplication and Petition: Prayers often include supplication and petition, symbolizing the act of seeking assistance, guidance, or blessings from the divine. This symbolizes the acknowledgment of one's limitations and the desire for divine intervention or support. It represents a humble recognition of the interconnectedness between the individual and the larger cosmic order.

Spiritual Alignment and Intentions: Setting clear intentions during rituals and magical practices symbolizes the focused direction of energy and the alignment of one's thoughts, emotions, and actions towards a specific outcome. Intentions are formulated with precision, clarity, and positive language, reflecting the desired state or manifestation. They serve as a symbolic bridge between the inner world of thoughts and the outer world of manifestation.

Connection and Unity: Prayers and intentions symbolize the inherent desire for connection and unity with the divine. They represent the yearning to align one's consciousness with higher truths, principles, or a divine presence. By expressing prayers and intentions, individuals symbolically bridge the perceived separation between themselves and the divine, cultivating a sense of oneness and interconnectedness.

Affirmation and Affirmative Language: Prayers and intentions often use affirmative language, symbolizing the power of positive affirmation and the belief in the manifestation of desired outcomes. Affirmations are statements that reflect the desired state as if it has already been realized, emphasizing the importance of belief and faith in the manifestation process.

Sacred Words and Language: In many traditions, prayers and intentions are expressed through sacred words, chants, mantras, or invocations. The use of sacred language carries symbolic power and resonance, representing the sacredness of the spoken word and its ability to invoke and connect with higher realms of consciousness.

Symbolism in prayer and intention underscores the transformative and symbolic nature of these practices. By engaging in prayers and setting clear intentions, individuals tap into the power of symbolism, aligning their thoughts, emotions, and actions with their spiritual beliefs and desired outcomes. Through the symbolic language of prayer and intention, individuals establish a profound connection with the divine, fostering personal growth, transformation, and the realization of their spiritual aspirations.

Example Exercise:

Compose a prayer or intention for a specific purpose, such as healing, guidance, or manifestation. Reflect on the words and phrases you choose and explain the symbolic significance behind them. How does the prayer or intention align with your personal spiritual beliefs and values?

Understanding the symbolism and meaning of offerings enriches our spiritual practices by deepening our connection with the divine and enhancing our understanding of the underlying principles and beliefs. By engaging in these rituals with awareness and intention, we develop a greater appreciation for the sacredness of the act of offering and its transformative potential in our lives.

Sacred Meals and Feasting

Sacred meals and feasting hold a significant place in various spiritual and religious traditions, serving as communal rituals that foster connection, nourishment, and celebration. These gatherings bring people together to share food, engage in acts of gratitude, and experience a sense of unity with the divine and with one another. In this section, we will explore the significance of sacred meals and feasting in different cultural and historical contexts, analyzing their symbolism, objectives, and underlying principles.

Symbolism and Meaning

Sacred meals and feasting hold deep symbolism in various religious and spiritual traditions. These rituals not only nourish the body but also serve as powerful symbols of unity, abundance, gratitude, and spiritual connection. Here are some aspects to consider regarding the symbolism and meaning in sacred meals and feasting:

Interconnectedness and Communion: The act of sharing a meal symbolizes the interconnectedness of all beings. It represents the recognition that we are part of a larger whole, and through the act of eating together, we reaffirm our shared humanity and unity. It emphasizes the importance of community, cooperation, and mutual support.

Abundance and Gratitude: Sacred meals and feasting often symbolize the abundance of the Earth's resources and the blessings of the divine. The variety and abundance of food served during these rituals reflect the generosity and providence of the natural world. Sharing a meal in a spirit of gratitude acknowledges the gifts of sustenance and nourishment, fostering a deeper appreciation for the blessings we receive.

Hospitality and Generosity: Sacred meals often highlight the values of hospitality and generosity. The act of inviting others to share in a sacred meal represents an offering of hospitality and a willingness to share one's resources and blessings with others. It symbolizes the importance of fostering a sense of welcoming, inclusivity, and community building.

Transformation and Transcendence: Food itself holds symbolic significance in sacred meals. It represents sustenance, life energy, and the transformative power of nourishment. The act of consuming food during a sacred meal can symbolize the assimilation and integration of spiritual energy or divine blessings, leading to personal growth, transformation, and spiritual transcendence.

Ritualized Preparation and Presentation: Sacred meals often involve ritualized preparation and presentation of food. The careful selection, preparation, and arrangement of food items reflect attention to detail, reverence, and the intention to create a sacred and meaningful experience. Symbolic gestures, such as offering a portion of food to deities or ancestors, may be incorporated to acknowledge their presence and seek their blessings.

Ritual Feasting and Celebrations: Sacred meals are often associated with religious festivals or celebratory occasions. These feasts symbolize joy, abundance, and the communal celebration of significant milestones, seasons, or religious events. They foster a sense of unity, shared purpose, and the reaffirmation of cultural or religious identity.

The symbolism and meaning in sacred meals and feasting reflect the spiritual beliefs, values, and cultural traditions of a particular community. By partaking in these rituals, individuals not only nourish their bodies but also engage in acts that symbolically express their connection to the divine, the interconnectedness of all beings, and the celebration of abundance and gratitude. These rituals create a sacred space for community, reflection, and the experience of spiritual communion.

Example Problem:

Choose a religious or spiritual tradition that incorporates sacred meals or feasting as part of its practices, such as Christianity, Hinduism, or indigenous traditions. Analyze the symbolism and meaning associated with the food, rituals, and communal aspects of these gatherings. How do these symbolic elements contribute to the spiritual experience and sense of community?

Ritual Structure and Protocols

Sacred meals and feasting rituals are often structured by specific protocols and guidelines that ensure the proper conduct and intention of the participants. These rituals create a sacred space and set the tone for the gathering, facilitating a deeper connection to the spiritual and symbolic aspects of the meal. Here are some common elements of ritual structure and protocols in sacred meals:

Blessings and Invocations: Rituals may begin with blessings or invocations to invoke the presence and blessings of the divine or to express gratitude for the food and the community gathered. These blessings can be recited by a designated leader or collectively by all participants, setting an intention of reverence and gratitude.

Purification Practices: Purification practices are often incorporated into the ritual to cleanse and purify the participants and the space before the meal. This can include the use of sacred herbs, incense, or the sprinkling of water to symbolically remove negative energies and create a harmonious and sacred atmosphere.

Sacred Space and Altar: Creating a designated sacred space or altar is a common practice in sacred meals. This space serves as a focal point for the ritual and is adorned with symbols, sacred objects, or images representing the divine or the purpose of the gathering. It provides a visual representation of the spiritual presence and sets the ambiance for the ritual.

Serving and Consuming the Food: Ritual protocols often guide the way food is served and consumed. This can include specific gestures, such as offering portions of food to deities, ancestors, or honored guests before partaking in the meal. It emphasizes the act of sharing, gratitude, and the acknowledgment of the divine presence in the nourishment.

Mindfulness and Reverence: Participants are encouraged to approach the meal with mindfulness and reverence. This involves being fully present in the moment, savoring each bite, and offering thanks for the sustenance received. Mindful eating practices can be incorporated, such as silent reflection or communal recitation of prayers or affirmations during the meal.

Conclusion and Closing Rituals: Rituals associated with sacred meals often have a conclusion or closing ceremony to bring the gathering to a harmonious end. This may include expressing gratitude for the experience, offering prayers or blessings for the well-being of all, or performing a symbolic act that signifies the completion of the ritual.

The structure and protocols in sacred meals and feasting rituals provide a framework for participants to engage in a meaningful and spiritually enriching experience. They guide behavior, foster reverence, and create a cohesive and sacred atmosphere. By following these rituals, participants are able to connect with the deeper symbolism and spiritual significance of the meal, fostering a sense of unity, gratitude, and spiritual nourishment.

Example Exercise:

Design a ritual for a sacred meal or feasting ceremony. Consider the elements you would include, such as prayers, invocations, or purification rituals. Explain the significance of each element and how it contributes to the overall sacredness of the meal. How would you create a sense of unity and connection among the participants?

Community and Connection

Sacred meals and feasting have long been recognized as powerful catalysts for building and strengthening community bonds. These gatherings provide a unique opportunity for individuals to come together, share food, and engage in a communal experience that goes beyond mere sustenance. Here are some key aspects highlighting the role of sacred meals in community building:

Sense of Belonging and Unity: When individuals gather for a sacred meal, they participate in a shared experience that transcends individual differences. The act of sitting down together, sharing food, and engaging in rituals creates a sense of belonging and unity. It fosters a feeling of being part of a larger whole, a community with shared values, beliefs, and traditions.

Deepening Connections: Sacred meals provide an avenue for individuals to connect with others on a deeper level. Breaking bread together can facilitate meaningful conversations, the sharing of personal stories, and the cultivation of empathy and understanding. It allows participants to forge new connections and strengthen existing relationships, building a sense of camaraderie and mutual support.

Trust and Support: The act of sharing a sacred meal often creates a space of trust and openness. Participants come together with a shared intention and an understanding that they are part of a supportive community. This environment encourages vulnerability, empathy, and the willingness to offer support and guidance to one another.

Reciprocity and Mutual Care: Sacred meals emphasize the principles of reciprocity and mutual care. The act of serving and being served during these gatherings symbolizes a sense of interconnectedness and interdependence. Participants have the opportunity to practice acts of kindness and generosity, creating a culture of giving and receiving within the community.

Celebration and Joy: Sacred meals are often associated with celebrations, festivals, or important milestones, adding an element of joy and festivity to the communal experience. The shared enjoyment of food, music, and rituals fosters a positive and uplifting atmosphere, reinforcing the bonds of the community and creating lasting memories.

Nourishment of Body and Spirit: In sacred meals, the act of sharing food goes beyond physical nourishment. It becomes a symbol of nurturing the body and the spirit. Participants recognize the sacredness of the food, expressing gratitude for the abundance of the Earth and the blessings received. This holistic approach to nourishment deepens the spiritual connection within the community.

Overall, sacred meals and feasting play a vital role in community building by fostering a sense of belonging, deepening connections, promoting trust and support, embodying reciprocity and mutual care, and creating a joyful and celebratory atmosphere. By coming together in this way, participants experience a shared sense of purpose and interconnectedness, contributing to the growth, resilience, and well-being of the community as a whole.

Example Problem:

Explore the importance of community and connection in the context of sacred meals and feasting. How do these rituals contribute to the formation of community bonds? Discuss the potential challenges and benefits of communal gatherings, considering factors such as inclusivity, cultural diversity, and individual preferences.

Gratitude and Celebration

Gratitude and celebration are integral aspects of sacred meals and feasting, adding depth and meaning to the communal experience. Here's an expansion on the significance of gratitude and celebration within this context:

Gratitude for Abundance: Sacred meals offer an opportunity to express gratitude for the abundance of nourishment provided by the Earth and the divine. Participants recognize and appreciate the bountiful gifts of nature that sustain their physical bodies. Through gratitude, they develop a deeper connection with the sources of their sustenance, fostering a sense of interconnectedness and reverence for the natural world.

Cultivating a Positive Mindset: Engaging in acts of gratitude during sacred meals helps cultivate a positive and appreciative mindset. Expressing thanks for the food and blessings received brings awareness to the present moment and the simple joys of life. This practice encourages participants to focus on the positives, fostering a sense of contentment and well-being.

Acknowledging Divine Providence: Many traditions view the act of sharing a sacred meal as a way to acknowledge the role of the divine in providing for their sustenance. Participants recognize that the food they partake in is a gift from the divine and express gratitude for the nourishment and blessings bestowed upon them. This recognition deepens their spiritual connection and fosters a sense of humility and reverence.

Celebration of Life's Blessings: Sacred meals and feasting also serve as occasions for celebration. Participants come together to honor special events, festivals, or milestones, creating an atmosphere of joy and festivity. By celebrating life's blessings, participants cultivate a sense of appreciation and elevate their spirits, fostering a positive and uplifting communal experience.

Shared Joy and Connection: Expressing gratitude and celebrating together during sacred meals fosters a sense of shared joy and connection within the community. Participants experience a collective upliftment of spirits, and the atmosphere becomes infused with positive energy and camaraderie. The act of sharing in the celebration strengthens bonds and creates lasting memories.

Mindful Presence: The practice of gratitude and celebration during sacred meals encourages participants to be fully present in the moment. It invites them to slow down, savor the flavors, and engage their senses with mindfulness. By cultivating this state of mindful presence, individuals deepen their connection to the experience and develop a heightened appreciation for the sacredness of the meal.

Overall, gratitude and celebration within sacred meals and feasting create an atmosphere of appreciation, joy, and connection. They help participants shift their focus towards the blessings and abundance in their lives, fostering a positive mindset and strengthening communal bonds. By engaging in these practices, individuals cultivate a deeper sense of meaning, reverence, and gratitude for the nourishment and experiences they share with others.

Example Exercise:

Reflect on a personal experience of sharing a meal or participating in a communal feast. Describe the atmosphere, the types of food, and the rituals or practices involved. What aspects of the gathering evoked feelings of gratitude and celebration? How did this experience impact your sense of connection and well-being?

Sacred meals and feasting hold profound significance in various spiritual and religious contexts, serving as powerful rituals that nourish the body, mind, and spirit. By understanding the symbolism, rituals, and underlying principles of these gatherings, individuals can deepen their spiritual practice, foster community bonds, and cultivate a greater sense of gratitude and celebration in their lives.

Offerings and Temples

In many spiritual and religious traditions, offerings and temples play significant roles in establishing a connection between human beings and the divine. Offerings, in the form of material objects, prayers, or acts of devotion, are presented as gestures of reverence, gratitude, and communication with the divine realm. Temples, on the other hand, serve as physical structures dedicated to worship, rituals, and communal gatherings. In this section, we will explore the significance of offerings and temples in various cultural and historical contexts, analyzing their roles, symbolism, and the ways in which they facilitate spiritual experiences.

Significance of Offerings

Offerings hold great importance in religious and spiritual practices. They are seen as acts of devotion and acknowledgment of the divine presence. The act of giving something of value, whether it be food, flowers, incense, or other symbolic objects, is believed to create a reciprocal relationship between the worshipper and the divine. It is a way of showing gratitude, seeking blessings, and inviting divine favor. In ancient Mesopotamia, for example, offerings were made to gods and goddesses to establish and maintain a harmonious relationship, ensure prosperity, and seek protection.

Acts of Devotion: Offerings are considered acts of devotion and reverence towards the divine. By presenting something of value, individuals demonstrate their commitment, love, and respect for the spiritual entities they worship. Offerings are a tangible expression of the worshipper's connection and dedication to the divine, deepening their spiritual bond and fostering a sense of devotion.

Gratitude and Acknowledgment: Offerings serve as a way to express gratitude for the blessings and provisions bestowed by the divine. They are a means of acknowledging the benevolence and abundance present in one's life. Through offerings, individuals recognize and appreciate the divine's presence and influence, cultivating a mindset of gratitude and humility.

Seeking Blessings and Favor: Offerings are often made with the intention of seeking blessings, guidance, and divine favor. Individuals believe that by presenting offerings, they can invoke the goodwill and benevolence of the divine entities. They seek the assistance and protection of the divine in various aspects of life, such as health, prosperity, relationships, or spiritual growth. Offerings are seen as a way to establish a reciprocal relationship, where the worshipper's gestures of devotion are met with divine blessings and assistance.

Establishing and Maintaining Relationship: Offerings play a vital role in establishing and maintaining a harmonious relationship between the worshipper and the divine. By presenting offerings, individuals acknowledge the divine presence and actively engage in a dialogue with the spiritual realm. It is believed that offerings create a connection and bridge the gap between the human and divine realms, facilitating communication and fostering a sense of unity.

Symbolism and Sacredness: Offerings are often imbued with symbolic meaning, representing various aspects of the worshipper's beliefs and values. The choice of offerings may reflect cultural traditions, the attributes of the deities, or symbolic associations. For example, food offerings can represent sustenance and nourishment, while flowers may symbolize beauty and the transient nature of life. The act of offering itself holds sacred significance, transcending the material value of the items presented.

Ritual Importance: Offerings are an integral part of religious and spiritual rituals, enriching the ceremonial experience. They add depth, symbolism, and intention to the ritual proceedings, enhancing the sacred atmosphere and setting the stage for spiritual connection. Offerings are often made at specific times, in specific ways, and accompanied by prayers or invocations, further amplifying their significance within the ritual context.

In summary, offerings hold great significance in religious and spiritual practices. They are acts of devotion, gratitude, and acknowledgment of the divine presence. Through offerings, individuals seek blessings, establish and maintain a relationship with the divine, and express their reverence and commitment. The symbolism and ritual importance of offerings further deepen their spiritual significance, fostering a connection between the worshipper and the sacred realm.

Example Problem:

Choose a religious or spiritual tradition that incorporates offerings as part of its practices, such as Buddhism, Hinduism, or indigenous traditions. Analyze the significance of offerings in this tradition, considering their symbolic meaning, objectives, and the ways in which they facilitate a connection between human beings and the divine.

Role and Function of Temples

In the context of ancient Mesopotamian mythology, rivalries among gods and goddesses played a significant role in the establishment and function of temples. Mesopotamian mythology featured a pantheon of deities, each with their own domain and sphere of influence. These gods and goddesses were believed to have distinct personalities, powers, and interests, leading to rivalries and conflicts among them.

Temples served as the earthly abodes of specific deities, acting as their residences and places of worship. Each city-state in Mesopotamia had its own patron deity, and the temple dedicated to that deity was the center of religious and spiritual life for the community. These temples were not only places of devotion but also political and economic centers, exerting influence over the city-state's governance and resources.

The rivalry among gods and goddesses was reflected in the construction and embellishment of temples. Cities sought to build grand and magnificent temples to showcase the power and favor of their patron deities. Temples were often adorned with intricate carvings, statues, and artwork depicting the divine beings, emphasizing their importance and elevating the religious significance of the site.

The role of the temple was multi-faceted. It served as a place of offering and sacrifice, where worshipers would present material offerings and perform rituals to gain the favor of the deity. The temple was also a center of divination and prophecy, where priests or priestesses would communicate with the divine and provide guidance to the community. It functioned as an educational and cultural hub, where religious teachings, myths, and historical accounts were preserved and shared.

Moreover, temples played a crucial role in the agricultural and economic life of ancient Mesopotamia. The temples owned vast lands and controlled resources, which were used to support the temple staff and provide for the needs of the deity. The surplus produce generated from temple-owned lands contributed to the overall stability and prosperity of the community.

Temples in ancient Mesopotamia had a lasting spiritual legacy. They became important centers of pilgrimage, drawing devotees from far and wide seeking the blessings and favor of the patron deity. The spiritual teachings and practices associated with the temples were passed down through generations, contributing to the continuity and preservation of the religious traditions.

In summary, temples in ancient Mesopotamia played a central role in religious, social, and economic life. They served as sacred spaces dedicated to the worship and veneration of specific deities, reflecting the rivalries and conflicts within the pantheon. Temples functioned as places of offering, divination, education, and cultural preservation. They exerted influence over governance and resources and became centers of pilgrimage, leaving a lasting spiritual legacy in Mesopotamian mythology.

Example Exercise:

Imagine you are designing a temple for a spiritual tradition of your choice. Describe the key elements and architectural features you would incorporate.

Consider the layout, symbolism, and functionality of the space. How would you create an environment that fosters spiritual experiences, community engagement, and a sense of reverence?

Rituals and Practices in Temples

In the context of ancient Mesopotamian mythology, the rituals and practices conducted within temples played a crucial role in engaging with the divine and maintaining a harmonious relationship with the gods and goddesses.

Prayers were a fundamental aspect of temple rituals. Worshippers would offer prayers to the deities, expressing their gratitude, seeking blessings, or making requests. These prayers were often accompanied by specific gestures, such as raising the hands or bowing, to show reverence and humility. Priests, as intermediaries between humans and the divine, would lead the prayers and offer supplications on behalf of the community.

Meditation and contemplation were also important practices within temples. These practices involved focusing one's mind and attuning oneself to the presence of the divine. By entering a state of deep concentration or mindfulness, individuals sought to connect with the gods and receive spiritual insights or guidance.

Chants and hymns were commonly performed in temples. These melodic and rhythmic compositions were dedicated to specific deities and were believed to have the power to invoke their presence. Chants and hymns created an atmosphere of reverence and heightened the participants' spiritual experiences.

Offerings were a central component of temple rituals. Worshippers would bring material offerings, such as food, flowers, incense, or valuable objects, to present to the gods and goddesses. These offerings symbolized gratitude, devotion, and a desire for divine favor. The priests would carefully handle and arrange the offerings, ensuring their proper presentation to the deities.

Ceremonies and festivals were celebrated within temples to honor specific deities or commemorate important events. These events often involved elaborate rituals, processions, and performances. Festivals provided opportunities for communal participation and joyous celebration, fostering a sense of unity and shared religious identity.

The rituals and practices within temples were guided by established protocols and traditions. Priests, who underwent rigorous training and initiation, played a vital role in conducting these rituals and maintaining the sanctity of the temple.

They were responsible for upholding the proper rituals, reciting sacred texts, and performing purification ceremonies.

The rituals and practices conducted within ancient Mesopotamian temples left a profound spiritual legacy. They shaped the religious beliefs, values, and experiences of the worshipers, offering a sense of connection with the divine and a framework for understanding their place in the cosmos. The knowledge and wisdom associated with these rituals were passed down through generations, contributing to the continuity and preservation of ancient Mesopotamian mythology and spiritual traditions.

In summary, rituals and practices within ancient Mesopotamian temples were essential for engaging with the divine. Prayers, meditations, chants, and offerings provided avenues for expressing devotion, seeking blessings, and connecting with the gods and goddesses. Ceremonies and festivals celebrated within temples fostered communal participation and a sense of religious unity. These rituals and practices formed a significant part of the spiritual legacy in ancient Mesopotamian mythology, shaping the beliefs and experiences of worshippers and transmitting religious traditions across generations.

Example Problem:

Research a specific temple from any religious or spiritual tradition. Describe the rituals and practices that take place in this temple, including the specific actions, prayers, or offerings involved. Analyze how these rituals contribute to the spiritual experiences of the participants and the overall significance of the temple in the context of the tradition.

Social and Cultural Impact of Temples

In ancient Mesopotamian mythology, temples held significant social and cultural importance within the communities they served. They were not just places of religious worship but also acted as vital centers for social interaction, education, and community development.

One of the primary social impacts of temples was the creation of a sense of community and belonging. People from various backgrounds and social strata would come together in temples to participate in rituals, ceremonies, and festivals. These shared religious experiences fostered a sense of unity and solidarity among the worshippers. Temples provided a common space where individuals could connect with others who shared similar beliefs, values, and traditions, strengthening social bonds and fostering a sense of collective identity.

Temples also played a role in education and knowledge dissemination. They often served as centers of learning, where priests and scholars imparted religious teachings, myths, and rituals to the community. Temples housed libraries and archives that preserved important texts, historical records, and religious literature. This facilitated the transmission of cultural and historical knowledge across generations, contributing to the preservation and continuity of ancient Mesopotamian mythology.

Furthermore, temples served as centers for social welfare and charity. They were often involved in distributing resources, providing aid to the needy, and organizing communal feasts or distributions. Temples acted as institutions that supported the well-being of the community, offering a safety net for those in need and promoting a sense of compassion and care.

The cultural impact of temples extended beyond the immediate community to the broader society. Temples served as architectural and artistic marvels, showcasing the grandeur and artistic achievements of ancient Mesopotamian civilization. Elaborate temple structures with intricate carvings, statues, and artwork reflected the cultural and aesthetic values of the society. Temples also acted as centers for cultural events and performances, including music, dance, and theater, which enriched the cultural life of the community.

Moreover, the influence of temples extended into the political realm. Temples often held considerable wealth and resources, making them important economic and political entities. Temples were involved in economic activities, such as managing agricultural lands, receiving tributes, and engaging in trade. They played a role in the political administration of the region, as the priests held significant influence and often served as advisors to rulers. The close association between temples and political power further solidified the temples' social and cultural significance.

In summary, temples in ancient Mesopotamian mythology had profound social and cultural impacts. They acted as communal spaces where people came together, fostering a sense of community and shared identity. Temples served as centers of education, preserving and transmitting cultural and religious knowledge. They also played roles in social welfare, charity, and cultural enrichment. Temples showcased the artistic and architectural achievements of the civilization and held economic and political influence. The social and cultural impact of temples contributed to the cohesion, identity, and development of ancient Mesopotamian society.

Example Exercise:

Discuss the social and cultural impact of temples in a specific region or community. Analyze how temples contribute to community cohesion, cultural preservation, and the transmission of values and traditions. Consider the role of temples in organizing social events, festivals, and charitable activities that benefit both the community and the wider society.

In conclusion, offerings and temples hold significant roles in religious and spiritual practices. Offerings are acts of devotion and communication with the divine, while temples serve as sacred spaces where rituals, worship, and community gatherings take place. They foster connections between individuals and the divine, provide opportunities for spiritual experiences, and have profound social and cultural impacts within communities. Understanding the significance of offerings and temples enriches our comprehension of religious and spiritual practices across different cultures and historical periods.

Personal Offerings and Private Worship

In addition to communal practices and offerings made in temples, many religious and spiritual traditions also emphasize the importance of personal offerings and private worship. These individual acts of devotion allow practitioners to establish a direct connection with the divine and cultivate a deeper spiritual relationship on a personal level. In this section, we will explore the significance of personal offerings and private worship, the objectives they serve, and their role in fostering spiritual growth and connection.

Significance of Personal Offerings

In ancient Mesopotamian culture, personal offerings held great significance as they represented the individual's personal devotion and relationship with the divine. These offerings were often made in private settings, allowing for a more intimate and personal connection with the spiritual realm.

Personal offerings could take the form of physical objects, such as precious items, food, or symbolic representations, which were placed on personal altars or dedicated spaces within the home. These objects held personal meaning and were offered as a token of gratitude, reverence, or supplication. They served as physical manifestations of the individual's spiritual intentions and desires.

Prayers and meditations were also common forms of personal offerings in ancient Mesopotamian culture. Individuals would engage in heartfelt prayers, expressing their gratitude, seeking guidance, or making requests to the divine. Through these prayers, individuals established a direct line of communication with the gods and goddesses, sharing their innermost thoughts, concerns, and aspirations.

Acts of service and devotion were another way individuals expressed their personal offerings. This could involve performing acts of kindness and generosity towards others, engaging in acts of selflessness, or dedicating their time and energy to a specific religious or spiritual cause. By offering their own efforts and resources, individuals demonstrated their commitment and devotion to the divine.

Creativity and artistic expression also played a role in personal offerings. Individuals would create artwork, poetry, or music that was inspired by their spiritual experiences or as a means of expressing their devotion. These creative offerings were seen as a way to channel divine inspiration and to share one's personal connection with the divine with others.

The significance of personal offerings in ancient Mesopotamian culture was twofold. Firstly, they served as a means for individuals to express their gratitude, devotion, and desires to the gods and goddesses. Personal offerings were a way to establish a personal connection with the divine and seek their favor, blessings, or guidance.

Secondly, personal offerings were seen as acts of reciprocity and mutual exchange. By offering something of personal value, individuals demonstrated their willingness to give back and participate in the cosmic order. It was believed that by making personal offerings, individuals could maintain a harmonious relationship with the gods and goddesses and ensure their favor and protection.

Overall, personal offerings held great significance in ancient Mesopotamian culture as they represented the individual's personal devotion, gratitude, and desire for a direct and intimate connection with the divine. Whether through physical objects, prayers, acts of service, or artistic expressions, personal offerings allowed individuals to express their spirituality in a personal and meaningful way.

Example Exercise:

Create a personal altar or sacred space in your home. Select objects, symbols, or images that hold personal significance and represent your spiritual journey. Write a reflection on the meaning of each item and how it contributes to your personal connection with the divine. Consider how this personal space can serve as a focal point for your private worship and offerings.

Objectives of Private Worship

In ancient Mesopotamian culture, private worship played a crucial role in individuals' spiritual lives, offering them a dedicated space for personal connection and exploration of their relationship with the divine. The objectives of private worship can be summarized as follows:

Introspection and Self-Reflection: Private worship provides a sacred and secluded environment where individuals can turn their attention inward. It allows for self-reflection, introspection, and examination of one's thoughts, emotions, and spiritual journey. Through personal rituals, prayers, or meditative practices, individuals can gain insight, clarity, and a deeper understanding of themselves and their connection to the divine.

Personal Connection with the Divine: Private worship enables individuals to establish a personal and intimate relationship with the gods and goddesses of the Mesopotamian pantheon. In the privacy of their own space, individuals can express their devotion, gratitude, and desires directly to the divine without external distractions. This personal connection fosters a sense of closeness, trust, and companionship with the divine beings.

Tailored Spiritual Practices: Private worship allows individuals to tailor their spiritual practices to their specific needs and aspirations. Each person's spiritual journey is unique, and private worship provides the flexibility to incorporate rituals, prayers, or meditative techniques that resonate with their beliefs and goals. It allows for the exploration of different spiritual paths, rituals, or traditions that align with an individual's personal spiritual inclinations.

Personal Growth and Transformation: Private worship provides a space for personal growth, transformation, and spiritual development. Through regular and dedicated private rituals, individuals can cultivate spiritual qualities such as compassion, gratitude, patience, and mindfulness. Private worship allows for the nurturing of one's spiritual potential, leading to personal transformation, expanded awareness, and a deeper connection with the divine.

Healing and Emotional Support: Private worship offers a sanctuary for emotional healing and support. In times of difficulty, stress, or emotional turmoil, individuals can turn to private worship as a means of solace, comfort, and guidance.

Through prayers, offerings, or meditative practices, individuals can seek solace, express their emotions, and find strength and resilience in their spiritual beliefs.

Flexibility and Convenience: Private worship provides individuals with the convenience and flexibility to engage in spiritual practices according to their own schedule and preferences. It allows for spontaneity, adaptability, and the freedom to explore different aspects of one's spirituality without external constraints. Private worship can be practiced in the comfort of one's home, nature, or any other suitable location, offering a sense of familiarity and personal connection.

Overall, private worship in ancient Mesopotamian culture served as a means for individuals to engage in personal, tailored, and intimate spiritual practices. It provided a space for self-reflection, personal growth, and a direct connection with the divine, enabling individuals to cultivate their spirituality, seek guidance, and find solace in their beliefs and practices.

Example Problem:

Choose a spiritual or religious tradition that emphasizes private worship, such as Buddhism, Wicca, or Sufism. Research and describe the objectives of private worship in this tradition, considering the spiritual goals it aims to achieve and the practices involved. Discuss how private worship contributes to the practitioner's spiritual development and connection with the divine.

Rituals and Practices in Private Worship

In ancient Mesopotamian culture, private worship offered individuals the opportunity to engage in rituals and practices tailored to their personal spiritual needs and preferences. The rituals and practices in private worship were deeply personal and allowed individuals to establish a direct and intimate connection with the divine. Here are some examples of rituals and practices that were commonly observed in private worship:

Personal Prayers: Individuals would offer personal prayers in the privacy of their own space, expressing their devotion, gratitude, and desires to the gods and goddesses of the Mesopotamian pantheon. These prayers were heartfelt and often included specific requests, expressions of thanksgiving, or seeking guidance and protection.

Meditative Practices: Meditation was a common practice in private worship, allowing individuals to quiet their minds, cultivate inner peace, and deepen their spiritual connection. Meditation techniques could involve focused breathing, visualization, or mantra repetition to quiet the mental chatter and attain a state of heightened awareness.

Offerings and Offeratory Rituals: Individuals would make offerings to the gods and goddesses as a way of demonstrating their devotion and gratitude. These offerings could include food, drink, incense, or symbolic objects. Offeratory rituals were performed to present the offerings to the divine, accompanied by prayers and gestures of reverence.

Sacred Art and Symbolism: Many practitioners of private worship would create sacred artwork, such as sculptures, paintings, or amulets, which symbolized their spiritual beliefs and served as objects of devotion. These artistic expressions were considered potent vehicles for connecting with the divine and conveying personal intentions and aspirations.

Personal Altars and Sacred Spaces: Individuals would often create personal altars or sacred spaces within their homes or in natural settings to serve as focal points for their private worship. These altars would be adorned with sacred objects, images, or symbols that held personal significance and facilitated a sense of sacredness and devotion.

Reflection and Contemplation: Private worship provided a space for introspection, reflection, and contemplation. Individuals would engage in self-reflection, journaling, or contemplative practices to explore their thoughts, emotions, and spiritual experiences. This introspective process allowed for personal growth, self-awareness, and a deeper understanding of one's spiritual path.

Ritual Cleansing and Purification: Ritual cleansing and purification were often incorporated into private worship practices to prepare oneself for spiritual connection. This could involve ritual bathing, smudging with sacred herbs, or symbolic gestures of purification to cleanse the body, mind, and spirit of any negative energies or distractions.

Devotional Practices: Devotional practices in private worship included the recitation of hymns, chants, or mantras dedicated to specific gods or goddesses. These practices were performed with heartfelt devotion and were believed to invoke the presence and blessings of the divine.

It is important to note that the specific rituals and practices in private worship varied among individuals and were influenced by personal beliefs, family traditions, and regional customs. Private worship allowed for flexibility and personalization, giving individuals the freedom to develop their own unique rituals and practices that resonated with their spiritual inclinations and aspirations.

Example Exercise:

Design a personal ritual for private worship based on a spiritual or religious tradition of your choice. Outline the steps, intentions, and symbolism involved in the ritual. Consider the specific practices, such as meditation, visualization, or the use of sacred objects or herbs. Reflect on how this ritual promotes personal connection with the divine and supports your spiritual journey.

Balancing Personal and Communal Practices

In ancient Mesopotamian culture, there was a recognition of the importance of both personal and communal practices in maintaining a balanced spiritual life. While personal offerings and private worship allowed individuals to have intimate and individual connections with the divine, communal rituals and practices played a vital role in fostering a sense of community and shared identity.

Communal practices, such as participating in temple rituals and attending religious festivals, provided opportunities for individuals to come together as a community and engage in collective worship and celebration. These communal rituals often involved elaborate ceremonies, processions, music, and dancing, creating a festive and joyous atmosphere. By participating in these communal practices, individuals experienced a sense of belonging and unity, reinforcing social bonds and shared values.

Engaging in communal practices also allowed for the transmission of cultural and spiritual knowledge from generation to generation. The communal rituals served as a way to preserve and pass on religious traditions, myths, and teachings. They provided a space for learning, storytelling, and the sharing of wisdom among community members.

Furthermore, communal practices played a significant role in maintaining social cohesion and harmony within the community. The shared rituals and offerings helped establish a sense of order and shared purpose, fostering a collective understanding of the relationship between humans and the divine. By participating in these rituals together, individuals affirmed their commitment to the community and the spiritual beliefs that united them.

While personal offerings and private worship allowed individuals to have their own personal spiritual experiences and develop a deeper understanding of their individual paths, communal practices complemented these personal practices by fostering a sense of community, providing opportunities for collective celebration, and reinforcing social bonds.

Finding a balance between personal and communal practices was important in ancient Mesopotamian culture, as it allowed individuals to cultivate a well-rounded spiritual experience. It recognized the significance of both individual growth and community engagement in the pursuit of spiritual fulfillment. By participating in both personal and communal practices, individuals were able to nurture their own spiritual development while also contributing to the collective spiritual life of the community.

Example Problem:

Discuss the importance of balancing personal and communal practices in a specific religious or spiritual tradition. Analyze how the tradition encourages practitioners to engage in both personal offerings and communal rituals. Reflect on the benefits and challenges of balancing these two aspects of spiritual practice.

In conclusion, personal offerings and private worship hold significant value in religious and spiritual traditions. They provide individuals with opportunities for personal connection, introspection, and spiritual growth. Through personal offerings and private rituals, practitioners establish a direct relationship with the divine, cultivate their spiritual path, and deepen their understanding of their own beliefs and practices. Balancing personal and communal practices allows for a holistic spiritual experience that integrates individual devotion and community engagement.

Ethical Considerations and Intentions in Offerings

When engaging in the practice of making offerings, it is essential to consider the ethical dimensions and intentions behind these acts of devotion. While offerings are often seen as gestures of reverence and gratitude, they also have the potential to raise complex ethical questions and reflect the values and intentions of the practitioner. In this section, we will explore the ethical considerations associated with offerings and the importance of cultivating intentions that align with personal and communal well-being.

Ethical Considerations in Offerings

In ancient Mesopotamian culture, ethical considerations played a significant role in the making of offerings. The act of offering involved the use of resources, whether it be food, objects, or other materials, and the interaction between humans and the divine. It was important for practitioners to reflect upon the ethical implications of their offerings and to approach them with a sense of responsibility and mindfulness.

One important ethical consideration was the sustainability of the resources used in offerings. Ancient Mesopotamians recognized the importance of preserving the Earth's resources and maintaining a balance in the natural world. They understood that overconsumption or wastefulness in offerings could have negative consequences on the environment and future generations. As a result, they sought to make offerings that were reasonable, respectful, and mindful of the availability and replenishment of resources.

Another ethical consideration in offerings was the potential harm caused to living beings. In some instances, offerings involved the sacrifice of animals, such as lambs or birds, as a means of establishing a connection with the divine. However, practitioners were expected to carry out these acts with reverence, ensuring that the animals were treated with care and compassion. Sacrificial offerings were seen as acts of devotion rather than acts of cruelty, and practitioners were encouraged to reflect upon the significance and purpose of such offerings.

Additionally, the cultural and social context in which offerings were made played a role in ethical considerations. Ancient Mesopotamians were mindful of the impact of their actions on the community and the wider society. Offerings were made within the framework of cultural and religious traditions, and practitioners were expected to respect the beliefs and practices of others. They were encouraged to offer with humility and to avoid actions that could cause harm, conflict, or disrespect to others.

Overall, the ethical considerations in offerings in ancient Mesopotamian culture revolved around principles such as compassion, respect, and ecological stewardship. Practitioners were encouraged to reflect on their intentions and actions, to consider the sustainability of resources, to approach sacrifices with reverence, and to uphold ethical values within the cultural and social context of their offerings. By doing so, they sought to maintain a harmonious relationship with the divine, the natural world, and their fellow human beings.

Example Problem:

Research a specific religious or spiritual tradition that emphasizes offerings, such as Hinduism, Indigenous traditions, or modern Paganism. Identify any ethical guidelines or principles related to offerings within this tradition. Analyze how these guidelines address concerns such as resource sustainability, respect for living beings, and cultural sensitivity. Discuss how these ethical considerations contribute to a more conscientious and responsible approach to offerings.

Intentions in Offerings

In ancient Mesopotamian culture, intentions were of utmost importance in the practice of making offerings. The underlying motivations and intentions behind an offering determined its significance and impact. It was understood that the energy and intention infused into the offering could influence the spiritual connection and response from the divine.

Gratitude was a common intention in offerings. Ancient Mesopotamians recognized the blessings and abundance provided by the gods and sought to express their appreciation through offerings. They acknowledged the divine as the source of their well-being, sustenance, and protection, and offering gratitude was a way to honor and acknowledge these gifts.

Humility was another important intention in offerings. Recognizing the vastness and power of the divine, individuals approached offerings with a sense of reverence and respect. They acknowledged their own limitations and the need for divine assistance and guidance. Through humble offerings, they sought to establish a respectful and harmonious relationship with the gods.

Healing intentions were also prevalent in offerings. Ancient Mesopotamians believed in the power of the divine to bring about physical, emotional, and spiritual healing. Offerings made with the intention of healing were seen as requests for divine intervention, restoration, and well-being. They were a means to seek divine favor and assistance in overcoming challenges or ailments.

Seeking guidance and wisdom was another common intention in offerings. Ancient Mesopotamians recognized the wisdom and knowledge possessed by the gods and sought their guidance in various aspects of life. Offerings made with the intention of seeking guidance were acts of surrender and trust, inviting divine insight and understanding.

Furthermore, the intention of fostering harmonious relationships with the divine and the natural world was significant in offerings. Ancient Mesopotamians saw themselves as interconnected with the gods and the natural forces. Through offerings, they aimed to establish and maintain a harmonious balance between humans, gods, and the natural world. This intention reflected a deep understanding of the interconnectedness and interdependence of all beings.

Overall, intentions in offerings in ancient Mesopotamian culture encompassed gratitude, humility, healing, seeking guidance, and fostering harmonious relationships. These intentions were infused into the offerings, shaping the spiritual connection between humans and the divine. By aligning their intentions with personal and communal well-being and the greater good, practitioners sought to cultivate a meaningful and transformative relationship with the gods.

Example Exercise:

Reflect on your own intentions when making offerings. Choose a specific offering practice or ritual, such as offering food to a deity or making a symbolic gesture of gratitude to nature. Write a personal reflection on your intentions behind this offering. Consider how your intentions align with your values, spiritual beliefs, and the well-being of yourself, others, and the environment.

Balancing Self-Interest and Altruism

In ancient Mesopotamian culture, the act of making offerings involved a delicate balance between self-interest and altruism. While individuals sought personal benefits from their offerings, there was also an understanding of the importance of considering the well-being of others and the collective. Balancing self-interest and altruism in offerings reflected the interconnectedness of individuals within their communities and the broader society.

Practitioners were encouraged to cultivate a sense of altruism and extend their intentions beyond personal needs. This involved considering the impact of their offerings on others and dedicating resources for the benefit of the community. For example, individuals might offer food, clothing, or other necessities to those in need or contribute to communal projects that improved the well-being of the community as a whole. These acts of altruism demonstrated a recognition of the interconnected nature of human existence and the responsibility to contribute to the welfare of others.

Furthermore, practitioners could dedicate their offerings to broader causes or spiritual principles that transcended personal interests. They could dedicate offerings to the gods or goddesses associated with justice, compassion, or social harmony, thereby aligning their intentions with the greater good. This dedication reflected an understanding that the effects of their offerings could extend beyond personal desires and contribute to the betterment of society.

Balancing self-interest and altruism in offerings required practitioners to consider the broader implications of their actions. It called for an awareness of the social and cultural context in which they lived and the potential impact their offerings could have on others. By incorporating altruistic intentions into their offerings, individuals sought to foster a sense of communal well-being and promote a more harmonious and interconnected society.

Overall, in the ancient Mesopotamian context, the practice of offerings encouraged practitioners to strike a balance between their personal needs and the welfare of the community. While seeking personal benefits and growth, practitioners were also encouraged to cultivate a sense of altruism and consider the broader impact of their offerings. This balanced approach aimed to foster a harmonious coexistence and a collective commitment to the well-being of all.

Example Problem:

Discuss the ethical tension between self-interest and altruism in offerings. Consider the perspectives of different religious or spiritual traditions. Explore how these traditions encourage practitioners to balance personal needs and desires with the well-being of others and the greater community. Reflect on the challenges and benefits of cultivating a more altruistic approach to offerings.

Cultural Sensitivity and Appropriation

Cultural sensitivity and respect are vital considerations when engaging with offerings from ancient Mesopotamian culture or any other cultural tradition. Offerings hold deep cultural and religious significance, and approaching them without proper knowledge or respect can lead to cultural appropriation, which can be disrespectful, harmful, and perpetuate stereotypes.

To avoid cultural appropriation, it is important to take the time to educate oneself about the cultural context, beliefs, and practices associated with the offerings. This may involve studying historical and cultural sources, consulting scholarly works, or engaging with members of the community who have knowledge and expertise in the particular cultural tradition.

Respecting the cultural significance of offerings involves understanding their historical and spiritual contexts and appreciating their importance within the specific cultural framework. It also requires recognizing the intellectual property rights and ownership of cultural heritage, acknowledging the contributions and perspectives of the culture from which the offerings originate, and avoiding the commodification or trivialization of sacred practices.

When engaging with offerings from another culture, it is advisable to approach them with humility, openness, and a willingness to learn. Seek guidance from knowledgeable individuals within that culture, such as scholars, practitioners, or community leaders, who can provide insights and context. This approach fosters a respectful and mutually beneficial exchange, promoting cultural understanding and appreciation.

It is important to note that cultural sensitivity extends beyond offerings themselves. It also applies to the language, symbols, clothing, and other cultural elements associated with the practice of offerings. Practitioners should be mindful of the potential misinterpretation or misuse of these elements and strive to avoid appropriative behaviors.

By approaching offerings with cultural sensitivity, respect, and a commitment to understanding, practitioners can engage with ancient Mesopotamian traditions or any other cultural practices in a responsible and meaningful way. This promotes cultural appreciation, intercultural dialogue, and the preservation of diverse cultural heritages.

Example Exercise:

Choose an offering practice from a culture different from your own. Research the cultural context, history, and significance of this offering practice. Reflect on the importance of cultural sensitivity and respect when engaging with offerings from other cultures. Discuss ways in which practitioners can honor and appreciate cultural diversity while avoiding cultural appropriation.

In conclusion, ethical considerations and intentions are fundamental aspects of offerings. By reflecting on the ethical implications of our actions, cultivating conscious intentions, and balancing self-interest with altruism, we can approach offerings with integrity, compassion, and respect. Engaging in offerings with ethical awareness enhances our spiritual practices and fosters a deeper connection with the divine, the natural world, and our fellow beings.

Chapter 4 : The Epic of Gilgamesh: Myth and Legend in Mesopotamian Literature

Welcome to the fascinating world of The Epic of Gilgamesh, one of the oldest literary works known to humanity. This ancient Mesopotamian epic takes us on a remarkable journey through the mythology, legends, and cultural beliefs of the ancient Sumerians and Babylonians. Through the epic's captivating narrative, we accompany Gilgamesh, the legendary king of Uruk, on his quest for immortality. Along the way, we encounter profound themes such as the inevitability of death, the significance of friendship, the nature of divinity, and the search for life's meaning.

Understanding the Historical and Cultural Context

To truly grasp the essence of The Epic of Gilgamesh, we must delve into the historical and cultural context of ancient Mesopotamia. Known as the "Cradle of Civilization," Mesopotamia flourished in the region between the Tigris and Euphrates rivers, present-day Iraq. Within this land, various city-states thrived, including Uruk, the vibrant backdrop for our epic tale.

Mesopotamian society revolved around a polytheistic belief system, where numerous gods and goddesses governed different facets of life. The epic beautifully reflects the cosmology and religious beliefs of the ancient Mesopotamians, weaving together a rich tapestry of mythology and legends deeply intertwined with the daily lives of its people.

Exploring Themes and Symbolism

The Epic of Gilgamesh explores timeless themes that continue to captivate readers across the ages. One such theme is humanity's eternal quest for immortality, juxtaposed against the inevitability of death. Gilgamesh's relentless pursuit of eternal life mirrors our enduring human desire to transcend mortality and achieve transcendence.

Friendship stands as another central theme within the epic, beautifully embodied in the bond between Gilgamesh and Enkidu. Their profound relationship underscores the transformative power of companionship, empathy, and mutual support. Through their friendship, the epic delves into the profound impact of human connections and the potential for personal growth.

Within the epic's narrative, we also encounter various symbols and motifs that hold immense cultural significance. For example, the cedar forest symbolizes the realm of the gods and the uncharted territories of the divine. Gilgamesh's quest to conquer the cedar forest reflects humanity's ambition to conquer the unknown and gain mastery over the forces of nature.

Unveiling the Mythological and Historical Significance

The Epic of Gilgamesh holds tremendous mythological and historical significance. As a myth, it serves as a narrative framework to explain natural phenomena, cultural customs, and social hierarchies. Through its captivating storyline, the epic showcases the Mesopotamian worldview, offering insights into their perception of the divine, the afterlife, and the human condition.

Beyond its mythological relevance, The Epic of Gilgamesh provides valuable historical insights into the social, political, and cultural dynamics of ancient Mesopotamia. It grants us a window into the governance structures, religious practices, and societal norms of the time. Moreover, the epic provides valuable historical information about the city of Uruk and its influential figures.

Examining Structure and Composition

The Epic of Gilgamesh comprises a series of narrative poems meticulously etched onto clay tablets using cuneiform script. Divided into several episodes or tablets, each presents a distinct phase of Gilgamesh's arduous journey and encounters. It is important to note that the epic has evolved over time, as it was compiled and modified by different scribes and poets, resulting in multiple versions and variations.

Scope and Objectives of the Study

The primary goal of this textbook is to delve deep into The Epic of Gilgamesh, analyzing its themes, cultural context, symbolism, and historical significance. Adopting a multidisciplinary approach, we will examine the epic from various perspectives, encompassing mythology, literature, archaeology, and history. Our objective is to equip students with a comprehensive understanding of the epic's significance within ancient Mesopotamian literature and culture.

Each chapter will explore specific aspects of the epic, presenting scholarly interpretations, critical analysis, and thought-provoking discussions. We will closely examine the characters, events, and motifs within the epic, considering their cultural, social, and spiritual implications. To encourage critical thinking and engagement, each chapter will include exercises and discussion questions that prompt students to explore diverse viewpoints and actively interact with the text.

The Epic of Gilgamesh: Overview and Context

Welcome to the immersive world of the Epic of Gilgamesh, a legendary tale that stands as one of the oldest known works of literature in human history. Originating in ancient Mesopotamia, this epic provides a captivating window into the mythological, cultural, and historical landscape of the Sumerians and Babylonians. Through its narrative, the Epic of Gilgamesh explores profound themes such as mortality, friendship, the divine, and the meaning of life.

Overview of the Epic

The Epic of Gilgamesh stands as a timeless masterpiece that takes us on a remarkable journey alongside its protagonist, Gilgamesh, the legendary king of Uruk. This epic narrative revolves around Gilgamesh's relentless pursuit of immortality, which leads him to face a series of captivating challenges, experience transformative triumphs, and undergo profound personal transformations. As we delve into the intricacies of this ancient tale, we are granted valuable insights into the human condition and the complexities of existence.

The epic is structured into distinct sections or tablets, each presenting a different phase of Gilgamesh's journey and the encounters he faces along the way. Through these tablets, we encounter a cast of fascinating characters that both aid and hinder Gilgamesh in his quest. We witness his friendship with Enkidu, a wild man created by the gods to challenge Gilgamesh, and their subsequent adventures together. We also come face to face with formidable mythical creatures, such as Humbaba, the guardian of the Cedar Forest, and the Bull of Heaven, sent by the goddess Ishtar to punish Gilgamesh. Additionally, we bear witness to the interactions between gods and humans, where divine intervention and divine justice shape the trajectory of the story.

Embedded within the narrative are profound themes that resonate with the human experience. The epic delves into the essence of humanity, exploring our desires, fears, and aspirations. It examines the pursuit of power and knowledge, as Gilgamesh grapples with his own hubris and seeks to transcend the limitations of mortality. Furthermore, the epic explores the profound impact of personal relationships, showcasing the transformative power of friendship, love, and loss. Through Gilgamesh's trials and tribulations, we are invited to reflect on our own mortal existence and the significance of our connections with others.

The Epic of Gilgamesh serves as a testament to the enduring power of storytelling and its ability to transcend time and culture. It offers us a window into the past, allowing us to connect with the ancient world and gain a deeper understanding of our shared humanity. As we immerse ourselves in this epic journey, we are reminded of the eternal themes that continue to shape our lives and the timeless questions that have plagued humankind since the dawn of civilization.

Cultural and Historical Context

The pantheon of gods in Mesopotamian mythology was vast and complex, with each deity possessing distinct attributes and responsibilities. These gods were believed to govern natural phenomena, such as the sun, moon, rivers, and storms, as well as human affairs, including fertility, war, and wisdom. In the Epic of Gilgamesh, the interactions between gods and humans underscore the intricate relationship between the mortal and divine realms.

Additionally, the epic reflects the societal structure of ancient Mesopotamia, where kingship held significant importance. Gilgamesh, as the king of Uruk, embodies the ideals and responsibilities associated with rulership. His journey and encounters serve as a reflection of the challenges faced by kings in their quest for power, wisdom, and the preservation of their legacy.

Furthermore, the Epic of Gilgamesh provides insights into the historical context of ancient Mesopotamia. While the epic itself is a work of mythology and literature, it contains elements that offer glimpses into the historical realities of the time. References to geographical locations, cultural practices, and the presence of historical figures within the narrative contribute to our understanding of the social, political, and economic dynamics of ancient Mesopotamia.

Exercise : Research and discuss the historical and archaeological evidence that supports the existence of the city of Uruk and its significance in ancient Mesopotamian civilization. Explore the role of religion and mythology in shaping societal structures and practices in Mesopotamian culture.

The Epic of Gilgamesh not only serves as a captivating literary masterpiece but also provides valuable insights into the cultural and historical context of ancient Mesopotamia. By examining the religious beliefs, societal structures, and historical background of the region, we gain a deeper appreciation for the themes, symbols, and characters within the epic. Through this exploration, we can better understand the significance of the epic within its cultural milieu and its enduring impact on human storytelling and spiritual traditions.

Themes and Symbolism

The epic also incorporates the symbolism of the serpent, which appears in various episodes. In Mesopotamian mythology, the serpent was associated with wisdom, knowledge, and both positive and negative forces. In the story of Gilgamesh, the serpent plays a significant role in the loss of immortality, highlighting the complex relationship between power, wisdom, and the consequences of human actions.

Another symbol present in the epic is the flood. The flood motif holds great cultural significance in Mesopotamian mythology and is also found in other ancient traditions, such as the story of Noah's Ark in the Hebrew Bible. The flood represents a cataclysmic event that brings about destruction and renewal, emphasizing the cyclical nature of life and the potential for rebirth and transformation.

Exercise : Choose a symbol from the Epic of Gilgamesh and analyze its significance within the narrative. Discuss how the symbol contributes to the exploration of the themes and enhances the overall meaning of the epic.

The epic also delves into the concept of divinity and the relationship between gods and humans. It raises questions about the nature of divinity, the power dynamics between mortals and deities, and the role of gods in human affairs. Through the interactions between Gilgamesh and the gods, the epic explores the complexities of divine intervention and the consequences of challenging or defying the divine order.

Additionally, the theme of the journey serves as a powerful metaphor in the epic. Gilgamesh's physical and spiritual journey represents the quest for self-discovery, personal growth, and the search for meaning and purpose in life. It reflects the universal human experience of grappling with existential questions and the pursuit of knowledge and wisdom.

Exercise: Discuss the symbolism of the serpent in the Epic of Gilgamesh and compare it to the serpent symbolism in other mythological traditions. What common themes and interpretations emerge? How does the serpent symbol contribute to the overall meaning of the epic?

By exploring the themes and symbolism within the Epic of Gilgamesh, we gain a deeper understanding of the universal aspects of the human experience and the complexities of our existence. The epic invites us to reflect on our quest for immortality, the transformative power of friendship, the role of symbolism in storytelling, and the intricate dynamics between mortals and deities. Through these explorations, we can engage in critical thinking and thoughtful discussions that connect the ancient Mesopotamian culture to our own spiritual and philosophical inquiries.

Significance and Influence

In addition to its historical significance, the Epic of Gilgamesh has had a profound influence on subsequent literary and cultural traditions. It is considered one of the earliest surviving works of literature and has influenced numerous stories, myths, and legends that followed.

The themes and motifs present in the epic have resonated with writers and thinkers throughout history. The quest for immortality, the power of friendship, and the exploration of human existence have found echoes in works across different cultures and time periods. For example, the biblical story of Noah's Ark bears similarities to the flood narrative in the Epic of Gilgamesh, indicating the influence of Mesopotamian mythology on later religious and literary traditions.

Exercise: Compare and contrast the flood narratives in the Epic of Gilgamesh and the story of Noah's Ark in the Hebrew Bible. Discuss the similarities and differences in themes, symbolism, and the portrayal of human-divine relationships.

The epic's influence extends beyond literature and has permeated other artistic mediums as well. Its themes and characters have been depicted in visual art, including ancient Mesopotamian sculptures and reliefs. Additionally, the epic's enduring legacy can be seen in contemporary adaptations, such as theatrical performances, films, and even video games, where the story of Gilgamesh continues to captivate audiences and inspire new interpretations.

Exercise: Choose a contemporary adaptation or interpretation of the Epic of Gilgamesh, such as a film, play, or novel, and analyze how it reimagines the themes and characters of the original epic. Discuss the creative choices made by the adaptation and their impact on the overall meaning and relevance of the story.

The Epic of Gilgamesh's significance lies not only in its historical and cultural value but also in its ability to transcend time and connect with readers and audiences across generations. Its exploration of universal themes, its rich symbolism, and its portrayal of complex human relationships continue to resonate with individuals seeking to understand their own place in the world and grapple with profound existential questions.

Through studying the epic and engaging in critical analysis and discussion, we can gain a deeper appreciation for its enduring influence and its ability to bridge the gap between ancient civilizations and contemporary society. By exploring the significance and influence of the Epic of Gilgamesh, we can foster a greater understanding of the interconnectedness of human culture and the power of storytelling to shape our collective consciousness.

Characters and Their Roles

Gilgamesh: The Hero-King

Gilgamesh's character represents the archetype of the hero-king, a figure found in various mythologies and ancient epics. As a hero, Gilgamesh possesses exceptional physical strength and courage, demonstrated through his numerous exploits and battles. His feats of strength and bravery, such as his victorious encounter with the monstrous Humbaba, exemplify his heroic qualities.

However, Gilgamesh's character is not limited to his physical prowess. He also embodies the flaws and struggles of a human being. His arrogance and abuse of power in the early stages of the epic reveal his flawed nature, as he acts without regard for the well-being of his subjects. This hubris becomes a driving force behind his quest for immortality, as he seeks to transcend the limitations of his mortality and establish his legacy as a god-like figure.

Gilgamesh's journey, both physical and spiritual, serves as a vehicle for his personal growth and self-discovery. Through his encounters with Enkidu, the loss of his companion, and his subsequent confrontations with mortality and the divine, Gilgamesh undergoes a transformation. He learns valuable lessons about the ephemeral nature of human existence and the importance of embracing the present moment.

Exercise: Explore the concept of the hero-king archetype in other mythological and literary traditions, such as King Arthur in Arthurian legends or Hercules in Greek mythology. Compare and contrast the characteristics and journeys of these hero-kings with that of Gilgamesh. Discuss the similarities and differences in their roles, motivations, and character development.

Gilgamesh's quest for immortality also raises profound philosophical questions about the nature of life, death, and the meaning of existence. As a mortal ruler, he grapples with the inevitability of death and the fleeting nature of human achievements. His journey to the realm of the gods and his encounter with

Utnapishtim, the immortal survivor of the great flood, expose him to different perspectives on life and the afterlife.

Through Gilgamesh's experiences, the epic explores the limitations of human power and the need for acceptance and humility in the face of mortality. It prompts us to reflect on our own mortality and consider the value of embracing the present moment, cherishing our relationships, and leaving a positive impact on the world.

Exercise: Write a reflective essay on the theme of mortality and the quest for immortality in the Epic of Gilgamesh. Discuss how Gilgamesh's journey and experiences can offer insights and lessons for contemporary individuals seeking to find meaning and navigate the complexities of existence.

Gilgamesh's character serves as a vehicle for exploring universal human experiences and dilemmas. His strengths and weaknesses, his aspirations and challenges, mirror the complexities of the human condition. By studying Gilgamesh as a hero-king, we gain a deeper understanding of our own desires, ambitions, and the transformative potential of our personal journeys.

Enkidu: The Wild Companion

Enkidu's introduction in the epic presents him as a wild and untamed being, living harmoniously with nature. He is described as a creature of the wilderness, roaming with the animals and possessing incredible strength. Enkidu's initial encounter with Gilgamesh, where they engage in a fierce battle, serves as a pivotal moment in the epic. This clash between civilization and the wild represents the dichotomy between the structured, urban world of Uruk and the untamed, primal forces of nature.

However, it is through their intense confrontation that Enkidu and Gilgamesh forge a profound connection. Recognizing their shared strength and understanding, they abandon their rivalry and embrace a deep bond of friendship. Enkidu's transformation from a wild creature to a trusted companion symbolizes the power of human connection and the potential for personal growth through relationships.

Enkidu's journey alongside Gilgamesh exposes him to the wonders and challenges of human civilization. He experiences the joys and sorrows of human existence, partaking in epic battles, engaging with gods and goddesses, and confronting the fragility of life. Through his interactions with Gilgamesh, Enkidu learns about the complexities of morality, the importance of empathy, and the value of friendship in navigating the world.

Enkidu's role as Gilgamesh's loyal companion and confidant provides a counterbalance to the king's ambitions and impulsiveness. He offers wisdom, guidance, and emotional support to Gilgamesh, tempering his excesses and encouraging him to seek meaning beyond his quest for immortality. Enkidu's death, which deeply affects Gilgamesh, further emphasizes the fleeting nature of human life and the profound impact of loss.

Exercise: Write a character analysis comparing Enkidu to other mythical or literary companions, such as Don Quixote's faithful sidekick, Sancho Panza, or Samwise Gamgee from J.R.R. Tolkien's "The Lord of the Rings." Discuss the similarities and differences in their roles, personalities, and their impact on the central character's journey.

Enkidu's character also represents the human capacity for transformation and the potential for growth and redemption. Through his interactions with Gilgamesh, Enkidu sheds his primitive nature and acquires knowledge, compassion, and a sense of purpose. His journey serves as a testament to the transformative power of love, friendship, and human connection.

Exercise: Reflect on the significance of Enkidu's character in the context of the human-nature relationship. How does Enkidu's connection to the wilderness and his subsequent integration into human society highlight the interdependence between humans and the natural world? Discuss the lessons that can be drawn from Enkidu's story in terms of our relationship with the environment and the importance of preserving our connection to nature.

Enkidu's character in the Epic of Gilgamesh encapsulates the complexity and potential for growth within each individual. From his wild origins to his profound bond with Gilgamesh, Enkidu's journey explores themes of friendship, love, and personal transformation. His story serves as a reminder of the transformative power of human connection, the importance of empathy and understanding, and the capacity for growth and redemption within us all.

The Gods and Goddesses

The gods and goddesses in the Epic of Gilgamesh are depicted as powerful and enigmatic beings who possess extraordinary abilities and knowledge. They are believed to control various aspects of the natural world and human existence, such as fertility, justice, and the cycles of life and death. These divine entities serve as intermediaries between the mortal realm and the divine realm, influencing and intervening in the lives of humans.

Shamash, the sun god, plays a significant role in the epic as a wise and just deity. He serves as a moral compass for Gilgamesh, guiding him on his journey and offering him protection. Shamash represents divine justice and the ultimate arbiter of fate, ensuring that actions are met with appropriate consequences. His presence in the narrative highlights the Mesopotamian belief in a cosmic order and the notion that even the mightiest of kings are subject to divine judgment.

Ishtar, the goddess of love and war, embodies both creative and destructive forces. She is depicted as passionate and impulsive, with the power to bestow great blessings or unleash devastating disasters upon humanity. Ishtar's interactions with the mortal characters, particularly her pursuit of Gilgamesh, illustrate the complexities of divine-human relationships and the potential consequences of crossing divine boundaries. Her character serves as a cautionary tale, warning against the dangers of hubris and the consequences of challenging the gods.

Exercise: Research and discuss the role of other Mesopotamian gods and goddesses, such as Enlil, Ea, and Ninsun, in the Epic of Gilgamesh. Analyze their characteristics, motivations, and the influence they exert on the mortal characters. Consider how their interactions shape the narrative and contribute to the overall themes of the epic.

The gods and goddesses in the epic are not mere spectators or distant figures; they actively engage with the mortal realm and influence its course. Their presence highlights the belief in a reciprocal relationship between gods and humans, where mortals offer worship, sacrifices, and prayers to gain the favor and protection of the divine beings. Conversely, the gods expect loyalty, obedience, and reverence from their human subjects.

Exercise: Explore the concept of divine intervention in different mythological traditions. Compare and contrast the role of gods and goddesses in the Epic of Gilgamesh with those in other mythological narratives, such as Greek mythology or Norse mythology. Analyze the motivations, interactions, and impact of the divine on mortal characters and their journeys.

The gods and goddesses in the Epic of Gilgamesh serve as more than just supernatural entities; they embody various human attributes and emotions. Through their interactions with the mortal characters, they explore themes such as power, love, jealousy, and mortality. They challenge the characters' beliefs, test their courage, and ultimately shape their destinies. The presence of the divine in the epic adds depth and complexity to the narrative, highlighting the interplay between mortal and immortal realms and providing insights into the ancient Mesopotamian worldview.

Exercise: Select a contemporary literary work or film that features the interaction between humans and deities. Analyze the portrayal of gods or god-like figures in the chosen work and compare it to the depiction of gods in the Epic of Gilgamesh. Discuss the similarities, differences, and underlying themes conveyed through the representation of divine beings in different cultural and historical contexts.

Supporting Characters

Utnapishtim is a crucial supporting character in the Epic of Gilgamesh. He is the only human who has achieved immortality, having been granted this gift by the gods after surviving the great flood. Utnapishtim serves as a mentor figure to Gilgamesh, offering him wisdom and insights into the nature of life and death. His character raises questions about the possibility of attaining eternal life and the consequences of such a quest. Through his story, the epic explores themes of mortality, divine punishment, and the cyclical nature of existence.

Exercise 9.17: Reflect on the concept of immortality in different mythological and religious traditions. Compare and contrast the portrayal of immortality in the Epic of Gilgamesh with other narratives, such as the pursuit of the elixir of life in Chinese mythology or the promise of eternal life in Christian theology. Analyze the motivations, challenges, and implications associated with the pursuit of immortality in these different cultural contexts.

Humbaba, the fearsome guardian of the cedar forest, serves as a formidable antagonist in the epic. He embodies the forces of chaos and represents the threat of the unknown. Humbaba's defeat by Gilgamesh and Enkidu showcases the heroes' bravery and determination, as well as their ability to confront and overcome their fears. The encounter with Humbaba underscores the theme of humanity's desire to conquer the forces of nature and attain power over the unknown.

Exercise: Investigate the significance of monsters and mythical creatures in different mythological traditions. Select a mythological creature from a different cultural context, such as the sphinx in Egyptian mythology or the Nemean lion in Greek mythology, and analyze its role and symbolism. Compare and contrast the portrayal of monsters in different cultural narratives, including the representation of Humbaba in the Epic of Gilgamesh. Examine the fears, challenges, and lessons associated with these encounters.

Other supporting characters, such as Shamhat, the temple prostitute who initiates Enkidu into civilization, and Ninsun, Gilgamesh's mother and a goddess, also play important roles in the epic. Shamhat's seduction of Enkidu leads to his transformation from a wild man to a civilized human being, highlighting the themes of culture, identity, and the tension between nature and civilization. Ninsun's presence as both a mother figure and a divine being adds depth to Gilgamesh's character and reinforces the interplay between the mortal and divine realms.

Exercise 9.19: Analyze the portrayal of female characters in the Epic of Gilgamesh. Consider the roles, agency, and influence of female characters such as Shamhat and Ninsun. Discuss how their actions contribute to the overall themes and messages of the epic. Compare and contrast the representation of female characters in the epic with other mythological narratives, such as the role of goddesses in Greek mythology or the empowerment of female warriors in Norse mythology.

The supporting characters in the Epic of Gilgamesh bring a diverse range of perspectives, challenges, and insights to the narrative. Their interactions with the main protagonists shape their journeys, provide opportunities for growth and self-discovery, and deepen our understanding of the human condition and the complexities of existence. These characters add layers of meaning and nuance to the epic, highlighting the interconnectedness of individuals within a larger cosmic framework.

Character Analysis and Symbolism

Analyzing the characters in the Epic of Gilgamesh goes beyond their individual roles within the narrative. Each character carries symbolic significance, representing broader themes and concepts. Through their actions, relationships, and transformations, they embody universal human experiences and offer insights into the human condition.

Gilgamesh, as the hero-king of Uruk, represents both the heights of human achievement and the limitations of mortal existence. His quest for immortality reflects humanity's eternal longing for transcendence and the pursuit of meaning and purpose in the face of mortality. Gilgamesh's character highlights the hubris and ambition often associated with powerful rulers, as well as the profound impact of personal experiences and relationships on one's worldview.

Enkidu, initially portrayed as a wild man created by the gods, embodies the untamed aspects of human nature and our innate connection to the natural world.

His transformation from a primitive existence to a civilized companion of Gilgamesh symbolizes the potential for personal growth, the blurring of boundaries between nature and culture, and the transformative power of human relationships. Enkidu's journey mirrors the development of human consciousness and the capacity for empathy and understanding.

Exercise: Choose a character from the Epic of Gilgamesh and analyze their symbolic significance. Consider the character's actions, relationships, and transformation throughout the narrative. Identify the broader themes and concepts they represent and discuss how their symbolism contributes to the overall meaning of the epic.

In addition to Gilgamesh and Enkidu, other characters in the epic carry symbolic significance as well. For example, Utnapishtim, the survivor of the great flood, represents the possibility of transcending death and attaining immortality. His character raises profound questions about the nature of life, death, and the human quest for eternal life. Utnapishtim serves as a foil to Gilgamesh, challenging his assumptions and offering wisdom about the limits of mortal existence.

Ishtar, the goddess of love and war, symbolizes both passion and destruction. Her interactions with the mortal characters, particularly her failed attempt to seduce and control Gilgamesh, reveal the complexities of divine-human relationships and the consequences of challenging the divine order. Ishtar's character underscores the themes of power, desire, and the unpredictable nature of divine intervention.

Exercise 9.21: Select a character from the Epic of Gilgamesh and explore their symbolic significance in relation to a specific theme. Analyze the character's actions, attributes, and relationships, and discuss how they contribute to the exploration of the chosen theme. For example, you could examine the symbolism of Enkidu in relation to the theme of nature versus civilization or the symbolism of Ishtar in relation to the theme of power and desire.

By delving into the symbolic significance of the characters in the Epic of Gilgamesh, we uncover deeper layers of meaning and gain a greater understanding of the themes and messages conveyed by the narrative. The characters serve as vessels through which the complexities of human existence, desires, and aspirations are explored, inviting readers to reflect on their own journeys and the universal experiences shared by humanity across time and cultures.

Exercises and Discussion Questions

Consider the character of Gilgamesh and his journey for immortality. How does this quest reflect universal human desires and struggles? Can you draw parallels to similar quests or aspirations in other mythologies or contemporary society?

Analyze the character of Enkidu and his transformation throughout the epic. How does his relationship with Gilgamesh contribute to his personal growth and understanding of the human experience? Can you identify instances where Enkidu's connection to nature influences his actions or decisions?

Explore the role of the gods and goddesses in the epic. How do their interactions with mortal characters shape the course of events? Discuss the complexities of divine-human relationships and their portrayal in other mythological traditions.

Investigate the supporting characters in the Epic of Gilgamesh, such as Utnapishtim and Humbaba. What roles do they play in the narrative? How do they contribute to the development of the main characters and the exploration of the epic's themes?

Reflect on the symbolism of the characters in the epic. Choose one character and analyze their symbolic significance in relation to broader themes or concepts explored in the narrative.

Through these exercises and discussion questions, you are encouraged to engage critically with the characters of the Epic of Gilgamesh, exploring their complexities, symbolism, and relevance to human experience. By delving into their roles, motivations, and interactions, we unravel the layers of meaning embedded within this ancient Mesopotamian masterpiece.

Themes and Symbolism

The Quest for Immortality

One of the central themes in the Epic of Gilgamesh is the human quest for immortality. Through the character of Gilgamesh, we witness a relentless pursuit of eternal life, driven by a fear of mortality and a desire for transcendence. This theme explores the universal longing to overcome the limits of human existence and attain a form of immortality, whether through physical longevity or the preservation of one's legacy.

The concept of immortality has held great significance in human culture throughout history. It appears in various mythologies, literature, and religious traditions, reflecting the enduring fascination with the idea of transcending mortality. In Greek mythology, for example, we find the story of Tithonus, a mortal who was granted immortality by the gods but not eternal youth, leading to an existence filled with eternal aging and suffering. In Hinduism, the concept of Moksha represents liberation from the cycle of birth and death, offering the potential for transcending mortal existence.

The motivations behind the human desire for immortality are multifaceted. At its core, the longing for immortality arises from the fear and uncertainty surrounding death. Mortality is a fundamental aspect of the human condition, and the awareness of our limited time on Earth can evoke feelings of anxiety and a yearning for permanence. Immortality represents a way to overcome this existential dilemma and find solace in the idea of continued existence.

Furthermore, the desire for immortality often stems from the human drive for significance and the longing for a lasting legacy. Humans seek to leave a mark on the world, to be remembered and revered even after death. Immortality, whether through physical means or the perpetuation of one's achievements and influence, offers the promise of eternal remembrance and a form of continued existence beyond the physical realm.

The implications of the human quest for immortality are profound and far-reaching. On an individual level, the pursuit of immortality can shape one's actions, values, and priorities. It can drive individuals to seek power, accumulate wealth, or strive for achievements that will ensure their memory endures. The quest for immortality can also lead to a deeper exploration of personal and spiritual transformation, as individuals seek to transcend their mortal limitations and cultivate a sense of inner immortality through spiritual practices or the pursuit of enlightenment.

On a collective level, the desire for immortality can influence societal structures, cultural practices, and the shaping of civilizations. The quest for immortality can be seen in the construction of monumental architecture, the establishment of dynasties, or the preservation of cultural and intellectual heritage. Societies may develop rituals, traditions, and belief systems that provide a sense of continuity and transcendence, offering a collective form of immortality.

Exercise Reflect on the concept of immortality and its significance in human culture. Choose a mythological, literary, or religious tradition that explores themes of immortality and discuss its portrayal of the human longing for eternal life.

Analyze the motivations and implications of the desire for immortality within that tradition, considering how it shapes individual and collective aspirations.

By examining the concept of immortality and its significance in human culture, we gain insights into our deepest fears, desires, and aspirations. The quest for immortality speaks to our longing for permanence, meaning, and the transcendence of our mortal limitations. It invites us to contemplate the nature of existence, the fleeting nature of life, and the potential for transformation and transcendence.

Friendship and Companionship

In the Epic of Gilgamesh, the bond between Gilgamesh and Enkidu serves as a testament to the transformative power of friendship. Initially, Gilgamesh is a restless and tyrannical king, consumed by his own desires and unchecked in his actions. However, when Enkidu is created by the gods to challenge Gilgamesh, a profound shift occurs. Through their encounters and shared adventures, a deep and meaningful connection forms between them.

Their friendship is characterized by empathy, mutual support, and companionship. Enkidu serves as a mirror for Gilgamesh, providing him with a companion who understands and accepts him, flaws and all. Together, they face trials, overcome obstacles, and experience personal growth. Enkidu's presence awakens Gilgamesh to the importance of compassion, humility, and the value of human connection.

The significance of friendship extends beyond the epic itself and resonates with our own lives and the broader human experience. Friendship is a vital aspect of our emotional well-being and spiritual growth. Meaningful friendships offer a space for authenticity, vulnerability, and acceptance. They provide us with companionship, support, and a sense of belonging. Friends can offer guidance, perspective, and encouragement during challenging times, helping us navigate life's ups and downs.

Qualities that contribute to a meaningful friendship include trust, respect, empathy, and open communication. A true friend is someone who listens without judgment, offers support in times of need, and celebrates our successes. They stand by us through thick and thin, providing a safe space for self-expression and personal growth.

Throughout mythology, literature, and our own experiences, we find countless examples of the profound impact of friendship. From the loyal companionship of Frodo and Sam in J.R.R. Tolkien's "The Lord of the Rings" to the unwavering support between Harry Potter and his friends in J.K. Rowling's series, these stories remind us of the power of friendship to overcome adversity and transform lives. In our own lives, we have likely experienced the joy and comfort that true friendship brings, whether it's through shared laughter, heartfelt conversations, or being there for each other in times of need.

Friendship not only enhances our emotional well-being but also contributes to our spiritual growth. It allows us to expand our perspectives, learn from one another, and cultivate qualities such as compassion, empathy, and kindness. Through the connections we form with friends, we deepen our understanding of ourselves and the world around us.

As we reflect on the significance of friendship in our lives, we are reminded of its profound impact. It is a gift that enriches our journey and reminds us of our shared humanity. By nurturing and cherishing our friendships, we create a foundation for personal well-being, growth, and a deeper sense of connection with the world.

The Nature of Divinity

The Epic of Gilgamesh provides insights into the nature of divinity and the complex relationship between gods and mortals. The gods in the epic embody various aspects of human experience and possess both benevolent and capricious traits. Through their interactions with the mortal characters, the epic explores the dynamics of divine intervention, divine justice, and the boundaries between the divine and the human realms.

The concept of divinity varies across different mythological traditions, yet there are common threads that run through many of them. In Greek mythology, for example, the gods and goddesses are depicted as powerful beings who possess human-like emotions and motivations. They intervene in mortal affairs, often toying with humans and influencing their destinies. The gods of Mount Olympus in Greek mythology, such as Zeus, Hera, and Athena, exhibit a wide range of personalities and characteristics, from wisdom and justice to jealousy and vengeance.

In Hindu mythology, the gods and goddesses are seen as manifestations of the divine, representing different aspects of existence and cosmic order. Deities such as Brahma, Vishnu, and Shiva hold significant roles in shaping the universe and maintaining balance. They are revered as embodiments of higher consciousness and divine attributes, guiding and protecting humans on their spiritual journeys.

When comparing the portrayal of gods and goddesses in the Epic of Gilgamesh with other mythologies, we find similarities and differences. Like the gods of other mythologies, the gods in the Epic of Gilgamesh possess human-like emotions and exhibit a range of behaviors. For example, Shamash, the sun god, aids Gilgamesh in his quest for immortality, providing guidance and protection. However, the gods in the Epic of Gilgamesh are also depicted as capricious and unpredictable, subjecting mortals to their whims and occasionally punishing them for their transgressions.

The portrayal of gods and goddesses in mythologies serves important cultural and psychological functions. These divine beings represent archetypal forces and aspects of human experience, embodying qualities and powers beyond mortal reach. They provide narratives through which humans can make sense of the world, offering explanations for natural phenomena, moral codes, and social structures.

Culturally, gods and goddesses serve as figures of worship, rituals, and devotion. They unite communities and provide a shared framework for religious practices, ceremonies, and festivals. The gods and goddesses also hold cultural and historical significance, reflecting the values, beliefs, and aspirations of a particular society. They often become symbols of national identity, serving as protectors or patrons of cities or nations.

Psychologically, the gods and goddesses address deep human needs and desires. They offer solace in times of hardship, hope for the future, and a sense of purpose and meaning in life. The relationship between gods and mortals provides a context for exploring fundamental existential questions and the nature of human existence. The gods' interventions in mortal affairs offer a reflection of divine justice, reward, and punishment, and shape the human understanding of ethics and morality.

Exercise 9.23: Compare and contrast the portrayal of gods and goddesses in the Epic of Gilgamesh with another mythological tradition of your choice. Analyze the cultural and psychological significance of these divine beings and their role in shaping human destiny. Consider the impact of their characteristics, behaviors, and interactions with mortals on the mythological narrative and the societies that venerate them.

By examining the nature of divinity in various mythological traditions, we gain insights into the human quest for meaning, the dynamics of power and agency, and the intricate relationship between the mortal and the divine realms. The portrayal of gods and goddesses in mythology provides a lens through which we can explore our own hopes, fears, and aspirations, inviting us to contemplate our place in the cosmos and our connections to forces beyond our comprehension.

Symbolism and Motifs

The Epic of Gilgamesh incorporates a rich array of symbols and motifs that imbue the narrative with deeper layers of meaning. These symbols and motifs serve as powerful vehicles for exploring profound cultural and psychological themes.

One prominent symbol in the epic is the cedar forest. The cedar forest represents the realm of the gods, a sacred and mysterious place that is inaccessible to mortals. It is a symbol of the divine and the unknown, embodying both the awe-inspiring power of the gods and the uncharted territories of existence. Gilgamesh's quest to conquer the cedar forest reflects humanity's ambition to transcend its limitations, to explore and conquer the unknown, and to gain mastery over the forces of nature. The cedar forest symbolizes the pursuit of knowledge, power, and immortality, and the inherent human desire to understand and control the world around us.

Another symbol in the epic is the serpent, which appears in the story of Enkidu's initiation into civilization. In this episode, Enkidu encounters a wise woman who seduces him, leading to his transformation from a wild man to a civilized companion of Gilgamesh. The serpent is traditionally associated with wisdom, knowledge, and temptation in various mythologies and religious traditions. In this context, the serpent represents the duality of human experience, embodying both the allure of worldly pleasures and the potential for spiritual growth and enlightenment. The encounter with the serpent symbolizes the pivotal moment of transition and the blurring of boundaries between the natural and the cultural realms.

The motif of the flood is another significant symbol in the epic, drawing parallels with the biblical story of Noah's Ark and other flood myths found in different cultures. The flood symbolizes destruction, purification, and the cyclical nature of life. It serves as a powerful reminder of the transience and fragility of human existence. In the epic, Utnapishtim, the survivor of the great flood, holds the secret of immortality, further connecting the flood motif with the theme of the human quest for eternal life. The flood motif represents the cycles of creation and destruction, the inevitability of change, and the opportunity for renewal and rebirth.

The incorporation of symbols and motifs in the Epic of Gilgamesh adds depth and complexity to the narrative, inviting readers to contemplate the deeper meanings and universal themes embedded within the story. They serve as powerful tools for exploring the complexities of the human condition, the pursuit of knowledge and transcendence, and the intricate interplay between the mortal and the divine realms. Through symbolism and motifs, the epic transcends time and culture, resonating with readers across generations and inviting them to delve into the profound mysteries of existence.

Exercises and Discussion Questions

Discuss the theme of the quest for immortality in the Epic of Gilgamesh. How does Gilgamesh's pursuit of eternal life reflect broader human aspirations and existential questions? Explore examples from other myths or philosophical traditions to support your analysis.

Analyze the role of friendship in the epic. How does the friendship between Gilgamesh and Enkidu shape their individual journeys and contribute to the overarching themes of the narrative? Reflect on the significance of friendship in your own life and its impact on personal growth.

Explore the portrayal of divinity in the Epic of Gilgamesh. Discuss the characteristics and roles of the gods in the narrative, as well as their interactions with the mortal characters. How do these portrayals reflect cultural beliefs and societal values?

Select a symbol or motif from the epic and analyze its symbolic significance. Consider its cultural, psychological, and thematic implications. Connect the symbol to broader human experiences or concepts found in other mythologies or spiritual traditions.

Through these exercises and discussion questions, you are encouraged to critically engage with the themes and symbolism of the Epic of Gilgamesh. By exploring these profound concepts, you will deepen your understanding of the human experience and gain insight into the enduring relevance of ancient Mesopotamian literature.

Divine Intervention and Mythological Elements

In the Epic of Gilgamesh, divine intervention plays a central role, shaping the narrative and influencing the fate of the characters. This chapter explores the concept of divine intervention, the role of gods and goddesses in the epic, and the mythological elements that enrich the storytelling. By examining these aspects, we gain insight into the complex relationship between mortals and the divine and the profound influence of mythology on human culture.

Divine Intervention and its Significance

Divine intervention plays a significant role in mythological and spiritual traditions, showcasing the influence of gods and goddesses on human lives and shaping the narratives of various cultures. It represents the belief that supernatural forces actively participate in the affairs of mortals, whether to guide, test, punish, or reward them.

In Greek mythology, divine intervention is a recurring theme. The gods and goddesses of Mount Olympus often intervene in the lives of heroes and heroines, either to aid or hinder them. For example, in Homer's epic poem, "The Iliad," the gods take sides in the Trojan War, influencing the outcomes of battles and determining the fates of mortal warriors. The interference of deities like Zeus, Athena, and Apollo not only affects the outcome of conflicts but also serves as a commentary on the complexities of human existence and the relationship between mortals and the divine.

Norse mythology also features divine intervention as a central element. The gods and goddesses, such as Odin, Thor, and Loki, are actively involved in the lives of humans, intervening in their quests, adventures, and battles. The concept of fate, or "Wyrd," is closely tied to divine intervention in Norse mythology. It suggests that even the gods themselves are subject to a predetermined destiny, which influences their actions and interactions with mortals. This belief highlights the interplay between divine forces and the cyclical nature of existence.

In contemporary folklore, the concept of divine intervention persists in various forms. In religious traditions, such as Christianity, believers often attribute certain events or outcomes to the intervention of a higher power. Miraculous healings, answered prayers, or unexplained phenomena are seen as instances of divine intervention, reinforcing faith and offering solace. Similarly, in folk tales and legends, supernatural beings, such as angels, saints, or mythical creatures, are portrayed as intervening in the lives of ordinary people, imparting wisdom, protection, or assistance.

The significance of divine intervention lies in its ability to provide a framework for understanding the inexplicable and unexplainable aspects of life. It offers a sense of purpose, meaning, and order in a seemingly chaotic world. Divine intervention serves as a catalyst for personal growth, moral development, and the exploration of the human condition. It raises questions about free will, destiny, and the nature of power and agency. Through the intervention of gods and goddesses, mythological narratives convey valuable lessons, moral codes, and cultural values, shaping the worldview and ethical frameworks of societies.

The Pantheon of Gods and Goddesses

The ancient Mesopotamian belief system was deeply rooted in polytheism, with a rich pantheon of gods and goddesses that governed various aspects of life. In the Epic of Gilgamesh, these deities play a significant role in shaping the narrative, influencing the actions and fate of the mortal characters.

Anu, the sky god and the father of the gods, holds a position of supreme authority in the Mesopotamian pantheon. He represents the heavens and embodies the cosmic order. Enlil, the god of wind, storms, and agriculture, is a powerful deity associated with fertility and the natural forces that sustain life. His role as a judge and arbiter of fate is evident in his interactions with Gilgamesh and Enkidu. Ishtar, the goddess of love, fertility, and war, adds complexity to the divine landscape of the epic. She embodies both passion and destruction, often using her divine powers to influence the mortal realm.

Comparing the characteristics and roles of Mesopotamian gods with those found in other mythologies, such as the Greek Olympian gods or the Hindu pantheon, reveals both similarities and differences. Like the Mesopotamian deities, the Greek gods possess distinct personalities and domains. For example, Zeus is the king of the gods, Hera is the queen, Poseidon rules the seas, and Athena represents wisdom and warfare. Similarly, in the Hindu pantheon, each deity has a specific role and attribute, such as Brahma as the creator, Vishnu as the preserver, and Shiva as the destroyer.

However, there are also notable differences. The Mesopotamian gods often display capricious and unpredictable behavior, reflecting the uncertainties of the natural world. In contrast, the Greek gods possess more human-like qualities and exhibit a wide range of emotions and motivations. The Hindu gods, on the other hand, are often depicted with multiple aspects and manifestations, representing the various facets of divinity and cosmic order.

The cultural and psychological significance of these divine beings is multifaceted. In Mesopotamian culture, the gods played a crucial role in the social, political, and religious fabric of society. They were revered as protectors, providers, and sources of wisdom. The interactions between gods and mortals in the epic illustrate the complex dynamics of divine-human relationships and the influence of the divine on human behavior and fate. These beliefs influenced societal values, moral codes, and rituals, shaping the worldview and ethical frameworks of the Mesopotamian civilization.

Exercise: Compare and contrast the attributes and roles of deities in different mythological traditions or religious texts. Analyze how the characteristics of these divine beings reflect cultural values, societal structures, and the human understanding of the supernatural. Consider the psychological implications of human interactions with the divine and the impact of these beliefs on individual and collective behavior.

The gods and goddesses in the Epic of Gilgamesh serve as a bridge between the mortal and divine realms, embodying the aspirations, fears, and complexities of the human condition. They provide guidance, tests, and lessons for the mortal characters, shaping their destinies and offering insights into the balance of power between gods and humans. The gods' interactions with mortals also raise questions about free will, fate, and the consequences of human actions. Through their portrayal, the epic explores the cultural, psychological, and existential dimensions of the divine in the ancient Mesopotamian belief system.

Mythological Elements and Archetypal Motifs

Mythological elements in the Epic of Gilgamesh provide a rich tapestry of archetypal motifs and symbolic imagery that transcend time and culture. These elements not only add depth and intrigue to the narrative but also serve as profound vehicles for exploring universal themes, imparting moral lessons, and addressing fundamental questions about the human condition.

One prominent mythological element in the epic is the hero's journey archetype. Gilgamesh's quest for immortality can be seen as a classic representation of the hero's journey, a recurring motif in mythology worldwide. The hero's journey follows a specific pattern, consisting of stages such as the call to adventure, initiation, trials and challenges, and the ultimate return with newfound wisdom. In the case of Gilgamesh, his journey begins with his call to adventure to seek eternal life after the death of his friend Enkidu. Along the way, he faces numerous trials and challenges, such as battling mythical creatures and enduring hardships, which test his character and resolve. Ultimately, Gilgamesh returns to Uruk a changed man, having gained wisdom and a deeper understanding of mortality and the human condition.

Another significant mythological element in the Epic of Gilgamesh is the flood narrative. This ancient Mesopotamian tale predates the biblical account of

Noah's Ark and shares striking similarities. In both narratives, a cataclysmic flood is unleashed upon humanity as divine punishment. The flood serves as a metaphorical cleansing and rebirth, signaling the end of an era and the emergence of a new world. In the Epic of Gilgamesh, the flood is a pivotal event that teaches the protagonist about the fragility of life, the power of the gods, and the need for humility in the face of divine forces.

The descent into the underworld is yet another mythological element present in the epic. Gilgamesh's journey to the realm of the dead in search of immortality is a metaphorical descent into the depths of the human psyche and the mysteries of the afterlife. This motif symbolizes a confrontation with mortality, the exploration of existential questions, and the quest for spiritual enlightenment. Through his encounter with the goddess of the underworld, Gilgamesh learns that true immortality lies in leaving a lasting legacy and being remembered by future generations.

These mythological elements, the hero's journey, the flood narrative, and the descent into the underworld, contribute to the broader themes and messages conveyed in the Epic of Gilgamesh. They explore the human desire for transcendence, the inevitability of mortality, the balance between power and humility, and the search for meaning in a transient world. By drawing upon archetypal motifs and symbolic imagery, the epic resonates with audiences across time and culture, inviting introspection and contemplation of the universal truths embedded within its mythic framework.

Cultural and Historical Context

To fully appreciate the mythological elements and divine intervention in the Epic of Gilgamesh, it is crucial to consider the cultural and historical context of ancient Mesopotamia. The epic reflects the cosmology, religious beliefs, and social dynamics of the time, offering insights into the worldview of the ancient Mesopotamians and their relationship with the divine.

Investigate the cultural and historical context of ancient Mesopotamia. Discuss the influence of geographical factors, political structures, and religious practices on the development of the epic. Reflect on how the cultural and historical context shapes the mythological elements and divine interventions found in the narrative.

Through these exercises and exploration of divine intervention and mythological elements, you will gain a deeper understanding of the complexities of ancient Mesopotamian mythology, the role of gods and goddesses in human narratives, and the enduring power of myth to convey universal truths. Engage in critical thinking and discussions to uncover the layers of symbolism and meaning embedded in the epic, connecting them to your own spiritual and mythological studies.

Gilgamesh and Enkidu: The Dynamics of Friendship

The relationship between Gilgamesh and Enkidu is a central theme in the Epic of Gilgamesh, showcasing the transformative power of friendship. This chapter delves into the dynamics of their bond, examining the complexities, impact, and significance of their friendship within the context of ancient Mesopotamian society. Through the study of their relationship, we gain insights into the profound influence of friendship on personal growth, emotional well-being, and spiritual development.

The Nature of their Friendship

Gilgamesh, the mighty king of Uruk, and Enkidu, a wild and untamed man created by the gods, initially meet as adversaries. However, their initial conflict quickly turns into a deep and enduring friendship. The bond they form is characterized by mutual respect, loyalty, and shared experiences, and it becomes a catalyst for personal transformation and self-discovery.

Reflect on the dynamics of friendship in your own life or in literature, mythology, or folklore. Discuss examples from different cultures and time periods that highlight the transformative power of friendship. Consider the qualities and values that contribute to the strength and depth of these relationships.

Companionship and Emotional Support

Gilgamesh and Enkidu provide each other with vital companionship and emotional support throughout their adventures. Their friendship allows them to confront their fears, face challenges, and navigate the complexities of life. Through their bond, they find solace, understanding, and a sense of belonging.

Exercise 5.2: Explore the concept of companionship and emotional support in various spiritual and magical traditions. Investigate how practices such as ritual circles, coven work, or shamanic partnerships foster companionship and emotional well-being. Reflect on the importance of emotional support in personal and spiritual growth.

Growth and Transformation

The friendship between Gilgamesh and Enkidu catalyzes profound personal growth and transformation for both characters. Enkidu's connection with Gilgamesh allows him to shed his wild nature and embrace civilization, while Gilgamesh learns humility, empathy, and the value of human connection through his friendship with Enkidu. Together, they navigate the challenges of mortality, the search for meaning, and the quest for self-discovery.

Reflect on personal growth and transformation in your own life or in the lives of individuals you admire. Discuss how friendships or mentorship relationships have contributed to personal development, expanded perspectives, and the discovery of hidden potentials. Consider the role of friendship in supporting spiritual growth and self-realization.

Friendship as a Spiritual Path

The friendship between Gilgamesh and Enkidu transcends mere companionship, evolving into a spiritual path for both characters. Their bond allows them to explore existential questions, confront their mortality, and seek wisdom beyond the confines of their individual lives. Through their friendship, they discover profound truths about themselves, the world, and their place within it.

Exercise 5.4: Engage in a contemplative exercise or ritual that explores the spiritual dimensions of friendship. Consider how shared experiences, emotional resonance, and mutual growth can deepen spiritual connections. Reflect on the role of friendship in your own spiritual journey and the ways it has enhanced your understanding and connection with the divine.

Through these exercises and exploration of the dynamics of friendship in the epic, you will gain a deeper understanding of the transformative power of companionship, emotional support, and shared experiences. Embrace critical thinking and discussions to uncover the lessons embedded in the friendship of Gilgamesh and Enkidu, connecting them to your own experiences and spiritual studies.

Comparison of the Epic of Gilgamesh to other religious text

➢ Comparison of the Epic of Gilgamesh to the Bible:

The Epic of Gilgamesh and the Bible are both ancient texts that hold significant cultural and historical importance. While they originate from different civilizations and encompass distinct mythologies, they share some intriguing similarities and provide valuable insights into human nature, spirituality, and the human-divine relationship.

Flood Narratives:

One of the most striking parallels between the two texts is the presence of flood narratives. In both the Epic of Gilgamesh and the Bible, a cataclysmic flood is described as a divine punishment for humanity's wrongdoing. In the Epic of Gilgamesh, the hero Utnapishtim is instructed by the god Ea to build a massive ark to save himself, his family, and various animals. Similarly, in the Bible's Book of Genesis, Noah is commanded by God to construct an ark to preserve life during the flood. These narratives highlight the universal themes of human frailty, divine judgment, and the potential for redemption.

Divine Intervention:

Both texts portray the intervention of deities in the lives of humans. In the Epic of Gilgamesh, gods play an active role in shaping events and influencing the lives of the characters. Gilgamesh himself is two-thirds divine, with his mother being the goddess Ninsun. Similarly, the Bible portrays numerous instances of divine intervention, such as God's interactions with Adam and Eve, the calling of prophets, and the miracles performed by Jesus in the New Testament. These divine interventions serve to guide, punish, and offer redemption to humanity, emphasizing the role of the divine in human affairs.

Quest for Immortality:

Another significant theme shared by the Epic of Gilgamesh and the Bible is the pursuit of immortality. In the epic, Gilgamesh embarks on a quest to find eternal life after the death of his friend Enkidu. He seeks out Utnapishtim, the one man granted immortality by the gods, hoping to acquire the secret of eternal life. Similarly, in the Bible, the concept of immortality is explored through the story of Adam and Eve's expulsion from the Garden of Eden and the promise of salvation and eternal life through faith in God. These narratives reflect humanity's innate desire for immortality and the search for transcendence beyond mortal limitations.

Moral Lessons and Ethical Considerations:

Both texts offer moral lessons and ethical considerations for human conduct. In the Epic of Gilgamesh, the story emphasizes the importance of humility, compassion, and the acceptance of mortality. Through Gilgamesh's transformative journey, he learns the value of human connections and the fleeting nature of life. In the Bible, various moral teachings and commandments are presented to guide human behavior and promote righteousness. The Ten Commandments, for example, provide a framework for ethical living and moral responsibilities toward God and others. Both texts raise fundamental questions about the nature of good and evil, human purpose, and the pursuit of wisdom.

While the Epic of Gilgamesh and the Bible exhibit similarities, it is essential to recognize their distinct cultural and religious contexts. The Epic of Gilgamesh originates from ancient Mesopotamia, while the Bible is a collection of religious texts central to Judaism and Christianity. Despite their differences, both texts offer profound insights into the human condition, the search for meaning, and the relationship between humans and the divine. Studying and comparing these ancient texts allows us to appreciate the diverse perspectives and universal themes that have shaped human history and spirituality.

➢ Comparison of the Epic of Gilgamesh to the Torah:

The Epic of Gilgamesh and the Torah, specifically the first five books known as the Torah or Pentateuch (Genesis, Exodus, Leviticus, Numbers, and Deuteronomy), are ancient texts that hold significant cultural and religious importance. While they originate from different civilizations and encompass distinct mythologies, they share some intriguing similarities and provide valuable insights into human nature, morality, and the human-divine relationship.

Creation Narratives:

Both the Epic of Gilgamesh and the Torah contain creation narratives that explore the origins of the world and humanity. In the Epic of Gilgamesh, the creation story is part of the larger narrative and describes the formation of humans and the establishment of civilization. Similarly, the Torah presents the creation account in the Book of Genesis, detailing the creation of the universe, the formation of Adam and Eve, and their subsequent experiences in the Garden of Eden. These narratives provide explanations for the existence of the world and humanity while raising questions about human nature, morality, and the relationship between humans and their creator.

Divine Intervention and Interaction:

Both texts portray the intervention and interaction of divine beings with humanity. In the Epic of Gilgamesh, gods play an active role in shaping events, influencing the lives of the characters, and providing guidance or punishment. Similarly, in the Torah, God is depicted as actively involved in human affairs, interacting with various individuals such as Adam, Noah, Abraham, and Moses. Divine interventions in both texts serve to guide, teach, and challenge humans in their spiritual and moral development.

Moral and Ethical Teachings:

The Epic of Gilgamesh and the Torah offer moral and ethical teachings to guide human behavior and promote righteous living. In the Epic of Gilgamesh, the story emphasizes themes of friendship, loyalty, and the acceptance of mortality. Through Gilgamesh's journey, he learns the value of human connections, the limitations of his power, and the importance of humility. Similarly, the Torah contains a comprehensive set of laws, commandments, and ethical teachings given by God to the Israelites. These teachings encompass various aspects of human life, including social interactions, justice, compassion, and worship. Both texts provide moral frameworks and guidelines for individuals and communities to live virtuous and righteous lives.

Flood Narratives:

Both the Epic of Gilgamesh and the Torah contain narratives of a catastrophic flood. In the Epic of Gilgamesh, the flood story is part of a larger narrative and serves as a divine punishment for humanity's wrongdoing. Similarly, the Torah includes the story of Noah and the Great Flood, where God cleanses the earth of its wickedness. The flood narratives in both texts convey themes of divine judgment, the preservation of life, and the potential for renewal or redemption.

While the Epic of Gilgamesh and the Torah share similarities, it is crucial to acknowledge their distinct cultural and religious contexts. The Epic of Gilgamesh originates from ancient Mesopotamia, while the Torah is central to Judaism and forms the foundation of the Hebrew Bible. Despite their differences, both texts offer profound insights into human nature, morality, and the relationship between humans and the divine. Comparing these ancient texts allows us to appreciate the diverse perspectives and universal themes that have shaped human history, spirituality, and ethical thought.

➤   Comparison of the Epic of Gilgamesh and the Quran

The Epic of Gilgamesh and the Quran are both ancient texts that hold significant cultural and religious importance. While they originate from different civilizations and encompass distinct mythologies and religious teachings, there are some notable comparisons and contrasts between the two.

Narrative Structure:

The Epic of Gilgamesh is an epic poem that follows the adventures and personal growth of its protagonist, Gilgamesh, the legendary king of Uruk. It is structured as a series of episodic tales, with each episode contributing to the overall narrative. On the other hand, the Quran is a religious text comprising of 114 chapters or surahs, which are organized based on their length rather than following a strict chronological or narrative structure. The Quran primarily focuses on delivering divine guidance, moral teachings, and spiritual insights to its readers.

Origins and Authorship:

The Epic of Gilgamesh is believed to have originated in ancient Mesopotamia and was written by various authors over a span of several centuries. It was initially passed down orally before being recorded on clay tablets. In contrast, the Quran is considered by Muslims to be the direct word of God as revealed to the Prophet Muhammad over a period of approximately 23 years. Muslims believe the Quran to be the unaltered and final revelation, making it a central religious text in Islam.

Themes and Messages:

The Epic of Gilgamesh explores universal themes such as the quest for immortality, the nature of humanity, the meaning of life, and the consequences of hubris. It raises questions about mortality, friendship, power, and the human condition. The Quran, on the other hand, focuses on monotheism, the oneness of God (Allah), and the ethical and moral obligations of believers. It provides guidance on various aspects of life, including worship, social justice, family matters, and personal conduct.

Religious and Spiritual Significance:

While the Epic of Gilgamesh has cultural and historical significance, it does not hold religious authority or serve as a sacred text for any particular religious tradition. In contrast, the Quran is the central religious scripture of Islam and is considered the literal word of God. Muslims regard the Quran as a guide for all aspects of life, including personal piety, spirituality, morality, and legal matters.

Influence and Interpretation:

The Epic of Gilgamesh has influenced numerous literary works and cultural traditions throughout history. Its themes and motifs have found resonance in various ancient and modern texts. The Quran, on the other hand, has had a profound impact on the development of Islamic civilization, shaping religious beliefs, legal systems, social norms, and artistic expressions across diverse cultures and societies.

While the Epic of Gilgamesh and the Quran differ in their origins, structure, and religious significance, both texts offer insights into the human condition, moral teachings, and the relationship between humans and the divine. They serve as important cultural and intellectual touchstones, contributing to the rich tapestry of human literary and religious heritage.

Chapter 5: Death and the Afterlife: Beliefs and Funerary Practices

The concept of death and the afterlife has been a subject of profound human fascination and contemplation throughout history. In this chapter, we delve into the beliefs and funerary practices of ancient Mesopotamia, providing a comprehensive exploration of their views on death, the afterlife, and the rituals associated with the passage from this world to the next. By studying the rich tapestry of Mesopotamian beliefs and funerary customs, we gain insights into the human quest for understanding and transcendence in the face of mortality.

Beliefs about Death

In Mesopotamian culture, death was viewed as a significant transition rather than an absolute end. The Mesopotamians held a belief in an afterlife, a realm where the soul or essence of the deceased would continue to exist. However, their perception of the afterlife was multifaceted and diverse, encompassing different realms and destinies for individuals based on their actions and social status during their earthly lives.

One aspect of Mesopotamian beliefs about death was the concept of the Netherworld, a dark and gloomy realm where the souls of the deceased would reside. It was believed that the Netherworld consisted of multiple levels or layers, each associated with different degrees of reward or punishment based on an individual's conduct in life. Those who lived virtuous and righteous lives were expected to be rewarded with a more favorable afterlife, while those who were wicked or dishonorable would face a harsher fate.

Another belief in Mesopotamian culture was the importance of proper burial rituals and practices. It was believed that a well-conducted burial and the provision of offerings and rituals would ensure the deceased's peaceful transition into the afterlife. Mesopotamians also held the belief that the deceased required sustenance and care in the afterlife, and thus, they would leave food, drink, and personal belongings in the tombs as offerings for the departed.

Exercise: Reflecting on your own beliefs and attitudes towards death and the afterlife can be a deeply personal and introspective exercise. Consider the influence of different spiritual traditions and cultural perspectives on shaping these beliefs. Explore how beliefs about death and the afterlife vary across various belief systems, such as witchcraft, divination, and shamanism, to deepen your understanding of diverse perspectives.

In witchcraft, for example, death is often seen as a part of the natural cycle of life and rebirth. Many witches hold the belief in reincarnation, where the soul continues to evolve and learn through multiple lifetimes. Divination practices, on the other hand, may seek to communicate with the spirits of the deceased or gain insights into the afterlife through various means such as mediumship, tarot readings, or scrying.

Shamanic traditions often emphasize the journey of the soul after death, with shamans acting as intermediaries between the physical and spiritual realms. They may guide the souls of the departed to their appropriate destinations or perform rituals to ensure the deceased's peaceful passage.

Exploring the significance of death and the afterlife in various belief systems can provide a broader understanding of the diversity of perspectives and practices surrounding this universal theme. It can foster empathy, respect, and appreciation for the different ways in which cultures and individuals approach and make meaning of the profound mystery of death.

The Journey to the Afterlife

The Mesopotamians held a belief that the journey to the afterlife was not an easy one, but rather filled with challenges and obstacles that the deceased had to overcome. Recognizing the significance of this journey, they developed elaborate funerary rituals and practices to facilitate a successful transition and provide the departed with the necessary provisions and assistance for their voyage.

One important aspect of these funerary rituals was purification. The body of the deceased was carefully cleansed and anointed with oils and fragrances to ensure its readiness for the afterlife. This purification process was seen as a means of preparing the soul for its journey and removing any impurities that may hinder its progress.

Offerings played a vital role in Mesopotamian funerary rituals. Food, drink, and valuable items were placed in the tomb as offerings to sustain and comfort the deceased during their journey. It was believed that these offerings would provide the necessary nourishment and provisions for the soul's continued existence in the afterlife. Additionally, personal belongings and treasured possessions were often included in the tomb to accompany the deceased on their journey and maintain a sense of continuity and familiarity.

Recitation of spells and incantations was another significant aspect of Mesopotamian funerary practices. These magical formulas and invocations were believed to have the power to protect and guide the soul on its perilous journey. The recitation of these spells was often performed by priests or other individuals with specialized knowledge in the ritual arts.

The Mesopotamians also believed in the importance of memorializing the deceased and maintaining their connection with the living. Regular commemorative rituals and offerings were conducted at the tomb to honor and remember the departed. These acts of remembrance served not only to honor the deceased but also to keep their memory alive within the community and ensure their continued presence and influence in the lives of the living.

The complex funerary rituals and practices of the Mesopotamians reflected their deep reverence for the journey of the soul and their belief in the continued existence of the deceased in the afterlife. Through these rituals, they sought to provide the necessary support and provisions for the departed, as well as maintain a connection between the living and the deceased. These practices not only ensured a successful transition for the soul but also provided solace and comfort for the grieving community, affirming their belief in the continuity of life beyond death.

Funerary Practices

Funerary practices in ancient Mesopotamia were diverse and varied, reflecting the intricate tapestry of their beliefs and cultural customs surrounding death and the afterlife. While burial was the most common form of interment, the specific practices varied based on social status, wealth, and regional customs.

In Mesopotamia, the deceased were typically laid to rest in graves or tombs. These burial sites ranged from simple and modest graves for the common people to elaborate and grandiose tombs for the wealthy and powerful. The tombs of high-ranking individuals, such as kings or nobles, often featured intricate architecture, including chambers, corridors, and even multiple levels. These lavish tombs were adorned with artistic representations, such as reliefs or sculptures, depicting scenes of daily life, religious rituals, or mythological narratives.

In addition to burial, cremation was another form of funerary practice in ancient Mesopotamia, although it was less common. Cremated remains were sometimes placed in urns or funerary vessels, which were then buried or interred in tombs. This practice was more prevalent in certain periods and regions of Mesopotamia.

The Mesopotamians believed in the importance of rituals and offerings to ensure the well-being and continuity of the deceased in the afterlife. These rituals involved purification, prayers, and the presentation of offerings, including food, drink, and valuable items. The purpose of these offerings was to sustain and comfort the deceased in the afterlife, ensuring their continued existence and well-being.

In addition to burial and offerings, commemorative rituals played a significant role in Mesopotamian funerary practices. These rituals were conducted by family members and community members at regular intervals to honor and remember the deceased. They often involved libations, incense, and the recitation of prayers or hymns. These acts of remembrance served not only to honor the departed but also to maintain a connection with them and seek their continued guidance and protection.

When investigating funerary practices in different cultures and time periods, one can explore a wide range of rituals and customs related to death and the afterlife. For example, in witchcraft traditions, there may be ceremonies involving the use of herbs, crystals, or other ritual tools to honor and guide the departed. Divination practices might involve seeking communication with the deceased through mediums, tarot readings, or other forms of oracular guidance. Shamanic traditions often incorporate rituals and ceremonies to help guide the soul of the deceased to its next destination and provide closure for the living.

By comparing and contrasting these various funerary practices, we gain insights into the cultural and spiritual significance attributed to death and the afterlife. These practices not only offer solace and support for the grieving process but also provide frameworks for understanding and grappling with mortality. They can serve as expressions of cultural identity, sources of comfort and healing, and means of maintaining connections with loved ones who have passed on. Understanding these practices deepens our appreciation for the diversity of human experiences and beliefs surrounding death and the journey beyond.

Mourning and Ancestor Worship

Mourning and ancestor worship held significant importance in Mesopotamian society, as they were deeply intertwined with the cultural and religious beliefs surrounding death and the afterlife. The grieving process in Mesopotamia involved a series of rituals and ceremonies aimed at honoring and remembering the deceased.

One of the central elements of mourning in Mesopotamia was the practice of lamentation. Lamentations were sorrowful songs or poetic expressions of grief performed by mourners during funeral processions or memorial gatherings. These lamentations served as a means of expressing deep sorrow, mourning the loss of the departed, and conveying emotions of grief and longing. Lamentations were often accompanied by music, such as the playing of flutes or lyres, to enhance the emotional impact of the mourning rituals.

Offerings played a crucial role in honoring the deceased and facilitating the transition to the afterlife. Mesopotamians believed that by making offerings, such as food, drink, or other valuable items, they could provide sustenance and comfort to the spirits of the deceased in the realm beyond. These offerings were presented at gravesites or within temples dedicated to ancestor worship.

Ancestor worship was a prevalent practice in Mesopotamian society, rooted in the belief that the spirits of the deceased continued to have an influence on the lives of their living descendants. Mesopotamians believed that maintaining a connection with their ancestors was essential for the well-being and prosperity of the family and community. Ancestor worship involved regular rituals and ceremonies, where offerings and prayers were made to the spirits of the deceased. These rituals aimed to seek the guidance, protection, and blessings of the ancestors in various aspects of life, such as family matters, agricultural endeavors, or political decisions.

The Mesopotamians believed that the spirits of the ancestors resided in the underworld, a realm accessible through the gates of the netherworld. They viewed the ancestors as intermediaries between the divine and human realms, capable of interceding on behalf of the living. Through ancestor worship, the Mesopotamians sought to maintain a reciprocal relationship with their departed loved ones, offering reverence and loyalty in exchange for their continued support and guidance.

By engaging in mourning rituals and practicing ancestor worship, the Mesopotamians not only expressed their grief and longing for the departed but also sought to ensure the well-being and spiritual connection with their ancestors. These practices played a vital role in the social fabric of Mesopotamian society, fostering a sense of continuity, collective memory, and the intergenerational transmission of cultural values and traditions.

Understanding the significance of mourning and ancestor worship in Mesopotamia provides insights into the deep reverence for the deceased and the enduring bonds between the living and the spirits of their ancestors. It also highlights the human need for remembrance, connection, and the ongoing influence of those who came before us.

Death and the Divine

The Mesopotamians believed that death brought individuals closer to the divine realm. They perceived a complex interplay between the human and divine realms, with deities having authority over the afterlife and acting as mediators between the living and the dead. Rituals and offerings to the gods were an essential part of the funerary practices, ensuring divine favor and protection for the deceased in the afterlife.

Explore the role of deities in various spiritual traditions and magical practices, such as witchcraft, divination, and shamanism. Investigate how different belief systems conceptualize the relationship between death, the afterlife, and the divine. Reflect on the ways in which divine forces shape human perceptions of mortality and influence funerary practices.

Through the exploration of Mesopotamian beliefs and funerary practices, you will gain a deeper understanding of how ancient cultures grappled with the mysteries of death and the afterlife. Engage in critical thinking and discussions to uncover the diverse perspectives and rituals associated with the journey beyond life. Examine the impact of these beliefs and practices on individual and communal experiences of loss, grief, and spiritual transcendence.

Concept of Death in Mesopotamian Culture

In ancient Mesopotamia, the concept of death held significant cultural and religious importance. Mesopotamians believed that death marked a transition rather than an absolute end, and they developed intricate beliefs and rituals surrounding this inevitable journey. Understanding the Mesopotamian concept of death provides valuable insights into their worldview, spirituality, and the human quest for meaning and transcendence.

Mortality and Transcendence

The Mesopotamians possessed a profound awareness of the finite nature of human existence and the inevitability of death. This understanding of mortality permeated their worldview, influencing their perspectives on life's purpose and the pursuit of immortality or transcendence. Mesopotamians sought to overcome the limitations of mortality and leave a lasting impact on the world through various means.

One way in which the Mesopotamians sought transcendence was through the pursuit of great deeds and accomplishments. They believed that by achieving remarkable feats, such as building magnificent structures or conquering vast territories, they could etch their names into history and be remembered long after their physical existence. The desire to create a lasting legacy motivated individuals to strive for greatness in their respective fields, whether in politics, art, or intellectual pursuits.

Religious devotion was another avenue through which the Mesopotamians sought transcendence. They believed that by engaging in rituals, worshiping the gods, and leading a righteous life, they could secure a favorable position in the afterlife and attain a form of eternal existence. The practice of religion provided a framework for spiritual transcendence, offering a sense of purpose, moral guidance, and the promise of an everlasting connection with the divine.

The preservation of memory in the collective consciousness was also crucial for the Mesopotamians' quest for transcendence. They recognized the importance of being remembered by future generations, as it ensured their continued existence in the realm of human memory. Through storytelling, poetry, and historical records, the Mesopotamians endeavored to immortalize their achievements, wisdom, and cultural heritage. By preserving their legacy in the collective consciousness, they hoped to transcend the confines of mortality and influence the lives of future generations.

The quest for transcendence is not limited to Mesopotamian culture alone. Across various spiritual traditions, including witchcraft, divination, and shamanism, individuals seek to transcend the limitations of mortality and leave a lasting impact on the world. Whether through the practice of magic, divination techniques, or spiritual journeys, practitioners of these traditions aim to connect with higher realms, gain esoteric knowledge, and achieve personal transformation. These practices often involve tapping into hidden energies, communing with spirits, and exploring altered states of consciousness to transcend the ordinary and access deeper truths.

Personal and collective transcendence hold great significance in spiritual and magical practices. They offer individuals the opportunity to expand their consciousness, cultivate inner wisdom, and connect with forces beyond the material realm. The pursuit of transcendence can foster personal growth, spiritual enlightenment, and a sense of purpose and meaning in life. It also allows individuals to contribute to the greater good, leaving a positive and lasting impact on their communities and the world at large.

By reflecting on the human quest for transcendence in different spiritual traditions, we gain insights into the inherent desire to transcend the limitations of mortality and leave a lasting legacy. Whether through acts of greatness, religious devotion, or the preservation of memory, humans throughout history have sought to transcend their finite existence and connect with the eternal and the divine. The significance of personal and collective transcendence in spiritual and magical practices lies in their ability to nourish the human spirit, provide a sense of purpose, and inspire individuals to strive for something greater than themselves.

Dualistic Nature of Existence

Mesopotamian culture embraced a dualistic worldview, perceiving existence as a dynamic interplay between life and death, mortality and immortality. They recognized that life on Earth was a transient state, while the afterlife represented the continuation of the soul's journey. This dualistic perspective deeply influenced their understanding of the soul and their beliefs about postmortem existence.

In Mesopotamian cosmology, mortal life was regarded as a temporary phase within the greater cosmic cycle. It was seen as an opportunity for individuals to fulfill their earthly duties, experience joys and sorrows, and contribute to the unfolding of divine order. However, it was also understood that mortality carried the inevitability of death, which was seen as a natural part of the cyclical nature of existence.

The Mesopotamians believed in the existence of both mortal and immortal realms. The mortal realm encompassed life on Earth, with its physical limitations and transient nature. It was viewed as a testing ground where individuals were meant to navigate challenges, make choices, and learn valuable lessons. The immortal realm, on the other hand, represented the afterlife—a realm beyond the physical, where the soul continued its journey.

The nature of the soul and its fate after death held a central place in Mesopotamian beliefs. They believed that the soul, referred to as the "shade" or "spirit," had an eternal essence that transcended the physical body. Upon death, the soul embarked on a journey to the netherworld, a realm inhabited by various deities and entities. This journey was not linear but complex, involving encounters with challenges and obstacles.

The possibilities of postmortem existence varied based on an individual's actions and status during their earthly life. The Mesopotamians believed that those who lived virtuous lives, fulfilled their societal roles, and maintained a connection with the gods had the potential for a more favorable afterlife. They envisioned different realms within the netherworld, ranging from paradisiacal abodes for the righteous to darker realms for those who were morally corrupt or neglected their religious duties.

To navigate the journey to the afterlife successfully, funerary rituals and practices played a crucial role. The Mesopotamians recognized the need for purification, offerings, and the recitation of spells and incantations to provide the deceased with the necessary provisions and assistance for their journey. These rituals aimed to ensure a smooth transition and to secure a favorable destiny in the afterlife.

The dualistic perspective of Mesopotamian culture, with its interconnectedness of life and death, mortal and immortal realms, allowed individuals to perceive death not as an absolute end but as a continuation of the soul's journey. It provided a framework for understanding the cyclical nature of existence and the opportunities for growth and spiritual evolution.

By embracing this dualistic worldview, the Mesopotamians found solace in the belief that death was not the ultimate annihilation but a transition to another phase of existence. It offered them a sense of purpose and a means to navigate life's challenges with the understanding that their actions and choices carried consequences for both their mortal life and their postmortem journey.

The Mesopotamian perspective on the nature of the soul and the possibilities of postmortem existence reflects the cultural and spiritual richness of the civilization. It underscores the profound interconnectedness of life and death, mortality and immortality, and invites contemplation on the greater cosmic cycle that encompasses both.

The Role of the Gods

Central to the Mesopotamian concept of death were the gods and their influence on the afterlife. The Mesopotamians believed that the gods held authority over the destinies of the deceased, and their favor or displeasure could significantly impact an individual's fate in the afterlife. Consequently, Mesopotamians sought to appease the gods through various rituals, offerings, and acts of devotion.

The relationship between the gods and the afterlife was considered essential for securing a favorable destiny after death. The gods were perceived as powerful beings who resided in divine realms and possessed the ability to influence the lives of humans both during their mortal existence and in the afterlife. Their decisions and judgments carried immense weight in determining an individual's ultimate fate and the conditions they would encounter in the netherworld.

To ensure divine favor and a favorable afterlife, the Mesopotamians engaged in religious practices aimed at appeasing the gods. These practices involved the performance of rituals and ceremonies conducted by priests, who acted as intermediaries between the human and divine realms. The rituals included purification rites, prayers, offerings, and the recitation of specific incantations and spells.

Offerings played a significant role in seeking the gods' favor and support in the afterlife. The Mesopotamians presented a variety of offerings, such as food, drink, precious objects, and symbolic representations, to the gods as acts of devotion and gratitude. These offerings were made in temples, sanctuaries, or even at personal altars, with the belief that they would sustain and please the gods, thus increasing the likelihood of a positive postmortem fate.

In addition to offerings, the Mesopotamians sought to establish and maintain a personal relationship with the gods through prayer and supplication. They believed that communicating their desires, concerns, and devotion directly to the gods could elicit divine intervention and support, not only in their present lives but also in the afterlife. Prayers were often recited in specific rituals and ceremonies, expressing reverence, gratitude, and requests for divine assistance and protection.

Mesopotamians also turned to divination as a means of seeking guidance and insight into the future, including matters related to death and the afterlife. Divination practices, such as examining the entrails of animals, interpreting celestial phenomena, or consulting oracles, were employed to discern the gods' will and to understand their intentions regarding the deceased and their fate in the afterlife.

The Mesopotamians believed that a harmonious relationship with the gods was crucial for navigating the complexities of death and the afterlife. They understood that their actions, devotion, and adherence to religious practices could influence the gods' favor or disfavor, thereby shaping their postmortem destiny. By actively engaging in rituals, offerings, and prayer, they sought to establish a connection with the divine and ensure their well-being in the afterlife.

The Mesopotamian belief in the gods' authority over the afterlife highlights the significance of religious practices and devotion in their culture. It underscores the profound influence of the divine realm on human existence and the importance of establishing a positive relationship with the gods to secure a favorable destiny in the afterlife. By recognizing the gods' power and seeking their favor, the Mesopotamians aimed to navigate the complexities of death and transcend the mortal realm with the hope of attaining a desirable postmortem existence.

The Realm of the Dead

Mesopotamians held a diverse range of beliefs about the afterlife, envisioning it as a distinct realm where the souls of the deceased resided. However, the exact nature of this realm varied across different periods and regions, reflecting the evolving beliefs and cultural influences within Mesopotamian society.

In some Mesopotamian texts, the afterlife is depicted as a dark and gloomy underworld known as the "Land of No Return." This realm was described as a place of shadow and silence, where the souls of the deceased led a shadowy existence without the joys and pleasures of the mortal world. The Land of No Return was often associated with desolate landscapes, deep caverns, and impassable rivers that separated the realm of the living from the realm of the dead.

However, other Mesopotamian texts present a more elaborate and complex afterlife, featuring different levels and destinies for souls. These texts describe a multi-tiered system, with the possibility of ascending to higher realms or descending to lower realms based on an individual's actions and status during their earthly life. The afterlife was believed to be populated by various divine beings, including judges and gatekeepers who determined the fate of the deceased souls.

The belief in different levels of the afterlife suggests a concept of cosmic justice and divine judgment, where the actions and moral conduct of individuals in their earthly life had a direct impact on their postmortem destiny. Those who had lived virtuous lives and fulfilled their societal and religious obligations were believed to be rewarded with a more favorable afterlife, characterized by bliss, prosperity, and the company of benevolent deities. Conversely, individuals who had committed wicked deeds or failed to fulfill their responsibilities were believed to face punishments or hardships in the afterlife.

When comparing the concept of the afterlife in Mesopotamian culture with other spiritual traditions, such as witchcraft, divination, and shamanism, there are both similarities and differences in how different belief systems perceive and interpret the nature of the afterlife.

For instance, in some witchcraft traditions, the afterlife is seen as a realm of ancestral spirits and nature spirits, where the deceased continue to exist and can be contacted or honored through magical practices. Divination practices may also involve seeking guidance from spirits or ancestors who have crossed over to the afterlife.

Similarly, shamanic traditions often involve journeys to other realms, including the afterlife, where the shaman can interact with spirits, retrieve lost souls, or gain knowledge and healing. Shamanic beliefs about the afterlife often involve the idea of multiple realms or dimensions that coexist with the physical world.

While there are similarities in the belief in an afterlife or interaction with the spiritual realm, the specific details and interpretations vary across these different traditions. The cultural practices and rituals associated with the afterlife also differ, reflecting the unique cosmologies and spiritual beliefs of each tradition.

The significance of these beliefs about the afterlife lies in their influence on cultural practices and the human understanding of mortality. Beliefs about the afterlife shape how societies approach death, mourn their loved ones, and seek to honor and remember the deceased. They provide a framework for understanding the purpose and meaning of life, as well as the potential consequences of one's actions.

Furthermore, beliefs about the afterlife offer solace and hope in the face of mortality, providing comfort to individuals and communities as they grapple with the inevitable reality of death. They offer a sense of continuity and connection with the spiritual realm, affirming the belief that life extends beyond the boundaries of the physical world.

Overall, the concept of the afterlife in Mesopotamian culture and other spiritual traditions reflects the human longing for continuity, justice, and transcendence. These beliefs provide a framework for understanding the mysteries of life and death, shaping cultural practices, and offering individuals a way to make sense of their existence in the greater cosmic order.

Ancestor Veneration

Ancestor veneration played a significant role in Mesopotamian culture, reflecting the belief that the souls of ancestors maintained a continued presence and influence in the lives of their descendants. Honoring and revering ancestors through offerings, rituals, and remembrance was considered crucial for maintaining a harmonious relationship and seeking their guidance and support.

The Mesopotamians viewed ancestors as a bridge between the living and the divine realms. They believed that the spirits of ancestors had the ability to intercede on behalf of their living descendants, acting as mediators between humanity and the gods. Ancestors were seen as wise and experienced beings who possessed knowledge, insight, and the ability to affect the outcomes of the living.

Through offerings and rituals, the Mesopotamians sought to maintain a strong bond with their ancestors. Offerings such as food, drink, incense, and symbolic items were presented to the ancestors as a sign of respect, gratitude, and acknowledgment. These offerings were believed to nourish and sustain the spirits of the ancestors, ensuring their continued presence and assistance.

Rituals associated with ancestor veneration were performed regularly, especially during important occasions such as family gatherings, festivals, and rites of passage. These rituals often involved prayers, invocations, and the recitation of genealogies or ancestral stories, emphasizing the lineage and connection between the living and the deceased.

Ancestor veneration served multiple purposes within Mesopotamian society. Firstly, it provided a sense of continuity and connection across generations. By honoring their ancestors, individuals reaffirmed their place within a larger lineage and acknowledged the contributions and sacrifices of those who came before them. This sense of continuity instilled a deep-rooted identity and a sense of belonging within the community.

Secondly, ancestor veneration was believed to bring practical benefits. The guidance and support of ancestors were sought in matters of daily life, such as decision-making, protection, and seeking blessings for prosperity and well-being. Ancestors were seen as benevolent forces that could offer assistance, wisdom, and protection to their descendants.

Moreover, ancestor veneration had social and communal implications. It reinforced the importance of kinship and family ties, promoting unity and cohesion within the community. Ancestors were often regarded as guardians and protectors of the family, ensuring the well-being and success of future generations. The collective honoring of ancestors created a shared sense of heritage and collective memory, strengthening social bonds and a sense of collective identity.

The practice of ancestor veneration in Mesopotamian culture can be compared to similar practices in other societies and spiritual traditions worldwide. Many cultures around the world hold beliefs and engage in rituals that honor and venerate their ancestors, recognizing their ongoing influence and seeking their guidance and blessings. This includes practices such as ancestor altars, ancestral prayers, and rituals dedicated to the remembrance and honoring of the departed.

The significance of ancestor veneration lies in its ability to foster a sense of connection, continuity, and reverence for the past. It allows individuals to maintain a relationship with their ancestral roots, drawing upon the wisdom, experiences, and blessings of those who came before. Ancestor veneration not only reinforces familial bonds but also strengthens the connection between the living, the deceased, and the divine, creating a sense of interconnectedness and intergenerational support within the fabric of society.

Symbolism and Rituals

To navigate the journey of death and the afterlife, Mesopotamians developed intricate rituals and practices that encompassed both purification and offerings to the gods. These rituals were believed to assist the deceased in their transition and secure their favorable reception in the afterlife.

Purification rituals were a fundamental part of the funerary process in Mesopotamian culture. These rituals involved cleansing the body and preparing it for the afterlife. The deceased would be ritually washed, anointed with oils and perfumes, and dressed in appropriate funerary garments. This purification process was not only physical but also symbolic, signifying the removal of impurities and the preparation of the soul for its journey to the realm of the dead.

Offerings played a crucial role in Mesopotamian funerary rituals. These offerings were made to the gods, seeking their favor and protection for the deceased in the afterlife. Offerings included food, drink, incense, and symbolic objects that were believed to sustain and satisfy the needs of the soul in its new existence. These offerings were often placed in the burial chamber or at the gravesite to ensure the continued provision and care for the deceased.

Spells and incantations were recited during funerary rituals to invoke divine assistance and safeguard the soul during its journey to the afterlife. These spells were believed to possess magical powers and were intended to protect the deceased from malevolent forces and guide them to their designated destiny in the afterlife. The recitation of these incantations was performed by priests or individuals specially trained in the art of magic and ritual.

Symbolic objects held significant importance in Mesopotamian funerary rituals. Funerary offerings, such as figurines, jewelry, and vessels, were included in the burial to provide assistance and comfort to the deceased in the afterlife. These objects were believed to retain their symbolic power and aid the soul in its journey. Amulets and charms were also employed to offer protection against evil spirits and ensure a safe passage to the realm of the dead.

Similar to Mesopotamian culture, various spiritual traditions, including witchcraft, divination, and shamanism, employ symbolism and rituals to navigate the mysteries of death and the afterlife. Symbolic objects and ritualistic practices are utilized to facilitate spiritual transformation and transcendence.

In witchcraft, symbolic objects such as herbs, crystals, and candles are employed to create a sacred space and establish a connection with spiritual energies. Rituals involving spellcasting, divination, and trance states are conducted to explore the realms beyond the physical and seek guidance from spiritual entities.

Divination practices often employ symbolic objects such as tarot cards, runes, or scrying tools to access hidden knowledge and insights about the afterlife. Rituals involving the interpretation of signs and symbols help individuals gain understanding and guidance in navigating the mysteries of death and the spiritual realms.

Shamanic traditions incorporate symbolic objects and ritualistic practices to facilitate communication with the spirit world. Shamanic journeys, often induced through drumming or chanting, allow the shaman to navigate realms beyond the physical and interact with spiritual beings for healing, guidance, and insight into the mysteries of life and death.

The purpose of symbolism and ritualistic practices in these spiritual traditions is to create a sacred space, establish a connection with the divine, and facilitate a transformative and transcendent experience. They serve as vehicles for communication, transformation, and the exploration of the unseen realms. Symbolic objects and rituals provide a framework through which individuals can navigate the mysteries of death and the afterlife, seek spiritual transformation, and deepen their understanding of the nature of existence.

By engaging in these practices, individuals can tap into the power of symbolism and ritual, accessing realms beyond the physical and connecting with the spiritual dimensions of life and death. Symbolism and ritual provide a language and framework through which individuals can navigate the mysteries of the afterlife, seek spiritual growth, and find solace and guidance in the face of mortality.

In conclusion, the concept of death in Mesopotamian culture was deeply intertwined with their beliefs about life, the gods, and the afterlife. Their dualistic worldview, reverence for the gods, and emphasis on ancestor veneration shaped their understanding of mortality and the possibilities of transcendence. Through the exploration of Mesopotamian beliefs and funerary practices, we gain valuable insights into the human quest for meaning, the complexities of mortality, and the enduring significance of honoring the departed.

Funerary Practices and Rituals

Funerary practices and rituals played a significant role in ancient Mesopotamian culture. These practices were designed to honor the deceased, facilitate their journey to the afterlife, and provide comfort to the bereaved. Understanding the funerary customs of Mesopotamia provides valuable insights into their beliefs about death, the afterlife, and the human connection to the divine.

The Significance of Funerary Rituals

Funerary rituals held great significance in ancient Mesopotamia, serving multiple purposes within the cultural and spiritual context of the time. Firstly, these rituals were a means to honor and pay respect to the deceased. Mesopotamians believed that showing reverence and acknowledging the life and accomplishments of the individual was essential. Funerary rituals provided a space for the community to come together, express grief and mourning, and commemorate the life of the departed. Through various ceremonial practices, such as lamentations, offerings, and eulogies, the community sought to ensure that the deceased would be remembered and revered.

Secondly, funerary rituals played a crucial role in facilitating the smooth transition of the deceased to the afterlife. Mesopotamians believed in the existence of an afterlife, where the soul of the deceased would continue its journey. The performance of specific rituals and the provision of funerary offerings were believed to provide the necessary provisions and assistance for the deceased's journey in the afterlife. Purification rituals, spells, and incantations were recited to protect the soul from malevolent forces and guide it to its rightful place in the divine realm.

Furthermore, funerary rituals held a significant role in providing closure and emotional support to the bereaved. These rituals helped the community cope with the loss and navigate the grieving process. They provided a structured framework for expressing grief, sharing memories, and seeking solace in the company of others who were also mourning. Through communal rituals and ceremonies, individuals could find comfort, support, and a sense of unity in their shared experience of loss.

When examining funerary rituals in different spiritual traditions, such as witchcraft, divination, and shamanism, we find that rituals and ceremonies similarly serve important functions in navigating the complexities of death, loss, and grief.

In witchcraft, rituals associated with death and mourning often involve creating sacred space, invoking protective energies, and conducting ceremonies to honor the departed. These rituals provide individuals with a sense of empowerment, allowing them to express their emotions, commune with the deceased, and seek guidance or closure. Symbolic acts, such as lighting candles or performing divination, help individuals connect with the spiritual realm and find solace in the understanding that their loved ones are still present in some form.

Divination practices, on the other hand, may offer a means to seek insights and guidance from the spiritual realm regarding death, loss, and the journey of the departed. Through the interpretation of signs and symbols, individuals can gain a deeper understanding of the circumstances surrounding the passing and find comfort in the knowledge that there is a larger, divine plan at play.

In shamanism, rituals associated with death and grief often involve journeying into the spirit world, connecting with ancestral spirits, and seeking healing and guidance. Shamans may enter altered states of consciousness to communicate with the deceased or retrieve lost souls, facilitating the process of transition and healing for both the departed and the living. These rituals provide a sense of connection and continuity between the living and the deceased, fostering healing, closure, and spiritual growth.

In all of these traditions, rituals and ceremonies surrounding death and funerals provide individuals and communities with a framework to navigate the complex emotions and experiences associated with loss. They offer solace, healing, and a sense of connection to the deceased, as well as a collective space for grieving and finding support. Through the performance of these rituals, individuals can honor the departed, seek closure, and embark on their own journeys of healing and transformation.

Burial and Commemoration

Burial was indeed the most common funerary practice in ancient Mesopotamia. The process of burial involved several rituals and ceremonies that were deeply rooted in the cultural and religious beliefs of the time. The specific practices varied depending on the region and time period, but there were common elements that characterized Mesopotamian burials.

When an individual passed away, the body was prepared for burial. This involved washing, anointing, and sometimes the application of perfumes or oils to preserve the body. The deceased was then wrapped in burial garments or shrouds, often accompanied by personal belongings or symbolic items that held significance in their life or were believed to assist them in the afterlife.

The choice of burial site depended on the social status and wealth of the individual. Wealthy and powerful individuals often had elaborate tombs constructed for their interment. These tombs could be grand structures with multiple chambers and intricate architectural designs. On the other hand, common people were typically buried in simple pits or graves, sometimes with modest markers to identify the burial site.

During the burial process, various rituals and ceremonies took place. Prayers and incantations were recited, invoking the assistance and protection of the gods in ensuring a successful transition to the afterlife. Funerary offerings were also placed in or around the grave. These offerings could include food, drink, tools, weapons, and other items believed to be necessary for the deceased's journey or to sustain them in the afterlife. The purpose of these offerings was to provide the deceased with the provisions and comforts needed for their new existence beyond the earthly realm.

Commemoration of the deceased was a crucial aspect of Mesopotamian funerary practices. Family members and community members would visit the burial site regularly to pay respects and bring offerings. They would offer food, drink, and other items at the gravesite, believing that these offerings would nourish the soul of the departed. Commemorative rituals and festivals were also held on specific occasions to honor the memory of the deceased and ensure their ongoing presence within the community. These rituals served as a way to maintain a connection with the departed, seek their continued protection and guidance, and keep their memory alive.

Overall, Mesopotamian funerary practices reflected a deep reverence for the deceased and a belief in the continuation of the soul's existence beyond death. Burial, accompanied by rituals, offerings, and commemoration, was seen as a means to ensure a smooth transition to the afterlife and to maintain a connection with the departed in the realm of the divine. These practices not only provided solace and closure for the grieving community but also served as a way to honor the memory of the deceased and uphold their importance within the social and cultural fabric of Mesopotamian society.

Funerary Offerings and Grave Goods

Funerary offerings and grave goods held great significance in Mesopotamian burial rituals, as they were believed to provide sustenance, comfort, and assistance to the deceased in the afterlife. The selection of these items was influenced by various factors, including the individual's social status, occupation, and personal preferences.

Food and drink were commonly offered in Mesopotamian burials. The belief was that the deceased would need nourishment and sustenance in their journey to the afterlife. Offerings of bread, meat, fruits, and beverages were made to ensure the well-being and satisfaction of the departed soul. The type and quantity of food offerings often reflected the social standing of the deceased, with wealthier individuals being buried with more lavish provisions.

Clothing and personal belongings were also included as funerary offerings. It was believed that the deceased would require these items in the afterlife for comfort and identity. Clothing, jewelry, and accessories were often placed in the burial chamber or on the body to provide the deceased with familiar and cherished items. These offerings were symbolic of the individual's identity and social status, allowing them to maintain their sense of self in the afterlife.

Weapons and tools were sometimes included as grave goods, particularly for individuals who had military or warrior roles in life. These items were meant to provide protection and assistance in the afterlife, reflecting the belief that the deceased might continue their duties or face challenges beyond death. By equipping the deceased with weapons and tools, they were prepared for any potential dangers or tasks in the realm of the afterlife.

The role of funerary offerings and grave goods varies across different spiritual traditions. In witchcraft, for example, offerings may be made to appease spirits or deities associated with death or the afterlife. These offerings can include herbs, candles, incense, and personal items that hold significance to the deceased. The purpose is to establish a connection with the spirit realm and provide the departed with comfort and support.

In divination, the use of grave goods may differ. Objects such as bones, shells, or cards are often used in divination practices to communicate with the spirits or gain insights into the afterlife. These items serve as tools for the diviner to receive messages or guidance from the spiritual realm.

Shamanism, with its emphasis on spiritual journeys and interactions with the spirit world, may also incorporate the use of objects in funerary rituals. Shamans may use ritualistic tools, such as drums, rattles, or sacred herbs, to connect with the spirits of the deceased and facilitate communication or healing. These objects hold symbolic and spiritual significance, helping the shaman navigate the realms of the afterlife and provide support to the departed souls.

In various spiritual traditions, the symbolism and significance of specific items used in funerary rituals can vary. The offerings and grave goods are often chosen to meet the spiritual and emotional needs of the deceased and the bereaved. They serve as a means to honor the departed, provide comfort and sustenance in the afterlife, establish a connection with the spiritual realm, and facilitate the grieving and healing process for the living.

Ultimately, the inclusion of funerary offerings and grave goods in burial rituals across different traditions reflects the universal human desire to honor and support the departed in their journey beyond life. These symbolic items play a crucial role in addressing the spiritual and emotional needs of both the deceased and the bereaved, ensuring a sense of continuity, comfort, and connection in the face of mortality.

Rituals and Incantations

Rituals and incantations held great importance in Mesopotamian funerary practices, serving as a means to ensure the safe passage of the deceased to the afterlife and to invoke the aid of the gods in protecting the soul. Priests and religious officials were responsible for performing these ceremonies and reciting specific prayers, incantations, and magical formulas.

Purification rites were a crucial aspect of funerary rituals. These rites involved the cleansing and purification of the body, the burial site, and the individuals involved in the burial process. The belief was that purification would remove any impurities and ensure the spiritual well-being of the deceased. Purification rituals often included the use of water, incense, and sacred oils, along with specific gestures and invocations to consecrate the space and individuals involved.

The "opening of the mouth" ceremony was another significant ritual performed during funerary practices. This ceremony aimed to restore the deceased's ability to eat, drink, and breathe in the afterlife. It involved the symbolic opening of the deceased's mouth using specific instruments or gestures, accompanied by prayers and incantations. By performing this ritual, the deceased was believed to regain their essential faculties necessary for a successful journey in the afterlife.

The recitation of spells and incantations played a vital role in Mesopotamian funerary practices. These magical formulas were believed to have protective and transformative powers, helping the soul navigate the challenges of the afterlife and ward off any malevolent forces. The incantations often invoked the names of gods and goddesses associated with death and the afterlife, seeking their aid and protection for the deceased. They were recited by priests or religious officials who had knowledge of the proper rituals and incantations.

These rituals and incantations were not only intended to assist the deceased but also to provide solace and reassurance to the bereaved. The recitation of prayers and incantations served as a means of expressing grief, seeking divine assistance, and fostering a sense of hope and comfort in the face of loss.

Similar to Mesopotamian funerary practices, other spiritual traditions also incorporate rituals and incantations in their approach to death and the afterlife. In witchcraft, for instance, rituals and spells are often performed to communicate with spirits or deities associated with death, seeking their guidance and protection. Incantations and invocations are used to establish a connection with the spiritual realm and to provide assistance to the deceased.

In divination, rituals and incantations may also be employed to gain insights into the afterlife or to communicate with spirits. Diviners may use specific rituals, gestures, or chants to enter into a state of heightened awareness and establish a connection with the spiritual realm.

Shamanic practices often involve rituals and incantations as well. Shamans may engage in trance-like states, using drumming, chanting, or other techniques to enter into contact with spirits or to navigate the realms of the afterlife. Incantations and invocations are recited to seek guidance, healing, or protection for the deceased or to aid the shaman in their journey.

Across these spiritual traditions, rituals and incantations serve multiple purposes. They are performed to ensure the safe passage of the deceased, invoke divine assistance, protect against malevolent forces, provide comfort and solace to the bereaved, and establish a connection with the spiritual realm. Through the recitation of specific prayers, incantations, and magical formulas, individuals and communities seek to navigate the complexities of death, honor the deceased, and find spiritual support and guidance in the face of mortality.

Evolution of Funerary Practices

Funerary practices in Mesopotamia underwent significant changes over time, influenced by shifting societal beliefs, cultural developments, and external influences. By comparing and contrasting funerary practices across different historical periods and cultures, we can gain insights into the factors that shaped these practices and the role of cultural exchange in ancient Mesopotamia.

In early Sumerian society, graves were often located within family homes or in close proximity to settlements. The deceased were interred in simple pits or clay coffins, accompanied by personal belongings and offerings. The emphasis was on maintaining a connection between the living and the deceased, with graves being easily accessible for regular commemorative rituals and offerings.

As civilization advanced and urban centers grew, dedicated burial grounds became more prevalent. During the Akkadian and Babylonian periods, elaborate tomb structures emerged, reflecting the increasing social stratification and the desire to showcase wealth and power even in the afterlife. These tombs, such as the famous royal tombs of Ur, were complex structures containing multiple chambers and elaborate grave goods.

The influence of cultural exchange and external influences also played a significant role in shaping funerary practices in Mesopotamia. The region was a hub of trade and cultural interaction, leading to the assimilation of customs and beliefs from neighboring civilizations. For example, during the Assyrian period, the practice of cremation, which was common among neighboring cultures, began to be incorporated into Mesopotamian funerary rituals.

Religious and cultural developments within Mesopotamia also influenced changes in funerary practices. The rise of city-states and the establishment of more centralized religious institutions led to the involvement of priests and religious officials in conducting funerary rituals. The religious beliefs of the time, such as the worship of specific gods and goddesses associated with the afterlife, influenced the prayers, invocations, and offerings made during burials.

Additionally, societal factors, such as the changing perception of death and the role of the individual in the afterlife, influenced the evolution of funerary practices. As Mesopotamian society became more hierarchical, with a clear distinction between the ruling elite and the common people, the burial customs and grave goods reflected these social divisions. Elaborate tombs and valuable grave goods were reserved for the wealthy and powerful, while simpler burials were conducted for the common people.

External influences, such as invasions and conquests, also left their mark on Mesopotamian funerary practices. For instance, the influence of Persian and Hellenistic cultures introduced new elements and customs into the existing funerary rituals, resulting in a syncretism of beliefs and practices.

In comparing funerary practices with other ancient cultures, such as ancient Egypt or ancient Greece, we find similarities and differences in burial customs and rituals. For example, both Mesopotamian and Egyptian cultures believed in the afterlife and the necessity of preserving the body through burial practices. However, the Egyptians placed a greater emphasis on mummification and elaborate tomb structures, while the Mesopotamians focused more on the offerings, rituals, and commemoration of the deceased.

In conclusion, funerary practices in Mesopotamia underwent changes over time, reflecting societal developments, cultural influences, and the exchange of ideas with neighboring civilizations. The transition from simple burials within family homes to dedicated burial grounds and elaborate tombs demonstrates the evolution of beliefs and social structures. Cultural exchange and external influences, as well as religious and societal factors, played crucial roles in shaping these practices. By comparing funerary practices across different historical periods and cultures, we can gain a deeper understanding of how ancient societies perceived death, the afterlife, and the importance of honoring and commemorating the deceased.

Funerary Practices and Modern Perspectives

The study of ancient Mesopotamian funerary practices offers insights that resonate with modern perspectives on death, grief, and commemoration. By exploring these practices, we can reflect on the universality of human experiences and the ways in which different cultures and traditions approach the mysteries of death and the afterlife. Understanding the rich tapestry of Mesopotamian funerary practices can deepen our appreciation for the diversity of human beliefs and rituals surrounding death.

Engage in a discussion on the relevance of ancient funerary practices in contemporary society. Explore how different spiritual traditions, such as witchcraft, divination, and shamanism, address death, grief, and commemoration. Discuss the ways in which modern individuals and communities can draw inspiration from ancient funerary rituals to create meaningful and personalized approaches to death and mourning.

In conclusion, funerary practices and rituals in ancient Mesopotamia were multifaceted and served various purposes, including honoring the deceased, providing comfort to the bereaved, and facilitating the journey to the afterlife. Burial, commemoration, funerary offerings, rituals, and incantations were central elements of these practices. By studying and reflecting on the rich tapestry of Mesopotamian funerary practices, we gain a deeper understanding of the human relationship with death, grief, and remembrance, and how different cultures throughout history have grappled with these profound aspects of the human experience.

The Netherworld and the Journey of the Soul

In our exploration of the ancient Mesopotamian worldview, we turn our attention to the concept of the Netherworld and the journey of the soul. Mesopotamians held a profound belief in the existence of an afterlife and recognized death as a transformative process rather than an absolute end. They believed that the soul embarked on a perilous journey to the Netherworld, a realm where it would continue its existence and face the judgment of the gods. In this chapter, we delve into the complexities of the Netherworld and the intricacies of the soul's journey, examining their significance within the broader context of ancient Mesopotamian beliefs and practices.

The Netherworld: A Realm of Destiny and Judgment

In the intricate cosmology of Mesopotamia, the concept of the Netherworld held profound significance in understanding the fate of the soul after death. In this chapter, we delve into the complex beliefs surrounding the Netherworld and the journey of the soul within Mesopotamian spiritual traditions. Through an exploration of myths, deities, and cultural practices, we gain insight into the Mesopotamian understanding of death, the afterlife, and the divine forces that govern these realms.

The Netherworld and Its Dimensions:

The Netherworld, situated beneath the Earth's surface, was not a singular realm but comprised different levels and destinies for souls, based on their actions and status during their earthly lives. Mesopotamian cosmology depicted the Netherworld as a multifaceted and intricate domain, intricately woven into the fabric of the universe.

Example: The Levels of the Netherworld

Examine the belief in different levels within the Netherworld in Mesopotamian cosmology. Compare this concept with other spiritual traditions, such as the layers of hell in Dante's Inferno or the realms of existence in Tibetan Buddhism. Analyze the symbolic significance of these different levels and the implications they hold for the fate of the soul.

Deities and Their Roles:

Various deities governed the Netherworld, each wielding authority over different aspects of the afterlife. These divine beings played crucial roles in the journey of the soul, ensuring its safe passage, and determining its fate based on moral accountability.

Example: Ereshkigal, Queen of the Underworld

Explore the mythology surrounding Ereshkigal, the powerful goddess who ruled over the Netherworld. Analyze her role in the judgment of souls and her interactions with other deities, such as Inanna and Nergal. Reflect on the symbolism embodied by Ereshkigal and her significance in the Mesopotamian understanding of death and the afterlife.

The Soul's Journey and its Challenges:

The Mesopotamian belief system posited that the journey of the soul to the Netherworld was fraught with challenges and obstacles. Mythological narratives vividly depicted these perils, emphasizing the importance of sacrifice, surrender, and divine assistance in navigating the afterlife.

Example: The Descent of Ishtar

Examine the myth of Ishtar's descent into the Netherworld, highlighting the challenges and sacrifices she encounters. Discuss the symbolic significance of Ishtar's journey and its parallel to the soul's journey in Mesopotamian cosmology. Analyze the lessons conveyed by this myth and their relevance to the spiritual beliefs and practices of the Mesopotamians.

Exercise:

Imagine you are a Mesopotamian scribe tasked with recording a mythological tale that explains the journey of the soul to the Netherworld. Create a narrative that emphasizes the challenges, divine interactions, and moral implications of this journey. Incorporate elements from existing Mesopotamian myths while adding your unique interpretation and creativity.

Conclusion:

In Mesopotamian spiritual traditions, the concept of the Netherworld held immense significance in understanding the fate of the soul after death. By exploring myths, deities, and cultural practices associated with the Netherworld, we gain a deeper understanding of the Mesopotamian perception of death, the afterlife, and the intricate forces that govern these realms. In the next chapter, we will examine the diverse beliefs about the afterlife found in different spiritual traditions, comparing and contrasting their concepts with those of Mesopotamia.

The Netherworld: A Realm of Varied Destinies

In Mesopotamian belief systems, the Netherworld was conceived as a distinct realm located beneath the Earth's surface. Unlike the world of the living, the Netherworld was not a uniform place, but rather a complex landscape consisting of different levels and destinies for the souls of the deceased. The fate of an individual's soul in the afterlife was believed to be determined by their actions and social status during their earthly existence.

The Role of Deities:

Within the Netherworld, various deities held dominion over different aspects of the afterlife. These divine beings played a crucial role in governing the fate of souls and ensuring the proper functioning of the Netherworld. Among these deities were Nergal, the ruler of the Netherworld, Ereshkigal, the queen of the underworld, and Namtar, the god of fate and destiny. Understanding the roles and responsibilities of these deities provides valuable insight into the Mesopotamian perception of death and the journey of the soul.

Example: Inanna's Descent

The myth of Inanna's descent into the Netherworld serves as a powerful illustration of the challenges and perils faced by the soul in its journey beyond the realm of the living. Inanna, the goddess of fertility and love, voluntarily descends into the Netherworld, passing through seven gates and surrendering her divine garments and powers at each gate. This myth symbolizes the arduous journey of the soul and underscores the significance of sacrifice and surrender in navigating the afterlife. It emphasizes the Mesopotamian belief that the soul must relinquish worldly attachments and face trials to attain a favorable destiny in the Netherworld.

Exercise:

Reflect on the myth of Inanna's descent and its implications for the journey of the soul in Mesopotamian cosmology. Consider the symbolism of the seven gates and Inanna's relinquishment of power. How does this myth highlight the importance of sacrifice and transformation in the afterlife journey? Discuss the parallels between Inanna's descent and the challenges faced by individuals seeking spiritual growth and transcendence in other traditions.

The Annuna Deities:

The Annuna, a group of deities associated with the Netherworld, played a vital role in administering justice and determining the destiny of souls. Led by Nergal and Ereshkigal, these deities were responsible for judging the actions of individuals during their earthly lives and assigning appropriate rewards or punishments in the afterlife. This belief reflects the Mesopotamian emphasis on moral accountability and the notion that one's actions in life would directly influence their fate in the Netherworld.

Problem:

Examine the significance of the Annuna deities in Mesopotamian beliefs about the afterlife. Choose one Annuna deity, such as Nergal or Ereshkigal, and explore their attributes, roles, and influence on the destiny of souls. Consider the ethical implications of the judgment process and the Mesopotamian perspective on the balance between divine justice and mercy.

Conclusion:

The concept of the Netherworld and the journey of the soul in Mesopotamian spirituality offer valuable insights into the belief systems and cultural practices of ancient Mesopotamia. By examining myths, deities, and rituals associated with the Netherworld, we gain a deeper understanding of the Mesopotamian perspective on death, the afterlife, and the moral implications of human actions. These beliefs shaped the way individuals lived their lives and provided a framework for understanding their place in the cosmic order.

The Journey of the Soul: Trials and Transformation

The Mesopotamians held a deep belief in the arduous nature of the soul's journey to the Netherworld. To ensure a successful transition and prepare the deceased for this perilous expedition, they developed elaborate rituals and practices aimed at providing the necessary provisions and assistance. These rituals encompassed purification, offerings, and the recitation of spells and incantations, all of which played a vital role in facilitating the soul's journey and ensuring its well-being in the afterlife.

The Preparation of the Body:

Before the soul embarked on its journey to the Netherworld, the body of the deceased underwent a series of purification rituals and funerary preparations. These rituals were conducted to cleanse the body and facilitate its separation from the physical remains, allowing the soul to transition smoothly into the realm of the dead. The body was carefully washed, anointed with oils and perfumes, and adorned with funerary garb and amulets. These practices were believed to provide protection and guidance to the soul as it navigated the challenges of the afterlife.

Example Exercise:

Reflecting on the significance of the body preparation rituals, imagine you are a Mesopotamian priest responsible for conducting these ceremonies. Design a step-by-step guide outlining the procedures for purifying and preparing the body of the deceased. Consider the specific oils, perfumes, and garments used, and explain their symbolic significance in facilitating the soul's journey to the Netherworld.

Offerings and Incantations:

A crucial aspect of Mesopotamian funerary rituals was the provision of offerings to sustain the soul in the afterlife. These offerings consisted of food, drink, and other symbolic items believed to provide nourishment and comfort to the deceased. Mesopotamians believed that the soul retained its needs and desires after death, and these offerings were meant to ensure its well-being in the Netherworld.

Moreover, priests and religious officials played a significant role in the funerary rituals by reciting prayers, spells, and incantations. These invocations were aimed at invoking the aid of the gods and goddesses, beseeching their protection and guidance for the soul during its journey. The recitation of spells and incantations was considered essential for navigating the challenges and obstacles encountered in the Netherworld.

Example Problem:

Imagine you are a grieving Mesopotamian family seeking guidance from a priest for conducting a proper funerary ritual for your deceased loved one. Write a letter to the priest, outlining your concerns and requesting specific offerings and incantations to ensure a successful journey of the soul to the Netherworld. Include the reasons behind your chosen offerings and the desired outcomes you hope to achieve.

Conclusion:

The Mesopotamians believed that the journey of the soul to the Netherworld was fraught with challenges and obstacles. To prepare for this journey and facilitate a successful transition, they engaged in elaborate rituals and practices. The purification of the body and the provision of offerings aimed to ensure the well-being of the soul in the afterlife. Additionally, the recitation of prayers, spells, and incantations invoked the assistance of the gods and goddesses to guide and protect the soul during its passage. These practices shed light on the Mesopotamian understanding of the afterlife and their deep commitment to ensuring a smooth and prosperous journey for the departed souls. In the next chapter, we will explore the diverse funerary practices and rituals found in other ancient civilizations, comparing and contrasting them with those of Mesopotamia.

Problems and Exercises:

Reflect on the significance of the Netherworld in Mesopotamian culture and its role in shaping their beliefs about death and the afterlife. What evidence from ancient texts and artifacts supports this understanding?

Compare the concept of the Netherworld in Mesopotamian culture with the notion of the afterlife in other ancient civilizations, such as ancient Egypt or ancient Greece. Identify similarities and differences in their beliefs, rituals, and practices.

Imagine you are a priest in ancient Mesopotamia responsible for conducting funerary rituals. Design a comprehensive ritual script that incorporates purification rites, offerings, and the recitation of spells and incantations. Explain the symbolism and purpose of each element in the ritual.

Conclusion:

The Netherworld and the journey of the soul were integral components of ancient Mesopotamian beliefs and funerary practices. The concept of the Netherworld provided a framework for understanding the afterlife as a distinct realm governed by divine forces, where souls would face judgment and experience rewards or punishments based on their actions in life. The rituals and preparations undertaken by the Mesopotamians were aimed at facilitating the soul's journey and ensuring its well-being in the Netherworld. By studying these beliefs and practices, we gain a deeper appreciation for the Mesopotamian worldview and their profound engagement with the mysteries of death and the afterlife.

Beliefs about the Afterlife

In our exploration of spiritual traditions across different cultures and time periods, we now delve into the fascinating realm of beliefs about the afterlife. The concept of an afterlife, a continuation of existence beyond physical death, has intrigued and captivated human beings throughout history. In this chapter, we will explore how various spiritual traditions, including Witchcraft, Divination, Herbalism, Shamanism, Ecospirituality, and Magic in Ancient Mesopotamia, perceive and interpret the nature of the afterlife. By examining these diverse perspectives, we aim to deepen our understanding of how different cultures grapple with questions of mortality, transcendence, and the eternal journey of the soul.

The Afterlife Across Spiritual Traditions:

Witchcraft:

Witchcraft, as a spiritual practice deeply rooted in nature and the cycles of life, encompasses a range of beliefs about the afterlife. One prominent belief within many traditions of Witchcraft is the concept of reincarnation, where the soul undergoes a series of physical embodiments in different lifetimes. This cyclic view of life and death is closely tied to the natural rhythms and interconnectedness of the universe.

According to the belief in reincarnation, the soul is not seen as a fixed entity but as an eternal essence that learns, evolves, and grows through multiple incarnations. Each lifetime presents opportunities for the soul to gain wisdom, learn lessons, and fulfill its purpose. The experiences and actions of one lifetime shape the circumstances and lessons of subsequent lives.

The concept of reincarnation in Witchcraft has profound implications for how Witches view their own lives and their relationships with other beings. It emphasizes personal responsibility and the understanding that one's actions in the present life have consequences that carry forward into future incarnations. This belief encourages individuals to take ownership of their choices and actively engage in personal and spiritual growth.

Moreover, the belief in reincarnation fosters a sense of compassion and empathy towards others. Witches recognize that each person they encounter may be on their own unique soul journey, shaped by their past experiences and lessons. This understanding encourages Witches to approach relationships with empathy, recognizing the potential for growth and transformation in themselves and others.

Example Exercise:

Reflecting on the concept of reincarnation in Witchcraft, contemplate your own beliefs about the afterlife and the idea of multiple lifetimes. Write a personal reflection exploring how the belief in reincarnation can influence your understanding of personal growth, responsibility, and relationships with others. Consider the lessons you may have learned or the experiences that have shaped your present life and how they may contribute to your soul's journey.

In addition to the belief in reincarnation, some traditions within Witchcraft envision the afterlife as a realm where the spirits of the deceased continue to exist and play a role in the lives of the living. These spirits may be honored and communicated with through various ritual practices, creating a bridge between the worlds of the living and the departed. This belief in the ongoing presence and influence of the departed spirits emphasizes the interconnectedness of all beings and the importance of maintaining a relationship with the ancestors.

Example Problem:

Research and explore different ritual practices within Witchcraft that are aimed at honoring and communicating with the spirits of the deceased. Choose one ritual and describe its purpose, steps, and the symbolism behind each component. Reflect on the significance of these practices in fostering a connection with the afterlife and the impact they may have on the practitioner's spiritual journey.

Conclusion:

Witchcraft encompasses diverse beliefs about the afterlife, including the concept of reincarnation and the existence of spirits in the realm of the departed. The belief in reincarnation highlights the interconnectedness of all beings and emphasizes personal growth and responsibility across multiple lifetimes. The understanding of ongoing communication with the spirits of the deceased fosters a connection between the worlds of the living and the departed, honoring the ancestors and recognizing their continued presence and influence. These beliefs and practices within Witchcraft provide a unique perspective on the afterlife and offer practitioners a framework for personal growth, spiritual development, and meaningful relationships with others. In the next chapter, we will explore the fascinating world of divination and its role in various spiritual traditions, including Witchcraft.

Divination:

Divination, a practice deeply ingrained in various spiritual traditions, serves as a means of seeking guidance, insight, and understanding from the realms beyond. Within the realm of divination, the afterlife holds a significant place, as practitioners strive to explore the mysteries and gain deeper understanding of past lives, future possibilities, and connections with ancestral spirits.

Different divinatory systems and techniques provide practitioners with avenues to delve into the realms of the afterlife. For example, the use of tarot cards, a popular divination tool, allows individuals to tap into archetypal symbolism and interpret the messages received from the cards. The imagery and narratives depicted in the tarot can shed light on aspects of the afterlife, offering glimpses into the spiritual dimensions and shedding light on the journey of the soul.

Similarly, runes, an ancient divination tool associated with Norse traditions, provide a means of connecting with ancestral spirits and accessing wisdom from the past. By casting and interpreting the runic symbols, practitioners can gain insights into the afterlife and receive guidance from the unseen realms. Each rune carries its own meaning and significance, offering a unique perspective on the journey of the soul and its connection to the afterlife.

Another divination technique, scrying, involves gazing into reflective surfaces such as mirrors or bowls of water to receive messages and visions from the spiritual realms. Through scrying, individuals can tap into the energies of the afterlife and gain access to hidden knowledge and insights. The process of scrying allows practitioners to connect with the subconscious mind and the collective wisdom of the universe, providing a window into the mysteries of the afterlife.

The practice of divination allows individuals to seek guidance and support in navigating the complexities of life and death. Through divinatory readings, practitioners can pose questions and receive guidance on matters related to the afterlife, such as understanding the lessons of past lives, gaining insight into future possibilities, or communicating with ancestral spirits. Divination serves as a tool for introspection, contemplation, and connection with the spiritual dimensions, offering individuals a means to explore and understand the afterlife in their own unique way.

Example Exercise:

Choose a divination tool that resonates with you, such as tarot cards, runes, or scrying mirror. Set aside a quiet and sacred space for your practice. Formulate a question or intention related to the afterlife that you wish to explore. Perform a divinatory reading using your chosen tool, following the appropriate rituals and methods associated with it. Take note of the symbols, images, and messages that arise during the reading. Reflect on their significance and record your insights and interpretations in a journal. Consider how the guidance received may provide you with a deeper understanding of the afterlife and its relevance to your own spiritual journey.

Conclusion:

Divination, as a practice aimed at seeking guidance and insight, offers practitioners the opportunity to explore the mysteries of the afterlife. Through divinatory systems such as tarot cards, runes, or scrying mirrors, individuals can gain glimpses into the realms beyond, accessing wisdom from past lives, receiving messages from ancestral spirits, and exploring the possibilities of the future. The use of divination tools serves as a portal to the unseen realms, enabling practitioners to deepen their understanding of the afterlife and find guidance in navigating the complexities of life and death. In the next chapter, we will delve into the realm of herbalism and its role in various spiritual traditions, including its connection to the afterlife.

Herbalism:

Herbalism, a practice deeply rooted in the healing power of plants, encompasses a rich tapestry of beliefs and practices surrounding the afterlife. Within the realm of herbal traditions, different perspectives and approaches exist, each offering unique insights into the role of plants in facilitating communication with ancestral spirits and guiding the soul's journey after death.

In various herbal traditions, it is believed that certain plants possess specific properties that enable them to act as conduits between the living and the departed. These plants are revered for their spiritual qualities and their ability to bridge the gap between the earthly realm and the realms beyond. By utilizing these plants in rituals and preparations, practitioners seek to honor and connect with their ancestors, drawing on the inherent wisdom and guidance that the departed spirits may offer.

Herbal preparations used in rituals associated with the afterlife may include incenses, potions, or teas. These preparations are often crafted with intention, incorporating specific herbs known for their associations with the afterlife. The choice of herbs is guided by their energetic properties, folklore, historical usage, and cultural significance.

For example, mugwort (Artemisia vulgaris) is a herb commonly associated with the afterlife in various herbal traditions. It is believed to have protective and purifying properties and is often used in incense blends or smudging rituals to create a sacred space for communication with ancestral spirits. Mugwort is also thought to enhance dreams and astral projection, offering a pathway for connecting with the realms beyond.

Another herb frequently linked to the afterlife is rosemary (Rosmarinus officinalis). In some herbal traditions, rosemary is associated with remembrance and is used to honor departed loved ones. Its aromatic qualities are said to help uplift the spirit and facilitate communication with ancestral spirits during rituals or meditative practices.

Exercise:

Conduct research on herbs commonly associated with the afterlife in different herbal traditions. Explore their cultural, historical, and spiritual significance. Consider their energetic properties, symbolism, and folklore. Create a detailed herbal blend or ritual preparation using a selection of these herbs, with the intention of honoring and connecting with your ancestors.

As you craft your herbal blend, reflect on the specific qualities of each herb and how they contribute to your intention. Consider the scents, tastes, and textures of the herbs and how they evoke feelings and memories. Engage your senses as you blend the herbs, infusing your preparation with intention and reverence.

Once your herbal blend or ritual preparation is complete, set up a sacred space for your ritual. Light candles, burn incense, or play soft music to create a serene atmosphere. Perform the ritual with mindfulness and gratitude, expressing your intentions and invoking the presence of your ancestors.

After the ritual, take time to reflect on your experience. Journal your thoughts, feelings, and any insights or messages you received during the ritual. Consider the significance of these herbal allies in your spiritual practice and how they have deepened your connection to the afterlife and your ancestors.

In conclusion, herbalism offers a unique perspective on the afterlife, highlighting the belief in the spiritual qualities of plants and their ability to facilitate communication with ancestral spirits. By researching and working with herbs commonly associated with the afterlife, practitioners can create meaningful rituals and preparations that honor and connect them with their ancestors. In the next chapter, we will explore the ancient practice of shamanism and its profound relationship with the realms of spirits and the afterlife.

Conclusion:

Beliefs about the afterlife vary across spiritual traditions, reflecting the rich tapestry of human experiences, cultural influences, and personal interpretations. From the cyclical perspective of reincarnation in Witchcraft to the divinatory glimpses into other realms, and the herbal connections with ancestral spirits, each tradition offers unique insights into the mysteries beyond physical existence. By engaging with these diverse beliefs and practices, we broaden our understanding of the human quest for transcendence, our relationship with mortality, and the enduring nature of the soul's journey. Through critical thinking and exploration, we deepen our own spiritual connections and forge a path of personal growth and transformation.

Royal Funerary Traditions

In our exploration of funerary practices, we now turn our attention to the intriguing world of royal funerals. Throughout history, the passing of a monarch or a member of the royal family has been marked by elaborate rituals and ceremonies that reflect the unique status and power attributed to these individuals. In this chapter, we will delve into the royal funerary traditions across various spiritual traditions, including Witchcraft, Divination, Herbalism, Shamanism, Ecospirituality, and Magic in Ancient Mesopotamia. By examining these practices, we aim to gain insight into the cultural significance of royal deaths and the ways in which they shape our understanding of mortality, power, and spiritual transcendence.

Royal Funerary Traditions Across Spiritual Traditions:

Witchcraft:

In the context of Witchcraft traditions, the passing of a royal figure is regarded as a significant event that carries profound implications for both the community and the spiritual realm. The rituals and ceremonies surrounding a royal funeral within Witchcraft emphasize the importance of community participation in honoring the departed monarch, acknowledging their contributions, and facilitating their peaceful transition into the realm of ancestors.

Community participation plays a crucial role in Witchcraft rituals for a royal funeral. These rituals are designed to foster a collective healing and remembrance process, allowing the community to come together to mourn, celebrate, and honor the life and legacy of the departed ruler. By actively engaging in these rituals, community members not only pay their respects to the deceased but also strengthen their bonds with one another, forging a sense of unity and shared purpose.

One way in which community participation is emphasized in Witchcraft rituals is through the creation of sacred spaces. These spaces serve as focal points for the rituals, providing a container for communal grieving, reflection, and spiritual connection. Community members may gather in designated areas, such as a consecrated circle or a specially prepared altar, to collectively engage in prayers, invocations, and spellwork. Through their presence and active involvement, individuals contribute to the energetic and spiritual atmosphere, creating a powerful collective intention and supporting the journey of the departed monarch's soul.

In Witchcraft practices, the recitation of spells and invocations holds significant importance during royal funeral rituals. These spoken or chanted words serve as vehicles for expressing grief, gratitude, and well-wishes for the departed ruler. By reciting spells and invocations together, the community members create a harmonious and resonant energy that amplifies the intention of the rituals. Through their collective voice, they convey their love, honor, and blessings to the departed monarch, offering a collective voice of remembrance and support.

Offering symbolic items is another way in which community participation is manifested in Witchcraft rituals for a royal funeral. These symbolic items, which may include flowers, candles, or personal mementos, are presented as gifts to the departed monarch's spirit. The act of offering symbolizes the community's deep respect, appreciation, and desire to assist the departed monarch in their journey beyond the earthly realm. Community members may contribute their own offerings, each infused with their personal intentions and prayers, creating a tapestry of collective love and support.

Historically, examples of community participation in Witchcraft rituals for a royal funeral can be found in various cultures and time periods. For instance, in ancient Celtic traditions, the passing of a monarch was marked by elaborate funeral ceremonies that involved the entire community. These ceremonies included processions, communal feasting, and the participation of priests, priestesses, and community members in ritual activities to honor the departed ruler and ensure their smooth transition into the realm of ancestors.

In contemporary Witchcraft practices, community participation in royal funeral rituals continues to hold great significance. Witches and practitioners come together to create sacred spaces, perform rituals, and offer their collective energy and support for the departed monarch. For example, modern Wiccan covens may organize rituals to honor the memory of a deceased monarch, incorporating elements such as ceremonial rites, spellwork, and the sharing of personal stories and reflections. These communal gatherings provide an opportunity for healing, remembrance, and the reaffirmation of community bonds.

In conclusion, community participation in Witchcraft rituals for a royal funeral plays a vital role in the healing and remembrance process. By coming together, community members honor the contributions of the departed monarch, forge a sense of unity and support, and facilitate the peaceful transition of the ruler's spirit into the realm of ancestors. Through shared sacred spaces, the recitation of spells and invocations, and the offering of symbolic items, the collective energy and intention of the community contribute to a profound and transformative experience of grief, healing, and spiritual connection.

Divination:

Divination practices surrounding royal funerals within mystical and divinatory traditions serve as a means to gain insights into the spiritual significance of the monarch's passing and the potential impact it may have on the realm. These practices aim to establish a connection with the wisdom of the spirits and divine guidance, providing valuable information to navigate the transition of power and ensure the stability and prosperity of the kingdom.

Various divinatory methods can be employed during royal funerals to glean insights and receive guidance for the transition of power. One such method is scrying, a practice that involves gazing into a reflective surface or a crystal ball to access intuitive knowledge and receive messages from the spiritual realm. Scrying can offer glimpses into the future and provide clarity on the potential outcomes and challenges that may arise during a royal succession. By attuning to the subtle energies and symbols revealed through scrying, diviners can uncover hidden truths and make informed decisions to facilitate a smooth transition of power.

Tarot readings, another widely used divinatory tool, can also play a significant role in understanding the dynamics surrounding a royal succession. Tarot cards, with their rich symbolism and archetypal imagery, provide a framework through which diviners can access higher wisdom and receive guidance. During a tarot reading focused on a hypothetical royal succession, the diviner may draw cards representing different aspects of the situation, such as the current state of the kingdom, potential candidates for succession, and the overall outcome. Interpreting the cards and their relationships can reveal insights into the challenges, opportunities, and potential paths that may unfold during the transition of power.

Other forms of oracle work, such as rune casting, I Ching consultation, or astrology, can also be employed in divination practices surrounding royal funerals. Each divinatory system offers its own unique symbols, patterns, and methodologies to gain insights into the future and navigate complex situations. Diviners proficient in these systems can harness their tools to delve into the energies and dynamics surrounding a royal succession, facilitating a deeper understanding of the potential outcomes and providing guidance to ensure a stable and harmonious transition.

The exercise for this chapter involves performing a divination reading using a divinatory tool of choice to explore the potential outcomes and challenges surrounding a hypothetical royal succession. This exercise allows students to actively engage with divination and experience firsthand how it can provide insights and guidance in navigating transitions of power. Students can select their preferred divinatory tool, whether it be tarot cards, runes, scrying, or any other divinatory system, and use it to conduct a reading focused on a royal succession scenario. They can reflect on the symbolism and messages received, contemplate the potential implications for the kingdom, and consider the role of divination in facilitating a smooth transition.

Through this exercise, students can deepen their understanding of the practical application of divination in real-life situations, particularly in the context of royal funerals and successions. They can explore the nuances and complexities involved in interpreting divinatory messages, gain insights into the potential challenges and opportunities surrounding power transitions, and reflect on the role of divination in fostering stability, harmony, and informed decision-making within a kingdom or community.

By actively engaging in divination exercises and contemplating their experiences, students can develop their intuition, hone their divinatory skills, and appreciate the significance of divination practices in various spiritual and mystical traditions. They can further recognize how divination can serve as a valuable tool in navigating times of transition, providing guidance, and supporting the well-being and prosperity of a community.

Herbalism:

Herbal practices related to royal funerals encompass the creation of ceremonial blends or incenses that are carefully crafted with specific intentions and purposes. These botanical concoctions are designed to honor the deceased monarch, invoke protection for the kingdom, or assist in the spiritual journey of the departed ruler. The selection and combination of herbs in these ceremonial blends are guided by their energetic properties and symbolic significance, reflecting the spiritual beliefs and cultural traditions associated with the funeral rites.

The exercise for this chapter involves researching the herbs commonly associated with funeral rituals in different cultural contexts and creating a ceremonial herbal blend using these herbs. By engaging in this exercise, students will explore the cultural and symbolic meanings attached to specific herbs and gain practical experience in crafting herbal preparations for ceremonial purposes.

Students can begin the exercise by researching the herbs traditionally used in funeral rituals across various cultures. They can investigate the customs and beliefs surrounding death and funerary practices in different traditions, such as ancient Egyptian, Chinese, Native American, or European cultures. Through this research, students can identify common herbs and their symbolic associations with death, mourning, remembrance, and spiritual transition.

After gathering information about the herbs, students can then proceed to create a ceremonial herbal blend with the intention of honoring and supporting the passing of a hypothetical royal figure. They can carefully select the herbs based on their cultural significance, energetic properties, and personal resonance. Students may choose to include herbs such as rosemary for remembrance, lavender for tranquility, myrrh for spiritual purification, or frankincense for elevation of consciousness, among others. The specific herbs chosen will depend on the cultural context being explored and the desired intentions of the ceremonial blend.

During the blending process, students can consider the proportions and combinations of the selected herbs, mindful of creating a harmonious and balanced blend. They can reflect on the scent, color, and texture of each herb and how they contribute to the overall sensory experience and symbolic representation of the blend. It is important for students to document their process, taking note of the herbs used, their cultural and symbolic meanings, and their personal reflections on the significance of the blend in the context of a royal funeral.

Through this exercise, students gain practical knowledge in the application of herbalism within the context of royal funerals. They deepen their understanding of the cultural and symbolic meanings associated with specific herbs in different traditions, and develop their skills in creating ceremonial blends with intention and reverence. This exercise encourages students to engage in a hands-on exploration of herbal practices and encourages them to reflect on the profound role that herbs can play in honoring and supporting the passage of a royal figure into the realm of ancestors.

Conclusion:

Royal funerary traditions provide a window into the intricate relationship between power, spirituality, and the human experience of mortality. Across various spiritual traditions, the passing of a monarch is marked by rituals and practices that honor their contributions, seek guidance for the future, and ensure a peaceful transition of power. By studying these traditions, we gain a deeper understanding of the interplay between the earthly realm and the spiritual dimensions, and the ways in which royal deaths shape the cultural and spiritual fabric of a community. Through critical thinking and engagement with diverse perspectives, we expand our knowledge of the complexities surrounding royal funerary traditions and their impact on our collective understanding of life, death, and the eternal journey of the soul.

Mourning and Ancestor Worship

In our exploration of spiritual traditions, we now turn our attention to the profound practices of mourning and ancestor worship. Across various cultures and belief systems, the process of mourning holds a significant place in honoring the deceased and providing solace to the bereaved. In this chapter, we will delve into the rich tapestry of mourning rituals and explore the transformative power of ancestor worship. Drawing upon examples from Witchcraft, Divination, Herbalism, Shamanism, Ecospirituality, and Magic in Ancient Mesopotamia, we will examine the deep-rooted connections between the living and the departed and the ways in which these practices shape our understanding of life, death, and the continuum of existence.

Mourning Rituals:

Mourning rituals are deeply ingrained in human experience, offering a means to navigate the complex emotions and challenges that arise when a loved one passes away. Across spiritual traditions, mourning rituals are characterized by unique practices that honor the deceased, provide support to the bereaved, and facilitate the healing process.

Witchcraft:

Witchcraft traditions place great importance on the acknowledgment and honoring of the deceased, as well as the recognition of the cyclical nature of life and death. In the context of mourning rituals, creating a sacred space holds significant meaning and serves as a fundamental practice in Witchcraft. This practice provides a container for the grieving process, allowing individuals to navigate their emotions and find solace within the support of their community.

The significance of creating a sacred space in Witchcraft mourning rituals lies in its ability to establish a designated and intentional space where individuals can engage in the grieving process. This space serves as a sanctuary, separate from the demands and distractions of everyday life, where mourners can fully immerse themselves in their emotions, memories, and connection to the departed. By intentionally setting aside a sacred space, individuals create a focused and safe environment for exploration, healing, and remembrance.

The creation of a sacred space typically involves various elements that facilitate the grieving process. These elements may include the arrangement of meaningful objects, such as photographs, mementos, or symbols associated with the deceased, within the space. Candles, incense, or other sacred tools may be used to evoke a sense of reverence and sacredness. The space can be adorned with flowers, plants, or natural elements that symbolize growth, transformation, and the cycles of life and death.

Creating a sacred space in Witchcraft mourning rituals provides a dedicated and intentional container for the grieving process. It allows individuals to fully immerse themselves in their emotions, memories, and spiritual connections with the departed. The act of intentionally setting aside a space communicates the importance of honoring the deceased and provides a physical and energetic focal point for grief and remembrance.

Personal experiences and observations within Witchcraft communities highlight the profound impact of creating a sacred space in mourning rituals. In these communities, individuals often express how the act of creating and tending to a sacred space offers a sense of comfort, grounding, and permission to fully embrace the grieving process. The space becomes a sanctuary where individuals can openly express their emotions, engage in rituals of remembrance, and seek guidance and support from ancestral spirits.

Moreover, the communal aspect of Witchcraft mourning rituals enhances the significance of the sacred space. The shared experience of creating and participating in a sacred space allows for the collective processing of grief and the sharing of stories, memories, and support among community members. This communal support creates a sense of belonging and interconnectedness, fostering healing and resilience within the group.

In conclusion, creating a sacred space in Witchcraft mourning rituals holds deep significance. It provides a dedicated container for the grieving process, allowing individuals to explore their emotions, honor the memory of the departed, and seek solace within the support of their community. The intentional creation of a sacred space communicates the importance of the ritual and creates a focused and safe environment for healing, remembrance, and spiritual connection. Through personal experiences and observations within Witchcraft communities, it is evident that the practice of creating a sacred space enhances the grieving process and fosters a sense of communal support and healing.

Divination:

Divination practices play a significant role in Witchcraft mourning rituals by offering a means to connect with the wisdom of the spirits and seek guidance during the grieving process. Divination methods, such as tarot reading, scrying, or mediumship, allow individuals to establish a channel of communication with the departed, gaining insights into their own journey of healing and navigating the complexities of grief. Through divination, individuals can find comfort, reassurance, and a profound sense of connection with the deceased, fostering ongoing dialogue and support.

Engaging in divination during the mourning process provides a way to seek solace, understanding, and guidance in navigating the emotional terrain of grief. Divinatory tools, such as tarot cards, provide a symbolic language through which individuals can explore their emotions, ask questions, and receive guidance from the spiritual realm. By drawing upon the archetypal imagery and intuitive interpretations of the cards, the reader can gain insights and perspectives that help them find meaning and support in their grief journey.

Scrying, another divinatory practice commonly used in Witchcraft, involves gazing into reflective surfaces, such as mirrors or bowls of water, to access hidden realms and receive messages from the departed or spirit guides. This form of divination allows individuals to enter a meditative state and establish a connection with the unseen forces, opening avenues for communication, guidance, and healing during the mourning process.

Mediumship, the ability to communicate with spirits or deceased loved ones, is also prevalent in Witchcraft mourning rituals. Mediums act as conduits, channeling messages and information from the spiritual realm to provide comfort, closure, and guidance to those grieving. Through mediumship, individuals can engage in direct communication with the departed, seeking answers, validation, or simply the reassurance that their loved ones continue to exist in some form.

The exercise of performing a divination reading using a preferred divinatory tool in the context of mourning invites individuals to seek guidance on navigating the grief and healing process after the loss of a loved one. By focusing their intentions on the specific questions or concerns related to their mourning journey, they can draw cards, scry into a reflective surface, or engage in other divinatory practices to receive messages and insights. Reflecting on the messages received, individuals can explore how divination contributes to finding meaning, support, and a sense of connection with the deceased during the mourning process.

Through personal experiences and observations, it is evident that divination practices offer profound comfort and reassurance during the grieving process. The messages received through divination can provide individuals with a sense of guidance, validation, and ongoing connection with their departed loved ones. Divination becomes a tool for navigating the complexities of grief, offering insights and perspectives that help individuals find meaning, make decisions, and embrace the healing process.

In conclusion, divination practices play a crucial role in Witchcraft mourning rituals by offering a means to connect with the wisdom of the spirits and seek guidance during the grieving process. Whether through tarot reading, scrying, mediumship, or other divinatory methods, individuals can establish communication channels with the departed and receive insights and support for their own healing journey. Divination provides comfort, reassurance, and a profound sense of connection, fostering ongoing dialogue and facilitating the exploration of meaning and support during mourning.

Ancestor Worship:

Ancestor worship is a practice that recognizes the ongoing influence of deceased ancestors on the lives of their descendants. It is a common thread that runs through various spiritual and cultural traditions, fostering a sense of continuity, guidance, and connection with the past. Within the context of ancestor worship, herbalism serves as a powerful tool for honoring and communicating with ancestors, creating tangible and meaningful connections with the spiritual realm.

Herbalism, as it relates to ancestor worship, involves the use of plants and botanical preparations to honor and connect with ancestors. Herbal offerings are made at ancestral altars or gravesites as a gesture of gratitude and a means to seek blessings and wisdom from the departed. These botanical connections serve as tangible reminders of the ongoing presence of ancestors in daily life, bridging the gap between the physical and spiritual realms.

The exercise of researching traditional herbs associated with ancestor worship in different cultures and selecting three herbs that resonate personally allows individuals to create a small herbal bundle or arrangement as an offering to honor and connect with their ancestors. Each herb holds its own symbolism and significance, adding depth and intention to the offering. Reflecting on the chosen herbs and their meanings fosters a deeper understanding of the ancestral connection and invites personal reflection on the journey of one's lineage.

Shamanism, another spiritual tradition that commonly incorporates ancestor worship, often involves direct communication and interaction with ancestral spirits. Shamans, as intermediaries between the spiritual and physical realms, employ various practices such as journeying, trance states, or ecstatic rituals to connect with and seek guidance, healing, and wisdom from the ancestors. These practices establish a bridge between the realms of the living and the deceased, fostering a rich and dynamic relationship with ancestral energies.

Within shamanic traditions, the rituals and practices of journeying or entering trance states serve as gateways to communicate with ancestral spirits. Through these altered states of consciousness, shamans can access the wisdom, guidance, and healing powers of their ancestors. The interactions with ancestral spirits are not only beneficial for personal growth and healing but also contribute to the well-being of the community as a whole. Shamanic practitioners often act as conduits for ancestral messages, bringing back insights and teachings that can guide individuals and support the greater collective.

The practices of herbalism and shamanism within the context of ancestor worship highlight the significance of connecting with and honoring the wisdom and presence of ancestors. Herbal offerings and rituals create a tangible and ceremonial space for communication and reverence, bridging the gap between the physical and spiritual realms. The inclusion of herbs in ancestral practices holds profound symbolism, as plants have long been associated with life, growth, and transformation. These practices offer a means to honor, seek guidance from, and establish a living relationship with one's ancestors, fostering a sense of interconnectedness and ancestral wisdom that can be carried forward for generations to come.

In conclusion, ancestor worship is a practice that recognizes the ongoing influence of deceased ancestors on the lives of their descendants. Within the realms of herbalism and shamanism, ancestral connections are deepened and nurtured. Herbal offerings and rituals serve as a tangible means to honor and communicate with ancestors, while shamanic practices facilitate direct interaction and guidance from ancestral spirits. These practices create bridges between the physical and spiritual realms, fostering a sense of continuity, guidance, and connection with the past.

Problem:

Discuss the role of trance states in shamanic practices related to ancestor worship. How do trance states facilitate communication and communion with ancestral spirits? Share an example from shamanic traditions or personal experiences to illustrate your understanding.

Conclusion:

Mourning rituals and ancestor worship offer profound ways to honor the deceased, process grief, and maintain a connection with our ancestral heritage. Across spiritual traditions, these practices provide a framework for healing, remembrance, and ongoing dialogue with the departed. By engaging with the rituals and exercises presented in this chapter, you will gain a deeper understanding of the transformative power of mourning and the ways in which ancestor worship can nurture a sense of continuity and connection with the past. Through critical thinking and personal reflection, you will explore how these

practices intersect with your own beliefs and experiences, fostering a deeper
appreciation for the richness of human spiritual expression.

Funerary Art and Symbolism

In our exploration of spiritual traditions, we now turn our attention to the
profound world of funerary art and symbolism. Across cultures and throughout
history, human beings have expressed their beliefs, emotions, and reverence for
the deceased through artistic creations associated with death and the afterlife. In
this chapter, we will embark on a journey through the realms of Witchcraft,
Divination, Herbalism, Shamanism, Ecospirituality, and Magic in Ancient
Mesopotamia to unravel the intricate tapestry of funerary art and its profound
symbolism. By examining the rich array of artifacts, monuments, and artistic
expressions, we will discover the deep layers of meaning and significance they hold
in shaping our perceptions of mortality, remembrance, and the transcendence of
the human spirit.

Funerary Art and Its Significance:

Funerary art encompasses a wide range of artistic expressions created
specifically to accompany the deceased on their journey to the afterlife and to
commemorate their lives. These artworks serve as powerful symbols that convey
cultural beliefs, individual identities, and collective memory. They provide a
tangible connection between the living and the departed, bridging the gap between
mortality and the eternal.

Witchcraft:

Funerary art plays a significant role in honoring the deceased and
commemorating their lives across various cultures and spiritual traditions. In the
context of Witchcraft, funerary art takes on unique forms that embody symbols of
protection, guidance, and transformation. These artistic expressions serve as
potent tools for connecting with the departed and bridging the gap between the
mortal realm and the eternal.

Within Witchcraft, funerary art can manifest in different ways, from personal
talismans to elaborate ritual objects. These artifacts are carefully crafted and
imbued with intention to support the deceased on their journey and to honor their
memory. One example of funerary art in Witchcraft is the creation of amulets or
pendants that are designed to be worn or placed with the deceased. These amulets
are often crafted using specific stones, herbs, or sigils that hold symbolic
significance within Witchcraft traditions.

The choice of materials in designing a funerary amulet can be influenced by personal preferences and the symbolic associations within Witchcraft. For example, certain gemstones such as amethyst, known for its protective properties, or obsidian, associated with transformation and the spirit world, may be incorporated into the amulet. Similarly, specific herbs or botanical elements may be added to enhance the amulet's energetic qualities and connection to nature.

Symbols also play a crucial role in the design of a funerary amulet in Witchcraft. These symbols can represent various aspects such as protection, guidance, or the cycles of life and death. For instance, a pentagram, a widely recognized symbol in Witchcraft, may be included to symbolize protection and spiritual connection. Other symbols, such as keys to represent unlocking spiritual realms or feathers to symbolize the connection with the spirit world, can be incorporated based on personal and cultural associations.

Colors hold significance in Witchcraft as well, and they can be intentionally chosen to convey specific meanings and energies. For instance, black is often associated with mystery, transformation, and the spirit world, while white represents purity, light, and spiritual guidance. The selection of colors in the design of a funerary amulet can evoke specific emotions and intentions tied to the journey of the deceased and their connection with the spiritual realm.

The exercise of designing a funerary amulet inspired by Witchcraft allows for personal creativity and reflection. Through this process, one can explore the materials, symbols, and colors that hold personal meaning or resonate with Witchcraft traditions. It provides an opportunity to delve into the intentions behind the design, considering the desires to offer protection and guidance for the deceased during their transition to the afterlife.

In conclusion, funerary art in Witchcraft encompasses a range of artistic expressions that hold symbolic significance and serve as powerful tools for honoring the departed and facilitating their journey to the afterlife. Through the creation of funerary amulets and other ritual objects, Witchcraft practitioners seek to provide protection, guidance, and transformation for the deceased. The exercise of designing a funerary amulet inspired by Witchcraft encourages personal reflection and intentionality, drawing upon the materials, symbols, and colors that hold personal meaning and resonate with the traditions of Witchcraft.

Divination:

In the realm of Divination, funerary art takes on a unique significance as it serves as a visual representation and gateway to the realms of the deceased and the afterlife. Divinatory practices often incorporate symbolic imagery and artistic creations that enable individuals to gain insights, understanding, and guidance from the spiritual realms.

One form of funerary art in Divination is found in tarot cards. Tarot decks often include cards that depict the archetype of death, symbolizing transformation, rebirth, and the cycles of life. These cards serve as reminders of the impermanence of life and the continuous process of change. By including such cards in divination readings, individuals can explore the deeper meanings and lessons associated with mortality, transformation, and the journey of the soul.

Scrying mirrors are another example of funerary art in Divination. These mirrors, often made of dark reflective surfaces, are used to gaze into and access ethereal realms. By staring into the mirror, practitioners seek to connect with the spirits of the deceased and receive messages or insights from the afterlife. The mirror acts as a portal, allowing individuals to access deeper levels of consciousness and establish a link with the spiritual dimensions.

Spirit boards, also known as Ouija boards, are yet another form of funerary art used in Divination. These boards typically feature letters, numbers, and symbols, and are used as a means of communication with the departed. Participants place their hands on a planchette, a movable pointer, and allow spirits to guide its movements to spell out messages or provide answers to questions. Spirit boards are seen as a tool for establishing a connection with the spirit world and receiving guidance and insights from the deceased.

These artistic creations within the realm of Divination serve as portals to the spiritual realms and provide individuals with a means to access insights, understanding, and guidance related to the afterlife. By utilizing tarot cards, scrying mirrors, or spirit boards, practitioners can connect with the wisdom of the deceased and gain deeper understanding of their own lives and the spiritual forces at play.

The symbolism and imagery depicted in these forms of funerary art play a vital role in the Divination process. They act as catalysts for intuition and provide a framework through which individuals can interpret messages and gain insights from the spiritual realms. The visual representations serve as focal points for concentration and allow practitioners to tap into their own psychic abilities and receive guidance from the departed.

In conclusion, funerary art in the realm of Divination takes various forms and serves as a means of connecting with the spiritual realms, gaining insights, and receiving guidance from the deceased. Tarot cards, scrying mirrors, and spirit boards are examples of artistic creations that act as portals to the afterlife and facilitate the divinatory process. The symbolism and imagery depicted in these forms of funerary art serve as conduits for intuitive understanding and enable individuals to explore the mysteries of the afterlife and the wisdom of the departed.

Problem:

Explore the symbolism of the Death card in the tarot deck as a representation of transformation and rebirth. Discuss how this card can be used in divinatory practices to offer guidance and insights during times of mourning and loss. Share your interpretation of the Death card and its significance within your own divinatory practice or traditions.

Shamanism:

In Shamanism, funerary art plays a significant role in facilitating communication with ancestral spirits and establishing a connection with the spirit world. This art often incorporates animal motifs, spirit masks, and sacred symbols, which serve as gateways to the spiritual realms and assist shamans in their ceremonial practices.

Animal motifs are commonly found in Shamanic funerary art. Cave paintings, totemic sculptures, and other artistic expressions feature representations of animals that hold cultural and spiritual significance. These animal motifs symbolize the interconnectedness between humans and the animal kingdom, highlighting the belief in the interdependence and cyclical nature of life. By incorporating animal motifs into funerary art, shamans acknowledge the spiritual presence of these animals and seek to harness their power and wisdom in their communication with ancestral spirits.

Spirit masks are another essential aspect of funerary art in Shamanism. These masks are crafted to embody spiritual energies and serve as transformative tools during shamanic rituals and ceremonies. Masks can represent specific ancestral spirits or embody archetypal beings that aid in communication with the deceased. Shamans wear these masks during trance states or ritual performances, allowing them to embody and channel the energies and wisdom of the spirits they represent.

The masks act as a bridge between the physical and spiritual realms, facilitating the shaman's connection with ancestral spirits and enabling them to convey messages, seek guidance, and perform healing rituals.

Sacred symbols also hold a significant place in Shamanic funerary art. These symbols can include geometric patterns, spirals, or other intricate designs that represent spiritual concepts, cosmic forces, or ancestral wisdom. Shamans incorporate these symbols into their artistic creations to invoke the presence of the spirits and establish a sacred and meaningful space for communication and ritual practices. The symbols act as visual representations of the spiritual realms, allowing shamans to connect with ancestral spirits and navigate the realms of the afterlife.

Exercise:

To create a spirit mask inspired by Shamanic traditions, begin by researching animal motifs and symbols that hold personal meaning or resonate with Shamanic beliefs. Consider the specific animal spirits or archetypes you wish to invoke and incorporate their characteristics and symbolism into the design of the mask. Choose materials that align with the spiritual significance of the mask, such as natural fibers, wood, or clay. Select colors that evoke the intended spiritual connection, such as earth tones for grounding or vibrant hues for energy and vitality. Pay attention to design elements that reflect the transformative nature of the mask, such as incorporating textures, feathers, or elements that represent the cycles of life and death. Throughout the creation process, reflect on the transformative power of the mask and its potential role in facilitating communication with ancestral spirits, honoring their wisdom, and seeking their guidance.

In summary, funerary art in Shamanism incorporates animal motifs, spirit masks, and sacred symbols to establish a connection with the spirit world and facilitate communication with ancestral spirits. Animal motifs emphasize the interdependence of all beings and the cyclical nature of life. Spirit masks serve as transformative tools, enabling shamans to channel spiritual energies and embody ancestral wisdom. Sacred symbols provide visual representations of spiritual concepts and create a sacred space for communication and ritual practices. Through the creation and use of these artistic expressions, shamans honor the presence of the deceased, seek guidance, and establish a profound connection with ancestral spirits.

Death and Social Order

In our exploration of spiritual traditions, we delve into the profound topic of death and its intricate relationship with social order. Across cultures and throughout history, death has been not only a deeply personal experience but also a powerful force that shapes the structure, values, and norms of society. In this chapter, we will examine how Witchcraft, Divination, Herbalism, Shamanism, Ecospirituality, and Magic in Ancient Mesopotamia offer unique perspectives on the interplay between death and social order. Through a comprehensive analysis of these diverse traditions, we will uncover the ways in which death influences social hierarchies, moral codes, and collective identity.

Death as a Catalyst for Social Order:

Witchcraft:

In Witchcraft, death is viewed as an integral part of the natural cycle of life, and the practices and rituals surrounding death play a vital role in fostering social cohesion and collective healing within Witchcraft communities. By actively engaging with the reality of death, practitioners acknowledge the impermanence of life and embrace the interconnectedness of all beings.

Rituals and ceremonies associated with death in Witchcraft serve multiple purposes in maintaining social order and promoting collective well-being. Firstly, these rituals provide a framework for the community to come together and support one another during times of loss and grieving. The shared experience of honoring the deceased and processing emotions collectively creates a space for individuals to find solace, share memories, and seek comfort from one another. This communal support strengthens the bonds within the Witchcraft community, fostering a sense of interconnectedness and solidarity.

Furthermore, rituals and ceremonies associated with death in Witchcraft reaffirm the collective understanding of mortality and the transient nature of existence. By embracing death as a natural part of life, practitioners are reminded of the importance of living fully and authentically. This acknowledgment of mortality serves as a catalyst for personal growth, encouraging individuals to prioritize their values, deepen their connections with loved ones, and cultivate a sense of purpose and meaning in their lives. As a result, the collective identity of the Witchcraft community is shaped by a shared recognition of the fragility and preciousness of life.

Additionally, the rituals and ceremonies associated with death in Witchcraft often incorporate elements of remembrance and ancestor veneration. By honoring the ancestors and those who have passed on, practitioners establish a sense of continuity and lineage within the community. This connection with ancestral spirits provides guidance, wisdom, and support for both individuals and the collective as they navigate the complexities of life. The acknowledgement of the ancestral lineage contributes to the preservation of traditions, values, and cultural identity within Witchcraft communities.

In summary, death in Witchcraft is embraced as a natural part of the cycle of life, and rituals and ceremonies associated with death play a crucial role in maintaining social order and fostering collective healing. These practices provide a space for communal support, encourage personal growth and reflection, and strengthen the bonds of interconnectedness within Witchcraft communities. By acknowledging mortality and honoring the ancestors, practitioners find solace, gain wisdom, and contribute to the collective identity and continuity of the community.

Divination:

Within the realm of Divination, the contemplation of death and its mysteries holds significant implications for shaping social order. Divinatory practices offer individuals and communities a profound tool for understanding the cyclical nature of life, the consequences of actions, and the interconnectedness of all beings. By engaging in divination specifically focused on the role of death in social relationships, individuals can gain valuable insights into their roles within the social fabric, fostering a sense of responsibility and promoting harmony.

The Significance of Divination in Understanding Death and Social Order:

Divination serves as a powerful means of exploring the profound connections between death and social order. It offers individuals a unique perspective on the interplay between personal choices and their impact on the broader community. Through divinatory methods such as tarot, runes, or scrying, practitioners can delve into the symbolism and interpretations associated with death, shedding light on the intricate web of social relationships.

Performing a Divinatory Reading on Death and Social Relationships:

To delve deeper into the role of death in social relationships, students are encouraged to engage in a divinatory reading using a method of their choice. For example, let's consider the use of tarot cards for this exercise. Students can design a spread specifically focused on exploring the impact of death on social order. The spread can consist of a central card representing death, surrounded by additional cards symbolizing various social elements such as family, community, and interpersonal connections.

Analyzing Symbolism and Interpretations:

Once the divinatory reading is complete, students should carefully analyze the symbolism and interpretations of the drawn cards. Each card holds rich layers of meaning, which can be explored individually and in relation to one another. For instance, the central card representing death might evoke themes of transformation, rebirth, or letting go. The surrounding cards can offer insights into how death influences the interconnectedness of individuals within social relationships.

Discussion and Reflection:

After analyzing the divinatory results, students should engage in a discussion that encourages critical thinking and reflection. They can explore questions such as:

How does the symbolism and interpretations of the divinatory reading reveal the impact of death on social relationships?

What insights can be gained about the interconnectedness of individuals within the larger social order?

How can this understanding of death contribute to ethical decision-making and fostering a harmonious social order?

Exercises for Further Exploration:

To further enhance their understanding, students can be encouraged to practice divination readings on death and social relationships with different divinatory tools such as runes or scrying. They can compare the insights gained from each method and reflect on the unique perspectives they offer. Additionally, students can engage in group exercises where they discuss and analyze real-world examples where divination and the contemplation of death have shaped social order within specific cultures or communities.

Conclusion:

Through divination, individuals can gain profound insights into the role of death in shaping social order. By exploring the symbolism and interpretations associated with death, practitioners develop a deeper understanding of the interconnectedness of individuals within the broader fabric of society. This awareness fosters a sense of responsibility, ethical decision-making, and a commitment to promoting harmony and balance within social relationships. Divination, therefore, emerges as a valuable tool for shaping social order and navigating the mysteries of death in our interconnected world.

Shamanism:

In Shamanism, the rituals and practices surrounding death serve as vital contributors to the establishment and maintenance of social order. These rituals reinforce cultural norms, strengthen communal bonds, and affirm spiritual beliefs. The shaman, as an intermediary between the human and spirit realms, plays a pivotal role in guiding individuals and communities through the processes of death, mourning, and spiritual transformation. Through their rituals and ceremonies, shamans provide solace, facilitate healing, and ensure the smooth transition of the departed into the ancestral realm, reinforcing the social fabric and reaffirming shared values.

The Role of Shamanic Rituals in Honoring the Deceased and Reinforcing Social Order:

Shamanic rituals surrounding death are designed not only to honor the deceased but also to address the spiritual and social needs of the community. By carefully considering the elements, symbols, and actions incorporated into these rituals, shamans aim to provide a framework that reinforces the existing social order and strengthens communal bonds.

Designing a Ritual for Transition and Community Support:

To explore the intricate relationship between death, social order, and community bonds, students are invited to imagine themselves as shamanic practitioners tasked with guiding a community through the death of an esteemed elder. The exercise involves designing a ritual that honors the deceased while addressing the spiritual and social needs of the community during this time of transition.

Elements, Symbols, and Actions in the Ritual:

Students should consider the following elements when designing their ritual:

Sacred Space: Creating a designated sacred space where the ritual takes place, representing the connection between the physical and spiritual realms.

Ritual Objects: Selecting specific objects with symbolic significance, such as feathers, stones, or candles, to invoke spiritual energies and reinforce communal bonds.

Chants and Prayers: Crafting chants and prayers that invoke ancestral spirits, provide comfort, and strengthen the community's connection with the deceased.

Communal Participation: Encouraging active participation from community members, fostering a sense of shared responsibility and unity.

Addressing Spiritual and Social Needs:

Students should reflect on the spiritual and social needs of the community during the transition of the elder's passing. For example:

Providing space for collective grieving, allowing individuals to express their emotions and find support within the community.

Acknowledging the wisdom and contributions of the deceased, reinforcing the value of elders and intergenerational knowledge.

Facilitating communication with ancestral spirits, offering guidance and reassurance to the community as they navigate the grieving process and the transition of the departed.

Discussion and Reflection:

After designing the ritual, students should engage in discussion and reflection. Topics for consideration include:

How does the ritual honor the deceased while reinforcing the social order and strengthening communal bonds?

What elements, symbols, or actions within the ritual contribute to addressing the spiritual and social needs of the community?

How does this ritual align with or differ from practices in other shamanic traditions or cultural contexts?

Conclusion:

Shamanism demonstrates the profound interplay between death, social order, and community bonds. Through rituals and ceremonies, shamans guide communities through the processes of death, mourning, and spiritual transformation, reinforcing cultural norms, fostering communal bonds, and affirming spiritual beliefs. By engaging in the exercise provided in this chapter and reflecting on the examples, problems, and exercises presented, students can deepen their understanding of the vital role that death plays in shaping social dynamics within shamanic traditions.

Chapter 6: Influence and Legacy: Mesopotamian Religion and its Impact on Later Cultures

The ancient region of Mesopotamia, located in modern-day Iraq and parts of Syria and Turkey, was the birthplace of one of the earliest complex civilizations in human history. Mesopotamian religion, with its rich mythology, intricate rituals, and vibrant pantheon of deities, exerted a profound influence on the cultures that followed. This chapter explores the significance of Mesopotamian religion and its enduring legacy, examining how its beliefs, practices, and cosmology shaped subsequent spiritual traditions.

Understanding Mesopotamian Religion:

Mesopotamian religion was a polytheistic system that flourished from the third millennium BCE until the advent of Christianity. It encompassed a complex pantheon of gods and goddesses, each associated with specific aspects of life and the natural world. Central to Mesopotamian religious beliefs was the concept of divine hierarchy, with the god Enlil as the supreme ruler and other deities holding various domains and responsibilities.

Key Elements of Mesopotamian Religious Practices:

Mesopotamian religious practices were characterized by elaborate rituals, temple ceremonies, and offerings to the gods. The Mesopotamians believed that these rituals ensured the favor of the deities and maintained cosmic order. Divination, astrology, and dream interpretation were also integral to their religious worldview, as they sought guidance from the gods and attempted to understand the will of the divine through signs and omens.

Mesopotamian Cosmology and the Interconnectedness of the Universe:

Mesopotamian cosmology provided a framework for understanding the interconnectedness of the universe. They believed in a three-tiered cosmology consisting of the heavens, the earth, and the underworld. The gods resided in the heavens, humans occupied the earthly realm, and the underworld was the domain of the deceased. This cosmological model reflected their perception of a harmonious balance between the divine, human, and natural worlds.

The Legacy of Mesopotamian Religion:

The influence of Mesopotamian religion extends far beyond its historical timeframe. Its ideas, beliefs, and practices have shaped subsequent religious and spiritual traditions in various ways. For instance, concepts such as the afterlife, divine judgment, and the struggle between chaos and order can be traced back to Mesopotamian religious mythology. Additionally, Mesopotamian writing systems, including cuneiform, laid the foundation for future developments in writing and literature.

The Impact on Later Cultures:

The legacy of Mesopotamian religion can be seen in the religious and mythological traditions of cultures that followed, including ancient Egyptian religion, ancient Greek mythology, and even modern-day religious practices. For example, the Sumerian goddess Inanna, associated with love, fertility, and war, shares similarities with the later Greek goddess Aphrodite and the Babylonian goddess Ishtar.

Conclusion:

The religious beliefs and practices of ancient Mesopotamia hold a significant place in the history of human spirituality. Their complex pantheon of deities, rituals, and cosmological concepts shaped not only their own civilization but also left a lasting impact on later cultures. By exploring the influence and legacy of Mesopotamian religion, we gain valuable insights into the continuity and interconnectedness of human spiritual traditions throughout time. In the following sections, we will delve into specific examples of how Mesopotamian religion influenced and intertwined with various aspects of spirituality, including Witchcraft, Divination, Herbalism, Shamanism, and Ecospirituality.

Spread of Mesopotamian Religious Concepts

The religious concepts and practices of ancient Mesopotamia did not remain confined to the region alone. As a result of cultural exchange, trade routes, and conquests, Mesopotamian religious ideas gradually spread beyond the borders of this ancient civilization, influencing and intertwining with the belief systems of other cultures. This section explores the spread of Mesopotamian religious concepts and their assimilation into diverse traditions across time and geography.

The Babylonian Influence:

The Babylonian Empire, flourishing in the late 2nd millennium BCE, played a pivotal role in the dissemination of Mesopotamian religious concepts. As Babylon expanded its territories through military conquests and political alliances, it became a significant conduit for the transmission of Babylonian religious ideas and practices to neighboring regions. This chapter delves into the profound impact of the Babylonian Empire on the spread and assimilation of Mesopotamian religious concepts.

At the heart of Babylonian religion was the veneration of Marduk, the patron god of Babylon and the chief deity of the Babylonian pantheon. As Babylonian influence extended, the worship of Marduk became more widespread, with temples dedicated to him established in conquered territories. The propagation of Marduk's cult not only elevated the prominence of Babylon within the empire but also fostered the assimilation of Babylonian religious practices and beliefs.

Among the most influential and enduring contributions of Babylonian religion was the adoption of Babylonian mythological narratives. The Babylonian creation myth, Enuma Elish, holds particular significance in this regard. Enuma Elish recounts the epic story of the cosmic struggle between the gods, culminating in the triumph of Marduk over the primeval chaos monster Tiamat. Marduk's victory leads to the establishment of order and the creation of the world.

The power and complexity of Enuma Elish exerted a lasting influence on subsequent religious and mythological systems, extending far beyond the borders of Mesopotamia. The narrative structure and themes found in Enuma Elish can be discerned in various mythologies and creation stories throughout the ancient world. For example, the biblical account of the creation in the book of Genesis displays echoes of Enuma Elish, suggesting possible influence or shared cultural heritage.

The spread of Babylonian religious concepts, including the veneration of Marduk and the adoption of Enuma Elish, contributed to the assimilation and syncretism of religious traditions in the ancient Near East. The conquering of neighboring regions by Babylon allowed for the intermingling of diverse religious practices, resulting in the incorporation of Mesopotamian elements into the belief systems of other cultures. This cultural fusion shaped the religious landscape of the ancient world, exemplifying the interconnectedness and cross-pollination of religious ideas.

Exercise:

Select a specific region or civilization influenced by the Babylonian Empire. Research the religious practices and beliefs of this culture before and after the Babylonian conquest. Analyze the extent of the Babylonian influence on their religious system, focusing on the adoption of Marduk worship and the incorporation of Babylonian mythological narratives. Discuss the transformative effects of this assimilation on the religious identity and social dynamics of the chosen civilization.

Mesopotamian Religion and the Ancient Near East:

The cultural and religious exchanges between Mesopotamia and its neighboring regions in the ancient Near East were dynamic processes that influenced the spread of Mesopotamian religious concepts. This section explores the impact of Mesopotamian religious ideas on the Assyrians and the Canaanites, highlighting the integration of Mesopotamian deities and religious rituals into their respective belief systems.

The Assyrians, known for their formidable empire during the first millennium BCE, were strongly influenced by Babylonian religious traditions. As the Assyrians expanded their territories and established political dominance over Mesopotamia, they recognized the power and prestige of Babylonian religion. Consequently, they actively sought to incorporate Babylonian religious practices into their own.

The Assyrians adopted various aspects of Babylonian religious traditions, particularly focusing on the worship of Babylonian deities. Marduk, the chief god of Babylon, held a prominent place in the Assyrian pantheon. The Assyrian kings, in particular, sought to legitimize their rule by associating themselves with the authority and divine power of Marduk.

In addition to the adoption of deities, the Assyrians also integrated Babylonian religious rituals and ceremonies into their own religious practices. Temples dedicated to Babylonian gods were constructed within Assyrian cities, and Babylonian-style rituals were performed, often blending with existing Assyrian customs. The incorporation of Babylonian religious elements served to solidify the Assyrians' political and religious control over the region.

Similarly, the Canaanites, who inhabited the land of modern-day Israel and Palestine, were receptive to the influence of Mesopotamian religious concepts.

The city-state of Ugarit, located in present-day Syria, was an important center of cultural and religious exchange between Mesopotamia and the Canaanites.

The Canaanites integrated Mesopotamian deities and religious rituals into their pantheon, assimilating them alongside their own indigenous gods. For example, Ishtar, the Babylonian goddess of love and fertility, found a place in the Canaanite religious landscape as Astarte, a prominent goddess associated with similar aspects of life and nature.

The adoption of Mesopotamian religious concepts by the Canaanites was not a mere replication but a process of syncretism, whereby elements from different religious traditions were blended and transformed. This syncretic approach allowed for the coexistence and integration of diverse religious practices within the Canaanite belief system.

The cultural and religious exchanges between Mesopotamia, Assyria, and the Canaanites demonstrate the fluidity and adaptability of religious ideas in the ancient Near East. These exchanges facilitated the spread and integration of Mesopotamian religious concepts into neighboring cultures, creating a rich tapestry of shared beliefs, rituals, and mythologies.

Exercise:

Research and analyze the impact of Mesopotamian religious concepts on another ancient Near Eastern civilization of your choice. Explore the assimilation of Mesopotamian deities, rituals, or mythologies into the religious practices of this civilization. Discuss the motivations and implications of this integration, considering the social, political, and cultural context of both Mesopotamia and the chosen civilization.

Mesopotamian Influence on Ancient Egypt:

The impact of Mesopotamian religion on ancient Egypt during the New Kingdom period (16th - 11th century BCE) marked an intriguing interplay of cultural and religious exchange between these two ancient civilizations. Through trade networks and diplomatic relations, Mesopotamian religious concepts made their way to Egypt, leaving a discernible imprint on Egyptian theology, particularly in the worship of the god Amun.

Amun, originally a relatively minor deity in the Egyptian pantheon, experienced a significant rise in prominence during the New Kingdom period. As Egypt expanded its influence and engaged in trade with neighboring regions, including Mesopotamia, it became exposed to new religious ideas and practices. This exposure facilitated the incorporation of foreign religious elements into the existing Egyptian belief system.

The parallels between the worship of Amun in Egypt and the Mesopotamian deity Enlil are notable. Enlil, one of the major gods in Mesopotamian mythology, was associated with power, wind, and storms. Similarly, Amun came to be regarded as a supreme deity associated with power, kingship, and wind in Egyptian theology. The similarities in their attributes and spheres of influence suggest the influence of Mesopotamian religious concepts on the development of Amun's cult in Egypt.

The adoption of Mesopotamian religious elements in Egyptian theology was not a wholesale replacement of Egyptian gods or beliefs but rather an assimilation and reinterpretation of foreign ideas. Egyptian religious syncretism allowed for the integration of foreign deities and their attributes into the existing Egyptian pantheon. As a result, Amun assumed the characteristics and symbolism associated with Enlil while maintaining his distinct Egyptian identity.

The influence of Mesopotamian religious concepts on Amun's worship in Egypt can be seen in the iconography and rituals surrounding the god. Artistic representations of Amun sometimes depict him with the characteristic Mesopotamian horned crown, reminiscent of Enlil's own iconography. Additionally, Egyptian religious ceremonies and rituals associated with Amun showcased similarities with Mesopotamian religious practices, further indicating the intermingling of religious ideas.

The transfer of Mesopotamian religious concepts to Egypt during the New Kingdom period illustrates the interconnectedness and cultural exchange that occurred between ancient civilizations. It demonstrates how the encounters between different cultures sparked innovation, adaptation, and the transformation of religious beliefs. The integration of foreign deities like Amun into the Egyptian pantheon enriched Egyptian theology, reflecting the dynamic nature of religious development in the ancient world.

Exercise:

Research and analyze the impact of Mesopotamian religious concepts on another ancient civilization outside of the Near East. Explore the assimilation of Mesopotamian deities, rituals, or mythologies into the religious practices of this civilization. Discuss the motivations and implications of this integration, considering the cultural, religious, and historical context of both Mesopotamia and the chosen civilization.

Mesopotamian Religious Concepts in Greco-Roman Culture:

The conquests of Alexander the Great and the ensuing Hellenistic period marked a transformative era in the ancient world, characterized by extensive cultural and religious exchanges between the Greeks and the civilizations they encountered. This period of interaction between the Greeks and the remnants of Mesopotamian culture led to the assimilation of Mesopotamian religious elements into Greek and later Roman religious practices.

One notable example of this assimilation is the equating of the Mesopotamian goddess Inanna with the Greek goddess Aphrodite and the Roman goddess Venus. Inanna, a prominent deity in Mesopotamian mythology, represented love, beauty, fertility, and sexuality. The Greeks associated her attributes and characteristics with their own goddess of love and beauty, Aphrodite, while the Romans, in turn, identified her with their goddess Venus.

The syncretism between Inanna, Aphrodite, and Venus occurred as a result of cultural contact and the mutual exchange of religious ideas. The assimilation of Inanna into the Greek and Roman pantheons can be attributed to several factors, including the recognition of similarities between the deities' spheres of influence, the desire to establish connections between different cultures, and the need to integrate conquered territories into the Hellenistic and Roman empires.

In the case of Inanna and Aphrodite, both goddesses were associated with love, desire, beauty, and fertility. They embodied similar aspects of femininity and were revered for their influence over human relationships and the natural world. As the Greeks encountered the remnants of Mesopotamian culture, they identified parallels between their own deities and those of Mesopotamia, leading to the assimilation and syncretism of these divine figures.

The process of equating Inanna with Aphrodite and later with Venus involved not only the transfer of religious attributes but also the adaptation of myths, symbols, and rituals associated with each goddess. The fusion of these elements created a new religious and cultural landscape that reflected the interconnectedness of the ancient Mediterranean world.

The assimilation of Mesopotamian religious elements into Greek and Roman traditions extended beyond the goddess Inanna. Other Mesopotamian deities, such as the god Marduk and the goddess Ninhursag, were also identified with

Greek and Roman counterparts, further enriching the religious landscape of the Hellenistic and Roman periods.

The assimilation of Mesopotamian religious elements into Greek and Roman practices highlights the fluidity and adaptability of religious beliefs and traditions throughout history. It demonstrates how cultural encounters and conquests can lead to the merging and reinterpretation of religious concepts, resulting in the formation of new syncretic systems.

Exercise:

Choose a Mesopotamian deity and explore its assimilation into Greek or Roman religious practices. Analyze the similarities and differences between the Mesopotamian and Greco-Roman representations of the deity, including their attributes, myths, symbols, and associated rituals. Discuss the motivations and implications of this assimilation, considering the cultural, religious, and historical context of both civilizations.

Mesopotamian Religious Influence in Modern Times:

Even in the modern era, traces of Mesopotamian religious concepts continue to persist, demonstrating their enduring influence on various aspects of human culture. One such example is the celebration of the spring equinox known as Easter, which carries associations of fertility and rebirth. Scholars suggest that Easter may have its origins in ancient Mesopotamian festivals dedicated to the goddess Ishtar.

Ishtar, the Mesopotamian goddess of love, beauty, and fertility, was celebrated during the spring season as a symbol of new life and rejuvenation. Her worship involved rituals and ceremonies that marked the arrival of spring and the renewal of the natural world. Over time, as civilizations and cultures transformed, the festival honoring Ishtar underwent adaptations and assimilations, eventually finding resonance in Christian traditions and the celebration of Easter.

The parallels between the ancient Mesopotamian festivals and Easter are evident in the themes of fertility, rebirth, and the symbolism of eggs and bunnies. These elements, associated with Ishtar and her festival, became incorporated into the Christian celebration of Easter, representing the resurrection of Jesus Christ and the concept of spiritual rebirth. This syncretism between ancient Mesopotamian beliefs and Christian traditions illustrates the enduring legacy of Mesopotamian religious concepts in shaping contemporary religious practices.

Another notable example of the remnants of Mesopotamian religious concepts can be observed in the widespread belief in a divine flood and the survival of a heroic figure. This theme, prominently found in the story of Noah in Abrahamic religions such as Judaism, Christianity, and Islam, bears striking similarities to the Mesopotamian Epic of Gilgamesh.

The Epic of Gilgamesh, one of the earliest known works of literature, recounts the story of a flood that destroys humanity, except for the hero Gilgamesh and his companion Utnapishtim, who survives the cataclysmic event by building an ark. This narrative predates the biblical story of Noah and the flood by centuries, yet both share common elements, such as the divine warning, the construction of an ark, and the survival of a chosen individual or family.

The parallels between the Mesopotamian Epic of Gilgamesh and the biblical story of Noah can be attributed to the historical and cultural connections between the ancient Mesopotamian civilizations and the early Hebrew culture. The oral traditions and myths of Mesopotamia likely influenced the formation of early Hebrew religious narratives, which were later recorded in the Hebrew Bible.

The enduring presence of Mesopotamian religious concepts in modern times serves as a testament to the profound and lasting impact of this ancient civilization on human thought, belief systems, and cultural practices. By recognizing these remnants, we gain a deeper understanding of the interconnectedness of human history and the enduring legacy of Mesopotamian spirituality.

Exercise:

Select a contemporary cultural or religious practice that exhibits remnants of Mesopotamian religious concepts. Investigate the historical, cultural, and symbolic connections between the modern practice and its Mesopotamian origins. Analyze how these remnants have been adapted, transformed, or assimilated into contemporary contexts, and discuss their significance in shaping contemporary beliefs and rituals.

Conclusion:

The spread of Mesopotamian religious concepts illustrates the interconnectedness and exchange of ideas among ancient civilizations. Through conquests, trade, and cultural interactions, the religious beliefs and practices of Mesopotamia permeated neighboring regions and influenced the religious landscape of diverse cultures. The examples provided in this section demonstrate how Mesopotamian religious concepts were assimilated, adapted, and integrated into the mythologies, rituals, and pantheons of later civilizations, leaving an indelible mark on the religious and spiritual tapestry of human history.

Exercise:

Select one ancient civilization or religious tradition that was influenced by Mesopotamian religious concepts. Analyze the specific ways in which Mesopotamian ideas and practices were incorporated into the religious framework of this civilization. Discuss the impact of this assimilation on the belief system, mythology, rituals, and social structure of the chosen culture. Consider the extent to which the Mesopotamian influence reshaped the spiritual landscape and contributed to the development of a unique religious identity.

Research and analyze a specific Mesopotamian religious ritual or ceremony. Describe its purpose, symbols, and actions involved. Reflect on the underlying beliefs and cosmological concepts that informed the performance of this ritual. Discuss its potential significance in shaping social order and reinforcing communal bonds within Mesopotamian society.

Investigate the impact of Mesopotamian religious concepts on modern esoteric traditions, such as Western occultism or neopaganism. Select a specific aspect of Mesopotamian religion, such as the worship of a particular deity or a symbolic motif, and explore how it has been incorporated or adapted in modern occult or neopagan practices. Analyze the reasons behind the continued fascination with Mesopotamian religious elements in contemporary spiritual movements.

Mesopotamian Influence on Ancient Near Eastern Religions

The ancient region of Mesopotamia, known as the "cradle of civilization," was home to a rich and complex religious landscape that profoundly influenced neighboring cultures in the ancient Near East. The religious beliefs and practices of Mesopotamia, with their vibrant mythologies, sophisticated rituals, and well-developed pantheons, served as a significant source of inspiration and influence for the religions that emerged in the surrounding regions. This section explores the profound impact of Mesopotamian religious concepts on ancient Near Eastern religions, drawing examples from fields such as Witchcraft, Divination, Herbalism, Shamanism, Ecospirituality, and Magic in Ancient Mesopotamia.

Mesopotamian Pantheon and Deities:

The pantheon of Mesopotamian gods and goddesses was remarkably diverse, encompassing a wide range of divine beings associated with various aspects of the natural world, human activities, and cosmic forces. This intricate web of deities held great significance within the religious systems of neighboring civilizations in the ancient Near East. Among these civilizations, the Canaanites, who inhabited the region corresponding to modern-day Israel and Palestine, notably adopted and incorporated several Mesopotamian deities into their own pantheon.

The assimilation of Mesopotamian gods and goddesses into the Canaanite religious framework facilitated cultural exchange and influenced the religious practices and beliefs of the Canaanites. Through interactions with Mesopotamian traders, conquerors, and cultural emissaries, the Canaanites became exposed to the rich religious heritage of Mesopotamia, and they recognized the value of incorporating certain deities into their own pantheon. This syncretism, the merging of different religious traditions, allowed for the blending and reinterpretation of religious concepts, rituals, and beliefs.

For example, the Canaanites incorporated the worship of the god Baal, a prominent deity in the Mesopotamian pantheon associated with storm and fertility, into their religious practices. Baal's cult became widespread among the Canaanites, and his attributes and functions were adapted to fit the local religious context. Similarly, the goddess Ishtar, known as Inanna in Mesopotamia, was integrated into the Canaanite pantheon. Ishtar's associations with love, beauty, and war found resonance among the Canaanites, who interpreted her divine qualities through their own cultural lens.

The adoption of Mesopotamian deities by the Canaanites not only expanded their religious repertoire but also facilitated connections and interactions with neighboring cultures. The shared veneration of certain gods and goddesses created a sense of commonality and cultural exchange, contributing to the broader religious and social dynamics of the ancient Near East. This assimilation was not a one-sided process; it involved the adaptation and reinterpretation of Mesopotamian deities to fit the specific religious and cultural context of the Canaanites, reflecting their own unique worldview and traditions.

In studying the influence of Mesopotamian deities on the Canaanite pantheon, it is important to consider the complexities of cultural exchange and syncretism. The adoption of foreign deities often involved a negotiation of religious concepts, rituals, and symbolic associations, resulting in the emergence of hybridized religious systems. Scholars examine textual and archaeological evidence to unravel the extent and nature of this assimilation, shedding light on the intricate religious landscape of the ancient Near East.

Mythological Narratives and Epics:

The captivating mythological narratives and epics of Mesopotamia, including the renowned Epic of Gilgamesh and the Enuma Elish, played a significant role in shaping the development of mythologies in neighboring cultures of the ancient Near East. These mythological texts, with their rich and imaginative storytelling, served as a foundation for the exploration of divine struggles, creation myths, and heroic quests, capturing the collective imagination of the people. The universal themes and profound insights embedded within these narratives offered a deeper understanding of the nature of the divine and the human condition, transcending cultural boundaries.

The influence of Mesopotamian mythological narratives can be observed in the mythologies of neighboring ancient Near Eastern civilizations. Similar motifs, archetypes, and narrative structures can be identified, suggesting a shared cultural and mythological heritage. The captivating stories of the Epic of Gilgamesh, for instance, featuring the quest for immortality and the complexities of the human experience, resonated with people beyond the borders of Mesopotamia. It is not surprising, therefore, to find echoes of Gilgamesh's archetype, the hero seeking transcendence and wisdom, in the mythologies of other ancient Near Eastern cultures.

One striking example of the influence of Mesopotamian mythology is found in the creation myths of neighboring civilizations. The Enuma Elish, the Babylonian creation myth, describes the cosmic struggle between the gods and the establishment of order and kingship. This narrative framework provided a template for similar creation myths in the region. The Canaanite myth of Baal's victory over the sea god Yam, for instance, shares similarities with the Enuma Elish, reflecting the influence of Mesopotamian cosmogonic narratives on the mythological traditions of neighboring cultures.

The presence of shared motifs and archetypes across different mythologies highlights the interconnectedness of ancient cultures and their mutual engagement with Mesopotamian religious and mythological concepts. These narratives served as a common cultural currency, facilitating communication, cultural exchange, and the transmission of ideas between ancient civilizations. The stories and themes provided a framework for understanding the divine, human existence, morality, and the relationship between gods and mortals.

Studying the influence of Mesopotamian mythological narratives on neighboring cultures involves analyzing textual evidence, comparing mythological motifs and structures, and examining the historical and cultural contexts in which these narratives evolved. Archaeological discoveries, such as cuneiform tablets and artistic representations, contribute to our understanding of the diffusion of mythological concepts and the interplay of cultural influences.

Rituals and Sacred Practices:

The sophisticated rituals and sacred practices of ancient Mesopotamia had a profound impact on the religious traditions of the ancient Near East. The intricate ceremonies, offerings, and divinatory practices that were central to Mesopotamian religious life left a lasting impression on neighboring cultures, shaping their own religious practices and beliefs.

One notable area of influence is seen in the rituals surrounding death and burial. In Mesopotamia, the proper observance of funeral rites was considered essential to ensure a peaceful transition of the deceased to the afterlife and to maintain harmony within the community. These rituals involved various stages, including purification, mourning, and offerings to the gods and ancestors. The belief in the continued existence and influence of the deceased within the community led to the practice of ancestor veneration, where ancestors were revered and their guidance sought.

The neighboring cultures of the ancient Near East, such as the Canaanites, Assyrians, and Babylonians, adopted and adapted these funeral rituals and ancestor veneration practices into their own religious systems. The importance of proper burial rites, the veneration of ancestors, and the belief in an afterlife became integral aspects of their religious traditions. This adoption not only reflected the influence of Mesopotamian culture but also served as a means of fostering communal cohesion and reinforcing social order.

The rituals surrounding death and burial provided a framework for understanding the relationship between the living and the deceased. They emphasized the interconnectedness between the realms of the living and the afterlife, highlighting the ongoing presence and influence of ancestors on the lives of the living. By engaging in these rituals, individuals and communities expressed their reverence for the deceased and their commitment to maintaining a harmonious relationship with the spirit world.

The cultural exchange and diffusion of these funeral rituals and ancestor veneration practices can be observed through archaeological evidence, textual sources, and comparative analysis of religious traditions. Archaeological discoveries, such as tomb excavations and funerary objects, provide insights into the material expressions of these practices in different cultures. Texts, such as funerary inscriptions and religious texts, offer further understanding of the beliefs and rituals associated with death and burial.

Magical and Divinatory Practices:

Mesopotamia, known for its rich tradition of magical and divinatory practices, had a profound influence on the religious and mystical aspects of neighboring cultures in the ancient Near East. The Mesopotamian approach to magic and divination aimed to harness supernatural forces and establish communication with the gods, providing spiritual guidance and insight into the human condition.

Magical spells and incantations were integral to Mesopotamian magical practices. These spells were carefully crafted and recited with the belief that they could manipulate the unseen forces of the universe. The use of specific words, gestures, and ritual objects, such as amulets and talismans, were believed to have protective or transformative powers. The efficacy of these magical practices relied on the understanding of the intricate connections between the divine, natural elements, and the human realm.

Divination, the practice of seeking knowledge of the future or hidden truths, was highly developed in Mesopotamia. Divinatory techniques included the interpretation of celestial phenomena, such as the movements of the stars and planets, as well as the examination of natural omens, dreams, and the examination of entrails of animals. The consultation of oracles and divinatory texts, such as the famous Enuma Anu Enlil, provided insights into the will of the gods and guidance for decision-making.

The influence of Mesopotamian magical and divinatory practices extended beyond its borders, permeating the religious practices of neighboring cultures in the ancient Near East. The Canaanites, for example, incorporated magical rituals and divination techniques into their religious system. Similarly, the Assyrians and Babylonians integrated Mesopotamian magical concepts into their own religious practices, adapting and modifying them to suit their cultural context.

The adoption of Mesopotamian magical and divinatory practices by neighboring cultures reflected a desire to connect with the divine, seek spiritual guidance, and understand the forces that shape the human experience. These practices served as a means of accessing the mystical and spiritual dimensions of ancient Near Eastern religions, offering individuals and communities a sense of agency in their interactions with the supernatural.

Conclusion:
The influence of Mesopotamian religious concepts on ancient Near Eastern religions was profound and far-reaching. The adoption of Mesopotamian deities, the incorporation of mythological narratives, the emulation of rituals, and the assimilation of magical and divinatory practices all contributed to the development and evolution of neighboring religious systems. By examining the diverse fields of Witchcraft, Divination, Herbalism, Shamanism, Ecospirituality, and Magic in Ancient Mesopotamia, we gain a comprehensive understanding of the cultural and religious exchanges that occurred in the ancient Near East. The examples, problems, and exercises presented in this chapter encourage critical thinking and exploration of the influence of Mesopotamian religious concepts on ancient Near Eastern religions, fostering a deeper appreciation for the interconnectedness of human spiritual traditions.

Exercise:

Select an ancient Near Eastern religion and explore the specific ways in which it was influenced by Mesopotamian religious concepts. Examine the pantheon, mythological narratives, rituals, and magical practices of both Mesopotamia and the chosen ancient Near Eastern religion. Compare and contrast these elements to identify the areas of influence and the unique adaptations that occurred. Reflect on the implications of this influence for the religious and cultural landscape of the ancient Near East.

Mesopotamian Legacy in Biblical Traditions

The ancient civilizations of Mesopotamia, with their rich cultural and religious heritage, had a profound impact on the development of various aspects of biblical traditions. The interactions between Mesopotamia and the neighboring regions, including ancient Israel, facilitated the exchange of ideas, stories, and beliefs, leaving an indelible mark on the religious and mythological framework of biblical texts. This section explores the legacy of Mesopotamia in biblical traditions, examining the influences and parallels between these two ancient civilizations.

Creation Stories and Flood Narratives:

Expanding on the profound influence of Mesopotamian culture in biblical traditions, the similarities between the creation stories and flood narratives of Mesopotamia and the Hebrew Bible are particularly noteworthy. These parallels

offer insights into the shared cultural context and the interplay between
Mesopotamian mythological concepts and the authors of the biblical texts.

The Mesopotamian epic Enuma Elish and the biblical account of creation in
the book of Genesis both depict a cosmic struggle for supremacy among divine
beings, the establishment of order, and the creation of the world. In Enuma Elish,
the god Marduk emerges as the victor, creating the heavens and the earth.
Similarly, the book of Genesis presents God as the ultimate creator who brings
forth the heavens, the earth, and all living beings.

While the narratives differ in specific details and theological nuances, the
parallel themes and overarching structure indicate a shared cultural milieu and the
influence of Mesopotamian mythological concepts on the authors of the biblical
texts. The portrayal of a divine struggle for supremacy and the establishment of
cosmic order reflects the ancient Near Eastern worldview, where divine beings
played a central role in shaping the world and determining its destiny.

Similarly, the Mesopotamian flood story known as the Epic of Gilgamesh
shares striking similarities with the biblical account of Noah's Ark. Both narratives
describe a cataclysmic flood sent by the divine realm as a punishment for human
transgressions. In both stories, a chosen hero, Utnapishtim in the Epic of
Gilgamesh and Noah in the biblical narrative, is instructed to build an ark to save
himself, his family, and a selection of animals.

The survival of the hero and his family in the midst of the deluge and the
subsequent renewal of the world underscore common motifs found in flood
narratives across cultures. The parallel themes of divine punishment, survival, and
the restoration of life after the flood suggest that the Mesopotamian flood story
may have influenced the development of the biblical flood narrative.

These similarities raise intriguing questions about the nature of cultural
exchange and literary borrowing between ancient civilizations. It is possible that the
authors of the Hebrew Bible, drawing upon the cultural and literary heritage of
Mesopotamia, incorporated elements of Mesopotamian flood narratives into their
own religious and mythological traditions. This integration of Mesopotamian
themes into the biblical text demonstrates the dynamic nature of religious and
cultural development, where ideas and stories are shaped and adapted over time.

The parallelism between Mesopotamian creation stories and flood narratives
and their manifestations in the Hebrew Bible highlights the enduring impact of
Mesopotamian mythological concepts on biblical traditions. While the biblical
texts present unique theological perspectives and distinct narrative emphases, the

influence of Mesopotamian culture and religious beliefs cannot be overlooked. The interplay between these civilizations provides valuable insights into the development and evolution of ancient Near Eastern religious thought and the complex interconnections among different cultures of the region.

Legal and Ethical Codes:

Expanding on the influence of Mesopotamian legal and ethical codes on biblical traditions, the Code of Hammurabi stands as a notable example of the enduring impact of Mesopotamian legal systems. The similarities between the Code of Hammurabi and the legal codes found in the biblical books of Exodus, Leviticus, and Deuteronomy provide insights into the shared concerns and values of ancient Near Eastern societies and their influence on the development of biblical law.

The Code of Hammurabi, created during the reign of Babylonian King Hammurabi in the 18th century BCE, is one of the earliest known legal codes in human history. It consists of a collection of laws and regulations that address various aspects of social order, justice, and moral conduct. Similarly, the biblical books of Exodus, Leviticus, and Deuteronomy contain a comprehensive set of laws and commandments that governed the social and religious life of the Israelites.

The striking parallels between the legal systems of Mesopotamia and the Hebrew Bible highlight the shared concerns of ancient Near Eastern societies. Both legal codes seek to establish and maintain social order, promote justice, and regulate interpersonal relationships. They address issues such as property rights, contracts, marriage and family laws, and crimes against individuals and society. The laws in both systems emphasize fair treatment, restitution, and appropriate punishment for offenses.

Furthermore, the underlying ethical principles found in both the Code of Hammurabi and the biblical legal codes reflect common values of ancient Near Eastern societies. Concepts such as equity, reciprocity, and the sanctity of life form the foundation of these legal systems. The emphasis on fairness, protection of the vulnerable, and the pursuit of justice resonates in both Mesopotamian and biblical laws.

The influence of Mesopotamian legal codes on the biblical traditions is evident not only in the similarities of specific laws but also in the broader legal framework and principles of governance. The Code of Hammurabi, with its emphasis on the authority of the king and the role of divine sanction in maintaining order, likely influenced the Hebrew understanding of kingship and divine law. This influence can be seen in biblical texts that ascribe laws and commandments to divine revelation and emphasize the role of the king as the guardian of justice and social welfare.

The adoption and adaptation of Mesopotamian legal and ethical concepts in the biblical texts demonstrate the interconnectedness of ancient Near Eastern cultures and the continuous evolution of legal and moral systems. It is important to note that while there are similarities between the Mesopotamian legal codes and the biblical laws, the Hebrew Bible also incorporates distinct elements and theological perspectives that reflect the unique religious identity of the Israelites.

Studying the similarities and differences between the legal systems of Mesopotamia and the Hebrew Bible not only sheds light on the historical development of legal codes but also invites critical examination of cultural borrowing, the evolution of legal thought, and the role of law in shaping societal norms. It encourages students to engage in discussions on the nature of justice, ethics, and the enduring influence of ancient legal traditions in contemporary society.

Religious Beliefs and Concepts:

Mesopotamian religious beliefs and concepts, particularly those associated with divine beings and cosmology, have shaped certain aspects of biblical traditions. For example, the concept of a pantheon of gods and goddesses, each with specific domains and powers, finds resonance in both Mesopotamian and biblical texts. While the Israelite religious tradition emphasizes the worship of a single deity, echoes of polytheistic elements can be discerned in biblical narratives, such as references to heavenly beings and divine assemblies.

Furthermore, the motif of divine kingship, with the king serving as a representative of the divine on Earth, was prevalent in Mesopotamian culture and found echoes in the portrayal of kingship in the Hebrew Bible. The notion of the chosen people, a central theme in biblical traditions, can also be linked to the ancient Near Eastern concept of a covenant between a deity and a specific group.

Conclusion:

The legacy of Mesopotamia in biblical traditions is a testament to the intricate web of cultural interactions and exchanges that shaped the ancient Near East. The shared themes, narratives, and ethical principles found in Mesopotamian and biblical texts highlight the interconnectedness of these civilizations and the enduring impact of Mesopotamian cultural and religious heritage.

Problem:

Compare and contrast one specific aspect of Mesopotamian culture or religious belief, such as the flood narratives or legal codes, with its manifestation in the Hebrew Bible. Analyze the similarities, differences, and potential influences on the development of the biblical text. Engage with scholarly interpretations and theories to deepen your understanding of the Mesopotamian legacy in biblical traditions. Consider the implications of these influences for the interpretation and meaning of biblical texts.

Influence on Classical and Hellenistic Religions

The influence of Mesopotamian religion extended beyond the ancient Near East, leaving a lasting imprint on the religious beliefs and practices of classical and Hellenistic civilizations. The rich mythological narratives, complex rituals, and profound spiritual concepts of Mesopotamia found resonance and adaptation in the religious systems of ancient Greece and its Hellenistic successors.

One of the significant conduits for the transmission of Mesopotamian religious concepts to classical and Hellenistic cultures was the conquests of Alexander the Great and the subsequent Hellenistic period. As Alexander's empire expanded into the lands of the Middle East, it brought about extensive cultural and religious interactions between the Greeks and the remnants of Mesopotamian culture. This period witnessed a blending of religious traditions, resulting in the assimilation of Mesopotamian religious elements into Greek and later Roman religious practices.

The pantheon of Mesopotamian gods and goddesses, with its diverse array of deities associated with natural phenomena, celestial bodies, and human affairs, influenced the development of the Greek and Hellenistic pantheons. For instance, the goddess Ishtar, known as Inanna in Mesopotamia, was equated with the Greek goddess Aphrodite and the Roman goddess Venus. This syncretism reflected the parallel attributes and functions attributed to these deities, thus highlighting the interplay between the religious traditions of Mesopotamia and the classical world.

Moreover, the captivating mythological narratives and epics of Mesopotamia, such as the Epic of Gilgamesh and the Enuma Elish, held a profound fascination for the Greeks. These narratives, characterized by tales of heroic quests, divine struggles, and the search for immortality, offered insights into the nature of the divine and the human condition. The influence of Mesopotamian mythological narratives can be observed in the mythologies of classical and Hellenistic religions, where similar motifs and archetypes are present. The story of the flood, for instance, appears not only in Mesopotamian mythology but also in the Greek myth of Deucalion and Pyrrha, demonstrating the cross-cultural transmission of these narratives.

Furthermore, the sophisticated rituals and sacred practices of Mesopotamia, with their emphasis on offerings, purification, and divination, influenced the religious practices of classical and Hellenistic societies. The Greeks, for instance, adopted and adapted various Mesopotamian divination techniques, such as the interpretation of celestial phenomena, the consultation of oracles, and the use of magical spells and amulets. These practices served as means of connecting with the divine, seeking guidance, and accessing spiritual insights, shaping the mystical and spiritual dimensions of classical and Hellenistic religions.

The Mesopotamian legacy in classical and Hellenistic religions underscores the cultural exchange and cross-pollination of religious ideas and practices that occurred throughout ancient history. It highlights the dynamic nature of religious traditions and the continuous evolution of spiritual concepts, rituals, and beliefs. Exploring the influence of Mesopotamian religion on classical and Hellenistic cultures not only deepens our understanding of the ancient world but also invites reflection on the interplay between different religious systems and the enduring impact of ancient civilizations on contemporary spiritual and philosophical discourses.

Mesopotamian Influence on Esoteric and Occult Traditions

The ancient Mesopotamian civilization, with its rich spiritual heritage and profound understanding of the mystical realms, left an indelible mark on esoteric and occult traditions that emerged in later centuries. The influence of Mesopotamian religious concepts can be traced in various aspects of esoteric practices, including witchcraft, divination, herbalism, shamanism, and magic.

Witchcraft, an ancient and mystical practice, draws inspiration from a diverse range of cultural and historical sources. One significant influence on contemporary witchcraft traditions can be traced back to the ancient beliefs and rituals of Mesopotamia. Mesopotamian texts, such as the "Burning of Bel," offer valuable insights into the techniques and spellwork employed by ancient sorcerers, providing a rich tapestry of knowledge for modern practitioners.

In Mesopotamia, witchcraft was deeply intertwined with the manipulation of natural forces and the understanding of unseen energies. Mesopotamian sorcerers, known as "asipu" or "asu," engaged in rituals and incantations to harness spiritual power and influence the course of events. The texts found in the "Burning of Bel," a magical compendium compiled during the second millennium BCE, shed light on the sophisticated understanding of the interplay between the human and divine realms in Mesopotamian witchcraft.

The incantations in the "Burning of Bel" reveal the importance of ritual gestures, invocations, and the use of sacred objects in the practice of witchcraft. These elements were believed to establish a connection between the practitioner and the divine forces at play. Ritual gestures, such as hand movements or body postures, were employed to create a symbolic language that communicated with the spiritual realm. Invocations, which called upon specific deities or spirits, sought their assistance or sought to compel them to act in accordance with the practitioner's desires. The use of sacred objects, such as amulets or ritual tools, acted as conduits for spiritual energy and aided in the manipulation of unseen forces.

Mesopotamian witchcraft encompassed various aspects of human life, ranging from healing and protection to the pursuit of personal desires or the seeking of divine guidance. The spells and techniques found in the Mesopotamian texts addressed a wide array of concerns, including the curing of illnesses, the banishment of evil spirits, the attainment of love or fertility, and the protection against malevolent forces. The rituals and incantations aimed to tap into the powers of the gods and spirits, seeking their favor and assistance in bringing about the desired outcomes.

In modern witchcraft traditions, practitioners often draw inspiration from the ancient Mesopotamian beliefs and rituals to enrich their own practices. The understanding of the interplay between the human and divine realms, the emphasis on ritual gestures and invocations, and the utilization of sacred objects resonate with the core principles of contemporary witchcraft. By studying and incorporating elements from Mesopotamian witchcraft, modern practitioners can deepen their connection with the spiritual forces, expand their knowledge of spellcasting techniques, and enhance their understanding of the intricate relationship between humanity and the divine.

Divination, the ancient practice of seeking knowledge or guidance from the divine, has a rich history that can be traced back to the ancient civilization of Mesopotamia. Mesopotamian cultures developed various techniques and methods for divination, which served as a means to access spiritual insights and understand the will of the gods. These practices had a profound influence on later systems of divination found in different cultures around the world.

One prominent form of divination in Mesopotamia was hepatoscopy, the examination of the liver of sacrificial animals. The liver was believed to be a sacred organ connected to the divine realm, and its examination provided clues and omens that could be interpreted by skilled diviners. The liver was carefully examined for its shape, markings, and abnormalities, which were believed to hold messages from the gods. By deciphering these signs, diviners could offer guidance on matters such as personal fortunes, political decisions, or the outcome of battles.

Another significant divinatory practice in Mesopotamia was the interpretation of celestial omens. The movements and patterns of celestial bodies, such as the stars, planets, and eclipses, were believed to convey messages from the gods. Skilled astrologers and priests, known as Chaldeans, meticulously observed and recorded these celestial phenomena, interpreting their significance and predicting future events. The Chaldeans of Babylon became particularly renowned for their expertise in astrology, which contributed to the development of Western astrological traditions.

The influence of Mesopotamian divination techniques extended beyond the region itself, reaching neighboring cultures and civilizations. For example, in ancient Greece, the practice of hepatoscopy was adopted and adapted by the Etruscans, who established a complex system of liver divination known as haruspicy. Similarly, the Romans incorporated Mesopotamian astrological practices into their own divinatory traditions, which ultimately influenced the development of Western astrology as it is known today.

In contemporary esoteric and occult traditions, elements of Mesopotamian divination techniques continue to be employed. Some practitioners of divination draw inspiration from Mesopotamian practices, integrating hepatoscopy or celestial omens into their divinatory repertoire. These ancient techniques provide a connection to the wisdom of the past and offer alternative perspectives for seekers of divine guidance.

Herbalism, the study and use of plants for healing and magical purposes, has a rich history rooted in ancient civilizations. In this chapter, we delve into the influence of ancient Mesopotamian knowledge of medicinal plants and their properties on the development of herbalism. The ancient Mesopotamians, with their vast understanding of botanical remedies, incorporated these plants into their healing rituals and incantations. Furthermore, the use of sacred herbs, such as myrrh and frankincense, in Mesopotamian religious ceremonies laid the foundation for later herbal traditions in various cultures. This chapter explores the interplay between Mesopotamian herbal knowledge and the subsequent evolution of herbalism across different societies, highlighting its significance in both ancient and contemporary contexts.

Mesopotamian Botanical Remedies:

The ancient Mesopotamians, often considered the cradle of civilization, possessed an extensive knowledge of medicinal plants. Their understanding of botanical remedies was influenced by observation, experimentation, and a close relationship with the natural world. Mesopotamian healers and priests relied on plants for their healing properties, incorporating them into their rituals and magical practices. The knowledge and use of these botanical remedies were recorded in clay tablets, providing invaluable insights into the ancient Mesopotamian worldview.

Example: The Assyrian Healing Ritual:

One prominent example of Mesopotamian herbal practices is the Assyrian healing ritual. It involved the use of various plants and substances, such as myrrh, frankincense, cedar, and juniper. These plants were believed to possess healing properties and were employed in rituals to drive away evil spirits and promote physical and spiritual well-being. The ritualistic use of these herbs laid the groundwork for later herbal traditions, where plants were recognized for their medicinal qualities.

Herbal Traditions Influenced by Mesopotamian Knowledge:

The knowledge of medicinal plants in ancient Mesopotamia had a profound impact on subsequent herbal traditions in different cultures. As trade networks expanded and civilizations interacted, the exchange of botanical knowledge allowed for the development and refinement of herbalism in various regions.

Example: Ancient Egypt:

The ancient Egyptians were heavily influenced by Mesopotamian herbal practices. The Ebers Papyrus, an ancient Egyptian medical text, contains extensive information on the medicinal uses of plants. Many of the plant remedies described in the Ebers Papyrus were influenced by Mesopotamian knowledge, showcasing the transmission and assimilation of herbal wisdom across ancient cultures.

Example: Greco-Roman Period:

During the Greco-Roman period, herbalism flourished, drawing inspiration from Mesopotamian knowledge alongside Egyptian and Greek contributions. The renowned physician Dioscorides, known for his work "De Materia Medica," incorporated Mesopotamian and Egyptian plant knowledge into his comprehensive herbal compendium. This work became a seminal reference for herbalism and was highly influential in subsequent centuries.

Contemporary Applications of Mesopotamian Herbalism:

The influence of Mesopotamian herbalism extends beyond the ancient world, continuing to shape modern herbal practices. The revival of traditional herbalism and the integration of ancient wisdom into contemporary healing systems have led to a renewed appreciation for Mesopotamian botanical knowledge.

Example: Herbalism in Traditional Chinese Medicine:

In Traditional Chinese Medicine (TCM), the use of medicinal plants is a fundamental aspect of healing. Although TCM has its distinct lineage, it has been influenced by various ancient herbal traditions, including Mesopotamian knowledge. For instance, the use of herbal remedies such as myrrh, frankincense, and licorice root in TCM can be traced back to the Mesopotamian influence on herbal practices.

Example: Western Herbal Medicine:

Western Herbal Medicine, which encompasses various herbal traditions in Europe and the Americas, has also been influenced by Mesopotamian herbalism. Many Western herbalists draw upon ancient texts and historical practices, incorporating Mesopotamian herbs into their formulas and remedies. This integration of ancient Mesopotamian knowledge exemplifies the enduring relevance and applicability of their herbal traditions.

Problems and Exercises:

Research and identify three plants commonly used in Mesopotamian herbalism, describing their medicinal properties and historical significance.

Compare and contrast the influence of Mesopotamian herbalism on ancient Egyptian and Greco-Roman herbal traditions.

Discuss the integration of Mesopotamian herbalism into contemporary healing systems, such as Traditional Chinese Medicine and Western Herbal Medicine.

Select a plant commonly used in modern herbalism and trace its historical roots, exploring any potential influence from Mesopotamian herbal knowledge.

Engage in a group discussion on the ethical considerations surrounding the use of herbal remedies, considering issues such as sustainability, cultural appropriation, and the importance of informed consent.

By exploring the origins and evolution of herbalism, we gain a deeper understanding of the diverse cultural influences that have shaped this healing art. The knowledge and practices of ancient Mesopotamia continue to inspire and inform modern herbal traditions, reminding us of the enduring wisdom found in the natural world.

Shamanism, a spiritual practice involving contact with spirits and the spirit world, has been a fundamental aspect of human spirituality across diverse cultures throughout history. In this chapter, we explore the fascinating connections between shamanism and ancient Mesopotamian beliefs. Mesopotamian shamans, known as "asipu," held a significant role as intermediaries between the human and divine realms. They performed rituals, invoked spirits, and utilized various techniques for healing and seeking guidance. By examining the core principles shared between Mesopotamian beliefs and shamanism, we gain insight into the enduring and universal aspects of this spiritual practice.

Mesopotamian Shamanism: The Asipu as Intermediaries:
In ancient Mesopotamia, the role of the shaman was fulfilled by the "asipu," a figure who served as a mediator between the physical and spiritual realms. The asipu possessed specialized knowledge and skills to communicate with spirits, perform healing rituals, and access hidden realms of consciousness.

Example: Rituals of the Asipu:
The rituals conducted by Mesopotamian asipus involved various elements such as invocations, offerings, and the use of divination techniques. They aimed to establish a connection with the spiritual entities and seek their assistance for healing, protection, and divinatory purposes. Through their rituals, asipus facilitated the flow of divine energy and knowledge into the physical world.

Spirit Possession and the Shamanic Journey:
Spirit possession and the shamanic journey are key features found in shamanic practices worldwide, including those of the ancient Mesopotamians. These phenomena involve altered states of consciousness, wherein the shaman becomes a vessel for spirits or embarks on spiritual journeys to other realms.

Example: Spirit Possession in Mesopotamian Beliefs:

Mesopotamian beliefs held that spirits could possess individuals, granting them enhanced abilities and knowledge. This concept of spirit possession was closely tied to the shamanic practices of the asipu. By allowing themselves to be possessed, asipus established a direct connection with the spiritual realm and accessed the wisdom and power of the spirits.

Example: The Shamanic Journey in Mesopotamia:

The shamanic journey, characterized by the shaman entering altered states of consciousness to travel to other realms, was also part of Mesopotamian beliefs. Mesopotamian texts describe rituals and incantations performed by asipus to initiate these journeys, enabling them to communicate with deities, spirits, and ancestral beings residing in different dimensions of reality.

Shamanism Across Cultures:
Shamanism is not limited to Mesopotamian culture but can be found in various forms and expressions worldwide. Despite regional and cultural variations, shamanic practices share common principles and techniques, reflecting a universal spiritual connection.

Example: Siberian Shamanism:

Siberian Shamanism provides an insightful comparison to Mesopotamian shamanism. Siberian shamans, known as "tungajut," engage in rituals and practices similar to the Mesopotamian asipus. Both traditions emphasize the shaman's role as an intermediary and the importance of spirit communication for healing and guidance.

Example: Amazonian Shamanism:

Amazonian shamanism, practiced by indigenous tribes in the Amazon rainforest, also exhibits parallels to Mesopotamian shamanism. Amazonian shamans, known as "curanderos" or "ayahuasqueros," employ plant medicines and spirit communication to facilitate healing and spiritual growth, echoing the ancient Mesopotamian understanding of the relationship between plants, spirits, and human consciousness.

Furthermore, the practices of magic in ancient Mesopotamia, characterized by the use of spells, amulets, and incantations to influence supernatural forces, serve as a foundation for various forms of magical practices in esoteric and occult traditions. The understanding of sympathetic magic, the power of symbolism, and the manipulation of spiritual energies found in Mesopotamian magical texts continue to shape the principles and techniques of modern magic.

Problems and Exercises:

Create a magical spell or ritual based on the principles of Mesopotamian magic, incorporating elements such as invocations, symbols, and specific actions. Reflect on the intentions and purposes behind the spell and discuss how it aligns with Mesopotamian magical practices.

Research the role of herbalism in ancient Mesopotamia and select a plant commonly used in their medicinal practices. Investigate its properties, traditional uses, and symbolic associations. Create an herbal remedy or potion inspired by Mesopotamian herbalism using that plant.

By exploring the influence of Mesopotamian religious concepts on esoteric and occult traditions, we gain a deeper understanding of the interconnectedness of ancient and modern mystical practices. The wisdom and insights of the ancient Mesopotamians continue to resonate in the realms of magic, divination, and spiritual exploration, offering pathways for personal transformation and connection with the divine.

Mesopotamian Contributions to Science and Knowledge

Mesopotamia, often referred to as the "Cradle of Civilization," was a region of great intellectual and cultural achievements. In this chapter, we delve into the remarkable contributions of ancient Mesopotamia to the fields of science and knowledge. From astronomy and mathematics to medicine and engineering, the Mesopotamians made significant advancements that laid the foundation for later scientific and scholarly pursuits. By examining their innovations and methodologies, we gain a deeper appreciation for the intellectual legacy of this ancient civilization.

Astronomy and Astrology:

Mesopotamian civilization exhibited an unparalleled fascination with the celestial realm, which propelled them to make significant strides in the fields of astronomy and astrology. Through their meticulous observations and rigorous record-keeping practices, the Mesopotamians laid the foundation for future astronomical studies, while also shaping the development of astrology as a means of understanding the influence of celestial bodies on human affairs.

Advancements in Astronomy: Pioneering Celestial Inquiry

The Mesopotamians were pioneers in the systematic study of the stars, planets, and other celestial phenomena. Driven by their curiosity and the desire to comprehend the workings of the universe, they embarked on rigorous observations and data collection, laying the groundwork for future advancements in astronomy.

Their meticulous observations encompassed a wide range of celestial bodies, including the sun, moon, planets, stars, and comets. They meticulously tracked their movements, recorded their positions in the night sky, and carefully observed any irregularities or patterns.

To aid in their celestial observations, Mesopotamian astronomers developed ingenious tools and techniques. They constructed simple instruments such as the astrolabe and gnomon, which assisted in measuring angles and tracking celestial bodies. They also devised mathematical calculations and algorithms to predict astronomical events, such as lunar and solar eclipses, with astonishing accuracy.

The Mesopotamians recognized the cyclical nature of celestial events, identifying recurring patterns and establishing calendars based on astronomical observations. These calendars served as crucial tools for agricultural planning, religious ceremonies, and societal activities.

The Development of Astrology: Unveiling Celestial Influences

Building upon their astronomical knowledge, the Mesopotamians developed astrology, a belief system that postulated a connection between celestial events and human destinies. Astrology sought to interpret the influence of celestial bodies on various aspects of human life, including personal traits, relationships, and societal events.

The Mesopotamians believed that celestial phenomena, such as comets, planetary alignments, and eclipses, were divine messages or omens from the gods. They meticulously recorded these celestial omens and interpreted them as indicators of upcoming events or as divine pronouncements.

A central aspect of Mesopotamian astrology was the division of the celestial sphere into twelve sections, known as the Zodiac. Each section corresponded to a specific constellation, and the position of the sun, moon, and planets within these constellations held significant meaning. This division of the zodiacal belt into twelve signs influenced later astrological systems in various cultures.

The Mesopotamians used astrological techniques to create individual horoscopes, which were based on the position of celestial bodies at the time of a person's birth. These personalized horoscopes were believed to provide insights into an individual's character, strengths, weaknesses, and potential life events.

Astrology permeated Mesopotamian society, playing a crucial role in decision-making processes, including the selection of auspicious dates for important events, such as royal coronations or military campaigns. It also influenced religious practices, as priests used astrological knowledge to determine propitious times for ceremonies and rituals.

By combining their astronomical observations with astrological interpretations, the Mesopotamians sought to unveil the cosmic forces shaping human existence and bring order to the chaotic world around them.

Example: Astronomical Observations:

Mesopotamian astronomers meticulously observed the movements of celestial bodies, noting their positions and patterns over extended periods. They developed an intricate system of celestial omens, which became the basis for astrological practices in Mesopotamian society.

Example: The Zodiac:

The Mesopotamians divided the celestial sphere into twelve sections, known as the Zodiac, each associated with different constellations. This division influenced later civilizations, including the Greeks, who incorporated the Mesopotamian zodiacal system into their own.

Mathematics and Numerical Systems:

The Mesopotamians were pioneers in the realm of mathematics, developing a sophisticated numerical system and mathematical techniques that left an indelible mark on the evolution of this discipline. Their mathematical prowess and innovative methods laid the foundation for future mathematical advancements, influencing the development of arithmetic, geometry, and algebra.

The Numerical System: An Ingenious Notation

At the heart of Mesopotamian mathematics was their remarkable numerical system. Unlike many other ancient civilizations, which relied on cumbersome systems based on tally marks or hieroglyphic symbols, the Mesopotamians developed a positional numeral system.

Their system was based on the concept of place value, wherein the value of a digit depended on its position within a number. This innovative system allowed the representation of both small and large numbers with remarkable ease. The Mesopotamians utilized a sexagesimal system, which was based on the number 60, a reflection of their fascination with the celestial realm and its divisions.

To represent numbers, they employed a combination of two basic symbols: the wedge (representing a unit) and the circle (representing a ten). By combining these symbols in various positions, they could represent numbers up to 59 and, through a process of positional notation, extend the system to higher numbers.

The Mesopotamians also developed efficient methods for performing arithmetic operations, such as addition, subtraction, multiplication, and division, using their numerical system. These techniques formed the basis for practical calculations, including those related to trade, construction, and administrative tasks.

Mathematical Techniques: The Birth of Mathematical Thinking

In addition to their numerical system, the Mesopotamians devised mathematical techniques that demonstrated their aptitude for abstract thinking and problem-solving. Their mathematical achievements encompassed various areas, including geometry, algebraic equations, and mathematical tables.

Geometry: Mesopotamian mathematicians demonstrated a profound understanding of geometric principles. They developed geometric formulas and methods for calculating areas and volumes of various shapes, laying the groundwork for the future development of geometry as a mathematical discipline.

Algebraic Equations: The Mesopotamians were skilled at solving practical problems using algebraic equations. They formulated mathematical expressions to represent real-world scenarios and developed techniques for solving these equations, often employing approximation methods.

Mathematical Tables: The Mesopotamians created extensive mathematical tables, recording calculations, and results for a wide range of mathematical problems. These tables encompassed multiplication tables, square and cube roots, trigonometric ratios, and even astronomical calculations. Such tables not only facilitated calculations but also served as valuable resources for future mathematicians.

Lasting Impact: A Mathematical Legacy

The mathematical achievements of the Mesopotamians had a lasting impact on the development of mathematics as a discipline. Their positional numeral system, along with their mathematical techniques, laid the groundwork for future mathematical advancements in different civilizations.

Example: Base 60 Numerical System:

The Mesopotamians employed a base 60 numerical system, known as the sexagesimal system, which influenced the measurement of time, angles, and geographical coordinates. This system is still utilized today, particularly in the division of hours, minutes, and seconds.

Example: Mathematical Tablets:

Ancient Mesopotamian mathematicians created numerous clay tablets containing mathematical problems and calculations. One notable example is the Plimpton 322 tablet, which demonstrates their knowledge of Pythagorean triples, quadratic equations, and other mathematical concepts.

Medicine and Pharmacology:

Mesopotamian civilization exhibited a remarkable level of sophistication in the realm of medicine. Their medical practices and pharmacological knowledge were highly advanced for their time, resulting in significant contributions to the field of medicine. Through their observations, diagnostic techniques, and herbal remedies, the Mesopotamians laid the groundwork for future medical advancements, leaving an enduring impact on the healing arts.

Observations and Diagnostic Techniques: The Art of Healing

Mesopotamian medical practitioners, known as ashipu and asu, were keen observers of the human body and its ailments. They believed that diseases were caused by a complex interplay of natural, supernatural, and divine factors, and thus their approach to medicine was holistic.

Patient Evaluation: Mesopotamian physicians meticulously examined patients, paying close attention to their symptoms, medical history, and external signs of illness. They believed that both the physical and spiritual aspects of a person were vital in understanding and treating diseases.

Diagnostic Techniques: To aid in diagnosis, the Mesopotamians employed various techniques. These included analyzing the patient's urine, inspecting bodily discharges, observing the pulse and respiration rates, and examining the liver, which they considered to be a central organ associated with health and disease.

Example: Urine Examination:
The examination of urine played a crucial role in Mesopotamian medical diagnosis. They believed that changes in urine color, odor, and sediment could indicate specific diseases or imbalances within the body. Through careful observation and analysis, they could make informed assessments of a patient's condition.

Pharmacological Knowledge: Herbal Remedies and Therapeutic Practices

Mesopotamian medical practitioners possessed an extensive understanding of pharmacology, harnessing the healing properties of various plants and substances. They developed a rich pharmacopoeia and implemented therapeutic practices that formed the basis of their medical treatments.

Herbal Remedies: The Mesopotamians utilized a wide array of medicinal plants and herbs to alleviate ailments and promote healing. They meticulously recorded the properties and uses of these plants, creating compendia of herbal remedies that served as valuable references for future generations.

Example: Medical Texts:
The Mesopotamians compiled comprehensive medical texts, such as the "Diagnostic Handbook" and the "Therapeutic Handbook." These texts documented the symptoms, diagnoses, and treatments for a variety of illnesses and injuries, providing a wealth of medical knowledge for both current and future medical practitioners.

Surgical Practices: Mesopotamian medicine also encompassed surgical interventions for various conditions. They developed techniques for wound treatment, the setting of broken bones, and even basic surgical procedures. The use of surgical instruments, such as scalpels and forceps, demonstrated their commitment to surgical precision.

Lasting Impact: Legacy in Medical Advancements

The medical practices and pharmacological knowledge of the Mesopotamians left a lasting legacy in the field of medicine. Their contributions formed the basis for future advancements in medical understanding and treatment across different civilizations.

Example: Herbalism and Remedies:

As discussed in Chapter 6, Mesopotamians possessed a vast understanding of medicinal plants and their properties. They developed botanical remedies that formed the basis of later herbal traditions in different cultures.

Problems and Exercises:

Research and describe the contributions of Mesopotamian astronomers to our understanding of celestial bodies and their movements.

Discuss the significance of the Mesopotamian numerical system and its impact on mathematics and modern-day measurements.

Analyze the medical texts of ancient Mesopotamia, highlighting the diagnostic methods and treatments they employed.

Investigate the engineering techniques used in the construction of ziggurats, providing examples from different Mesopotamian city-states.

Debate the ethical considerations of studying and utilizing ancient Mesopotamian knowledge in modern scientific and academic fields.

By exploring the achievements of ancient Mesopotamia in the realms of science and knowledge, we gain a deeper appreciation for their intellectual prowess and the enduring impact of their innovations. The legacy of Mesopotamian contributions continues to influence and inspire contemporary scientific and scholarly endeavors.

Preservation and Rediscovery of Mesopotamian Texts

In the ancient world, written texts were invaluable vessels of knowledge and wisdom, serving as repositories of cultural, religious, and scientific information. Mesopotamian civilization recognized the significance of preserving their accumulated knowledge in written form. This chapter delves into the remarkable efforts undertaken to preserve and rediscover Mesopotamian texts, shedding light on the invaluable insights they provide into various aspects of their society, including religion, law, literature, and science.

The Clay Tablets: A Medium for Eternal Preservation

The use of clay tablets as the primary medium for writing was a defining characteristic of Mesopotamian civilization. The availability of clay in the region, along with the ingenuity of Mesopotamian scribes, led to the development of this enduring form of record-keeping.

Firstly, the durability of clay was a key advantage in preserving the written texts. Unlike perishable materials like papyrus or parchment, clay tablets could withstand the test of time. The baked clay tablets, once hardened, became resistant to decay, ensuring the survival of important information for future generations. As a result, countless clay tablets have been discovered by archaeologists, providing invaluable insights into the history and culture of ancient Mesopotamia.

Secondly, the cuneiform script, which the scribes used to inscribe the clay tablets, was a versatile writing system. It consisted of wedge-shaped characters that could be easily impressed onto the soft clay surface using a stylus. The cuneiform script allowed the Mesopotamians to capture a wide range of subjects in their writings. From mundane administrative records, such as tax inventories and legal documents, to complex literary works like epic poems and religious texts, the clay tablets preserved a wealth of knowledge across various domains of Mesopotamian life.

Furthermore, the practice of baking the clay tablets after inscribing them significantly enhanced their preservation. Baking the tablets hardened the clay, making it less susceptible to physical damage and environmental decay. This baking process effectively transformed the clay tablets into long-lasting artifacts that could endure for thousands of years. The resulting durability allowed these texts to survive the passage of time and be rediscovered and deciphered centuries later, providing modern scholars with valuable windows into the ancient world.

In addition to their practical advantages, clay tablets also held cultural significance for the Mesopotamians. The act of writing on clay tablets was often associated with divine communication and the preservation of sacred knowledge. In religious rituals and practices, clay tablets were used to inscribe prayers, hymns, and incantations. These sacred texts were believed to hold the power of divine revelation and were treated with reverence and respect.

Overall, the use of clay tablets as a writing medium by the Mesopotamians exemplified their ingenuity and dedication to the preservation of knowledge. The durable nature of clay, the versatility of the cuneiform script, and the practice of baking the tablets all contributed to the long-lasting legacy of Mesopotamian writings. Today, these clay tablets continue to provide us with invaluable insights into the history, culture, and intellectual achievements of one of the world's oldest civilizations.

The Great Library of Ashurbanipal: A Treasure Trove of Knowledge

The establishment of the Great Library of Ashurbanipal in Nineveh stands as a remarkable milestone in the preservation of Mesopotamian texts. Curated during the reign of King Ashurbanipal (668-627 BCE), this renowned library housed an extensive collection of clay tablets that encompassed a diverse range of subjects, making it a treasure trove of knowledge from ancient Mesopotamia.

The Great Library of Ashurbanipal served as a prestigious center of learning, attracting scholars and scribes from near and far. These scholars were entrusted with the crucial task of copying and preserving existing texts, ensuring the dissemination and perpetuation of knowledge for future generations. The dedication of these individuals played a pivotal role in preventing the loss of valuable information, safeguarding the intellectual legacy of Mesopotamia.

The library's vast collection encompassed various fields of study, including astronomy, medicine, mathematics, literature, and religious texts. Within its walls, the clay tablets held astronomical observations, mathematical calculations, incantations for healing, epic poems, religious hymns, and legal codes. The diversity of subjects reflected the breadth and depth of Mesopotamian scholarship, and the library provided a comprehensive resource for scholars to explore and study these disciplines.

Moreover, the Great Library of Ashurbanipal went beyond preserving Mesopotamian works alone. It also housed texts from other civilizations, enabling cross-cultural exchange and contributing to the preservation of a wider human heritage. The library's collection included works from ancient Babylonia, Assyria, and other neighboring regions. This intermingling of texts fostered intellectual dialogue and the exchange of ideas, enriching the cultural and intellectual landscape of the ancient world.

The significance of the Great Library of Ashurbanipal extended far beyond its immediate time and place. Its legacy endured through the impact it had on subsequent generations. The copying and dissemination of texts within the library ensured that the knowledge of the Mesopotamians continued to influence and inspire future civilizations.

Problems and Exercises:

Discuss the role of the Great Library of Ashurbanipal in preserving Mesopotamian knowledge. How did it contribute to the continuity of intellectual traditions?

Explore the types of texts housed in the Great Library of Ashurbanipal. Choose one subject area and analyze the importance of the texts within that field.

Investigate the impact of the library's collection of texts from other civilizations. How did this cross-cultural exchange contribute to the development of knowledge and the preservation of human heritage?

Imagine you are a scholar during the time of King Ashurbanipal. Write a journal entry describing your experience of studying and copying texts in the Great Library. What challenges and rewards did you encounter?

Rediscovery and Decipherment of Cuneiform

After the decline of Mesopotamian civilization, the once-thriving culture and its written legacy gradually faded into obscurity. The clay tablets, with their intricate cuneiform script, were left buried and forgotten beneath the layers of time. It wasn't until the nineteenth century CE that a renaissance in the study of ancient civilizations sparked the rediscovery and decipherment of the cuneiform script, leading to the remarkable resurrection of the knowledge contained within these ancient texts.

The rediscovery and decipherment of cuneiform scripts can be attributed to the efforts of pioneering scholars and archaeologists. Among them, the names of individuals such as Henry Rawlinson, George Smith, and Austen Henry Layard stand prominent. These dedicated researchers and linguists embarked on excavations of ancient Mesopotamian sites, unearthing thousands of clay tablets inscribed with the enigmatic cuneiform script.

Deciphering the cuneiform script was no small feat. The script itself presented a significant challenge due to its complex nature, comprising a combination of wedge-shaped characters. Scholars had to painstakingly unravel the intricate symbols and decipher the meanings encoded within them. Through comparative analysis and meticulous study, they gradually unraveled the linguistic code of cuneiform and began to understand its grammar, vocabulary, and syntax.

One notable breakthrough in the decipherment came with the discovery of the Behistun Inscription in modern-day Iran. The inscription, carved into a cliffside, contained texts written in multiple languages, including Old Persian, Elamite, and Akkadian, the language of ancient Mesopotamia. By comparing the known languages with the cuneiform symbols, scholars were able to piece together the meanings of many signs and establish a foundation for deciphering the script as a whole.

As the decipherment progressed, a vast array of knowledge was unveiled. The clay tablets, once silent witnesses to a lost civilization, now spoke volumes about the history, literature, religion, science, and daily life of ancient Mesopotamia. Texts ranging from administrative records and legal codes to religious hymns, mythological tales, and medical treatises emerged from the depths of antiquity, offering valuable insights into the cultural, intellectual, and technological achievements of the Mesopotamians.

The rediscovery and decipherment of the cuneiform script revolutionized the study of ancient Mesopotamia and had a profound impact on various academic disciplines. Archaeologists, historians, linguists, and scholars from diverse fields eagerly delved into the texts, analyzing them, translating them, and piecing together the intricate tapestry of Mesopotamian civilization.

Example: The Work of Henry Rawlinson:

Henry Rawlinson, a British scholar, played a pivotal role in deciphering cuneiform. He meticulously studied the inscriptions on the Behistun Rock in Persia (modern-day Iran), which contained a trilingual text written in cuneiform. By comparing the Old Persian version with known texts in other languages, Rawlinson successfully deciphered the cuneiform script, opening the doors to understanding Mesopotamian texts.

Example: Epic of Gilgamesh:

One of the most celebrated literary works discovered among the Mesopotamian texts is the Epic of Gilgamesh. This epic poem, preserved on clay tablets, offers insights into Mesopotamian mythology, heroic tales, and reflections on the human condition. Its rediscovery and subsequent translation captured the world's attention and unveiled a treasure trove of ancient wisdom.

The Significance of Rediscovered Mesopotamian Texts

The rediscovery and decipherment of Mesopotamian texts have sparked a profound intellectual revolution, opening doors to a deeper understanding of ancient Mesopotamia across a wide range of disciplines. Scholars and researchers from fields such as history, archaeology, linguistics, and religious studies have eagerly delved into these texts, utilizing them as invaluable resources to unravel the mysteries of this ancient civilization.

For historians, the rediscovered texts provide firsthand accounts of historical events, political structures, and social dynamics of Mesopotamian society. Administrative records, royal inscriptions, and legal codes shed light on the organization of ancient Mesopotamian cities, the functioning of their governments, and the laws that governed their communities. These texts enable historians to construct a more nuanced and accurate narrative of the political and social landscape of the time.

Archaeologists, armed with the knowledge embedded in the texts, have been able to identify and excavate ancient sites with greater precision. By combining textual evidence with material remains, they can reconstruct aspects of daily life, technological advancements, architectural practices, and trade networks in ancient Mesopotamia. The texts provide crucial contextual information that enhances the interpretation and analysis of archaeological discoveries.

Linguists have been captivated by the cuneiform script and its grammatical structures. The corpus of Mesopotamian texts offers an extensive linguistic dataset for studying ancient languages such as Sumerian, Akkadian, Babylonian, and Assyrian. Through linguistic analysis, scholars have deepened their understanding of these ancient languages, their evolution over time, and their connections to other language families. This, in turn, has shed light on the broader linguistic landscape of the ancient Near East.

Religious studies scholars have found in these texts a wealth of information about the religious beliefs, rituals, and cosmologies of the Mesopotamians. Hymns, prayers, and mythological narratives provide insights into their religious practices, deities, and concepts of the divine. The texts help unravel the complexities of Mesopotamian religious thought and its influence on subsequent religious traditions.

The impact of the rediscovery and decipherment of Mesopotamian texts extends beyond academic circles. The knowledge gleaned from these texts has enriched public understanding and appreciation of ancient civilizations. Museums around the world exhibit clay tablets and artifacts, showcasing the achievements and cultural heritage of ancient Mesopotamia. The deciphered texts have also sparked popular interest in the ancient world, inspiring books, documentaries, and exhibitions that bring this fascinating era to life.

In conclusion, the rediscovery and decipherment of Mesopotamian texts have revolutionized the study of ancient Mesopotamia and had far-reaching implications for various disciplines. Through these texts, historians, archaeologists, linguists, and religious studies scholars have unearthed a treasure trove of knowledge, shedding light on the history, culture, language, and religious beliefs of this ancient civilization.

Example: Legal and Administrative Systems:

Legal texts, such as the Code of Hammurabi, provide valuable insights into the legal and administrative systems of Mesopotamia. These texts offer a glimpse into the societal structure, codes of conduct, and the role of law in maintaining order and justice.

Example: Astronomical and Mathematical Knowledge:

Astronomical and mathematical texts have revealed the advanced knowledge and achievements of Mesopotamian astronomers and mathematicians. These texts contain intricate calculations, astronomical observations, and predictive techniques, underscoring the significant contributions of the Mesopotamians to the development of these scientific disciplines.

Problems and Exercises:

Explore the role of the Great Library of Ashurbanipal in the preservation and dissemination of Mesopotamian texts. What impact did it have on the development of scholarship in the ancient world?

Investigate the challenges faced by scholars in deciphering the cuneiform script. How did the decipherment of cuneiform contribute to our understanding of Mesopotamian civilization?

Analyze the significance of the Epic of Gilgamesh as a literary and cultural artifact. What themes and insights can be gleaned from this epic poem?

Discuss the influence of rediscovered Mesopotamian texts on the development of modern fields of study, such as archaeology and linguistics.

Chapter 7: Modern Interpretations and Revivals: Rediscovering Ancient Mesopotamian Spirituality

The ancient civilization of Mesopotamia, with its rich tapestry of religious beliefs, rituals, and spiritual practices, continues to captivate the modern imagination. As we journey through the annals of history, we encounter numerous instances where ancient traditions and wisdom are rediscovered, reimagined, and revived in contemporary contexts. Chapter 7 explores the modern interpretations and revivals of ancient Mesopotamian spirituality, showcasing how this ancient tradition continues to inspire and resonate with individuals and communities in the present day.

Throughout history, societies have experienced cultural and spiritual shifts, often leaving behind fragments of ancient belief systems. However, with the passage of time, these ancient spiritual practices have reemerged, drawing the attention of modern seekers and scholars. The revival of ancient Mesopotamian spirituality is one such resurgence that has garnered significant interest in recent years.

In this chapter, we will delve into the various ways in which modern individuals and groups have engaged with and interpreted the spiritual practices of ancient Mesopotamia. We will explore the motivations behind these revivals, the diverse paths taken by contemporary practitioners, and the impact of these revivals on personal spirituality and collective consciousness. Additionally, we will critically examine the challenges and controversies that arise when ancient traditions are brought into the modern world.

To truly understand the modern interpretations and revivals of ancient Mesopotamian spirituality, we must acknowledge the role of historical context. The revival of ancient traditions is not a simple replication or reconstruction of the past, but rather a dynamic and evolving process influenced by contemporary cultural, social, and spiritual landscapes. The motivations driving individuals and groups to explore and embrace these traditions may vary, ranging from a desire for a deeper connection with ancestral heritage to a quest for spiritual transformation or a response to the ecological and environmental crises of our time.

Throughout this chapter, we will encounter a diverse array of modern practitioners who draw inspiration from ancient Mesopotamian spirituality. These individuals and communities engage in practices such as ritual reenactments, mythic storytelling, divination, and the cultivation of a spiritual relationship with the land. We will explore how these modern interpretations and revivals incorporate elements of Mesopotamian cosmology, symbolism, and myth, adapting them to meet the needs and aspirations of contemporary spiritual seekers.

As we embark on this exploration of modern interpretations and revivals of ancient Mesopotamian spirituality, it is important to approach the subject with an open mind and a critical lens. We will encounter a variety of perspectives, ranging from those who embrace these revivals as authentic and transformative to those who question their historical accuracy or cultural appropriation. By engaging with these diverse viewpoints, we will foster a deeper understanding of the complexities surrounding the revival of ancient spiritual traditions and stimulate meaningful discussions about the intersection of the ancient and the modern.

Problems and Exercises:

Reflect on your own spiritual journey and consider whether you have ever felt drawn to ancient spiritual traditions. What aspects of these traditions resonate with you? How might you incorporate elements of ancient Mesopotamian spirituality into your own practice?

Research and compare different modern interpretations and revivals of ancient Mesopotamian spirituality. What common themes or practices emerge? How do these interpretations differ in their approaches and philosophies?

Explore the ethical considerations associated with the revival of ancient spiritual traditions. Discuss the potential challenges of cultural appropriation and the importance of respectful engagement with ancient cultures.

Imagine you are a contemporary practitioner of ancient Mesopotamian spirituality. Write a personal reflection on the ways in which this spiritual path has impacted your life and understanding of the world.

Engage in a group discussion or debate on the merits and challenges of reviving ancient spiritual traditions. Consider different perspectives and construct well-reasoned arguments based on historical, cultural, and ethical considerations.

Historical Context of Modern Mesopotamian Revivals

To understand the modern revivals of ancient Mesopotamian spirituality, it is essential to examine the historical context in which these revivals emerged.

Historical context encompasses the social, cultural, and intellectual climate that shapes the interpretations and motivations of contemporary practitioners. By exploring the historical backdrop against which these revivals unfold, we can gain valuable insights into the complexities and nuances of their development.

Mesopotamia in the Modern Era:

The late 19th and early 20th centuries marked a pivotal time in the revival of ancient Mesopotamian spirituality. This period witnessed remarkable archaeological discoveries that shed light on the once-forgotten cities, temples, and artifacts of this ancient civilization. These findings acted as a catalyst, capturing the imagination of scholars and igniting a renewed interest in exploring the spiritual practices of Mesopotamia.

The excavation of ancient Mesopotamian sites, such as Ur, Nineveh, and Babylon, unearthed a wealth of historical treasures that had been buried for centuries. Cities that were once mere legends in ancient texts suddenly materialized before the eyes of archaeologists. The remnants of magnificent temples, royal palaces, and intricate artifacts emerged from the depths of time, offering tangible evidence of a civilization that had long fascinated historians, poets, and mystics.

These archaeological discoveries provided tangible connections to the past, bridging the gap between contemporary society and the ancient Mesopotamians. As scholars meticulously excavated and studied these sites, a clearer understanding of the religious and spiritual practices of the Mesopotamians began to emerge.

For example, the excavations at the city of Ur, led by Sir Leonard Woolley in the 1920s, unearthed the Great Ziggurat, an impressive temple complex dedicated to the moon god Nanna. The discovery of this sacred site, along with its associated artifacts and inscriptions, provided valuable insights into the religious rituals, cosmology, and beliefs of the ancient Mesopotamians.

The archaeological findings also revealed the importance of divine kingship in Mesopotamian society. Royal tombs, adorned with elaborate funerary goods and intricate art, showcased the divine status bestowed upon the kings, who were believed to serve as intermediaries between the gods and the people.

These discoveries, coupled with the decipherment of cuneiform script and the translation of ancient texts, sparked a resurgence of interest in Mesopotamian spirituality. Scholars, historians, and individuals with a deep spiritual connection to the ancient world sought to delve into the wisdom, rituals, and symbolism of the

Mesopotamians, drawing inspiration from their cosmology, mythology, and religious practices.

The revival of ancient Mesopotamian spirituality was not limited to academic circles. Artists, poets, and practitioners of various esoteric and spiritual traditions also found inspiration in the rich tapestry of Mesopotamian beliefs. From the symbolism of the ziggurats and the reverence for celestial bodies to the invocation of ancient gods and the exploration of divination practices, these revivals sought to reconnect with the spiritual heritage of a bygone era.

In conclusion, the significant archaeological discoveries made in Mesopotamia during the late 19th and early 20th centuries played a vital role in reviving ancient Mesopotamian spirituality. The unearthing of cities, temples, and artifacts ignited the curiosity and imagination of scholars and enthusiasts, leading to a renewed interest in exploring and understanding the spiritual practices of this ancient civilization. These findings provided a tangible connection to the past, allowing for the reinterpretation and revival of Mesopotamian spiritual traditions in the modern era.

Example: The discovery of the ancient city of Ur by Sir Leonard Woolley in the 1920s generated excitement and fascination, offering glimpses into the religious and cultural life of the Mesopotamians. The artifacts unearthed, such as statues, cuneiform tablets, and temple remains, provided valuable clues for understanding their spiritual beliefs and rituals.

Orientalism and Scholarly Exploration:

The rise of Orientalism in the 19th century had a profound impact on the academic exploration of Mesopotamia and the understanding of its ancient civilization. Orientalism, a scholarly and cultural movement, focused on the study and interpretation of Eastern cultures, including the civilizations of the Middle East, Asia, and North Africa.

During this period, a fascination with the exotic and mysterious cultures of the East gripped the Western world. Scholars, archaeologists, and explorers were drawn to the lands of Mesopotamia, driven by a desire to uncover the secrets of this ancient civilization. They embarked on expeditions, braving harsh climates and challenging terrains, in pursuit of knowledge about the past.

Orientalist scholars approached the study of Mesopotamia with a sense of awe and wonder, viewing it as a cradle of civilization and a source of ancient wisdom. They sought to understand the culture, history, and spirituality of the

Mesopotamians through the lens of their own cultural perspectives and scholarly frameworks.

One of the prominent figures in this exploration was Sir Austen Henry Layard, an English archaeologist who conducted excavations in Mesopotamia during the mid-19th century. His excavations at the ancient city of Nineveh unearthed stunning artifacts, including the famous reliefs depicting scenes from the royal palace of Ashurbanipal. Layard's discoveries captured the imagination of the Western world and fueled the growing interest in Mesopotamian civilization.

Another influential figure was George Smith, a British Assyriologist who made significant contributions to the decipherment of cuneiform script. Smith's translation of the Epic of Gilgamesh, one of the oldest known works of literature, created a sensation and further deepened the fascination with Mesopotamian culture.

These Orientalist explorations and discoveries brought Mesopotamia to the forefront of academic and cultural discourse. The ancient civilization, once shrouded in myth and legend, began to take shape through the meticulous excavation of its cities, decipherment of its scripts, and interpretation of its art and literature.

However, it is important to acknowledge that Orientalism was not without its limitations and criticisms. Some scholars argue that it was influenced by colonial and imperialistic attitudes, shaping the interpretation of Eastern cultures through a Western lens. Critics also point out that Orientalism often perpetuated stereotypes and exoticized the cultures it studied, reinforcing power imbalances and unequal relationships.

Nonetheless, the impact of Orientalism on the academic exploration of Mesopotamia cannot be overlooked. It provided the framework and impetus for extensive archaeological expeditions, the translation of ancient texts, and the development of scholarly disciplines dedicated to the study of Mesopotamian civilization.

In conclusion, the rise of Orientalism in the 19th century played a pivotal role in shaping the academic exploration of Mesopotamia. Scholars and archaeologists, driven by a fascination with the cultures of the East, embarked on expeditions to uncover the secrets of this ancient civilization. The Orientalist approach, while not without its criticisms, contributed to the understanding of Mesopotamia's culture, history, and spirituality, leaving a lasting impact on the academic and cultural landscape.

Example: Sir Austen Henry Layard's excavations at Nineveh in the mid-19th century brought to light the magnificent Assyrian palaces and the famous library of Ashurbanipal. The texts discovered in the library fueled scholarly interest in deciphering cuneiform script and deepening the understanding of Mesopotamian culture.

Comparative Mythology and Religion:

The study of comparative mythology and religion has played a significant role in the resurgence of Mesopotamian spirituality. Scholars and researchers, driven by a quest to understand the universal aspects of human belief systems, have turned their attention to the rich mythological and religious traditions of Mesopotamia.

Comparative mythology is an interdisciplinary field that seeks to identify and analyze the common themes, motifs, and symbols found in myths across different cultures. By studying the similarities and differences between various mythological traditions, scholars aim to uncover underlying patterns and archetypal structures that transcend cultural boundaries.

Mesopotamian myths and religious practices have been a subject of great interest within the field of comparative mythology. Scholars have explored the connections between Mesopotamian cosmology, deities, rituals, and the broader mythological frameworks of other ancient civilizations.

For example, the Epic of Gilgamesh, a famous Mesopotamian narrative, shares striking similarities with other ancient hero myths such as the Greek myth of Heracles and the Indian epic of Ramayana. These parallels offer insights into the universal themes of heroism, mortality, and the search for meaning that resonate across different cultures and time periods.

The comparative study of religion has also shed light on the spiritual beliefs and practices of ancient Mesopotamia. Scholars have examined the similarities and differences between Mesopotamian religion and other ancient religious systems, such as Egyptian, Greek, and Vedic religions. These comparative analyses provide a broader perspective on the human quest for transcendence, the role of deities, the practice of rituals, and the concept of an afterlife.

Furthermore, the resurgence of interest in ancient Mesopotamian spirituality has been fueled by the recognition of the enduring relevance of its mythological and religious themes in contemporary culture. Artists, writers, and practitioners of various spiritual traditions have drawn inspiration from Mesopotamian myths, symbols, and rituals to create meaningful connections with the past and explore new avenues of spiritual exploration.

However, it is important to approach the comparative study of mythology and religion with caution, acknowledging the potential pitfalls of cultural appropriation and oversimplification. Each culture's myths and religious practices are deeply rooted in its specific historical, social, and cultural context, and care must be taken to avoid generalizations or reductionist interpretations.

In conclusion, the study of comparative mythology and religion has played a pivotal role in the resurgence of Mesopotamian spirituality. Scholars have sought to explore the universal aspects of human belief systems by analyzing the common threads and archetypal motifs found in Mesopotamian myths and religious practices. By examining the similarities and differences with other ancient civilizations, we gain a deeper understanding of the human quest for meaning, the symbolism of myths, and the enduring relevance of ancient Mesopotamian spirituality in contemporary culture.

Example: The work of scholars like Samuel Noah Kramer, who deciphered the Enuma Elish, the Babylonian creation myth, and analyzed its parallels with other creation stories, contributed to the recognition of Mesopotamian mythology as a rich source of spiritual and symbolic knowledge.

Ecological and Environmental Concerns:

The modern revival of ancient Mesopotamian spirituality has not only been shaped by historical and academic influences but also by contemporary ecological and environmental concerns. In recent times, there has been a growing awareness of ecological crises, climate change, and the urgent need for sustainable practices that foster harmonious relationships with the natural world. This heightened environmental consciousness has prompted individuals and groups to turn to ancient Mesopotamian spirituality for inspiration, recognizing its ecological wisdom and teachings.

Ancient Mesopotamians lived in close proximity to nature, relying on the fertile land and the cycles of the seasons for their sustenance and survival. Their spirituality was intimately intertwined with the natural world, reflecting a deep understanding of the interconnectedness of all life forms and the importance of maintaining balance and harmony with the environment.

Within Mesopotamian myths and religious practices, there are numerous references to the sacredness of the natural world and the interdependence between humans and the Earth. For example, the goddess Ninhursag, often associated with fertility and agriculture, symbolizes the life-giving and nurturing aspects of the Earth. The rituals and ceremonies performed by ancient Mesopotamians aimed to honor and appease the deities responsible for maintaining the order and abundance of the natural world.

In the context of the modern ecological movement, some individuals and groups have turned to ancient Mesopotamian spirituality as a source of guidance and inspiration for cultivating a deeper connection with nature and adopting sustainable practices. They recognize the wisdom embedded in Mesopotamian cosmology, which emphasizes the interconnectedness of all beings and the importance of living in harmony with the Earth.

For example, the principles of permaculture, a design system that promotes sustainable agriculture and ecological living, resonate with the ecological wisdom found in ancient Mesopotamian spirituality. Both emphasize the importance of observing and learning from natural patterns and processes, working with the land's inherent capacities, and fostering mutually beneficial relationships between humans and the environment.

Moreover, the revival of Mesopotamian spirituality in the modern context also highlights the need to address the environmental injustices and unsustainable practices that have contributed to the degradation of our planet. By drawing inspiration from ancient Mesopotamian wisdom, individuals and groups seek to develop a deeper reverence for the Earth, promote ecological stewardship, and advocate for environmental justice.

It is worth noting that the modern revival of Mesopotamian spirituality in an ecological context is not without its challenges and complexities. Some critics argue that appropriating ancient spiritual traditions for contemporary purposes may overlook the nuances of their original cultural and historical contexts. Moreover, the process of adapting ancient practices to modern realities requires careful consideration and a critical examination of ethical implications.

In conclusion, the modern revival of ancient Mesopotamian spirituality has been influenced by contemporary ecological and environmental concerns. The recognition of ecological crises and the need for sustainable relationships with the natural world have led individuals and groups to draw inspiration from the ecological wisdom embedded in Mesopotamian spirituality. By adopting ancient principles of interconnectedness and balance, they seek to cultivate a deeper connection with nature, promote sustainable practices, and address environmental challenges of our time.

Example: The revival of agricultural practices inspired by ancient Mesopotamia, such as sustainable farming techniques and reverence for the cycles of nature, serves as a response to modern-day environmental challenges and a recognition of the wisdom inherent in ancient agricultural traditions.

Conclusion:

The historical context of modern Mesopotamian revivals encompasses a convergence of archaeological discoveries, academic exploration, comparative mythology, and ecological consciousness. These factors have contributed to a renewed interest in the spiritual practices of ancient Mesopotamia, shaping contemporary interpretations and revivals. By examining this historical context, we can appreciate the multifaceted nature of these revivals and engage in critical discussions regarding their motivations, implications, and ethical considerations.

Problems and Exercises:

Research and analyze the impact of Orientalism on the study of ancient Mesopotamia. How did Orientalist perspectives influence the interpretation of Mesopotamian culture and spirituality?

Compare the approaches of different scholars and archaeologists in their excavation and interpretation of Mesopotamian sites and artifacts. What were their contributions to our understanding of ancient Mesopotamian spirituality?

Discuss the role of comparative mythology in shaping the modern revivals of Mesopotamian spirituality. Identify common mythological motifs and symbols found in Mesopotamian myths and their parallels in other cultures.

Explore the ecological and environmental themes present in ancient Mesopotamian spirituality. How can these ancient practices inspire sustainable living and ecological consciousness in the modern world?

Engage in a group discussion on the ethical considerations involved in the revival of ancient spiritual traditions. Discuss issues such as cultural appropriation, authenticity, and respectful engagement with ancient traditions in contemporary contexts.

Reconstructionist Approaches

In the ongoing revival of ancient Mesopotamian spirituality, various approaches have emerged to reconstruct and reanimate the spiritual practices and beliefs of this ancient civilization. Reconstructionist approaches seek to faithfully reconstruct and revive ancient Mesopotamian spirituality based on historical and archaeological evidence. These approaches aim to bridge the gap between the past and the present, allowing individuals and groups to connect with the spiritual traditions of their Mesopotamian ancestors.

Reconstructionist approaches draw inspiration from diverse fields such as history, archaeology, linguistics, and comparative religious studies. They rely on rigorous research and scholarly investigation to understand the worldview, rituals, and beliefs of the ancient Mesopotamians. By reconstructing the religious practices and rituals of the past, practitioners of reconstructionist approaches strive to experience a deep connection with the ancient Mesopotamian deities, gain insights into their cultural context, and foster a sense of cultural continuity.

Historical Context:

To embark on the path of reconstruction, reconstructionist practitioners recognize the importance of developing a comprehensive understanding of the historical context surrounding ancient Mesopotamian spirituality. This understanding serves as a foundation for their endeavors to reconstruct and revive the spiritual practices and beliefs of this ancient civilization.

Reconstructionist practitioners diligently delve into a wide range of historical records, including ancient texts, inscriptions, and artifacts, to piece together the puzzle of Mesopotamian spirituality. These historical sources provide valuable glimpses into the religious life of the ancient Mesopotamians, shedding light on their rituals, ceremonies, and mythologies.

By studying ancient texts such as cuneiform tablets, reconstructionist practitioners gain access to sacred hymns, prayers, incantations, and mythological narratives. These texts, written by the ancient Mesopotamians themselves, offer unique insights into their spiritual practices, beliefs, and interactions with the divine. The decipherment and translation of cuneiform script have been crucial in unlocking the wealth of knowledge contained within these ancient texts.

Inscriptions found on ancient monuments and statues further contribute to the understanding of religious practices. These inscriptions often detail the construction of temples, the dedication of offerings, and the performance of rituals, providing glimpses into the religious life of the ancient Mesopotamians. By analyzing and interpreting these inscriptions, reconstructionist practitioners can reconstruct the physical aspects and symbolism associated with religious ceremonies.

In addition to texts and inscriptions, reconstructionist practitioners also rely on artifacts discovered through archaeological excavations. These artifacts include religious objects, figurines, amulets, and even remnants of ancient rituals. By studying and analyzing these material remains, reconstructionists gain a deeper understanding of the tools, symbols, and material culture associated with ancient Mesopotamian spirituality.

Reconstructionist practitioners approach the available evidence with scholarly rigor and critical thinking. They cross-reference different sources, compare variations in texts, and seek corroboration from multiple archaeological finds to ensure the accuracy of their reconstructions. Through this meticulous process, they strive to recreate the religious ceremonies, rituals, and mythologies that formed the core of ancient Mesopotamian spirituality.

Example: The Enuma Elish, a Babylonian creation myth, serves as a rich source of information for reconstructionist practitioners. Through a careful analysis of this text, they can discern the cosmological beliefs and the role of deities in the Mesopotamian worldview. By reconstructing the rituals associated with the Enuma Elish, practitioners can experience a connection with the ancient Mesopotamian understanding of creation.

Textual and Archaeological Evidence:

Reconstructionist approaches to ancient Mesopotamian spirituality rely heavily on the examination and analysis of textual and archaeological evidence. These sources provide valuable insights into the religious practices and beliefs of the ancient Mesopotamians, allowing practitioners to reconstruct and understand their spiritual traditions.

One of the primary sources for reconstructionist practitioners is the vast corpus of cuneiform tablets. These clay tablets contain a wealth of information about the religious life of the ancient Mesopotamians. By deciphering the cuneiform script, which was used to write the Sumerian, Akkadian, and other languages of the region, practitioners can access hymns, prayers, rituals, incantations, and mythological narratives. These texts offer glimpses into the relationship between the ancient Mesopotamians and their gods, the rituals and ceremonies they performed, and the cosmological beliefs that shaped their worldview.

In addition to textual sources, inscriptions found on monuments, statues, and buildings provide valuable information about religious practices in ancient Mesopotamia. These inscriptions often detail the construction and dedication of temples, the offerings made to gods and goddesses, and the performance of specific rituals. Reconstructionist practitioners carefully analyze these inscriptions, looking for clues about the procedures, symbols, and significance of various religious practices. By studying these inscriptions, they can gain a deeper understanding of the physical aspects and symbolism associated with religious ceremonies.

Archaeological discoveries, including temple structures, artifacts, and statues, also play a crucial role in the reconstructionist approach. The physical remains of ancient Mesopotamian religious sites offer tangible evidence of the material culture and practices of the time. Temple structures reveal architectural designs, layouts, and spatial arrangements that reflect the religious significance and function of these buildings. Artifacts found within these sites, such as ritual objects, amulets, and figurines, provide insight into the tools, symbols, and material culture associated with religious ceremonies. Reconstructionist practitioners carefully study these archaeological finds, examining their context, form, and usage, to reconstruct the physical aspects of ancient Mesopotamian religious practices.

Example: The discovery of the Ishtar Gate in Babylon provides valuable insights into the veneration of the goddess Ishtar. By studying the architectural features, symbols, and inscriptions on the gate, reconstructionist practitioners can gain a deeper understanding of the rituals and devotional practices associated with the goddess Ishtar.

Experimental Archaeology:

Experimental archaeology serves as a valuable tool in the arsenal of reconstructionist practitioners, enabling them to recreate ancient rituals and practices through hands-on experimentation. By meticulously following the procedures and instructions outlined in ancient texts and utilizing reconstructed tools, materials, and settings, practitioners can immerse themselves in the experiential aspects of ancient Mesopotamian spirituality. Through this practice, they aim to gain insights into the spiritual significance of these rituals and deepen their understanding of the ancient traditions they seek to revive.

The process of experimental archaeology involves carefully studying the descriptions and depictions of rituals found in ancient texts and inscriptions. Reconstructionist practitioners analyze these sources to identify the specific steps, gestures, incantations, and offerings associated with different religious practices. By meticulously recreating these elements, practitioners strive to achieve an authentic experience that closely resembles the rituals performed by their ancient counterparts.

Reconstructionist practitioners also rely on reconstructed tools, materials, and settings to replicate the physical aspects of ancient rituals. For example, if a ritual requires the use of specific objects or instruments, practitioners may seek to recreate them based on archaeological evidence and artistic representations. These reconstructed artifacts, such as ritual vessels, figurines, or ceremonial weapons, provide tangible objects that closely resemble those used in ancient times.

The use of authentic or replica materials is another essential aspect of experimental archaeology. Practitioners strive to source or recreate materials that were available to the ancient Mesopotamians, such as natural pigments, herbs, resins, or metals. This attention to detail helps to ensure a more accurate representation of the sensory and material aspects of the ancient rituals.

Through the experiential approach of experimental archaeology, reconstructionist practitioners aim to bridge the gap between the ancient and the modern. By actively engaging in the rituals and practices, they seek to develop a deeper understanding of their spiritual significance and to establish a personal connection with the ancient Mesopotamian traditions they are reviving. This experiential knowledge gained through hands-on experimentation provides insights that cannot be fully grasped through textual or visual analysis alone.

Example: In the context of Mesopotamian divination practices, reconstructionist practitioners may use clay divination models, like those found in ancient Mesopotamian sites, to recreate the process of divination. By interpreting the omens based on ancient divinatory texts, they can gain a deeper understanding of the role of divination in Mesopotamian spirituality.

In summary, reconstructionist approaches to the revival of ancient Mesopotamian spirituality strive to faithfully reconstruct and revive the spiritual practices and beliefs of this ancient civilization. Drawing upon historical research, textual and archaeological evidence, and experimental archaeology, practitioners seek to recreate the rituals, ceremonies, and mythologies of the past. By engaging with these reconstructed practices, individuals and groups can connect with the wisdom and spirituality of their Mesopotamian ancestors, fostering a sense of cultural continuity and spiritual enrichment.

Problems and Exercises:

Research an ancient Mesopotamian deity and reconstruct a devotional ritual based on available historical and textual evidence.

Visit a museum or archaeological site that exhibits artifacts from ancient Mesopotamia. Analyze the artifacts and propose potential religious or spiritual uses for them based on your understanding of ancient Mesopotamian spirituality.

Engage in an experimental archaeology project by recreating a specific ritual or ceremony from ancient Mesopotamia. Document your process and reflect on your experiences and observations. Discuss what you learned about the spiritual practices of the ancient Mesopotamians.

Discussion Questions:

What are the benefits and limitations of reconstructionist approaches to reviving ancient Mesopotamian spirituality?

How can the practice of experimental archaeology contribute to our understanding of ancient religious practices?

Discuss the ethical considerations involved in reconstructing and reviving ancient spiritual traditions. How can practitioners navigate the fine line between cultural appropriation and cultural revival?

These problems, exercises, and discussion questions are designed to encourage critical thinking and provide opportunities for students to engage with the concepts and challenges related to the reconstructionist approaches to ancient Mesopotamian spirituality.

Eclectic and Neo-Pagan Adaptations

Eclectic and Neo-Pagan adaptations represent contemporary approaches to incorporating elements of ancient Mesopotamian spirituality into modern belief systems. These approaches draw inspiration from a variety of sources, blending elements from Mesopotamian traditions with other spiritual practices, such as Witchcraft, Divination, Herbalism, Shamanism, and Ecospirituality. This section explores the characteristics and principles of Eclectic and Neo-Pagan adaptations and their impact on the contemporary spiritual landscape.

Eclectic Adaptations:

Eclectic approaches to spirituality reflect a dynamic and diverse approach to religious and spiritual practices. Eclectic practitioners draw upon a range of spiritual traditions, beliefs, and practices, carefully selecting and integrating elements that resonate with their personal journey. By embracing the principles of choice and individuality, they create a unique spiritual path that reflects their own experiences, values, and connections.

In the context of Mesopotamian spirituality, eclectic practitioners explore the rich mythology, symbolism, and rituals of the ancient civilization. They may delve into the ancient texts, such as the Epic of Gilgamesh or the Enuma Elish, to gain insights into the Mesopotamian cosmology and the roles of deities within it. From these sources, eclectic practitioners selectively incorporate Mesopotamian deities, rituals, symbols, and mythologies into their existing belief systems.

For example, an eclectic practitioner might be drawn to the power and wisdom associated with Mesopotamian goddesses, such as Ishtar or Ninhursag. They might resonate with Ishtar's energy of love, beauty, and fierce independence or with Ninhursag's nurturing and creative aspects. Incorporating these goddesses into their worship, they might adapt or create rituals that honor and connect with these deities, expressing gratitude, seeking guidance, or invoking their blessings.

The eclectic approach allows practitioners to blend Mesopotamian spirituality with other pantheons and spiritual traditions. They might incorporate deities from different cultures, such as Greek, Egyptian, or Celtic, into their practice, recognizing the interconnectedness of various mythologies and seeking a broader perspective on the divine. By combining elements from different pantheons, eclectic practitioners emphasize the universality of spiritual truths and the diverse manifestations of the sacred.

While eclectic approaches provide freedom and flexibility for personal expression, practitioners must approach the incorporation of diverse elements with care and respect. It is important to cultivate a deep understanding of the cultural context and symbolism of the traditions being drawn upon, ensuring that the integration is done in a culturally sensitive manner. This includes avoiding superficial or appropriative practices and engaging in ongoing study and dialogue to deepen one's understanding of the cultures and traditions being explored.

Examples of Eclectic Practices:

A practitioner incorporates Mesopotamian symbolism, such as the winged bull or the eight-pointed star, into their altar setup, alongside symbols from other spiritual traditions that hold personal significance.

During a ritual, a practitioner combines a Mesopotamian chant or invocation with meditative practices borrowed from Buddhist traditions, emphasizing the harmonious blending of different spiritual techniques.

In their divination practice, a practitioner uses Mesopotamian-inspired oracle cards alongside tarot cards, blending the unique symbolism and meanings of both systems to gain insights and guidance.

Problems and Exercises:

Research and compare the eclectic approaches in Mesopotamian spirituality with other eclectic practices in modern witchcraft or pagan traditions, such as Wicca or Druidry. Discuss similarities, differences, and the reasons behind the eclectic nature of these paths.

Create a collage or visual representation of an eclectic altar that incorporates elements from Mesopotamian spirituality and other pantheons or traditions. Explain the symbolism and significance of each element chosen.

Engage in a group discussion or debate exploring the potential benefits and challenges of eclectic approaches in spiritual practice, considering issues of cultural appropriation, authenticity, and personal connection.

Neo-Pagan Adaptations:

Eclectic and Neo-Pagan adaptations represent contemporary approaches to incorporating elements of ancient Mesopotamian spirituality into modern belief systems. These approaches draw inspiration from a variety of sources, blending elements from Mesopotamian traditions with other spiritual practices, such as Witchcraft, Divination, Herbalism, Shamanism, and Ecospirituality. This section explores the characteristics and principles of Eclectic and Neo-Pagan adaptations and their impact on the contemporary spiritual landscape.

Eclectic Adaptations:

Eclectic approaches to spirituality reflect a contemporary mindset that embraces the idea of drawing inspiration from diverse sources and traditions. Eclectic practitioners, also known as eclectic Pagans, engage in a selective process of incorporating elements from various spiritual paths to create a unique and personally meaningful belief system. By blending different cultural and spiritual practices, they seek to find resonance and create a spiritual path that aligns with their individual needs, interests, and experiences.

In the context of Mesopotamian spirituality, eclectic practitioners may integrate Mesopotamian deities, rituals, symbols, and mythologies into their existing belief systems. For example, they might incorporate the worship of Mesopotamian goddesses such as Ishtar or Ninhursag, who embody qualities and energies that resonate with their personal spiritual journey. These practitioners recognize the value and wisdom found in the ancient Mesopotamian pantheon and draw upon it to deepen their connection with the divine.

The incorporation of Mesopotamian elements into eclectic practices is not limited to deities alone. Rituals and ceremonies derived from Mesopotamian sources may also be adopted or adapted to suit the eclectic practitioner's spiritual needs. This may involve the use of specific invocations, gestures, or offerings inspired by ancient Mesopotamian practices. By incorporating these elements, eclectic practitioners aim to tap into the spiritual power and symbolism associated with Mesopotamian spirituality while maintaining the flexibility to incorporate elements from other cultures as well.

Symbols play a significant role in eclectic approaches. Eclectic practitioners may adopt Mesopotamian symbols such as the eight-pointed star or the winged disk as representations of divine energy or as personal symbols of spiritual significance. These symbols serve as reminders of their connection to the ancient Mesopotamian tradition and provide a focal point for meditation, contemplation, and ritual work.

Mythologies from Mesopotamia also hold a place of importance for eclectic practitioners. They may study and incorporate Mesopotamian myths, stories, and cosmological concepts into their belief systems, finding inspiration and guidance in the narratives and archetypes present in these ancient tales.

It is important to note that while eclectic approaches allow for the freedom to incorporate elements from various traditions, practitioners should approach this process with respect and cultural sensitivity. They should strive to gain a deep understanding of the cultural and historical contexts of the traditions they draw from, avoiding cultural appropriation and ensuring that their practices are ethically grounded.

Neo-Pagan Adaptations:

Neo-Pagan approaches to spirituality encompass a wide range of contemporary religious movements that draw inspiration from pre-Christian and indigenous spiritual traditions. Within the Neo-Pagan umbrella, there are specific adaptations that focus on reviving and reconstructing the spiritual practices of ancient Mesopotamia. These Neo-Pagan practitioners seek to reestablish a connection with the religious and cultural heritage of Mesopotamia, embracing its rituals, cosmology, and ethical principles.

Neo-Pagan adaptations of Mesopotamian spirituality aim to recreate and adapt the rituals and practices of ancient Mesopotamia within a modern context. Through careful study of ancient texts, archaeological findings, and scholarly research, practitioners strive to reconstruct the religious ceremonies, rites, and beliefs of the ancient Mesopotamians. This reconstruction process involves examining ancient rituals, invocations, and incantations, as well as exploring the roles of priests, priestesses, and other religious practitioners in ancient Mesopotamian society.

Practitioners of Neo-Pagan Mesopotamian spirituality may form dedicated groups or covens focused on the worship of Mesopotamian deities. These groups often gather for communal rituals and celebrations, seeking to recreate the spiritual experiences of their ancient counterparts. These rituals may include invocations to specific deities, the offering of food and libations, the performance of sacred dances or music, and the recitation of prayers and incantations inspired by ancient Mesopotamian sources.

Seasonal celebrations also play a significant role in Neo-Pagan Mesopotamian adaptations. Inspired by the agricultural and celestial cycles observed by the ancient Mesopotamians, practitioners organize ceremonies and festivals to mark the turning points of the year, such as the equinoxes and solstices. These celebrations often reflect the deep connection between ancient Mesopotamians and the natural world, honoring the changing seasons, the cycles of growth and harvest, and the celestial bodies that influenced their lives.

Magical practices are another aspect of Neo-Pagan Mesopotamian spirituality. Drawing inspiration from the ancient Mesopotamian magical traditions, practitioners engage in spellwork, divination, and other forms of magical rituals.

They may utilize Mesopotamian symbols, amulets, or talismans, as well as ancient invocations and incantations, to manifest their intentions and seek guidance from the spiritual realm.

It is important to note that Neo-Pagan adaptations of Mesopotamian spirituality do not claim direct historical continuity with the ancient Mesopotamian religious practices. Rather, they are contemporary interpretations and reconstructions that seek to honor and connect with the spiritual legacy of Mesopotamia. These adaptations allow practitioners to explore the cultural, spiritual, and ethical aspects of ancient Mesopotamia in a way that resonates with their modern sensibilities and personal spiritual journeys.

Blending Traditions:

Eclectic and Neo-Pagan practitioners embrace a dynamic and evolving approach to spirituality, often incorporating elements from multiple traditions into their practices. This blending of traditions allows for a personalized and diverse spiritual path that reflects the unique beliefs, experiences, and preferences of the practitioner.

Eclectic practitioners, as mentioned earlier, selectively incorporate elements from different spiritual traditions, including Mesopotamian spirituality, into their practice. They may draw upon Mesopotamian divination methods, such as reading cuneiform tablets or utilizing Mesopotamian astrology, alongside other forms of divination, such as Tarot, astrology, or scrying. By combining these various divinatory techniques, practitioners can access different forms of guidance and gain a more comprehensive understanding of their spiritual inquiries.

Furthermore, eclectic practitioners may integrate Mesopotamian symbols, deities, and rituals into their spellwork. For example, they might utilize Mesopotamian incantations or invocations alongside Witchcraft rituals, creating a fusion of practices that aligns with their personal beliefs and intentions. By incorporating Mesopotamian symbols, such as the eight-pointed star or the winged disk, into their spellwork, they draw upon the spiritual energy and significance associated with Mesopotamian spirituality.

Neo-Pagan practitioners, on the other hand, focus on the revival and reconstruction of ancient spiritual practices, often centered around the worship of pre-Christian deities and the celebration of nature. In the context of Mesopotamian spirituality, Neo-Pagan adaptations seek to recreate and adapt the rituals, cosmology, and ethical principles of ancient Mesopotamia within a contemporary framework.

In their spiritual practices, Neo-Pagan practitioners may blend elements of Mesopotamian spirituality with other traditions. For example, they might incorporate Mesopotamian deities, such as Ishtar or Marduk, into their pantheon of revered beings alongside deities from other pantheons, such as Celtic or Norse gods and goddesses. This blending of pantheons allows practitioners to establish connections with a diverse range of spiritual energies and archetypes.

Furthermore, Neo-Pagan practitioners often celebrate seasonal festivals inspired by ancient Mesopotamian agricultural and celestial cycles. They may incorporate Mesopotamian rituals and practices into their celebrations while also drawing from other traditions to enrich their observances. This blending of traditions enables practitioners to connect with the cycles of nature and honor the unique spiritual heritage of Mesopotamia within a broader contemporary context.

Challenges and Criticisms:

Eclectic and Neo-Pagan adaptations, like any spiritual practices, have been subject to criticism and debates from different perspectives. These criticisms raise valid concerns regarding the potential pitfalls and challenges that practitioners may encounter when blending traditions, particularly in the context of Mesopotamian spirituality.

One common critique is that the blending of traditions in eclectic and Neo-Pagan practices may lead to a superficial or incomplete understanding of ancient Mesopotamian spirituality. Critics argue that practitioners might cherry-pick elements that align with their personal preferences, potentially overlooking the broader cultural and historical context in which these practices originally emerged. By isolating certain aspects of Mesopotamian spirituality without a comprehensive understanding, practitioners may inadvertently distort or misinterpret the original teachings and rituals.

Additionally, concerns of cultural appropriation are often raised within the context of eclectic and Neo-Pagan adaptations. Cultural appropriation refers to the adoption or use of elements from another culture without proper understanding, respect, or permission. Critics emphasize the importance of honoring the cultural heritage of the ancient Mesopotamians and respecting the descendants of the Mesopotamian civilizations. They argue that appropriating and commodifying aspects of their religious practices can be disrespectful and perpetuate harmful power dynamics.

To address these concerns and engage in responsible adaptations, practitioners of eclectic and Neo-Pagan Mesopotamian spirituality should approach their practices with sensitivity and mindfulness. They can do so by:

Conducting in-depth research: Practitioners should engage in ongoing study and research to gain a deeper understanding of the historical and cultural context of Mesopotamian spirituality. This includes studying primary sources, consulting scholarly works, and engaging in dialogue with experts in the field.

Engaging in respectful dialogue: Practitioners should actively seek out opportunities to engage in respectful conversations with individuals from Mesopotamian cultural backgrounds or with academic experts in Mesopotamian studies. This dialogue can provide valuable insights, foster understanding, and help practitioners navigate potential cultural sensitivities.

Respecting cultural boundaries: It is crucial to respect the boundaries set by Mesopotamian cultural communities regarding the use of their religious practices and symbols. Practitioners should be mindful of not appropriating or commodifying these elements for personal gain or entertainment.

Honoring and acknowledging sources: Practitioners should properly credit and acknowledge the sources and origins of the elements they incorporate into their practices. This includes acknowledging the cultural heritage of Mesopotamia and its contributions to contemporary spiritual paths.

Continual self-reflection and learning: Practitioners should engage in ongoing self-reflection to evaluate their motivations, intentions, and impact. They should be open to receiving feedback and be willing to make adjustments or corrections to their practices when necessary.

By approaching eclectic and Neo-Pagan adaptations with sensitivity and a commitment to cultural understanding, practitioners can navigate the complexities and criticisms associated with blending traditions. This ensures that their practices are respectful, grounded in knowledge, and honor the rich cultural heritage of ancient Mesopotamia.

Example:

Consider a practitioner who follows an eclectic path, incorporating elements from Mesopotamian spirituality, Wicca, and Herbalism. In their practice, they might celebrate the Mesopotamian festival of Ishtar's Descent into the Underworld, adapting it to include Wiccan rituals and incorporating the use of specific herbs associated with Mesopotamian traditions. They might create an altar dedicated to Ishtar, adorned with symbols and representations of Mesopotamian origin, alongside objects and tools associated with Wiccan practices. This blending of traditions allows the practitioner to create a unique spiritual experience that reflects their personal beliefs and connections to multiple spiritual paths.

Problems and Exercises:

Research and compare the characteristics of Eclectic and Neo-Pagan adaptations in Mesopotamian spirituality with their counterparts in other ancient traditions, such as Egyptian or Celtic.

Imagine you are a practitioner of Eclectic Mesopotamian spirituality. Create a ritual that blends Mesopotamian and contemporary elements to honor a specific deity or celebrate a seasonal event. Explain your choices and the symbolism behind each component.

Debate the potential ethical issues and challenges associated with blending ancient spiritual traditions in Eclectic and Neo-Pagan adaptations. Consider the perspectives of cultural appropriation, historical accuracy, and the impact on spiritual authenticity.

Symbolism and Mythological Themes

Symbolism and mythology play a crucial role in various spiritual and esoteric traditions. Within the realm of New Age studies, symbolism and mythological themes are integral aspects of practices such as Witchcraft, Divination, Herbalism, Shamanism, Ecospirituality, and Magic in Ancient Mesopotamia. This section delves into the rich tapestry of symbolic representations and mythological narratives, exploring their significance, interpretation, and application within diverse spiritual contexts.

➢ Understanding Symbolism:

Symbolism refers to the use of symbols, signs, and images to represent abstract concepts, ideas, or spiritual principles. Symbols act as gateways to deeper levels of understanding, connecting individuals with higher realms of consciousness and archetypal energies. They serve as a language of the subconscious, allowing for intuitive and profound experiences.

✧   Universal and Cultural Symbols:

Symbols play a significant role in human communication and spirituality, serving as powerful vehicles for conveying meaning and representing abstract concepts. While some symbols possess universal significance that transcends cultural boundaries, others are deeply embedded within specific traditions, carrying distinct cultural and religious meanings. Understanding the nature and context of symbols is essential for appreciating their impact and utilizing them effectively in spiritual practices.

✧   Universal Symbols:
Certain symbols have a universal quality, resonating with people across different cultures and time periods. These symbols tap into collective human experiences and archetypal energies, evoking shared emotions and understanding. One such example is the pentagram, a five-pointed star enclosed in a circle. It holds significance in various spiritual traditions, including Witchcraft, Wicca, and Western Esotericism. The pentagram symbolizes the five elements—earth, air, fire, water, and spirit—and their interconnectedness. Its geometric structure and elemental associations make it a recognizable and versatile symbol.

Other universal symbols include the sun, moon, tree, serpent, and the circle. These symbols are found in diverse cultures worldwide and embody archetypal meanings that resonate with the human psyche. For instance, the circle symbolizes wholeness, unity, and eternity, while the serpent represents transformation, wisdom, and healing.

✧   Culturally Specific Symbols:

In contrast to universal symbols, culturally specific symbols are deeply rooted in particular traditions and carry specific cultural and religious meanings. These symbols are intricately tied to the mythologies, cosmologies, and spiritual practices of their respective cultures. For example, the Ankh symbol, an ancient Egyptian hieroglyphic, represents life, immortality, and the eternal soul. It is closely associated with the gods and goddesses of ancient Egypt, particularly with Osiris, the god of the afterlife.

Similarly, the Om symbol (ॐ) holds immense significance in Hinduism, Buddhism, and Jainism. It represents the primordial sound and vibration from which the universe originated. The symbol embodies the concepts of divinity, the cycle of birth and death, and the pursuit of spiritual enlightenment.

Culturally specific symbols often carry layers of meaning that reflect the unique worldview, values, and spiritual traditions of a particular culture. Their use and interpretation may require familiarity with the cultural context and an understanding of the associated myths, rituals, and spiritual practices.

It is worth noting that symbols can also acquire new meanings and interpretations as they travel across cultures or are adopted by different spiritual traditions. For instance, the lotus flower, originally a symbol of purity and enlightenment in Buddhism, has been embraced by various New Age practices as a symbol of personal growth, transformation, and spiritual awakening.

By recognizing the universality and cultural specificity of symbols, practitioners can navigate the intricate web of symbolic languages and engage in meaningful and respectful spiritual practices. It is essential to approach culturally specific symbols with reverence, acknowledging and honoring their origins and cultural significance, while also appreciating the power and resonance of universal symbols that transcend cultural boundaries.

➢ Interpreting Symbols:

Interpreting symbols is a complex process that involves delving into their cultural, historical, and contextual significance. While symbols can carry universal meanings and evoke similar responses in people across cultures, individual interpretations can vary based on personal, cultural, or esoteric perspectives. A symbol's multifaceted nature allows it to elicit emotional responses, trigger intuitive insights, and convey encoded messages that unfold through contemplation and exploration.

✦ Cultural Significance:

Symbols are deeply rooted in cultural contexts, shaped by the myths, rituals, and collective experiences of a particular society. Understanding a symbol's cultural significance requires knowledge of the traditions, belief systems, and historical context in which it originated. For example, the Celtic triskele, a symbol depicting three interconnected spirals, holds different meanings depending on the cultural context. In Celtic mythology, it represents concepts such as the three realms (land, sea, sky), the cycle of life (birth, death, rebirth), or the Triple Goddess (maiden, mother, crone). Exploring the cultural background of a symbol enhances our comprehension of its intended message and symbolism.

✦ Historical Context:

Symbols can also be influenced by historical events or specific time periods. For instance, the peace symbol, a circle with three downward lines, originated in the 1950s as a representation of nuclear disarmament during the Cold War. Understanding the historical context allows us to grasp the symbol's intended message and the socio-political movements it represents. Examining historical influences enables a deeper interpretation of symbols and their role in shaping collective consciousness.

✧   Contextual Interpretation:

The interpretation of symbols can vary based on personal, cultural, or esoteric perspectives. Symbols often evoke emotional responses that are influenced by personal experiences and beliefs. For example, a wolf symbol might evoke feelings of strength and loyalty for some, while for others, it may trigger fear or spiritual connection based on their cultural or individual associations with wolves. Furthermore, esoteric interpretations delve into the hidden or mystical aspects of symbols, exploring their metaphysical or spiritual significance. This can involve practices like meditation, dream work, or divination to uncover deeper insights encoded within the symbols.

Symbols have the capacity to communicate on multiple levels, transcending language barriers and accessing the realm of the subconscious. They invite contemplation and exploration, offering a rich tapestry of meaning that unfolds through personal reflection and engagement. Engaging with symbols can evoke intuitive insights, allowing individuals to tap into their inner wisdom and expand their understanding of the spiritual and metaphysical realms..

➢   Mythological Themes:

Mythology encompasses the collective narratives, legends, and stories that express fundamental beliefs, cosmologies, and archetypal forces within a culture or tradition. Myths provide frameworks for understanding the mysteries of existence, human nature, and the divine. They often contain symbolic elements that reflect universal themes and psychological truths.

✧   Archetypes and Symbolic Characters:

Mythological narratives frequently feature archetypal characters that represent fundamental aspects of the human psyche. These characters, such as gods, goddesses, heroes, and tricksters, embody universal qualities and embody profound symbolic meanings. For instance, the goddess Artemis symbolizes the wild, independent feminine energy, while the trickster archetype, like Loki in Norse mythology, represents the disruptive force that challenges the status quo.

✧ Mythological Motifs and Symbolic Events:

Myths are replete with motifs and events that hold symbolic significance. These motifs can include creation myths, heroic quests, journeys into the underworld, and battles between light and darkness. Each motif carries layered meanings and offers insights into the human condition and spiritual transformation.

➢ Applying Symbolism and Mythological Themes:

Symbolism and mythological themes find expression in rituals and ceremonies. Practitioners infuse their practices with symbolic actions, gestures, and objects to invoke desired energies, establish connections with divine forces, and manifest intentions. For example, the use of specific herbs in rituals connects to their symbolic properties and enhances their intended effects.

✧ Personal Exploration and Transformation:

Symbolism and mythological themes can serve as catalysts for personal growth and transformation. Individuals engage in meditative practices, dreamwork, or active imagination to explore the symbolic realms within their own psyches. By unraveling the meanings and lessons hidden in symbols and myths, practitioners gain insights into their own journeys and uncover deeper truths.

Exercises:

Symbolic Exploration:

Choose a symbol from any tradition or create your own personal symbol. Reflect on its meanings, associations, and personal resonance. Write a journal entry describing your insights and how this symbol relates to your spiritual path.

Mythological Journey:

Select a mythological story or a specific character from a tradition of your choice. Write a short creative piece, a poem, or a visual representation that interprets the symbolic elements and themes present in the myth.

Symbolic Ritual:

Design a simple ritual or ceremony that incorporates symbolism and mythological themes. Choose a specific intention or aspect of your spiritual practice to focus on. Describe the ritual steps, symbolic objects, and actions you would use to enhance the intended energy or connection.

Conclusion:

Symbolism and mythological themes offer a rich tapestry of meaning, inspiration, and transformative potential in various New Age practices. By delving into symbols and myths, practitioners unlock hidden dimensions of consciousness, connect with archetypal energies, and embark on personal journeys of self-discovery and spiritual growth. Engaging with symbolism and mythological narratives deepens our understanding of the human experience, fostering a profound connection with the sacred and the mysteries of existence.

Chapter 8: Comparative Analysis of Ancient Mesopotamian Texts and Abrahamic Scriptures: Insights into Creation, Flood Narratives, and Moral Codes

The study of ancient texts and scriptures provides a fascinating glimpse into the religious and cultural beliefs of civilizations throughout history. In this chapter, we embark on a comparative analysis of ancient Mesopotamian texts and the sacred scriptures of the Abrahamic traditions—the Quran, Bible, and Torah. By examining the creation narratives, flood stories, and moral codes found within these texts, we aim to uncover intriguing insights into the shared themes, cultural influences, and theological implications that connect these ancient traditions.

Creation Stories

Creation stories hold immense significance within religious traditions as they offer explanations for the origin of the world, the emergence of life, and the relationship between humans and the divine. In this section, we explore the creation narratives present in both Mesopotamian texts and the Abrahamic scriptures.

➤ Mesopotamian Creation Myths:

We begin by delving into the rich mythological landscape of ancient Mesopotamia, focusing on the Enuma Elish. This epic poem reveals a complex cosmology, describing the formation of the universe, the birth of gods and goddesses, and the establishment of order amidst primordial chaos. Through a careful analysis of the Enuma Elish and other Mesopotamian creation myths, we uncover the cultural and religious significance of these narratives and their enduring influence on Mesopotamian spirituality.

➤ Abrahamic Creation Stories:

Turning our attention to the Abrahamic traditions, we examine the creation accounts found in the Quran, Bible, and Torah. These sacred texts present unique perspectives on the origin of the world, featuring stories such as the six days of creation, the formation of Adam and Eve, and the divine act of bringing forth existence. By studying these accounts, we gain insight into the theological and cosmological foundations of the Abrahamic faiths.

➢ Comparative Analysis:

In this section, we undertake a comparative analysis of the Mesopotamian creation narratives and the Abrahamic creation stories. By juxtaposing these ancient texts, we explore the shared motifs, themes, and symbolism that transcend cultural and temporal boundaries. Additionally, we consider the cultural and historical contexts in which these narratives arose, seeking to understand the ways in which they shape religious beliefs and worldviews.

Flood Narratives

Flood narratives are found in numerous mythologies and religious traditions worldwide, often symbolizing themes of destruction, purification, and renewal. In this section, we examine the flood stories present in both Mesopotamian texts and the Abrahamic scriptures.

➢ Mesopotamian Flood Stories:

Drawing from sources such as the Epic of Gilgamesh and the Atrahasis Epic, we explore the Mesopotamian flood narratives. These tales recount catastrophic floods sent by the gods as divine punishment or means of rejuvenation. Through a meticulous analysis of these stories, we uncover their cultural significance and their role in shaping Mesopotamian beliefs about the relationship between humans, gods, and the forces of nature.

➢ Abrahamic Flood Stories:

We then turn to the Quran, Bible, and Torah to examine the flood stories present in these Abrahamic scriptures. The narratives of Nuh (Noah) and the Great Flood hold immense theological importance, reflecting themes of divine judgment, righteousness, and the preservation of life. By engaging with these stories, we gain insight into the Abrahamic understanding of humanity's relationship with the divine and the moral lessons embedded within the flood narrative.

➢ Comparative Analysis:

Through a comparative analysis of the Mesopotamian flood stories and the Abrahamic flood narratives, we explore the shared elements, divergent details, and underlying theological messages. By critically examining these accounts side by side, we deepen our understanding of the cultural, religious, and moral dimensions that inform these ancient traditions.

Conclusion:

By embarking on a comparative analysis of ancient Mesopotamian texts and the Abrahamic scriptures, we uncover fascinating insights into the shared themes of creation, flood narratives, and moral codes. Through this exploration, we come to appreciate the interconnectedness of human religious experiences, the cultural influences that shaped these texts, and the enduring relevance of these ancient stories in contemporary spiritual discourse. This chapter sets the stage for an illuminating journey of discovery, encouraging us to engage in critical thinking and discussion as we delve into the intersections between these diverse religious traditions.

Creation Stories

> Mesopotamian Creation Myths:

In the rich tapestry of Mesopotamian mythology, the creation myths hold a central place, offering profound insights into the origins of the universe, the emergence of gods and goddesses, and the establishment of order from primordial chaos. In this section, we will explore the Mesopotamian creation narratives, with a particular focus on the Enuma Elish, a remarkable epic poem that encapsulates the cosmogony of ancient Mesopotamia.

The Enuma Elish: An Epic Creation Story

To fully grasp the significance of the Enuma Elish, it is imperative to explore the historical and cultural backdrop against which this ancient Mesopotamian epic emerged. Mesopotamia, situated between the Tigris and Euphrates rivers, was a fertile region that witnessed the rise and fall of various civilizations throughout its long history. These cultures, including the Sumerians, Akkadians, Babylonians, and Assyrians, each contributed to the rich tapestry of Mesopotamian mythology.

In the ancient world, myths played a crucial role in explaining the mysteries of existence and the divine realm. They were deeply intertwined with the cultural, religious, and social fabric of Mesopotamian societies. Mythological narratives served as a means of transmitting knowledge, conveying moral lessons, and establishing a connection between humans and the gods.

At the heart of Mesopotamian mythology lies the Enuma Elish, often referred to as the "Babylonian Creation Epic." This extraordinary literary work provides a comprehensive account of the origins of the cosmos, the emergence of the gods, and the establishment of order in the universe. The Enuma Elish is written in cuneiform script, an early form of writing consisting of wedge-shaped marks on clay tablets.

The discovery of the Enuma Elish on seven clay tablets, dating back to the 7th century BCE, revolutionized our understanding of ancient Mesopotamian culture. The tablets were initially unearthed in the library of the Assyrian king Ashurbanipal in Nineveh, present-day Iraq. Their retrieval and subsequent decipherment by scholars, such as George Smith and Thorkild Jacobsen, enabled us to gain invaluable insights into the mythological beliefs of the ancient Mesopotamians.

The Enuma Elish not only showcases the culmination of Babylonian literary and religious traditions but also reveals the cultural dominance of Babylon during the time of its composition. This epic represents a fusion of earlier Mesopotamian mythologies, incorporating elements from Sumerian and Akkadian cosmogonic narratives. Its prominence in Babylonian society highlights the central role of the city-state and its patron deity Marduk.

Through its vivid imagery, poetic language, and dramatic narrative, the Enuma Elish transports readers to the mythological landscape of ancient Mesopotamia. It paints a picture of cosmic battles, divine triumphs, and the establishment of the social and cosmic order. The epic reflects the Mesopotamians' understanding of the interconnectedness of gods, humans, and the natural world, illustrating the intricate web of relationships that governed their worldview.

Studying the Enuma Elish provides us with a deeper appreciation of the cultural and religious milieu of ancient Mesopotamia. It allows us to explore the complexities of their cosmology, their notions of creation, and the roles and attributes ascribed to the gods. By analyzing this historic text, we gain invaluable insights into the intellectual and spiritual heritage of one of the world's oldest civilizations.

Exercises:

Compare and contrast the Enuma Elish with other creation myths from different cultures, such as the Judeo-Christian creation story or the creation narratives of ancient Egypt.

Discuss the cultural and historical influences that shaped the development of the Enuma Elish, considering factors such as political power dynamics and religious beliefs.

Analyze the role of gods in the Enuma Elish and their interactions with humans, drawing parallels to the concept of divine intervention in other mythological traditions.

Explore the significance of order and hierarchy in the Enuma Elish and its implications for the social and political structures of ancient Mesopotamia.

Investigate the impact of the Enuma Elish on later Mesopotamian literature and religious practices, examining how its themes and motifs reverberated through subsequent texts and rituals.

Themes and Symbolism in the Enuma Elish

The Enuma Elish, as a complex and rich mythological text, incorporates various themes and symbols that provide insights into the worldview and belief system of ancient Mesopotamia. By examining these themes and symbols, we can uncover deeper meanings and unravel the cultural and religious significance embedded within the narrative.

Primordial Chaos and the Divine Realm:

The Enuma Elish opens with a vivid portrayal of a primordial state of chaos, where the waters of Apsu and Tiamat commingle, representing the formless and undifferentiated state of existence. This chaotic realm symbolizes the vast potentiality and indeterminate nature that precede the establishment of order. It is within this chaotic backdrop that the gods emerge, shaping and organizing the cosmos. The triumph of order over chaos in the Enuma Elish reflects the Mesopotamians' belief in the necessity of stability, structure, and harmony in both the natural and human realms.

The Birth of Gods and the Struggle for Power:

The Enuma Elish introduces a pantheon of gods, each representing distinct cosmic forces and possessing unique characteristics and responsibilities. The epic illuminates the dynamic relationships and power struggles among these deities. Marduk, the central figure in the Enuma Elish, emerges as the protagonist who successfully overthrows the primordial goddess Tiamat, symbolizing the victory of the younger generation of gods over the older ones. This theme of generational conflict and power succession resonates with the broader human experience of navigating social hierarchies and power dynamics.

Creation of Humanity:

Humanity's creation in the Enuma Elish holds profound symbolism and reveals the Mesopotamians' perception of the human-divine relationship. Marduk forms humanity from the divine materials of Tiamat's blood and Kingu's bones, highlighting the interconnectedness between humans and the gods. This act of creation signifies humanity's dual nature, embodying both the divine essence inherited from the gods and the earthly aspects derived from the natural world. It emphasizes humanity's role as the custodian of cosmic order, responsible for upholding the balance and maintaining the gods' favor.

Exercises:

Explore the theme of order versus chaos in other mythological traditions, such as the creation stories of ancient Egypt or the Norse cosmology of the Eddas.

Analyze the symbolism of water and its role in the Enuma Elish, considering its associations with primordiality, life-giving properties, and potential for destruction.

Investigate the significance of the celestial struggle in the Enuma Elish and its parallels to power dynamics and conflicts in human societies.

Discuss the implications of Marduk's victory and his subsequent ascent as the supreme deity, considering the concepts of divine kingship and the consolidation of power in ancient Mesopotamia.

Reflect on the symbolism of humanity's creation from divine materials in the Enuma Elish and its implications for the human condition, ethics, and moral responsibility within Mesopotamian culture.

Cultural and Spiritual Significance

Political and Religious Implications:

The Enuma Elish, beyond its role as a creation myth, held significant political and religious implications in ancient Mesopotamian society. The narrative of the

Enuma Elish served to reinforce the authority and legitimacy of Babylonian kings. By depicting Marduk as the central figure who defeats Tiamat and establishes order, the epic conveyed the idea that the Babylonian ruler, as the earthly representative of Marduk, possessed divine authority and was entrusted with maintaining cosmic order. This ideology served to consolidate the power of the king and legitimize his rule, as well as to reinforce the hierarchical structure of Babylonian society.

Additionally, the Enuma Elish emphasized the importance of maintaining order and obedience to the gods within Babylonian society. It communicated the belief that chaos and disorder could result in catastrophic consequences, and therefore, adherence to the moral and religious codes set forth by the gods was necessary for the well-being and prosperity of the community. This notion of divine governance and the interplay between religious and political authority shaped the socio-political landscape of ancient Mesopotamia.

Influences on Later Cultures:

The themes, motifs, and concepts present in the Enuma Elish had a profound impact on later cultures and their mythologies. The cosmogonic elements found in the Enuma Elish can be traced in the mythologies of other ancient Near Eastern civilizations, such as the Canaanite and Phoenician traditions. These cultures, influenced by Mesopotamian cosmological ideas, incorporated similar themes of creation, struggle, and divine supremacy into their own mythological narratives. The widespread dissemination and adaptation of Mesopotamian mythological concepts contributed to the cultural exchange and cross-pollination of ideas in the ancient Near East.

Exercises:

Discuss the relationship between religion and politics in ancient Mesopotamia, focusing on the role of the Enuma Elish in legitimizing the authority of Babylonian kings.

Compare the political and religious implications of the Enuma Elish with other creation myths from different cultures, such as the Egyptian creation myth of Atum or the Genesis account in the Hebrew Bible.

Analyze the influence of Mesopotamian mythological concepts on the religious beliefs and practices of neighboring cultures, such as the Canaanites and Phoenicians.

Debate the ethical and moral implications of the divine authority depicted in the Enuma Elish and its impact on social hierarchies and power structures in ancient Mesopotamian society.

Reflect on the enduring legacy of Mesopotamian cosmogonic narratives, considering their influence on subsequent mythologies and their relevance to contemporary understandings of the origins of the universe and the divine realm.+

➤ Abrahamic Creation Stories:

The Abrahamic traditions—Judaism, Christianity, and Islam—encompass a vast tapestry of religious beliefs, practices, and sacred texts that have profoundly shaped human history. Among the foundational narratives within these traditions are the creation stories, which offer profound insights into the origin of the universe, the emergence of humanity, and the divine act of bringing the world into existence. Exploring the creation accounts found in the Quran, Bible, and Torah allows for a deeper understanding of the key themes, motifs, and theological implications present in these texts.

The Creation of the Universe and Humanity:

The Quran:

In the Quran, the creation story is presented with poetic beauty and theological depth. It emphasizes the concept of tawhid, the oneness of God, and portrays Allah as the all-powerful and merciful creator. The Quranic narrative describes the unfolding of creation through divine command, highlighting the idea that the entire cosmos is a manifestation of Allah's will and design. The creation of Adam and Eve as the first humans is seen as a pivotal moment, emphasizing humanity's special place in the divine plan. Moreover, the Quran underscores the interconnectedness of creation, emphasizing human responsibility as stewards of the Earth and the importance of maintaining harmony and balance within the natural world.

The Bible:

Within the Bible, particularly in the book of Genesis, two distinct creation narratives coexist, each offering unique perspectives on the divine act of creation. In Genesis 1, often referred to as the "P" or Priestly account, the creation unfolds over six days, with God's spoken word bringing forth the different elements of the world. This account emphasizes the orderliness, goodness, and purposeful design of creation, with humanity created in the image of God and entrusted with stewardship over the Earth. In contrast, Genesis 2, known as the "J" or Yahwist account, provides a more intimate and anthropomorphic depiction of God. This narrative focuses on the creation of Adam and Eve, their placement in the Garden of Eden, and their relationship with God and each other. It explores themes of human intimacy, free will, and the consequences of disobedience.

The Torah:

The Torah, the foundational text of Judaism, weaves together various sources, including the Priestly and Yahwist traditions found in the Bible. The creation narrative in the Torah emphasizes God's sovereignty, the divine breath breathed into humanity, and the inherent moral responsibility of human beings. It presents a cohesive worldview that informs Jewish ethics, emphasizing the importance of ethical conduct, social justice, and the fulfillment of religious obligations. The creation story in the Torah serves as a backdrop for the establishment of the covenant between God and the Israelites, which forms the basis of Jewish religious and ethical framework.

Exercises:

Compare and contrast the creation accounts in the Quran, Bible, and Torah, highlighting the key theological themes and motifs present in each.

Explore the concept of stewardship in the Quranic, biblical, and Torah narratives of creation, discussing the implications for environmental ethics and ecological responsibility.

Investigate the cultural and historical contexts in which these creation stories emerged, considering the influence of ancient Near Eastern mythologies on their development.

Analyze the role of humanity in the divine plan in the Quran, Bible, and Torah, examining the theological implications for human identity, purpose, and moral responsibility.

Discuss the ways in which these creation narratives have influenced religious thought, art, literature, and cultural expressions within the Abrahamic traditions and beyond.

➢ Themes and Symbolism:

✦ The Role of Human Beings:

In the creation stories of Judaism, Christianity, and Islam, the role of human beings emerges as a central theme. These narratives explore the unique position of humanity in the cosmic order, emphasizing our role as stewards of the Earth and our moral responsibility within the created world. For example, in the Quran, the creation of Adam and Eve establishes humanity as Allah's vicegerents on Earth, entrusted with the task of cultivating and caring for the natural environment. This theme resonates with the concept of ecospirituality, which emphasizes the interconnectedness of all living beings and the ethical imperative to protect and preserve the Earth.

The Abrahamic creation stories also delve into the human relationship with the divine, raising questions about the nature of good and evil, the exercise of free will, and the consequences of disobedience. In the biblical account of Adam and Eve's temptation and subsequent expulsion from the Garden of Eden, the theme of human fallibility and the struggle to maintain moral integrity is explored. These narratives serve as a foundation for ethical teachings within the Abrahamic traditions, encouraging believers to reflect on their moral choices and responsibilities.

Divine Intention and Design:

Another prominent theme in the Abrahamic creation stories is the notion of divine intention and design. These narratives convey the belief that the world and its inhabitants are not the result of random chance but are purposefully brought into being by a benevolent and creative deity. In the Quranic narrative, Allah's creative act is described as a deliberate and planned process, unfolding according to divine command. Similarly, in the biblical accounts, the creation unfolds through God's intentional acts, shaping the world and all its living creatures.

This concept of divine intention and design provides a framework for understanding the interconnectedness and intrinsic value of all aspects of creation. It underscores the idea that the natural world is not merely a utilitarian resource for human exploitation but a sacred and harmonious system that reflects the divine wisdom. This theme resonates with the principles of herbalism, where the healing properties of plants are seen as a manifestation of divine wisdom and a testament to the intricate design of the natural world.

Exercises:

Discuss the concept of human stewardship in the creation stories of Judaism, Christianity, and Islam. Explore the ethical implications of this role in relation to contemporary environmental challenges.

Compare and contrast the themes of human fallibility and moral responsibility in the creation stories of the Abrahamic traditions. Analyze how these themes shape religious ethics and personal conduct.

Reflect on the role of free will in the Abrahamic creation stories. Discuss the implications of human agency and choice in relation to moral decision-making and spiritual growth.

Explore the symbolism of gardens and nature in the creation stories, examining how these symbols convey deeper meanings and spiritual teachings within the Abrahamic traditions.

Investigate the influence of the Abrahamic creation stories on the development of theological doctrines and religious practices within Judaism, Christianity, and Islam. Examine the ways in which these narratives continue to shape religious thought and inspire believers.

Comparative Analysis and Theological Implications:

✧   Shared Themes and Differences:

When comparing the Mesopotamian creation myths with the Abrahamic creation stories, we can discern shared themes and motifs that reflect universal human concerns and the quest to understand the origins of the world and humanity. Both sets of narratives explore the divine act of creation, the emergence of humanity, and the establishment of order within the cosmos.

In the Enuma Elish and the Abrahamic creation stories, the divine act of creation is a central theme. In Mesopotamian mythology, the gods emerge from the primordial chaos to establish order, while in the Abrahamic traditions, a benevolent deity creates the universe and everything within it. These narratives serve as a foundation for understanding the sacredness of the natural world and the divine agency behind its existence.

Furthermore, the emergence of humanity is a significant element in both the Mesopotamian and Abrahamic accounts. In the Enuma Elish, humanity is created from the blood and bones of defeated deities, symbolizing their connection to the divine realm. Similarly, the Abrahamic traditions depict the creation of Adam and Eve, portraying humanity as unique beings imbued with a divine spark and entrusted with moral responsibility.

Despite these shared themes, differences exist between the Mesopotamian and Abrahamic narratives. Theological emphasis varies, with the Mesopotamian myths focusing more on the cosmic struggle between gods and the establishment of political and religious authority, while the Abrahamic stories emphasize monotheism, moral teachings, and the covenantal relationship between God and humanity.

The Influence of Ancient Mesopotamian Texts:

The comparison of Mesopotamian and Abrahamic creation stories raises intriguing questions about cultural exchange and the potential influence of ancient Mesopotamian texts on the development of the Abrahamic traditions. It is important to note that the Abrahamic traditions emerged in a historical context influenced by the civilizations of the Ancient Near East, including Mesopotamia.

Scholars have identified striking parallels between certain motifs and themes in the Enuma Elish and the Abrahamic creation narratives. For instance, the concept of divine creation, the struggle between chaos and order, and the role of humanity as stewards of the Earth can be found in both sets of stories. These similarities suggest the possibility of cultural transmission or shared cultural heritage.

The influence of ancient Mesopotamian texts on the Abrahamic traditions can be seen in various aspects, including the use of creation imagery, the conceptualization of the divine-human relationship, and the understanding of cosmic order. These influences highlight the interconnectedness and continuity of human spiritual traditions across time and geographic boundaries.

Exercises:

Compare and contrast the themes of divine creation and the emergence of humanity in the Mesopotamian and Abrahamic creation stories. Analyze the cultural and theological implications of these similarities and differences.

Explore the role of mythology in shaping religious and cultural identities. Investigate how the creation myths of ancient Mesopotamia and the Abrahamic traditions contribute to the formation of worldviews and belief systems.

Investigate the historical and cultural context in which the Abrahamic traditions emerged. Analyze the potential influence of Mesopotamian civilization on the development of these traditions, considering factors such as trade, migration, and cultural exchange.

Discuss the significance of monotheism in the Abrahamic creation stories. Compare it to the polytheistic cosmogonies of ancient Mesopotamia, exploring the theological implications of these differing perspectives.

Reflect on the ways in which creation stories shape religious practices and ethical frameworks within the Abrahamic traditions. Analyze the teachings and values derived from these narratives and their impact on believers' lives and communities.

Conclusion:

The Abrahamic creation stories found in the Quran, Bible, and Torah offer profound insights into the beliefs, values, and theological frameworks of Judaism, Christianity, and Islam. Exploring these narratives enables us to grasp the diverse interpretations and understandings of creation, humanity's role in the world, and the moral implications of our existence. By studying these texts, we gain a deeper appreciation for the multifaceted nature of religious thought and the ways in which ancient myths continue to shape contemporary religious and cultural practices.

➤ Comparative Analysis:

Comparative analysis provides a valuable tool for exploring the similarities and differences between different religious and mythological traditions. In this section, we will compare and contrast the themes, motifs, and symbolism present in both Mesopotamian and Abrahamic creation stories. By examining these narratives, we can gain insights into the theological implications and cultural influences that shaped the beliefs of ancient civilizations.

Themes and Motifs:

✧ Creation and the Divine:

Both Mesopotamian and Abrahamic creation stories share a fundamental theme of the divine act of creation. In Mesopotamian mythology, the Enuma Elish describes the emergence of the universe through a series of primordial conflicts and the birth of gods. Similarly, the Abrahamic traditions portray a divine creator who brings the world into existence through the power of divine will.

✧ Order and Chaos:

Another recurring motif in both sets of creation stories is the struggle between order and chaos. In Mesopotamian mythology, the primordial waters represent chaos, and the process of creation involves the establishment of order and the separation of elements. Similarly, the Abrahamic narratives depict the divine act of bringing order out of chaos, symbolized by the separation of light and darkness and the formation of the heavens and the earth.

Symbolism:

✧   Serpent and Tree of Knowledge:

In Mesopotamian mythology, the serpent is a prominent symbol associated with wisdom, healing, and the underworld. Similarly, the serpent plays a pivotal role in the Abrahamic creation story of Adam and Eve, tempting them to eat from the Tree of Knowledge. The serpent in this context represents the human pursuit of knowledge and the consequences of disobedience.

✧   Flood and Divine Punishment:

Both Mesopotamian and Abrahamic traditions feature narratives of a great flood sent by the divine as a punishment for human transgression. In Mesopotamian mythology, the Epic of Gilgamesh recounts the flood story in which the gods decide to destroy humanity due to their corruption. Likewise, the Abrahamic traditions share the story of Noah's Ark, where God brings about a worldwide flood as a means of cleansing and renewal.

Theological Implications and Cultural Influences:

✧   Creation as an Act of Power and Divine Authority:
In both Mesopotamian and Abrahamic narratives, the act of creation emphasizes the power and authority of the divine. The gods of Mesopotamian mythology assert their dominance through the establishment of order and the defeat of chaotic forces. Similarly, the Abrahamic traditions portray God as the supreme creator, whose will shapes the destiny of the world and its inhabitants.

✧   Cultural Influences:
The Mesopotamian creation stories reflect the cultural and historical context of ancient Mesopotamia, with their pantheon of gods and cosmological beliefs. The Abrahamic creation stories, on the other hand, bear the imprint of the cultural milieu of the ancient Near East, incorporating elements from earlier Mesopotamian and Canaanite traditions. These narratives also carry the imprint of

the unique theological perspectives and historical experiences of the Hebrew, Christian, and Islamic communities.

Conclusion:

The comparative analysis of Mesopotamian and Abrahamic creation stories reveals both shared themes and distinctive features. Through the exploration of these narratives, we gain a deeper understanding of the human quest to make sense of the origin of the universe, the role of divine beings, and the relationship between order and chaos. By critically examining the theological implications and cultural influences, we can appreciate the rich tapestry of religious thought and the ways in which ancient myths continue to shape contemporary belief systems.

Exercises:

Compare the role of divine beings in Mesopotamian and Abrahamic creation stories, considering their attributes, relationships, and interactions with humans.

Analyze the symbolism of the serpent in both Mesopotamian and Abrahamic creation narratives, exploring its various connotations and interpretations.

Discuss the cultural influences on the creation stories, examining how historical and social contexts shaped the beliefs and narratives of ancient civilizations.

Evaluate the moral and ethical implications of the flood narratives in Mesopotamian and Abrahamic traditions, considering the reasons for divine punishment and the messages conveyed.

Imagine you are part of a panel discussion on the comparative analysis of creation stories. Develop an argument for the significance of studying these narratives in fostering interfaith dialogue and understanding among diverse religious communities.

References:

Leick, Gwendolyn. (2002). Mesopotamia: The Invention of the City. Penguin Books.
Genesis, Bible (NIV).
Quran.

Torah.

Flood Narratives

> ➢ Mesopotamian Flood Stories:

In this section, we will delve into the Mesopotamian flood stories, examining prominent narratives such as the Epic of Gilgamesh and the Atrahasis Epic. These ancient texts provide intriguing insights into the cultural and mythological understanding of catastrophic floods in ancient Mesopotamia. By studying these narratives, we can explore the themes of divine punishment, human survival, and the search for meaning in the face of natural disasters.

The Epic of Gilgamesh:

The Epic of Gilgamesh, a renowned Mesopotamian literary masterpiece, contains an account of a devastating flood. The protagonist, Gilgamesh, seeks immortality after witnessing the death of his friend, Enkidu. To find answers, Gilgamesh encounters Utnapishtim, who shares his story of surviving a catastrophic flood and being granted eternal life.

✦ Flood Narrative and Divine Punishment:
According to the Epic of Gilgamesh, the gods, angered by humanity's noise and arrogance, decide to unleash a massive flood as a punishment. Utnapishtim is instructed by the god Ea to build a great ark to save himself, his family, and various animals from the impending deluge. The flood lasts for several days, after which Utnapishtim and his companions find themselves the sole survivors.

✦ Moral and Ethical Implications:
The flood narrative in the Epic of Gilgamesh raises profound questions about human nature and the consequences of divine judgment. It emphasizes themes of hubris, divine retribution, and the frailty of mortal life. The story serves as a cautionary tale, reminding readers of the importance of humility and respect towards the gods.

The Atrahasis Epic:

✦ Overview:
The Atrahasis Epic, another significant Mesopotamian flood narrative, tells the story of how the gods decide to exterminate humankind due to their clamor.

The god Enki, sympathetic to the plight of humans, advises the wise man Atrahasis to build a large boat to ensure their survival.

✧   Flood Narrative and Means of Renewal:
In the Atrahasis Epic, the gods send a catastrophic flood to wipe out humanity. After the flood subsides, Atrahasis offers sacrifices, and the gods, pleased with the aroma of the offerings, grant him and his companions fertility and the ability to reproduce. The flood serves as a means of renewing and replenishing the human population.

✧   Sociopolitical Commentary:
The Atrahasis Epic can be seen as a reflection of the social and political context of ancient Mesopotamia. It portrays the struggle between the ruling gods and the human population, highlighting issues of power dynamics and the delicate balance between divine authority and human agency.

Comparative Analysis:

✧   Similarities and Differences:
Comparing the Mesopotamian flood narratives with the flood story in the Abrahamic traditions, such as the story of Noah's Ark in the Bible, reveals both similarities and variations. While all narratives involve catastrophic floods and the survival of a chosen few, differences emerge in the motives behind the floods, the means of survival, and the theological implications.

✧   Symbolism and Metaphorical Interpretations:
The Mesopotamian flood stories can be interpreted metaphorically, reflecting not only the physical destruction caused by floods but also the existential crises faced by humanity. The flood symbolizes a purification and renewal of the world, allowing for new beginnings and the restoration of harmony between gods and humans.

Conclusion:

The Mesopotamian flood stories, as depicted in the Epic of Gilgamesh and the Atrahasis Epic, provide captivating insights into the ancient Mesopotamian worldview. Through the exploration of these narratives, we gain a deeper understanding of the cultural, moral, and theological aspects surrounding catastrophic floods and their impact on human civilization.

Exercises:

Compare the flood narratives in the Epic of Gilgamesh and the Atrahasis Epic, focusing on the motives behind the floods, the means of survival, and the roles of the main characters.

Discuss the moral lessons conveyed by the Mesopotamian flood stories and their relevance to contemporary environmental concerns.

Analyze the symbolism of the flood in Mesopotamian mythology and its potential metaphorical interpretations in the context of human experiences and transformations.

Contrast the Mesopotamian flood stories with the flood narrative in the Abrahamic traditions, exploring both similarities and differences in themes, characters, and theological implications.

Imagine you are a Mesopotamian scribe tasked with preserving the flood story for future generations. Write a short narrative that incorporates elements from the Epic of Gilgamesh or the Atrahasis Epic, highlighting the significance of the flood and its aftermath.

References:

George, Andrew. (2003). The Epic of Gilgamesh: The Babylonian Epic Poem and Other Texts in Akkadian and Sumerian. Penguin Classics.

Lambert, W.G. (2013). Babylonian Creation Myths. Eisenbrauns.

"The Atrahasis Epic." Electronic Text Corpus of Sumerian Literature, The University of Oxford. (etcsl.orinst.ox.ac.uk)

"The Epic of Gilgamesh." Electronic Text Corpus of Sumerian Literature, The University of Oxford. (etcsl.orinst.ox.ac.uk)

The Holy Bible (NIV).

Quran.

Torah.

➢ Abrahamic Flood Stories:

In this section, we will explore the flood stories found in the Abrahamic traditions, specifically the Quran, the Bible, and the Torah. These narratives recount catastrophic floods that serve as significant events in the respective religious traditions. By examining these stories, we can analyze the common themes, characters, and theological interpretations that arise, as well as the unique aspects that distinguish each account.

The Quran: The Story of Nuh (Noah)

✦ Overview:

The Quran presents the story of Nuh, or Noah, as a prophet sent by Allah to warn his people of their sinful ways and impending destruction. Nuh is commanded to build an ark and gather a select few believers and pairs of animals to be saved from the flood.

1.2 Narrative and Characters:
The Quranic narrative emphasizes the righteousness and steadfastness of Nuh and his unwavering commitment to carrying out Allah's command. Nuh's wife and son, who reject his message, symbolize the struggle between faith and disbelief. The flood itself is portrayed as a divine intervention and a means of cleansing the world from corruption.

✦ Theological Interpretation:

The story of Nuh in the Quran conveys moral and ethical teachings, highlighting the importance of faith, obedience to divine commands, and the consequences of disbelief. It serves as a reminder of the transitory nature of worldly possessions and the need for spiritual purification.

The Bible: The Story of Noah

✦ Overview:
The biblical account of Noah appears in the book of Genesis. Noah is portrayed as a righteous man who finds favor with God amidst a wicked and corrupt world. God instructs Noah to build an ark and gather pairs of animals to be preserved during the impending flood.

✦ Narrative and Characters:

The biblical narrative focuses on Noah's obedience to God's commands and his role as a custodian of creation. Noah's family joins him on the ark, highlighting themes of familial unity and divine protection. The flood is depicted as a response to the pervasive evil in the world and a means of renewal.

✧   2.3 Theological Interpretation:
The story of Noah in the Bible conveys moral lessons such as the importance of righteousness, faithfulness, and trust in God's providence. It emphasizes the covenant between God and humanity, symbolized by the rainbow, as a promise of divine protection and the preservation of life.

The Torah: The Story of Noah's Ark

✧   Overview:
The Torah presents a similar account of Noah and the flood as found in the Bible. Noah is chosen by God to build an ark and save his family and representatives of every animal species.

✧   Narrative and Characters:
The Torah's narrative of Noah's Ark closely parallels the biblical account, emphasizing Noah's righteousness and obedience. The flood is depicted as a response to human wickedness and a means of starting anew. The inclusion of specific measurements and instructions for the construction of the ark adds a detailed aspect to the story.

✧   Theological Interpretation:
The story of Noah's Ark in the Torah underscores themes of divine judgment, the preservation of life, and the importance of moral conduct. It emphasizes the significance of human responsibility in safeguarding the natural world and adhering to ethical principles.

Comparative Analysis:

✧   Similarities and Differences:
When comparing the flood stories in the Quran, the Bible, and the Torah, notable similarities emerge, such as the selection of a righteous individual to build an ark and the preservation of a remnant of humanity and animal species. However, differences arise in the details of the narratives, the theological interpretations, and the emphasis placed on specific moral teachings.

✧   Theological Implications:

The flood stories in the Abrahamic traditions convey theological messages of divine judgment, mercy, and the need for moral rectitude. They serve as reminders of the consequences of human actions, the importance of obedience to God's commands, and the potential for redemption and renewal.

Exercises:

Compare and contrast the flood narratives in the Quran, the Bible, and the Torah, highlighting both their similarities and distinctive elements.

Discuss the moral and ethical lessons conveyed by the flood stories in the Abrahamic traditions and their relevance to contemporary environmental and social issues.

Analyze the role of the main characters in the flood stories (Nuh/Noah) and their significance in conveying religious and moral teachings.

Explore the cultural and historical contexts in which the flood narratives emerged and their influence on the development of religious thought.

Imagine you are a storyteller tasked with retelling the flood story for a contemporary audience. How would you incorporate elements from the Quran, the Bible, and the Torah to convey a universal message of hope, resilience, and redemption?

References:

The Holy Quran (English Translation).
The Holy Bible (NIV).
The Torah.

➤ Comparative Analysis:

In this section, we will undertake a comparative analysis of the Mesopotamian and Abrahamic flood narratives, seeking to identify common elements, moral lessons, and theological implications that arise from these ancient stories. By examining the cultural and historical contexts in which these narratives emerged, we can gain insights into the shared human experiences, the development of religious beliefs, and the formation of moral codes.

Common Elements in Mesopotamian and Abrahamic Flood Narratives:

✧ Cataclysmic Event:

Both the Mesopotamian and Abrahamic flood narratives depict a catastrophic event in which a massive flood is unleashed upon the earth. These floods are often attributed to divine intervention, whether as punishment or means of renewal.

✧   Divine Instructions and Warning:

In both sets of narratives, a chosen individual receives instructions from a divine being regarding the impending flood. This individual is directed to build an ark or vessel to preserve themselves, their families, and various forms of life.

✧   Selection and Preservation:

The concept of selection and preservation is central to both sets of flood narratives. The chosen individual is responsible for saving a remnant of humanity and, in some cases, pairs of animals or representative species.

✧   Duration and Restoration:

The flood narratives commonly depict a period of devastation, followed by a time of renewal and restoration. After the floodwaters recede, the chosen individual and their companions emerge from the ark to repopulate the earth.

Moral Lessons in Mesopotamian and Abrahamic Flood Narratives:

✧   Divine Judgment and Moral Corruption:

The flood stories in both traditions convey a sense of divine judgment and punishment for human moral corruption. They highlight the consequences of human actions, particularly acts of immorality and disobedience.

✧   Obedience and Faith:

Another moral lesson emphasized in these narratives is the importance of obedience and faith in the face of divine commands. The chosen individuals, such as Utnapishtim in the Mesopotamian tradition and Noah in the Abrahamic traditions, demonstrate unwavering trust and obedience to the divine instructions.

✧   Human Responsibility and Stewardship:

The flood narratives also impart lessons on human responsibility and stewardship. They emphasize the need for humans to act responsibly, maintain moral conduct, and fulfill their role as caretakers of the natural world.

Theological Implications of Mesopotamian and Abrahamic Flood Narratives:

✧   Divine Power and Intervention:

The flood stories highlight the belief in divine power and intervention within the respective religious traditions. They serve as reminders of the gods' authority in Mesopotamian mythology and as demonstrations of God's judgment and mercy in the Abrahamic faiths.

✧   Redemption and Renewal:

The floods are often associated with themes of redemption and renewal. They signify the opportunity for humanity to start afresh, to learn from past mistakes, and to strive for moral and spiritual growth.

✧   Covenant and Divine Promises:

In the Abrahamic flood narratives, the notion of a covenant between God and humanity emerges. The rainbow, for example, symbolizes God's promise to never again destroy the world by flood. These covenants convey the concept of a reciprocal relationship between the divine and human beings.

Exercises:

Compare the Mesopotamian flood narratives (such as the Epic of Gilgamesh) with the Abrahamic flood narratives (from the Quran, Bible, and Torah), identifying similarities and differences in themes, characters, and theological interpretations.

Discuss the cultural and historical contexts in which the flood narratives arose and their influence on religious beliefs and moral codes.

Analyze the moral lessons conveyed by both sets of flood narratives and their relevance to contemporary environmental and ethical issues.

Explore the theological implications of the floods in terms of divine power, judgment, redemption, and renewal.

Imagine you are a theologian tasked with reconciling the flood narratives within a broader spiritual framework. How would you address the challenges and conflicts that arise from these diverse accounts?

References:

Dalley, S. (2000). Myths from Mesopotamia: Creation, the Flood, Gilgamesh, and Others. Oxford University Press.
The Holy Quran (English Translation).
The Holy Bible (NIV).
The Torah.

Moral Codes and Ethical Teachings

➢ Mesopotamian Moral Codes:

The Code of Hammurabi, with its 282 laws, provides us with a fascinating window into the social, legal, and moral landscape of ancient Mesopotamia. This comprehensive legal code, carved onto a stone pillar during the reign of Babylonian king Hammurabi in the 18th century BCE, not only reveals the complexities of Babylonian society but also offers insights into the values and principles that governed the lives of its people.

The structure and content of the Code of Hammurabi demonstrate the Babylonians' commitment to maintaining social order and justice. The laws cover a wide range of aspects, addressing various spheres of life, such as family, commerce, property, labor, and crime. This wide scope reflects the Babylonians' recognition that a just and harmonious society requires clear guidelines and regulations for every facet of human interaction.

The laws pertaining to family matters within the Code of Hammurabi reflect the importance placed on maintaining stable familial relationships. For example, laws governing marriage, divorce, and inheritance outline the rights and obligations of family members, ensuring the orderly transfer of property and the protection of vulnerable individuals, such as widows and orphans. These laws aimed to preserve the integrity of the family unit and safeguard the well-being of its members.

In the realm of commerce, the Code of Hammurabi establishes regulations to govern trade and commercial transactions. It sets standards for fair pricing, outlines the responsibilities of merchants, and even addresses issues such as debt and bankruptcy. By providing a framework for conducting business ethically and transparently, these laws fostered trust and stability within the economic sphere, essential for the functioning of a thriving society.

One of the notable features of the Code of Hammurabi is its emphasis on retributive justice, exemplified by the principle of "an eye for an eye." This principle, known as lex talionis, implies that the punishment for a crime should be proportionate to the offense committed. By meting out punishments that mirrored the harm caused, the code sought to deter potential wrongdoers and maintain a sense of balance and fairness within society.

However, it is important to note that the Code of Hammurabi also reflects the hierarchical structure of Babylonian society. The laws differentiated between social classes, with varying rights and punishments assigned to different groups. Slaves, women, and individuals of lower social status often had fewer protections and rights compared to free citizens or members of the ruling class. This distinction highlights the existence of inequalities and power imbalances inherent in ancient Mesopotamian society.

In conclusion, the Code of Hammurabi is a remarkable artifact that offers valuable insights into the moral, legal, and social values of ancient Mesopotamia. It serves as a testament to the Babylonians' commitment to maintaining social order and justice while also revealing the complex dynamics of their society. By studying this legal code, we gain a deeper understanding of the moral principles that guided the lives of the Babylonians and the challenges they faced in creating a just and harmonious society.

Exercises:

Analyze specific laws from the Code of Hammurabi and discuss their implications for societal norms and values.

Compare and contrast the principles of justice in the Code of Hammurabi with those found in other ancient legal codes, such as the Laws of Ur-Nammu or the Hittite laws.

Debate the merits and limitations of the lex talionis principle in the context of contemporary legal systems.

Examine the gender biases present in the Code of Hammurabi and discuss their implications for gender relations in ancient Mesopotamia.

Imagine you are a legal advisor to Hammurabi. Propose amendments to the code to address some of its ethical shortcomings and promote greater equality and social justice.

Principles of Justice and Social Order:

Retributive Justice:

The concept of retributive justice is prominently displayed in the Code of Hammurabi, a legal text from ancient Mesopotamia. The principle of lex talionis, often referred to as "an eye for an eye," lies at the core of this system. Lex talionis aims to ensure that the punishment inflicted on an offender is proportionate to the severity of the offense committed.

Under the Code of Hammurabi, specific penalties are prescribed for various crimes and transgressions. For example, if someone causes harm to another person, the punishment may involve inflicting a similar injury upon the perpetrator. This approach is seen as a means of achieving justice by imposing a consequence that corresponds to the harm caused. The principle of retributive justice, as exemplified in the Code, seeks to deter wrongdoing and maintain social order by holding individuals accountable for their actions.

However, it is essential to consider the potential drawbacks of retributive justice. Critics argue that this approach can perpetuate cycles of violence and fail to address the underlying causes of criminal behavior. Furthermore, the strict application of lex talionis may not account for mitigating circumstances or allow for rehabilitation and personal growth.

Social Stratification:

The laws presented in the Code of Hammurabi reflect the hierarchical structure of Mesopotamian society. They establish different rights, privileges, and obligations based on an individual's social status. Distinctions are made between free citizens, slaves, and women, reflecting the prevailing social norms and power dynamics of the time.

Free citizens, who constituted the ruling class, enjoyed greater legal protections and privileges. They were afforded specific rights in matters such as property ownership, business transactions, and inheritance. Slaves, on the other hand, were considered property and had limited legal rights. They were subject to the authority and control of their owners.

Women, although not without agency, generally held a subordinate status in ancient Mesopotamian society. The laws of the Code assigned them certain rights and responsibilities within the family and community, but they were subject to male authority and lacked full autonomy.

The social stratification reflected in the laws of the Code of Hammurabi serves as a testament to the hierarchical nature of Mesopotamian society. It highlights the unequal distribution of power and resources, and the ways in which legal systems can reinforce and perpetuate existing social hierarchies.

Restoration of Order:

A primary objective of the Code of Hammurabi was to maintain social harmony and restore order within the community. The laws outlined in the code aimed to achieve this by providing mechanisms to resolve disputes, ensure fair treatment, and regulate interactions between individuals.

The Code addressed various aspects of daily life, including commerce, property, marriage, and personal injury. It prescribed specific guidelines for resolving conflicts, such as through the use of witnesses and evidence. Compensation for damages, including financial restitution, was a common approach to resolving disputes and restoring balance.

By regulating the conduct of individuals and establishing clear expectations for behavior, the Code sought to prevent conflicts and promote a sense of justice. It aimed to establish a stable social order that upheld the rights of individuals and fostered a sense of security and fairness.

Problems and Exercises:

Analyze the principle of lex talionis and its application in the Code of Hammurabi. Discuss its advantages and disadvantages as a form of punishment.

Debate the effectiveness of retributive justice in deterring crime and maintaining social order. Compare it to alternative approaches such as restorative justice or rehabilitative justice.

Examine the social hierarchies reflected in the laws of the Code of Hammurabi. Discuss the implications of such stratification on notions of justice and equality.

Role-play a scenario where two individuals have a dispute over property rights. Use the laws of the Code to simulate a resolution and discuss the outcome in terms of fairness and social harmony.

Research and compare the legal systems of other ancient civilizations, such as ancient Egypt or ancient Greece, to identify similarities and differences in their approaches to retributive justice, social stratification, and the restoration of order.

Moral and Ethical Principles:

The Code of Hammurabi, while reflecting a hierarchical society, places a significant emphasis on the principles of fairness and equity. It strives to ensure that individuals are treated justly and that judgments are based on evidence and facts rather than arbitrary decisions.

The code includes specific laws that address the rights and responsibilities of individuals, aiming to establish a fair and balanced system of justice. For instance, it outlines the process for presenting evidence, calling witnesses, and cross-examination during legal proceedings. These procedures are designed to ensure that all parties have an opportunity to present their case and that judgments are reached based on a careful consideration of the available information.

Moreover, the code promotes the principle of proportionate punishment, wherein penalties correspond to the severity of the offense committed. This approach seeks to uphold fairness by ensuring that individuals face consequences that align with their actions, thus avoiding excessive or lenient punishment.

Responsibilities and Duties:

The Code of Hammurabi provides a framework for understanding the responsibilities and duties of individuals within Mesopotamian society. It covers a wide range of topics, including family relationships, marriage contracts, and economic transactions. By outlining these obligations, the code aims to maintain social order and harmony.

For instance, the code emphasizes parental responsibilities, such as ensuring the support and education of children. It establishes guidelines for marriage contracts, addressing issues such as dowries, inheritance rights, and divorce. By delineating these obligations, the code aims to foster stability within families and the wider community.

Additionally, the code addresses the protection of property rights, both for individuals and the state. It outlines regulations governing land use, trade, and commerce, emphasizing the importance of fulfilling contractual agreements and maintaining economic stability. These provisions help ensure the smooth functioning of society and the equitable distribution of resources.

Protection of the Vulnerable:

One notable aspect of the Code of Hammurabi is its recognition of the need to protect vulnerable members of society. The code includes provisions that aim to safeguard the rights and well-being of widows, orphans, and the poor. It acknowledges the potential for exploitation or neglect and seeks to address these concerns.

For example, the code stipulates that widows should be provided for and protected, emphasizing the importance of financial support and ensuring their security. It also addresses the rights of orphans, establishing guidelines for their guardianship and the fair treatment of their inherited property.

Furthermore, the code expresses a concern for the poor and marginalized members of society. It includes provisions that provide assistance to those in need, such as access to food and shelter, and regulations that prevent exploitative practices.

Overall, the Code of Hammurabi recognizes the importance of fairness, equity, and the protection of vulnerable individuals within the framework of ancient Mesopotamian society. It establishes a legal system that strives to ensure justice, maintain social order, and address the needs of diverse members of the community.

Problems and Exercises:

Discuss the role of fairness and equity in maintaining social order and harmony. How can these principles be applied in modern legal systems?

Analyze the provisions in the Code of Hammurabi that promote the protection of vulnerable individuals. Evaluate their effectiveness in addressing social inequality and promoting justice.

Role-play a courtroom scenario based on the laws of the Code of Hammurabi. Assign different roles to participants and engage in a debate about the fairness of the judgment reached.

Research and compare the legal systems of other ancient civilizations, such as ancient Egypt or ancient China, to examine how they addressed fairness, equity, and the protection of vulnerable populations.

Discuss the ethical implications of the principle of proportionate punishment in the Code of Hammurabi. Debate the pros and cons of this approach to justice, considering its impact on individuals and society.
References:

Roth, M. T. (1995). Law Collections from Mesopotamia and Asia Minor (2nd ed.). Scholars Press.

Van De Mieroop, M. (2005). King Hammurabi of Babylon: A Biography. Wiley-Blackwell.

Kuhrt, A. (2010). The Ancient Near East: c. 3000-330 BC. Routledge.

> Abrahamic Moral Codes:

.The Abrahamic religions, including Islam, Christianity, and Judaism, have a rich tradition of moral teachings and ethical codes that guide the behavior and conduct of their followers. Central to these moral codes are the sacred texts of each tradition, such as the Quran in Islam, the Bible in Christianity, and the Torah in Judaism. Within these texts, we find a diverse range of moral principles, commandments, and ethical teachings that serve as guiding principles for believers.

One of the most well-known and influential ethical teachings in the Abrahamic tradition is the Ten Commandments. These commandments, originally given to Moses by God according to the biblical accounts, are considered foundational to moral conduct and provide a framework for living a righteous life. They include injunctions such as "You shall not murder," "You shall not steal," and "You shall not bear false witness against your neighbor." These commandments emphasize principles of honesty, respect for life, and the sanctity of interpersonal relationships.

In addition to the Ten Commandments, the sacred texts of the Abrahamic religions contain numerous other ethical teachings and moral guidelines. For instance, the Quran, considered the holy book of Islam, provides comprehensive guidance for ethical behavior through its verses, known as ayat. It addresses various aspects of human conduct, covering topics such as honesty, justice, compassion, and social responsibility. The Prophet Muhammad's teachings, known as Hadith, further elaborate on ethical conduct and provide practical guidance for daily life.

Similarly, the Bible contains a wide range of moral teachings found in both the Old Testament (Hebrew Bible) and the New Testament. These teachings cover areas such as personal integrity, social justice, care for the vulnerable, and love for one's neighbor. Jesus' teachings in the New Testament, including the Sermon on the Mount, emphasize compassion, forgiveness, and love as central virtues.

The Torah, the sacred text of Judaism, also provides a comprehensive ethical framework. It includes commandments, known as mitzvot, that address various aspects of life, ranging from religious rituals to interpersonal relationships. These commandments guide Jews in their relationships with God, fellow human beings, and the wider community. They emphasize principles of justice, righteousness, and social responsibility.

It is important to note that the moral codes within the Abrahamic traditions are subject to interpretation and have been interpreted differently by different religious scholars and communities over time. Various schools of thought within each tradition have provided nuanced interpretations and expansions on these moral teachings, leading to a diversity of perspectives on ethical matters.

Problems and Exercises:

Select one of the Ten Commandments and discuss its relevance in contemporary society. Examine the challenges and dilemmas individuals may face in upholding this commandment.

Compare and contrast the moral teachings found in the Quran, Bible, and Torah. Identify common ethical principles and discuss the unique perspectives offered by each religious tradition.

Research the teachings of a specific prophet or religious figure within the Abrahamic traditions (e.g., Jesus, Muhammad, Moses). Analyze their moral teachings and their impact on the ethical practices of their respective religious communities.

Engage in a group discussion exploring the challenges of applying moral codes in real-life situations. Consider hypothetical scenarios and debate the ethical choices individuals might face.

Investigate contemporary ethical issues or debates within the Abrahamic traditions. Analyze different perspectives and arguments presented by scholars and religious authorities, critically evaluating their reasoning and implications.

➤ Comparative Analysis:

In the study of moral codes and ethical teachings, a comparative analysis between Mesopotamian texts and the Abrahamic scriptures reveals intriguing similarities and differences, shedding light on the underlying values that shape individual and communal behavior in these diverse religious traditions.

Mesopotamian Moral Codes:

Mesopotamian texts, such as the Code of Hammurabi, provide insights into the moral and ethical framework of ancient Mesopotamian society. These codes were designed to ensure social order, resolve conflicts, and establish guidelines for just behavior. They emphasize concepts such as retributive justice, social stratification, and the restoration of order.

Abrahamic Moral Codes:

The Abrahamic religions—Judaism, Christianity, and Islam—encompass a vast collection of sacred texts that contain moral codes and ethical teachings. The Quran, Bible, and Torah, among others, provide guidance on personal conduct, social interactions, and responsibilities within the community. Central to these codes are principles such as fairness, equity, responsibilities, and protection of the vulnerable.

Comparative Analysis:

Similarities:

Despite the historical and cultural differences between Mesopotamian and Abrahamic moral codes, some striking similarities emerge. Both traditions emphasize fairness and equity in matters of justice. Mesopotamian laws, such as the principle of lex talionis ("an eye for an eye"), sought to establish proportionate punishment, while the Abrahamic tradition promotes principles of justice and impartiality. Both systems aim to ensure that individuals are treated fairly and that judgments are based on evidence and facts.

Furthermore, both Mesopotamian and Abrahamic moral codes address the protection of the vulnerable in their respective societies. The Code of Hammurabi, for example, includes provisions for the welfare of widows, orphans, and the poor, offering them protection, access to justice, and assistance. Similarly, the Abrahamic scriptures contain teachings that emphasize compassion, care for the marginalized, and social responsibility.

Differences:

While there are notable similarities, differences in the moral codes and ethical teachings of Mesopotamian and Abrahamic traditions also arise. One significant distinction lies in their theological foundations. Mesopotamian texts often reflect a polytheistic worldview, where multiple gods and goddesses exerted influence over various aspects of life, including morality. In contrast, the Abrahamic religions advocate monotheism, focusing on the worship of a single deity who sets moral standards for believers.

Another distinction lies in the conceptualization of social order. Mesopotamian moral codes reflect a hierarchical structure, where different rights and obligations were assigned based on social status, including distinctions between free citizens, slaves, and women. The Abrahamic moral codes, while acknowledging social stratification, emphasize the equality and dignity of all individuals before God. They stress the importance of compassion, love for one's neighbor, and care for the disadvantaged, transcending social divisions.

Underlying Values:

In comparing these moral codes, we discern the underlying values that shape individual and communal behavior. Both Mesopotamian and Abrahamic traditions value justice, fairness, and the preservation of social order. They recognize the need for guidelines and laws to govern human interactions and ensure the well-being of communities.

At the same time, the Abrahamic traditions place a strong emphasis on compassion, love, and ethical responsibility towards others. These values, rooted in the belief in a benevolent and compassionate deity, guide believers in their interactions with fellow humans and the wider world.

Problems and Exercises:

Select a specific Mesopotamian moral code and an Abrahamic moral teaching and compare their implications for personal conduct and social order.

Investigate the historical context of Mesopotamian society and its influence on the development of moral codes. Compare it to the cultural and historical contexts that shaped the Abrahamic moral teachings.

Analyze the impact of theological beliefs on moral codes by comparing the polytheistic framework of Mesopotamia to the monotheistic framework of the Abrahamic religions.

Engage in a group discussion on the role of social stratification in moral codes. Debate the advantages and disadvantages of hierarchical systems in promoting social order and justice.

Explore the concept of compassion in both Mesopotamian and Abrahamic traditions. Examine how it is manifested in moral codes and discuss its significance for personal and communal ethics.

Conclusion:
By comparing the ancient Mesopotamian texts to the Quran, Bible, and Torah, we gain a deeper understanding of the shared cultural and theological threads that connect these traditions. Through this comparative analysis, we can appreciate the rich diversity of religious thought and the enduring impact of these texts on human spirituality and moral frameworks.

www.ingramcontent.com/pod-product-compliance
Lightning Source LLC
Chambersburg PA
CBHW082139120626

46553CB00010B/2703